WINTER
IN CHINA:
AN AMERICAN LIFE

WINTER
IN CHINA:
AN AMERICAN LIFE

Bert Stern

To order additional copies of this book, contact:
Xlibris LLC
1-888-795-4274
www.Xlibris.com
Orders@Xlibris.com
602636

Contents

ACKNOWLEDGMENTS

When I came to China in the fall of 1984 this book was there, waiting to be written. Though the living Robert Winter was decrepit and often out of touch with the present, his colleagues and former students had preserved lively impressions of his teaching, collegiality, courage in behalf of humane causes, and talent for getting in and out of trouble. I dedicate this book to them, in deep gratitude for the time they gave me out of their busy lives.

The following people, whom I interviewed in 1984-85 and 1987 gave me my first perspectival view of Robert Winter. My warmest thanks to them all, and apologies to any I may have omitted. Tollef Ås, Martin Bernal, Chao Hsiung-hao, Lin Chao, Liu Da-Mien, Chen Deison, Lao Deng, Wang Feng-xin, Li Fun-ning, Dorothy Gaylord, Chou Li-Kate, Wang Minyuan, Ernest Young, Fu Yi, Wang Shi-ren, Walter Tzeisberger, Wang Wei, Marty White, Yang Zho-han, Yang Zhou-han, Tang Xi-jian, Zhang Xiao-bin, Liu Xuan.

Peking University and Wabash College were generous in their support of this project, and the Rockefeller Archive Center (especially archivist Tom Rosenbaum) gave me access to and guided me through a wealth of letters and reports that broadened and deepened my understanding of Winter's rich life. And a phone call from Roland Chou helped me revive this project from a deep slumber.

Deep thanks to Rujie Wang, who planted the seed for this biography in me long ago. Thanks also to my friends Peter Frederick and Steve Charles, early aiders and abettors. David E. Kendall of Williams and Connolly carried on in my behalf a long battle with the FBI over their records of Robert Winter. My very warm thanks to him.

Finally, my wife and children gave me the kind of love that's the ultimate support. And above all, loving thanks to my daughter Anna, who, as a child, was with me at the beginning of this journey and, as an astute and caring daughter, was with me at the end.

Cover image: "Fisherman at Tsingtao," oil painting by Robert Winte

PREFACE

This journey began in September 1980, when Wabash College, where I taught English, received a letter from Robert Winter, who identified himself as the college's oldest alumnus. Despite the fact that no one had heard from him in some seventy-five years, his claim proved to be true. He explained that he'd been teaching in China's major universities for the better part of that time.[1]

The purpose of his letter was to recommend Rujie Wang for admission to the college. Winter had been tutoring Rujie for several years and thought he was ready for an American education. Rujie proved worthy of Winter's praise. More than an excellent student, he was an able and willing teacher. We talked about books and about Robert Winter, who had been a colleague of Rujie's parents and, for several years, his tutor. I was intrigued by Winter, this mysterious old man who had gone to China in 1923 and lived there almost continuously, except for a brief visit to the States during WWII. Of course, we also talked about China. In that context, I was a beginning student, long interested in Tang Dynasty poetry, Asian spiritualism (I'd traveled in India), and the Cultural Revolution, but generally ignorant.

I had Red Stars in my eyes in those days. I'd been an academic in the company of academics long enough to believe that, as a class, we might all be made more interesting and more developed human beings if we hung out a bit more with "the peasants," sharing their work and the conditions of their lives. I'd spent a couple of years living in a crude cabin without plumbing, and I valued what I'd learned there about a simpler and less comfortable lifestyle among "less cultivated" neighbors from whom I had a lot to learn. I'd also done some hard traveling in Mexico and other countries in Central America and thought of myself as the kind of intellectual whom Mao might view as less in need of cultural reform

9

than many of my colleagues. Soon I met enough of Mao's victims to know how unforgivably romantic I was about Mao's China.

But for the while, I was full of all kinds of illusions, and even Rujie's stories about his own experiences as a member of the Red Guard didn't quite rid me of them. For example, he had been one of a ring of Red Guards shouting abuse and accusation against his own father, who was a well-known scholar-professor at Peking University. But the intensity of Rujie's stories about the tumultuous days of the Cultural Revolution fascinated me. The security of tenure and the sense of confinement I felt in a small men's college set among the cornfields of Indiana had made my life feel humdrum. At a certain point, I knew, in the way that one knows once or twice in a lifetime, exactly what my life needed that I needed to go to China.

My wife, who had already lived for several years in Japan, also lit up at the prospect. As for our five-year-old daughter, Anna . . . well, twenty years earlier I'd taken two young children with me to Thessaloniki (where I taught at the university for two years as a Fulbright scholar) and that uprooting hadn't hurt them, so I was ready once gain to test my faith that travel broadens, even in the case of children.

All that was missing was the teaching job, and Rujie got that for me. His parents were both honored, semiretired professors in the English Department, and through them I gained a one-year appointment. The message from Peking University was curt: "University President invites you to teach next academic year. Formal invitation forthcoming." The reality of the huge leap that awaited me for that moment overwhelmed me. I think I turned white. Robert Bly, who was visiting the college at the time, said three words to me that had a great and permanent effect on my life: "That's just fear." For the first time I realized that it wasn't fear but panic that was the problem.

As we started up the ramp to the plane at Kennedy, that same anticipatory shock struck Anna. "I'll go for the summer but not for a year," she announced and grabbed onto the ramp rail like a vice. I had to detach her physically, not without a bit of anguish. She didn't settle down until the stewardess brought us a meal. Fascinated with the adventure of peeling aluminum foil from her meal tray and discovering the (to her) magic foods beneath, Anna seemed to decide that there might be something good in this after all.

There's a lot to say about our early days in China: how Anna was enrolled in a kindergarten school that taught five hundred children, and didn't speak at all for several months until she could speak competent kindergarten Chinese; how we explored the campus on bicycles and discovered the Empress Xu Ci's summer palace, adjacent to the campus; and how its ruined palace and broken monumental beasts became a favored playground for Anna. Early on, we were too ignorant to experience culture shock. The surface presented to us was unruffled, uniformed in Mao suits, and even visibly militaristic, as when, twice a day, the university loudspeakers barked out orders and cadences for exercise drills in which all able-bodied people were required to participate. There were also what remained mysteries for a while: for example, that my students would bring me official slips of paper that I had to sign and that were returned to the minor official who sat at the door of our visitor's dormitory—but it took me some months to take in the fact that the Cultural Revolution was only nominally over, and that both my students and my colleagues were held fast in a system that allowed them only slight leeway.

It took a while for several reasons. Though I had many private conversations with students, those were necessarily limited to my area of understanding. As that area expanded, a few students, including the brilliant young man who served as a kind of personal guide and cultural translator, began to teach me things. For example, the young man pointed to a newspaper photo of a group of high Party officials and explained that one face was missing and that this was the only clue that a serious political upheaval had taken place. On another occasion, he told me of a painter who was arrested because his version of a traditional scene contained some strokes of black beyond the standard ones, and this was understood by the authorities as political criticism. So I slowly discovered that China's oppressive government didn't end with Mao.

Another reason why it took me some time to pierce the veil of Communist authoritarianism is that, along with other "foreign experts," we were taken on field trips for a while, many of which exulted the benevolence of authority. For example, on a visit to a Red Army base, where we witnessed men in some kind of commando training perform impressively on obstacle courses and in hand-to-hand combat, we were also shown how the army served as protectors and helpers to the people of the countryside. We came away with the impression that China was authoritarian but benign. We'd been presented with what an Austrian friend described to me as a *Gastspiel,* and it worked quite well with us for a while. After all, at that time, even seasoned experts like John Fairbank could feel sympathy for Mao's revolution, just as Robert Winter initially did.

All this happened in the late summer and fall of 1984. And then what turned out to be the real story for me began, with my first visit to Robert Winter, whose house was on the southern edge of the campus. When I met him, Winter was ninety-seven, bedridden as the result of a bicycle accident two years earlier. He was often comatose or bewildered and a most unlikely candidate for interviewing. My first visit to him was official: my purpose was to deliver him a message from Lewis Salter, then president of Wabash College, along with an honorary doctoral certificate awarded by Salter (which was soon hanging above Winter's headboard, whether at his behest or not, I don't know).

Winter fascinated me from the start (more of that first visit in chapter 18), and I knew almost at once that I'd visit and, insofar as possible, interview him often. My thinking was in part self-serving. As I said, my knowledge of Chinese history was negligible, and I saw the prospect of living, guided by Winter's experience, through a good part of China's especially turbulent twentieth century. But I also had another less self-interested motive. Winter was trapped, hopelessly, by infirmity and circumstance—and he knew it and often complained about it and asked me the impossible favor of freeing him. Telling his story, it seemed to me, was the only way I had of giving him a kind of freedom. He was obsessed with doubts as to whether he'd lived a worthy life, and long before I knew much about that life, I *felt*—for what that's worth—that he had.

At first, the story I could piece together was ghostly. In his mind, characters and events from different periods merged with one another into odd archetypes. Worse, for a while, I didn't know enough Chinese history even to attempt to shape our interviews but was forced to take what came and make what I could of it.

These interviews could be emotionally unsettling for both of us. For me, there was the dreamlike quality of riding my bicycle down a sunny path that winds between lily ponds to a little house on the northern edge of the university campus, in a spot that not so long ago was part of the imperial hunting grounds. At the door, I would be greeted by Winter's servant, a woman called Wang, who was not really very glad to see me because my visits would leave the old man animated and difficult to pacify. Still, she always treated me kindly, hoping that she might find in me another protector, her destiny having always depended on the kindness of gentlemen.

Inside the house, she would lead me through the small antechamber where she and her husband lived, down a short hallway that opened to the right onto a closet-like space where Winter once kept his study, into the old man's bedroom. The room, windows closed tight, with one pane replaced by a stout square of wood so that the old man could not break it in one of his rages, smelled stale. Often he would be asleep, a big man in a quilted Chinese jacket, whose padded body seemed to spill over the frame of his small bed but whose face was gaunt, nearly cadaverous.

A classic carved teak cabinet covered one wall. (How Winter managed to preserve it through the wars and exiles he endured, I can't imagine.) Other vestiges of his earlier lives hung on walls. There was a Qing Dynasty painting that depicted a mustachioed man in a red cloak leading a camel through snowy mountains. Both the man and the camel stare with a kind of sublime haughtiness at the clear mountain sky. It is a traveler's picture, and it celebrates solitude and fearless quest. Across from it hung what Wang Min-yuan told me was a self-portrait in oil that depicts Winter as he was perhaps fifty years earlier: big, boldly mustachioed like the horseman, and very handsome in an imperious, British kind of way. Another painting by Winter, which I now own, showed a young fisherman looking directly at us, holding a small seahorse in his right hand. His expression is unmistakably erotic.

There were only a few other things: a scroll whose characters read, "Give up the old, / Start something new. / A hundred flowers are open," a pennant and a certificate of merit from Wabash College that hung on the wall at Winter's feet, and the color TV set that offered Winter one of the last remaining windows out of the room.

*   *   *

In that room, we had the most extraordinary conversations. On one of my visits, he reflected on "the people who influence me now." These people, he said, "are not all a good influence. I understand that. They have their faults, some faults. But my correction of these faults may not be better . . . . It's as if China has already seen its future, no matter what I say or do." From the lips of a man so old and utterly powerless, so long past influencing anybody but me, the words sounded absurdly inflated, if not mad. I had to remind myself that Winter's mind was no longer time bound. At a given moment, he might speak out of any of the many time frames in which he had lived. The people who influenced him included, indiscriminately, his attendants, the university authorities most directly responsible for his well-being, and the Chinese government itself. His words made compelling sense when I reflected that he had worked for years at the heart of institutions in which the intellectual and political future of China was being forged.

I suppose that this is the first coherent form that emerged for me from these interviews: that brooding over this little room was an enormous history that ranged through continents and through a dialectic of high hopes and shattered illusions that had carried both East and West to the moment in which we stand today. Along those lines, this slumbering, shattered figure of a man took on allegorical properties for me.

Winter's task, as he and both his Eastern and Western employers had understood it, was to interpret to one another two cultures—the one he had been born into and had half renounced, and the one he had tried to make his own and had half embraced. He had "lived in China longer than anyone and understood China best," as one of his former students told me. He had hoped to write a book that would contribute to the deepening understanding between the two countries.

Indeed, the prospect of a new culture, melded of the elements of an East and West each imperfect in themselves, had been very much in the minds of intellectuals on both sides of the Atlantic—men like John Dewey, Bertrand Russell, and I. A. Richards in the West, and Liang Ch'i'chao, Liang Shu-ming, and Hu Shih in the East had all written about such a new culture, until the flames of war grew so intense that all such thoughts burned to cinders. In any case, by the time that the inchoate civil wars, the anti-Japanese war, the war between the Guomindang and the Communists, the Korean and Vietnamese Wars, and the Cultural Revolution were ended, Winter was eighty-five years old.

More than once, he said to me, "Can't you think of some way to get me out of here?" Of course I could not. This house, these attendants, this terrible state of mind and body, were where his life had carried him and could carry him no farther. He was like a great fish washed up on the shore, breathing out his last anguish. I could not think of any way to get him out of here, except to imagine his life as accurately as I could, moving from his dead present to his vital past.

*   *   *

One spring day, after I had finished teaching an afternoon class, I rode my bike out to Winter's house. I had promised I would take him for a walk in his wheelchair, now that the flowers were beginning to bloom, miraculously, out of the arid Beijing soil. Winter had not been out of his house in nearly a year, and he was desperate to leave his room. The day when we arranged the walk, he told me that he did not want to talk about the past. "I'd rather have something new . . . . There must be change . . . . I don't think anything could be worse than the past."

He meant not that the past was bad—he specifically did not want to be misunderstood in that way—but that he was trapped in a series of dull and unchanging days, watching his deterioration. He was a little like the Cumaean Sibyl, shrunken, hanging in a bottle. But unlike her, he did not want to die. Only a few days earlier, he had glimpsed out of his window a crumpled sheet of polyurethane discarded in front of his old house, which was nearly all he could see from his window. "What is that white object out there?" he wanted to know. I explained, but he was still very agitated. "What is it for? Has somebody died?" No, it is nothing, trash discarded by workmen. "Is it for me?" he persisted.

But on the day when we planned our outing, he forgot all this. "Are you superstitious?" he asked me. I told him that I was not. Some of those who had taken him for walks in the past, he explained, were, and for that reason they had refused to wheel him across bridges or past water, where evil spirits lurked. But since Winter's home is situated in the midst of several small lotus ponds, it would be impossible to take him very far without crossing a bridge or passing by water.

As it turned out, the evil spirits seemed to be working independently of bridges, for on the scheduled day of the walk, a big Beijing wind had blown up, and I went to tell him that we would not be able to go out, what with the Gobi dust and all. When I got there, however, it turned out that the weather didn't matter. The sons of a former servant of Winter—a man now dead with whom Winter had carried on an extended feud—had been in what was left of his garden, digging up flowers and stealing the trellis that held up a big old lilac bush. Now Winter didn't know who I was, or care, though he had it vaguely in mind that I was the winner of a speech contest. Livid, his body more animated than I had ever seen it, he shouted orders to me: "Don't sit there. Time is wasting. Call the authorities. No. Go at once."

The old man's terrible state of mind, which had become chronic, had one obvious central cause. The worst thing that could happen to him had happened. He had become immobile. For him, even through most of his long old age, life and mobility had been synonymous. "As I remember it," he told me once, "I lived a wonderful life, walking around this place, as

far as you can see, and to the waterside, to the *shue*." He brooded a little,
then went on:

> I'm quite a different person since I was not able to walk. When
> I was able to walk I could go anywhere—here and here and
> here—to see what it was like. Now I don't go anywhere, don't
> see anything. I think it is very bad not to be able to walk . . . .
> So long as I could walk the world was very interesting. I could
> go into any corner and examine any bit of something that I
> couldn't see from a distance. I found it more interesting than I
> would have found a corresponding place in America.

Winter often talked about his anxiety over whether he had been
"good enough"—a broad phrase that I took to mean, had he ably
discharged the moral and intellectual duties that came his way? (Perhaps
too it reflected remorse over his sometimes unbridled homosexual
passion, though he never talked about such episodes with me.) So it
was my notion that we would reconstruct his life together and that in
the realized form of what he had been he would find an escape from
the self-doubt that haunted him. On my first visit, he told he that he
had wanted "to blot himself out." He never had personal ambitions,
he said; he had "wanted to be nothing." Why did people come to see
him now? He really wanted to know. And though he had wanted to be
"nothing"—an ambition replete with all sorts of Oriental ambiguities—
now he wanted to know from me, from anyone, whether his life had
meant anything and what people thought of him. He wanted to hear
a redeeming judgment, for it was obvious that this former Catholic
sometimes feared that he had been cast into a kind of actual hell because
of his homosexuality. His servant, Wang, who had once been a prostitute,
and he, he once said, had been thrown together like this as punishment
for each other's sins.

Some of his remorse had come down a more secular avenue, by way
of the many struggle sessions (aggressive interrogations) to which he had
been subjected, during which he was repeatedly instructed that actions
he had performed, values he had held in the past, were evidence of his
antirevolutionary tendencies. So I imagined that we would construct
between us a world that we could walk around in together, examining the
bits of things, redeeming his past.

Yet, to borrow from T. S. Eliot, how could I "shore these fragments against [his] ruin?" I feared that I had come too late. The true shapes of Winter's life were already dissolving; some had already dissolved. He was like a poem stuck on the tip of my tongue, a dream on waking. Once, as I left the home of Gladys Yang and her husband Yang Xian-yi, the prolific English translators of Chinese literature, Mrs. Yang wished me luck on my biographical project but shook her head ruefully: "You're dealing in clouds," she said. And so I was—an old man's fragmented memories, a few newspaper stories, the anecdotes of his remaining friends, most of them aged or aging men and women themselves.

Sometimes Winter tried hard to participate. "Ask me any questions," he would say. So I did, but he would have forgotten the episode or person or period I asked about, and he would apologize, and fall back to brooding over his own ruin. "There's something queer about me that I don't understand," he told me one day. "You see, I seem to mix up fairy tales and facts."

Yet in his more lucid moments, he knew that I wanted to write his biography, and he wanted that too:

> I'm an American who has tried to be a Chinese. But I'm not a good one. And what I fear is that I'm not good enough. So somebody will come out and make it clear whether I'm good enough or not good enough. And somehow I feel that you are an important person in my life. The question is whether you are enough or not.

*   *   *

Fortunately, my year in China (1984-1985) was the beginning of an era of new openness, or so it seemed then. Had I arrived a few years earlier—or, in the light of Tiananmen, two years later—I would have gotten little cooperation for my project. Others who had attempted to get the story earlier had been turned away, told that there was no story there, or that they had come too late to get it. I, on the contrary, enjoyed the cooperation of the university authorities. Through them, I was able to obtain some of Winter's papers—though not the most critical ones, as I later discovered—and photos he had managed to preserve in two albums. With the cooperation of the authorities, I was also able to interview people who had known Winter in his prime.

I learned much from these interviews. From Professor Li Fu-ning, then chairman of the English Department of Peking University, I heard a complete outline of Winter's life delivered in impeccable sentences and rounded paragraphs). This charted for me the interviewing work I had to do while I was still in China. And from the dozens of people I interviewed in Peking and in Tientjin, I heard anecdotes that helped me recover pieces of the lost life. But perhaps the single moment, which, in retrospect at least, seems to have been ripest was when an elderly professor named Zhou told me that Winter had once been connected with a Rockefeller Foundation project called the Orthological Institute of China.

Correspondence with J. William Hess, then associate director of the Rockefeller Archives, gave me access to reports and letters that Winter had written to Rockefeller Foundation officers and to friends like I. A. Richards during the first half of the '40s. Through Mr. Hess, I also discovered part of a diary Winter had kept while teaching at Lianda, the remarkable university in exile in Kunming formed by students and professors after Japanese occupation closed the northern schools. The diary was especially exciting to me because I had been hearing for nearly a year—even from eyewitnesses—what a shame it was that the Red Guard had burned this document during the Cultural Revolution.

Immediately upon my return to the States in the summer of 1985, I visited the archives and unearthed thousands of pages of documents, enough to warrant a second visit in the following summer. Since much of this material had to do with the Orthological Institute itself, I was drawn into an extended secondary examination of that project, as it hatched out of the book called *The Meaning of Meaning* that I. A. Richards and C. K. Ogden published in 1923, the same year that Winter sailed to China.

Then, in late December 1986, I was able to return to China for a visit of several weeks, on the occasion of Winter's hundredth birthday, Chinese reckoning. (For a detailed account of the celebration, see chapter 18). Despite his deteriorating condition, Winter and I had a few talks during the several weeks that I was in Beijing. During the last of these, I told him that I had written a story about him for the *China Daily*, and I asked him if he wished to hear it. He said that he did, but after a sentence or two, it was obvious that he could not keep his attention fixed, so I stopped. When I prepared to leave, he made me promise that I would come back. I promised, and then he took my hand and kissed it.

The following day, two weeks after his birthday, he went into a coma. I was in his room when the doctor arrived and, detecting a faint heartbeat, called for an ambulance to transfer him to the university hospital. The last time I saw him alive, two English Department cadres were carrying him in a stretcher down the winding walk past what had once been his garden.

On that same cold, clear day, Wang, his nurse, her finger to her lips, brought me a pile of his papers that had remained hidden in the house. Walter Zeisbrger,[2] who was standing next to me, surreptitiously handed me his large briefcase and I dropped the papers in. They included a copy of his diary, self-criticisms he had written during antirightist campaigns in the '50s, as well as some letters. Later I found an extensive file of additional letters in the Rockefeller Archives, and that was that except the FBI files I obtained with the help of an FOI suit initiated for me by my former student David Kendall of Williams and Connolly in Washington, D.C. Like Winter's memory, the documentary material provided rich but fragmented glimpses into his long life in China that began in 1923.

*   *   *

Bob Winter, as his friends called him, was a man famous in his world. His "freakish glands," in Emily Hahn's[3] words, for a long time prevented him from showing any signs of advancing age. His brilliant gossip and verbal exhibitionism made him a delightful entertainer, a conversationalist among conversationalists who often managed to silence even Ms. Hahn herself. Winter naturally drew to his side companions like Ms. Hahn, as well as the eminent Chinese scholar John Fairbank and the renowned literary critic I. A. Richards, not to mention a host of Chinese scholars of equal stature.

As China's history evolved, Winter lived a variety of lives—university lecturer, Rockefeller Foundation cultural ambassador without portfolio, gardener, health food advocate, and amateur zookeeper par excellence. During the anti-Japanese war, he even had a fling at espionage, a trade he took to as he took to everything else he did—brilliantly, zestfully, and humanely. The story of how he rescued a Mongolian Living Buddha from Japanese hands should become a classic of spy literature, and there are a half dozen other stories equal to this, involving everything from gunrunning to smuggling radios and weapons to the Communist guerillas of Shantung province. As Ms. Hahn, writing in the '40s, put it, "Romance in China is not dead. Bob was this romance personified."[4]

With the Communist victory in 1949, the romance quickly faded. Once Winter decided to remain in China, he found himself increasingly treated (better say mistreated) like a Chinese intellectual. This meant that he was subject to the same antirightist campaigns that periodically terrorized them. Even before the Cultural Revolution, he was subjected to intense struggle sessions. In the course of these, Winter became half convinced—though only in his darkest moments—that the work he had done for the Rockefeller Foundation, and even the espionage efforts he carried out against the Chinese, might somehow be evidence of his antirevolutionary leanings. In fact, after he became disillusioned with Mao's revolution, he regularly passed on to American authorities such political information as he was privy to, which was considerable.

There was a short period when he had high hopes for the Communist regime, which at least offered an alternative to the corrupt and violently repressive regime of Chiang Kai-shek. These hopes quickly died. Already in his sixties at the time of Liberation, Winter spent his last decades in China in a subdued light. His remaining teaching duties (which officially ended in 1957) were reduced to the tasks of writing exercises for English readers and providing pronunciation models for young speakers of English. Yet if his spirit was chastened, it was certainly not extinguished—not, at least, until his ninety-fourth year, when he broke his hip and became bedridden. Until then, he was still at least the monument of his glittering past—an old China hand par excellence, whom Sinophiles of every nation came to visit when the political atmosphere allowed and who still cut a certain figure: this big, silver-haired American, riding his bicycle in all kinds of weather, swimming every summer noon in nearby Kunming Lake, where his talent for reading a newspaper and smoking a cigarette while he floated on his back drew large crowds around him.

Writing in 1941, George Orwell remarked that "modern literature is essentially an individual thing. It is either the truthful expression of what one man thinks and feels, or it is nothing." Yet, he added, as soon as one puts this notion into words "one realizes how literature is menaced. For this is the age of the totalitarian state, which does not and probably cannot allow the individual any freedom whatever." I think that this same formula applies to the liberal humanism that Winter embodied. Not only did he believe in the individual freedoms that the literature he taught explored and endorsed, but he also believed in the power of culture to overcome violence and the tendency toward totalitarianism itself. For him, as for other thinkers in the interlude between the great wars, the merging of Eastern and Western cultures represented the possibility of bridging the abysses that separated nations and races and signaled a movement toward a larger cultural order that could make for peace.

In the long run, however, the flames of war annihilated such teaching. Humanism was subsumed by terrorism in a variety of forms, and as manifest in a variety of striving ideologies and nation states. So Winter lived to see the core of his educational principles mocked by world history. That core, as he once expressed it in his diary, was that "The chief aim of education should be . . . to see to it that the desire for domination over others does not arise."

My book is about suffering, about the chastening of a man's Western ideals and his slow resignation to the long patience of the Orient. Yet there survived in him, almost to the end, the rebellious conviction that, despite the superior powers of history, the awakened, cognizant individual, even when his view opposes that of the status quo, can be right, and thus that opposition to absolute power can also be right, however dangerous.

CHAPTER ONE:

HOOSIER IN EXILE

That winter the raids came between ten in the morning and three in the afternoon, and he planned around them, working for a couple of hours in the morning and from three to six in the afternoon. He got used to carrying on his person the things that were important to him. In his suitcase were his typewriter, his glasses, a briefcase containing the records of the Orthological Institute of China, which he directed, and a trenchcoat to put under him in the ditches where he sought shelter from shrapnel. "It had all become a kind of routine, mere child's play," he wrote home, "compared to what is happening in Europe."

Still, for a "tenderfoot" like himself—he had come down to Kunming from Peking only two months ago—it was not pleasant to "see stupefied women sitting like watchdogs in the craters where their families had blown up." Since he had no family, Robert Winter was spared such watches. The worst personal loss that he had suffered occurred shortly after his arrival in November 1940, when thieves broke into his room and split open his trunks with crowbars. Thus he had lost all the personal possessions (including his Hermes portable typewriter) that he had managed to keep with him during his recent fourteen-day truck ride up the Burma Road, through a saga of bombed-out bridges, black water fever, interminable official delays, drivers who themselves tried to steal his baggage, and the sobering experience of watching "five trucks a day plunge over the precipice or lying at the foot after they had plunged."[1]

He resembled a harlequin, dressed in odds and ends of clothing given to him by friends—though in Kunming, in the winter of 1940-1941, even a graying, gaunt American in motley who stood over six feet was no odd sight in the welter of soldiers, local citizens, tribal people down from the mountains, and university students and professors who had migrated, in many cases on foot, from Peking more than one thousand miles to the northeast in order to preserve their universities after the Japanese seized the physical plants back in the north.

Ordinarily, the air raid warnings came early enough to allow the city's inhabitants to make their way through the east gate to the wooded hills half an hour away. Occasionally though, the planes managed to get around the first line of spotters and would be over the town before the earliest warning had finished sounding. Then it was pandemonium. People ran through the narrow east gate with valuables on their heads.

> Old women with babies strapped on their backs, opium smokers with their pipes, cripples, students with packages of books, house-wives with bound feet clutching a clock to their bosom or some other valuable tied in their person somewhere are all mixed up with the cars of the rich and the trucks belonging to the larger offices.[2]

Just a few weeks before Winter arrived, his closest friend, a Scotsman named Arthur Pollard-Urquhart, had died as a result of the complications that resulted from a bad cut on his left knee he had gotten when a truck knocked him down in the press at the gate.[3]

Winter himself cut a rather comic figure when the siren blew and he and his assistant ran for the hills, carrying between them the heavy office typewriter he had borrowed from the British Consulate to replace the Hermes he had lost. Sometimes he got caught short—once at the local cemetery, where he lay among the tombs to dodge shrapnel, suffering from several degrees of fever from the local typhus that he had gotten from the bite of a rat while he was asleep. As a Chinese friend had said to him, "There is no time here now to be old, ill, or to die."[4]

It was the sciatica, which developed from the lumbago he contracted on the Burma Road, that almost did him in. One day, just a week after he arrived in Kunming, half crippled already, he fell behind the crowd that poured through the gate, and he never got as far as the wooded hills. Instead, when the planes came in on that particular December day, he was sitting in the wet rice fields, where he had to remain while the planes, having used up their machine gun ammo, dove into the crowd dropping hand grenades. Two students were killed, but Winter, lucky as usual, watched one pilot make two passes at him, going wide with his grenade both times. Thus Winter suffered no harm, except that the all-clear did not sound for six hours and he limped home cold and drenched. The next day, unable to move without agony, he was relieved by his friend the British consul's kind loan of a hot water bottle. It was a good day in Kunming when one's woes could be relieved by the application of a hot water bottle.

Through all of this, Winter drew a kind of comfort from the Chinese, who had been stripped of everything, even of their traditional reverence for the dead. Now there were no funerals. Bodies were disposed of "as quietly and quickly as possible," and Winter learned of the death of Mr. Pirey, "an old French gentleman who had kept an English school in Kunming for many years," only because he happened to pass a group of twenty-odd students running out of a gate with a coffin on their shoulders. A small cotton flag on a bamboo stick gave his name in Chinese and said that they were taking his body out for burial.

There was so much to adjust to, yet "the surprising thing is that most people, and particularly Chinese, adjust themselves very quickly. Possibly the enforced physical exertion and tension leave little room for emotions. I am not able to sleep after a day of horrors, but I have not noticed that the students are affected in the same way. In my case, it may be caused partly by the unaccustomed altitude."[5]

Winter had come to China seventeen years ago as a kind of cultural emissary who could talk about Shakespeare and Dante, Michaelangelo and Montaigne, Beethoven and Mozart with a clarity and passion that commanded attention. And he had come to learn as well as to teach. In China, he had discovered a level of everyday culture and courtesy that he had found sadly absent in the West. But now all thoughts of culture were driven out of mind. One's business was simply to survive. And even though one managed to do that physically, emotional survival exacted a high price. One had either to muffle one's thoughts and feelings in gray or to remain open to horrors that allowed little space for other guests of the imagination:

The raid over, coming back to the city from the hills, one encountered

> the clay bust of a woman, armless and smiling . . . leaning against the foot of a tree. Across the road, on a bubbly black pool in the dust, crawling with flies, float white grains of rice. From the centre, a little hand, an inch long, is pointing

at the sky. Cover her face . . . . Why do they make the boxes
so narrow. It doesn't matter, when there are only bits to be
shovelled in, but this naked fat man, whose shoulders are still
entire, has to be forced in with the shovel . . . . Before my door
a man is kneeling, his bottom high in the air, like an Arab at
prayer. His head is gone. They say it is my carpenter . . . . A
woman has climbed to the highest point of the ruins of her
house, and her face, hot and shining from digging in the tangle
of beams and wires, catches the last ray of the sun. "Pitched
past pitch of grief." [6] Depths of suffering in her eyes. Irony,
futility, on her lips . . . .

Tonight, when you have turned the key in the lock, slipped the
ready cartridge back into its clip, blown out the candle, and you
sink down, your eyes, the mouth of a bottle suddenly overturned,
will go on dripping till you are on your feet again. Your bed a
rack, where "thoughts against thoughts in groans grind."[7]

Yet Winter continue to witness and report from the heart of a misery
that most Western residents of China had long since put behind them. By
1940, it was very apparent that China would never again be the paradise
for emigré aesthetes that it had been before the war. But he stayed and
he taught, though he recognized that his attitude would "suggest to most
persons the strange behaviour of Gide's Séquéstrée de Poitiers who, when
rescued from a dark and filthy room where she had been locked up for
over twenty years, resisted all efforts of her nurses to cut off her matted
hair and to give her a bath and, as far as I know, begged continuously for
the rest of her life to be allowed to return to her 'dear little den.'"[8]

Why did he stay? He pondered the question with his friend I. A.
Richards, who had begun to hint to him that it was time to get out.
Was it mere conditioning, like Séquestrée's? Was it a kind of "dramatic
instinct" that made him fear "the dullness of an orderly world?" Did he
stay because "on the rough canvas of these lower physical levels" he was
"spared the finicky lines of useless worries at the corners of the mouth
and eyes?" Was it mere vanity? The weekly lectures on poetry that he was
delivering at Lianta, the university in exile in Kunming, had had to move
constantly to larger and larger halls to accommodate the crowds.

Did he remain in China out of "sheer funk at having fallen eighteen years behind the times and at the effort required to sweep the cobwebs from the brain? Or a secret horror of becoming American in the sense of what one hears over the radio? Or fear that literature would cease to mean as much in more favorable surroundings?" Or was it because of the sheer impossibility of walking out on people who literally kept themselves alive to defend their country "with soup brewed from the marrow of their dead fellow's bones." He could not easily turn away from them after that, "before the show is over, no matter how dishonest and callous many of them may be."[9]

He stayed for all these reasons and one more. He had found a place in China. In Peking, he belonged to a university that valued him and that, in some roundabout Chinese way, would keep him from starving while saving his face. "It is certain," he told Richards, that China is the only country in the world where I could count on any such thing, and this knowledge partly compensates for the disadvantages of living here."

So, at fifty-seven years old, he declared himself irreversibly an inhabitant of a realm about as far from his birthplace in Crawfordsville, Indiana, as it was possible to get, where his alienation from his country and its people began.

                          *   *   *

When he was almost ninety, Robert Winter wrote: "It seems that I entered this world in the midst of terrorism and after some [time] shall [leave] it in the midst of terrorism." 1890, the year of Winter's birth, was devastating for his family. First they got news that their oldest son, John, a railroad man who had been named after his father, had died in a train accident out west, near Florence, Colorado, where he was buried. He was just twenty. Toward the end of November, the youngest child, Max, died at eight months, of pneumonia. But the death that hurt them most was the death of father John, also by pneumonia, just nine weeks before Max followed him to the grave. Robert Winter, though he was only three at the time, remembered this disastrous year as the beginning of hysteria in his mother "that went on till she died."[10]

Winter would enjoy much mothering of a certain sort during his childhood years, but he knew no fathering. His only memory of John was of an afternoon when he was led, into the parlor by an older sister: "and there was what I had never seen before but it was a coffin, and she held me up to look at the face of a dead man and told me he was my father. So I never knew him except that one minute I was lifted up to look at him dead."[11]

This stark moment initiated him into the deep solitude of the boy who is fatherless. All his life, Winter would do what he could to surround himself with people, and all his life he would be alone. All his life he would reach out toward men, and the formative experiences of his life would result from an extraordinary series of male friendships. But as a child, he lived in the company of women.

Despite the family's heavy losses, the modest, two-story house that John (a carpenter by trade) had built for them on Wabash Avenue, just west of Wabash College, still bulged at the seams—though unfortunately not with wage earners. John had left behind him, besides his widow Katherine, who was already forty, a family of eight children, six of them girls. Only the two eldest daughters—Katherine, who was twenty-two, and Margaret, or Maggie, who was five years younger—were employed, at a downtown store, D. W. Rountree's. Mother Katherine stayed at home to raise the other girls—Anna, Josephine, Mary, and Elizabeth, ranging from fifteen to five years old—and the two surviving boys.

Frank, at seven the older son, fended for himself as well as he could, away from that household of women. That left Robert (the ninth born), at four the family's youngest and favored male, to live the life of a pasha and to develop in the bargain those defects of character that such a life imposes. One of Winter's old friends remembers him saying after some fit of temper: "I am such a beast because I was absolutely spoiled in my childhood. I was raised to be a tyrant. If I lifted a finger, they served me."[12] So Winter grew up without having to struggle against a restricting male will. On the rare occasions when he was opposed, he had only to run out of the house and lie down in the road, waiting to get run over by a passing cart or carriage, to persuade the delinquent female to tend at once to his needs. His easy rise to power must have contributed to the indifference bordering on contempt that he showed toward his family. But it was not merely the absence of a father that caused Winter to grow up spoiled and without positive family feeling. Though through most of his life he would exercise the passion for gardening that he had learned from his mother and would also share her taste for gossip, he disliked her from an early age.[13]

It is hard to imagine how a woman as burdened as Katherine Winter could have provided the fatherless boy with the emotional upbringing he needed. But she also had certain personal qualities that Winter would live to blame her for. Needing whatever she could find to prop herself up, Katherine was convinced that she derived from gentile Alsatian stock, and she liked to put on airs. In fact (or so Winter was convinced as a man) her family were "ordinary people . . . not distinguished in society in any way. But she didn't want people to think that we were just ordinary workers, so pretended that in Germany we were a distinguished family—and other things that were not true—to give us better standing in America."[14]

Katherine's high measure of her worth helped keep the family afloat during the difficult years when they all lived on two salesclerks' salaries. It may even have instilled in Robert that sense of natural aristocracy, which as a man he displayed even while he practiced his own deep principles of democracy. But during his childhood, the most visible result of his mother's pride was that it isolated Robert from the local boys whom she taught him were his inferiors. Later he would remember her snobbery with an almost physical distaste.

But what repelled Winter most was Katherine's admiration for her elder brother who had died with Custer. He never tired of retelling the story. "My mother was born in 1834," he reflected he was eighty-nine years old. She

> married at 16 (1850), and then began to produce children every other year during the years that Americans were murdering hundreds of thousands of Indians until December 1890 when they murdered Tatanka Yotanka (Sitting Bull), two weeks before my third birthday. That month (Dec 1890) my father, my eldest brother, and a baby brother all died and I can still remember (more vividly [than] I can remember what happened yesterday) my mother's hysteria that went on till she died. Her own elder brother whom she must have been particularly fond of had run away to Montana to help Custer murder Indians and from the age of three she boasted to me how he carried in his belt the scalps of the Indians he killed until in 1876 he was caught with a small group of whites. When their horses were killed they stood while the Indians galloped round them in a huge circle at tremendous speed and picked them off with arrows one by one. Then closed in and scalped him in turn. It seems that I entered this world in the midst of terrorism and after some [time] shall [leave] it in the midst of terrorism.

Though Winter, with his customary flair for dramatic heightening, is a little off in dating the series of deaths that struck the family in 1890, the rest sounds right. Or at least, it is hard for me to escape from the spell the old man cast over me when he first told me the tale. As he brought it to a close, lying in the bed he no longer left, he came back from the remote past and looked at me: "The greatest mystery of my life which I never cleared up is how I—a small child four or five years old—knew it was wrong to kill the Indians. Nobody told me. It was as if I just knew without being told . . . . My mother and her brother thought that they should all be killed—all the so-called Indians, the natives of America. And why should I as a little child of four or five feel that I wanted to know them? Could I have been born with that?"[15]

*   *   *

"Could I have been born with that?" The question was not rhetorical. Winter's death was approaching. He looked straight at me: he wanted to know. But who can say what we are born with? What is certain is that quite early he learned to hate the snobbery and petty vanity and savagery that often masks itself as civilization. In childhood, he also learned what would become one of his life's shaping motives: to prefer the Indian to his exterminator, to despise orthodox notions of respectability, and to be a reluctant member of the middle class. Indeed, he would grow up not merely to sympathize with the oppressed, the castaway, but to experience himself as one.

"The thing that I think very interesting that I remember about myself now is this: that for a small child I understood these society things so well. I knew when my mother pretended we were something we were not. And then my uncle ran away to Oregon and there they killed the Indians." Winter had begun that early to experience the pains suffered and the pleasures enjoyed by persons who see things with their own eyes.

Thus he grew up as a solitary. "When I was a little boy I played about," he told me, "but my mother didn't want me to play with other boys."[16] Believing in her own social superiority, she also believed in his. In later years, Winter dropped his middle name, Karl, in a kind of final recoil against his mother's burgherly airs. So, with few ties to the past and the born exile's flimsy attachment to his native ground, Winter had begun to practice his odd fate.

*   *   *

Crawfordsville, the west central Indiana town where Winter grew up, with its population of just over six thousand, was a kind of natural paradise for boys—up to a certain age. Not five minutes walk from his home on Wabash Avenue was Crawford's Woods, where Winter liked to explore and climb trees, usually alone. Also near at hand was Sugar Creek, which ran through the town through dramatic gorges and the dense woods of sugar maples that gave the creek its name. It was in Sugar Creek that he learned to swim—one of the many skills that would become part of his legend.

It was also the first of many waters that would grace the landscape for him. He had a Chinese taste in such matters: he found no landscape without a lake or running water truly beautiful. Oddly, Winter's feeling for the landscape and for the earth seems to be another of the characteristics that he shared with his mother. The one activity he recalls enjoying with her was puttering in the garden that she kept excellently. Here he learned the skill that would be one of his lesser claims to fame in China.

Farming was even more native to Crawfordsville than gardening. The earth was level and fertile and had already begun to make fortunes for the men who farmed it and who could raise from it as much as twenty-five bushels of wheat or sixty bushels of Indian corn per acre. In other ways too, the earth had laid a ground of prosperity around the town. The creek provided power for the many grist and sawmills in the area and for the celebrated woolen mills run by a man named Yount. In the autumn, local men and boys earned spare cash (as they still do) digging "sang" for export to Oriental ginseng markets.

Culturally too, the city had resources to stir a booster's heart, though through works that fell below the standards of high literary art. General Lew Wallace, who had spent a short time at the preparatory academy of Wabash College when he was a boy of nine, came back there to live after accomplishing his varied career as Civil War general of clouded reputation (Grant complained that at Shiloh, Wallace had led his troops in the wrong direction on the first day of the battle). Back home, he built himself an exotic study and wrote historical romances, including the enormously successful *Ben-Hur*. His presence helped to activate such local writers as Maurice Thompson, who, with a few others, helped

maintain the town's claims to the title "the Athens of Indiana." As Mary
Hannah Krant, under the pen name of Ben Offield, put it with perhaps
less than a booster's passion in the August 5, 1876, issue of the town
paper, "Crawfordsville, as everyone knows, is literary . . . . The citizens
of Crawfordsville have great respect for their small city which they are
somewhat surprised that all the world does not share." Such insularity
would be the bane of Robert Winter.

But for all its bright airs, this new Athens, like the old, had its dark
corners. Rich in churches, Crawfordsville nevertheless outdid them with
saloons—some twenty-three of them were once located on a single block
of North Green Street. Along with them, enough prostitution thrived to
keep the newspapers full of outraged editorials. One whole area of town,
called Fiskeville, was famous as a red-light district, and the one public
school in that part of town, Fiskeville School (also called the Whitlock
School) closed early in the new century for lack of trade. The illicit
children of the prostitutes tended not to get schooling.

Winter's own recollections of the town are colored with woods and
sex. Crawford's Woods were modest, hardly more than a clump of trees.
But even as an old man, Winter could still see himself, whenever he had
a chance to get away from his family, "crossing the street and entering
Crawford's Woods and roaming it and climbing a tree that no one else
could climb."

He would shin up "the lower part and then it was just like climbing
stairs, the branches leading to the top. And from there I could see the
world." And from there, he added, in the half befuddled state of his last
years, "I met the most extraordinary things that nobody could climb but
I." The city was reeking with sex, he said, and that fact was mixed up
in his mind with trees. "A cherry tree grew outside my back door," he
told me once. "And you know how I learned about sex? The only way of
climbing that tree to where there were branches was shinning up the tree
with my arms and legs around it and I would stick there, quivering with
excitement, before I could get my breath to slide down the tree. I learned
sex from that tree."[17]

He also remembered, truly or falsely, that immigrant women were
brought into town as servants and were sometimes forced to serve as
prostitutes. The whole of Crawford's Woods, he said, "was full of little
patches of low trees, and under the shade of them there was a woman
under each one, earning her living all day long." And he would be
perched in his tree, high above, looking down.

This outdoor brothel, the prostitution, overt and covert, made a strong impression on the boy. Men used women against their wills, and "there was nothing in the law to prevent it." In those days, he half remembered, "the countries could borrow girls from another country, to live in their house and do the work for them. And these screams came from a room where they borrowed a girl from another country—there was nothing in the law to prevent it—and had a room where they tied these girls." Then he reflected: "You know, it's astonishing, having lived as long as I have, to know how much better the world is. Everybody [was] doing things that people would be shot for today." That was the only time I ever heard him argue the case for moral progress.

Winter's mother "was very fond of gardening and was always out in the garden planting flowers."[18] Every Sunday morning he was out there with her, and sometimes, he said, a beautiful neighbor woman would pass by and turn the corner to the grocery, though the grocery didn't open on Sunday. And as she went past, the woman would sing out to Winter's mother, who was planting flowers with the boy: "I'm paying my grocery bill." That meant, Winter explained, "that she was going around to the grocery, which closed its door on Sunday. I don't know if there were one or two heads of that grocery. I think there were two brothers, and they simply took turns jumping on her the whole day . . . . The whole town was simply reeking with sex, but it was almost death to admit it," he told me. On Sundays "there'd be loud laughter, and a little horse wagon would go by my house, full of whores taking a day off by riding around the town. Everyone knew what it was, and everyone laughed and waved to them as they went by. They didn't see any harm in that." And then, in the kind of stream-of-consciousness style of his later years, he added: "Only I could climb that tree."[19]

A pubescent boy in a town reeking of sex that no one talked about, looking down from that tree onto a brothel al fresco, where immigrant women, tied to trees, gave themselves to rough customers, in the pointillist light—an odd but oddly archetypal American figure. Perhaps some of this is remembered fantasy or something he invented when he was old and his mind addled. But these were his memories, and up to his senior year in high school, they are all I have.

Winter's high school classbook remembered him as a "powder puff and fashion plate," and one class wit encapsulated him with a couplet:

A beauty doctor's life he'll lead,
And all the fashion columns read

—a wildly inaccurate prophecy, except insofar as it may have expressed a tacit observation that he already had traits that marked him as gay.

Before Winter left high school, he had begun to find windows that opened to other worlds not only in books but also in foreign languages. When Winter was in his early teens, a next-door neighbor brought back with him from Europe a French wife, who never troubled to learn English. She often invited the boy over and give him things to eat. Then she would talk to him. When her husband died suddenly, the boy became the woman's only real companion. So by the time he entered Wabash College in his hometown of Crawfordsville—this in 1905—Winter knew not only the Latin and Greek he had learned in high school, but he also spoke French nearly as well as English.[20]

When Winter graduated from high school in 1905, he was a big-eared boy, a bit younger looking than his classmates. His face is bright, reflective, and openly expectant, unlike the faces of his male classmates, which are masked in varying degrees of manly-jawed Horatio Algerism. They look ready for suitable employment. But an employer would be taking a chance with Winter. He looks too sensitive, and although his gaze is direct, his face is a shade too intimate.

Happily, he was not seeking employment but instead embarking on a college career that would prove formative. By his sophomore year, and again in the year following, he already served the college as an instructor—first of Greek (this to take the place of Ezra Pound) and then of French. Late in the spring semester of his sophomore year, he played the role of a priest of Zeus in a college production of *Oedipus Tyrannus*.[21] In the college literary magazine, he published both poetry and prose. One of his poems, a Miltonic effort in quatrains called "Pan-Worship," invites its readers, while "The sprightly robin warbles loud in glee, / [And] the soaring lark sings out her shrill sweet song / to "Cease groping after vague gods wearily, / Come worship Pan; Spring may not tarry long." In another, a fragment called "Apollo and Daphne" and written in Spenserian stanzas, the stage is set for the nymph's aborted ravishment, though that scene does not appear.[22]

In his senior year, Winter served as literary editor of the Wabash magazine known as *The College Board*. And during his last semester at Wabash, he wrote an essay on Thackeray that closed with an impassioned defense of the wisdom of the heart:

In these days of the scientific method some advocates of the old school have almost feared that art might be extinguished; what should be a mean has become an end and the novel approaches a scientific treatise on the genus Homo. But this will work out its own destruction in the end. Knowledge is necessary but it must be kept subordinate; the artist's function is to see and feel; not to miss the slightest shade or line of what he sees about him, but to give it to us as his eyes see it, as his heart feels it, but not merely as his mind knows it.[23]

At Wabash, Winter learned to transform into strengths the eccentricities that already marked him. Known for the while as Bobbie, in his senior year he had the honor of composing the class poem, being elected to Phi Beta Kappa, and being appointed the Fowler Duhme fellow in English. He had also been appointed university scholar in comparative literature at Columbia University. A Wabash newspaper story about this appointment praised him both as "a natural literary genius" and as one who had "taken practically all the English courses here and is exceptionally well qualified for the work which the scholarship will afford him."[24] No doubt he was, but, presumably because he could not afford to study in New York, he remained instead for another year at Wabash to take his MA during the brief period when the college awarded that degree, and, after a year away, returned again to serve the college as an instructor in 1913-1914.

But Winter's deepest experience at Wabash occurred when he fell under the influence of the brilliant young instructor of Romance languages, Ezra Pound, during the few months the young poet taught before being fired. The meeting with Pound was one in a series of chance meetings that helped chart the course of Winter's life. Though the contact between them was brief, the two men continued to correspond for a year afterward, principally, Winter told me, about the concept of literary periods. "The whole thing had an importance in my life much greater than it should have had for the very short meetings I had with him," Winter said.[25]

The last of those meetings between the two young men (Pound was only two years older than Winter), on the night before Pound's departure from Wabash, gave Winter his first glimpse of the exhilarations of exile.

As Winter remembers the scene, it was tamer but even more hilarious than Pound's own famous account of how he sheltered a girl abandoned by a traveling vaudeville troupe. Pound was living at the time in a boarding house on Grant Avenue, "where they usually put teachers who had no family." Crawfordsville, Winter remembers, seventy-five years after the fact, "was then a little uncivilized village."

> Some wild puritan from the college went to see Pound and found one of the local women teachers in his room asking him some questions about phonetics. He immediately rushed back to Wabash headquarters and ordered them to write an official letter to Pound demanding that he leave town by the next train!!! A few hours later I happened to go to see Pound and he showed me the letter and then picked up a volume of Browning's poems and read to me the poem, "Seen by a Contemporary," which begins "I only knew one poet in my life" and goes on to say how a man watched "a man on the streets of Valladolid" [Valladolid] who walked up and down observing and taking notes about everything and who was, of course, a poet, but who was thought to be a spy! Then Pound said goodbye, left Crawfordsville and went to Italy. We wrote to each other for about a year. In one of his letters he said that I was the most civilized person in Crawfordsville. Then he met T. S. Eliot and stimulated him to be a good poet. I fled from the USA. I kept Pound's letters as my most precious possession. By that last evening with Pound, I had suddenly been awakened!!! Without Pound I probably would now be an idiot crawling about in Crawfordsville. As it is I am a belligerent atheist in China![26]

Pound praised Winter, though perhaps faintly, as "the most civilized man in Crawfordsville."

The poet's immediate legacy to Winter was more practical. The *Crawfordsville Journal* of February 15, 1908, mentions Pound's departure, adding that Professor Haines would take over his classes in French and that Robert Winter would relieve Haines of one of his classes in Greek. So it was through Pound that Winter obtained his first teaching job.

Despite these evidences of his precocity, Winter won from his Wabash classmates the kind of acceptance that he had failed to win in high school. The caption under his picture in the college yearbook reads: "He is truly great that is little in himself and that maketh no account of any height in honor"—an odd anticipation of the Oriental gauges of character against which Winter would later measure himself.

*   *   *

In 1909-1910, while he was earning the MA degree, Winter worked as a teaching fellow in English. The recognition and encouragement he had received not only from Wabash but from Columbia University, even though he was unable to put that latter to use, must have had the young man thinking about an academic career. But he was restless, and after completing that year of teaching and graduate studies, he walked out of his mother's house, got on a train without a ticket, arrived in New York, and soon after booked passage to England. (That, at least, is the chronology as the Rockefeller Foundation—and the FBI from them—have it.)

Winter didn't like England very well; it was too much like the U.S. So he moved on to Paris where he took classes at the Sorbonne and lived in a room "that was almost not a room for a human being to live in." In Paris he was acquainted with anarchist circles, and he may have known Victor Serge. The only job offers he had in Paris were dozens of invitations (all rejected) to throw bombs at important people or important buildings."[27] This would have been his second encounter with terrorism, though it would hardly be his last.

From 1911-1912 he studied at the University of Naples. Then he sailed back home. But as soon as he "got into America," he told me he felt he had made a mistake. "All my life since then I've felt that America is a bad place to live in." Whenever he returned, he said, no sooner did his feet touch his native soil than he wished to be gone again. In 1912, however, Winter still had more than a decade to live in America before he would leave it once and for all. For the first year of this period, he was "in business." Then, from 1914-1916, he worked as the head of Romance Language Departments in Howe School, Indiana. For the next three years, he taught French and Spanish at Evanston Township High School in Evanston, Illinois, where he served on the advisory committee to the school magazine, *The Evanstonian*, and as faculty advisor to the French Club, and playing the lead in a French comedy called *Rosalie*. He also gave a number of dramatic readings, including Maeterlinck's *Ariane et Barbe-bleue*, which was received with great interest by an incipient feminist reviewer, who found in Ariane a figure of "the modern woman, ever inquiring and demanding reasons," and in the other women characters "the submissive type of women in the Middle Ages, who obeyed instinctively and unquestioningly."[28]

Winter was a bright light among the French set of Evanston students, who not only wrote enthusiastically about his readings and translations, but also thanked him for giving them a foundation for a true appreciation of French literature.[29] He seemed to enjoy his liberated life in Evanston. Dorothy Gaylord, wife of one of Winter's later colleagues in China, remembers him saying, "I just went farting down Michigan Avenue for all I was worth."[30]

While he was at Township High, during the great epidemic of 1918 that killed twenty million people, Winter fell ill with influenza. One day, as he returned to his rented rooms, he dropped unconscious just inside the door. His landlady tried to get a doctor, but every one she called was himself in the hospital with the flu, so she called a woman teacher Winter knew and she came and nursed him, following instructions from the hospitals as to how to do it. After three days in a coma, Winter recovered, but he was left with a scar on his right bronchial tube that would become his Achilles' heel. (Almost sixty years later, he would attribute to this illness the repeated bouts of flu that he suffered each winter at Peking University during his later years.)

In December 1919, *The Evanstonian* printed an editorial on "The Shantung Question."[31] It was signed by a student, "Katherine F. Brammer, '20," but the style of prose and thought suggests the likelihood that Winter, who as one of the paper's faculty advisors and who had already begun to cultivate an active interest in things Chinese, had lent a hand. The piece is remarkably well informed about a chapter in Chinese history that would prove critical to China's long struggle toward modern identity.

The gist of the matter was that, at the end of WWI, in which China had fought on the side of the Allies, the Allies had rewarded her by taking Shantung, which had been part of the German "sphere of influence," and transferring it to Japan instead of returning it, as China had hoped. In the Council of Foreign Ministers, where the question was settled, the United States had opposed that outcome, but only feebly. Young people in China reacted to this decision by the Allies as a "National Humiliation." On May 4, 1919, some three thousand students gathered in an inflammatory meeting at Peking University and marched downtown, where they attacked and set fire to the house of Ts'ao Ju-lin, the member of China's Foreign Affairs Commission whom the students considered principally responsible for the sell out to Japan. Though Ts'ao was not at home, the students did find Chang Tsung-hsiang, the Chinese minister to Japan, and beat him into insensibility.

The immediate upshot was the arrest of thirty-two students, one of whom died of injuries three days later. The long-term effect was that this episode, which came to a climax on the fourth of May (giving the movement its name), would come to be known as the beginning of the modern Nationalist movement in China.

Given the complexity of this affair, it is remarkable that in Evanston, Illinois, not many months after the outbreak of events that would eventually transform the face of modern China, a young American high school student, with the help of her faculty advisor, argued, in *The Evanstonian*, in defense of the Shantung decision, that "what China as a republic needs is a great national unity. If Shantung were returned to China without the vigorous action of the Chinese themselves, it is doubtful whether unity could be achieved. This is the question: shall China work out her own salvation or shall other nations step in and decide her destiny for her?"[32] Robert Winter could hardly have known that this question would decide not only China's destiny but his own.

Yet unawares, he was moving toward his destiny. In the fall of 1918, he moonlighted at Northwestern University as a teaching assistant in French, for which services he received $50 extra a month.[33] This job lasted only through the fall semester, but by 1920, he had obtained a full-time university appointment at the University of Chicago, this one carrying the title of assistant professor of romance languages—though his teaching assignment was to the Junior College Department of the university high school, where he taught French and Spanish to students with minimal previous training or none.[34] Winter couldn't have been happy with these menial positions. Stuck in an academic cul de sac, he could not have known that he was on the brink of the adventure that gave his life its ultimate form.

*   *   *

In Chicago, as in Crawfordsville, Winter's most important experience was a meeting with a remarkable young poet, Wen Yiduo who came to Chicago to study at the art institute. Wen's second book, *Red Candle*, just published in China, would establish him as his country's first and foremost modernist, and, after he abandoned poetry in 1928 for political reasons, he would go on to become a brilliant classical scholar, whom Robert Payne called "perhaps the greatest and most representative, and certainly the most beloved in modern China."[35] More sadly, after his later role as a high effective opponent of Chiang Kai-shek's Nationalist regime, he would end as a political martyr.

Wen, who was twenty-four, and Winter, eleven years his senior, met through some painters they both knew. Winter had Wen over for dinner several times. On one occasion, they were joined by the poet Eunice Tietjens and her husband, Cloyd Head. Eunice, recently returned from China, had just published a volume of poetry which she wrote in a traditional Chinese form, and most of the conversation concerned Chinese verse technique. But what Winter remembered best was

> Wen's fiery indignation about an incident which had occurred the day before at the [Art Institute]. He was making a sketch and he had paused for a moment to consider what he had done. Some American students passed, and, without asking his permission, took up his sketch, looked at it for a moment, then threw it down without a word and went on . . . . Wen would not have been offended if they had told him that his sketch was bad, but their throwing the sketch down instead of laying it down on the table he could only interpret as a deliberate insult.[36]

Wen and Winter discovered that, for all their differences, they had a world in common—a world of painting and poetry and of democratic ideals. Together, they haunted the art institute. As to poetry, Wen's special passion was for the poems of John Keats, who became his poetic mentor, and who influenced Winter's early poems. Around this convergence of taste, their friendship blossomed into a work relationship. Winter asked Wen to collaborate in a translation of the young Chinese poet's new work written in Chicago, that appeared in his second book, *Red Candle*. Winter also wanted Wen to work with him translating Chinese classical poetry.

The friendship between the two was not purely aesthetic. They shared a fierce loyalty to liberal democratic principles and a hatred against opression. Wen had visited Chinatowns in America and knew something about American institutionalized racism. He lived for the day when the Chinese nation would stand on its own feet, an equal among equals. He also dreamed of equality between all nations and opposed parochial nationalism, which in his own country he had seen as standing in the way of China's acquisition of Western advanced technology and sciences. Bob Winter shared Wen's democratic principles and protested strongly against racism when the university ordered him to lower the grades of black and Jewish students. He also felt great sympathy toward the Eastern oppressed nations and great admiration for their ancient cultures. As he later told Lu Xuan, he already knew that he wished to devote his life to bridging the cultures of the West and that of the East and to fighting for the cause of equality between nations.

Thus the friendship between Winter and Wen developed on the basis of shared tastes and ideals, despite the fact that Wen, as he said of himself, normally was not "good at socializing." Later, both men would see their utopian dreams turn to nightmares. But in Chicago in the early '20s, they spoke of dreams. As Winter remembers it: "I told him that I'd dreamed of a world—and then I described the kind of world. And he said, 'If that's what you want, you should go to China.' So I took a boat to China at once."[37]

Wen's own impression of their short but intense friendship, set down in a letter he sent in late November 1926, to Liang Shi Qiu, a friend still in China who would later join him in America, fills the picture out. Wen wrote that he had found Winter "really an interesting man . . . one of the Americans who are extremely warm toward China." Winter's character, Wen told Liang, he could "describe by a simple story":

Winter had a very big Chinese inverted iron bell, and whenever he could not fall asleep, he would bring it to his bed and listen to the sound coming from knocking it. He is a celibate. If he finds any girl fall in love with him, he will keep himself away from her. I think that must be the result of a failure in a love affair when he was young. I think so because when I asked him for his poems, he said he had once been very romantic in his boyhood, but one day he destroyed all his writings and never wrote any poem after that. However, he likes poems very much. I still have all his translations of Baudelaire.

Whenever Wen called on him, Wen said, they would "talk till one or two o'clock after midnight. Then I say goodbye to him, go to get my overcoat from another room. There, we start another talk. While we walk together to the door, we talk on. We open the door, we continue our talking, then I get to the stairs, we go on with our talk. At last I have to say 'I do need to go to bed now.' We finally have a chance to say 'good night' to each other and part."

By the time that this friendship began, Winter was already a passionate Sinophile. When Wen first visited his house, Winter held up a lantern to a painting on the wall and asked Wen to guess who it was. Wen correctly guessed Lao Zi (Lao Tzu) and was dazzled by the quality of this work by a man who had never studied painting. Winter had also copied several very large Indian figures of the Buddha, and these paintings too hung on the walls of his room. Except for a few pieces of furniture, Wen noted with pleasure, all Winter's things were from China, India, and Japan. Winter also burned various kinds of Oriental incense on the occasions of Wen's visit.[38]

Wen's lengthy account of his new American friend had a purpose. Winter had told him that he could not remain in the States any longer and that he wanted to come to China. In mid-November, a few weeks before Wen wrote to Liang Shi Qiu, Wen's friend Zhang Jing-yue (who was learning French from Winter at the time) and Wen had jointly written a letter to President Cao of Tsinghua University (which was just reconstituting itself from a preparatory school). Now Wen wrote to Liang Shi Qiu in the hope that President Cao might give Winter's candidacy a boost: "If you find a way to have a 'push,' that will be significant for Tsinghua University. I've never seen such an American."

As Wen put it to Liang Shi Qiu, "The most important thing is that [Winter] says he couldn't be in the States any longer and wants to come to China." Winter was certainly drawn to Wen's account of the new political and intellectual ferment that burst loose in China as a result of the May Fourth Movement, just as he was repelled by America's greed and racism. Just a few months before he departed, Winter said he was told by the head of his department to mark down the exam papers of the Jews and Negroes in his class, lest the university be overrun by them.

But it is also possible that Winter was in some kind of trouble. Wen's statement that "he couldn't be in the States any longer" implies real urgency, possibly connected with a homosexual liaison. An odd twist to the story is that, according to Lu Xuan, Wen said nothing to Winter about his letters to China, presumably preferring to wait until he had received replies. But Winter seems to have booked passage to China impetuously. Some months before Wen wrote in his behalf, he applied for "a passport to visit Japan and China for an intended stay of twelve months for the purpose of travel and study." The passport was issued to him on July 27, 1923, by the Department of State, Washington. And on August 21, 1923, he departed the United States at San Francisco aboard the *Trujo Maru*.

CHAPTER TWO:

ARRIVALS

On September 1, 1923, roughly two years after the founding of the Chinese Communist Party, Winter arrived in Nanking after an eleven-day voyage, to remain there for the better part of two years. If he did not stay longer, this was not because the city lacked charms. Located on the southern banks of the Yangtse River and at the foothills of the Zinin (Purple and Gold) Mountains, Nanking enjoys a lovely setting. Founded in the eighth century BC, in an area that has been inhabited for some six thousand years, it has a richly layered history.

From 229 CE, Nanking has been the capital of six imperial dynasties. Destroyed and renewed many times, Nanking would also be the bloody site of the massacre launched against it by the Japanese in 1937, four months after their invasion of China. It was in Nanking that in AD 762, the poet Li Po ended his life of driven exile, and it was here that the Qing dynasty ended in 1911, when delegates from seventeen provinces met to elect Dr. Sun Yat-sen president of the new republic. And in 1925, it was in Nanking, at his request, that Sun Yat-sen, though a native of Guangzhou, would be buried. A city so deeply etched by time had its special appeal for the deracinated Hoosier, himself raised in a town that was scarcely seventy years old when he was born.

Winter had languished in America partly because, like many an American intellectual, including Ralph Waldo Emerson, he sensed that here "things are in the saddle and ride mankind." The China that Wen Yiduo had described to him offered an appealing alternative. Of course, part of the appeal was in the idealized image of an ancient, harmonious, traditional civilization, with its alluring rituals and music, through which the spirit was made amenable with the Way. In that China, nature, rather than an enemy to be conquered, was a companion and coequal, our destiny and our source. This China made its appeal to Winter as to other Western men of letters as an alternative to the ever more imperious positivism of the West. And even to the very dualism that allows "things" to reign.

But it wasn't quite that simple. Winter also came to a China in ferment that, under the impact of the May Fourth Movement, was turning to Western ideas (including positivism) for guidance and power even as she struggled to preserve her own ancient culture and, with it, her identity. Not surprisingly, the first important friend Winter made in Nanking played his part in this struggle, albeit a reactionary part.

Soon after he settled in Nanking, Winter was teaching classes in English and French at the National Southeastern University, where he made a friend of Wu Mi, perhaps through their mutual friend, Wen Yiduo. Wu would become China's "most famous—or notorious—professor of foreign languages,"[1] and it was also Wu Mi, Winter told me sixty years later, who performed for Winter the service that Winter had performed for Wen Yiduo, by initiating him into those secrets of the culture that only intelligence and imagination could disclose.

In certain respects Wu Mi proved an odd guide to the Western stranger just arrived. During this period when all Chinese intellectuals took positions, Wu Mi was associated with a group devoted to the propagation and study of traditional literature and scholarship and to the idea of "national essence" (kuo-ts'ui). This "nativist" group stood opposed to the New Tide Movement, who were dedicated to purging what was dead in Chinese civilization and adapting what was alive in the West, especially critical thought. The New Tide people, led by the Dewey disciple Hu Shih, hoped to create a vital, modern China, but Wu Mi shocked literary progressives by opposing the colloquial literature movement that was part of the New Tide and by writing in classical Chinese, thus showing himself to be doubly reactionary.[2]

But Winter's new friend, a man of paradoxes, had come to his reactionary positions by the progressive path of Western studies. Like many of the best Chinese humanists of his generation, Wu Mi had studied in America, where, at Harvard, he became a convert to Irving Babbitt's New Humanism. Especially appealing to this man whose own unbridled appetites sometimes made him a figure of public ridicule was Babbitt's notion that the arts of the humanities tutor the ethical will and thus help us to put checks upon appetite. The study of the classics accomplishes this, Babbitt held, both by tempering the will with reason and by teaching respect for the wisdom of our ancestors.

Though Wu Mi had freighted himself with this rather grave intellectual baggage, he did not allow it to dampen his lively and contradictory temperament. Like Winter, Wu was an appealingly colorful personage, and, like Winter, he was passionate about English and European literature. Further, he shared Winter's interest in comparative studies and was fond of exploring the similarities and differences between Greco-Roman civilization, Christian culture, India's Buddhist philosophy, and the teachings of China's Confucianists.

So the breadth of Wu Mi's interests naturally engaged Winter, who was himself a man interested in nearly everything. And the two did important work together, designing a program in English literature that would set the curriculum not only in Nanking but at Tsinghua University as well.[3]

But in one important way Wu Mi differed from Winter: Wu Mi was a "nativist," whose essential passion was for the ancient stream of his own culture. Wu wrote poems in the ancient style and was one of two leading authorities on *Dream of the Red Chamber*, China's greatest novel. The American, on the other hand, never showed much positive interest in American culture, and his literary tastes, typical of the educated taste of the time, leaned toward English and continental literature. His America (despite the fact that Winter remained democratic to his bones) was rather like Pound's—an America whose saving remnant could be addressed as Pound addresses them in "The Rest":

> O helpless few in my country,
> O remnant enslaved!
>
> Artists broken against her,
> A-stray, lost in the villages,
> Mistrusted, spoken against,
>
> Lovers of beauty, starved,
> Thwarted with systems,
> Helpless against the control;
>
> You who can not wear yourselves out
> By persisting to successes,

You who can only speak,
Who can not steel yourselves into reiteration;

You of the finer sense,
Broken against false knowledge,
You who can know at first hand,
Hated, shut in, mistrusted;

Take thought:
I have weathered the storm,
I have beaten out my exile.[4]

One of the things that Pound meant by "beaten out" was that he
had broken a trail out of the moribund—though not without the help
of such exiled predecessors as Whistler and Henry James. Now, at the
head of a trail in many respects more forbidding than Pound's, Winter
was preparing to beat out his own. I do not know when he read the poem
(Pound published it in 1913), but Winter, who in his ninety-fifth year
said that without Pound he "probably now would be an idiot crawling
about in Crawfordsville,"[5] must have read it as addressed directly to him.

Winter was fortunate enough to have as his guide at this stage a man
with whom he shared not only cultural and intellectual interests but
also a type of temperament. Though Wu Mi sometimes took the role of
the upright Confucian scholar, upholder of the old morality, he often
acted the iconoclast in his personal life. Wu sometimes called himself
"the Matthew Arnold of the East," and he has been characterized, like
Arnold, as a "classicist in form, a romantic in sentiment."[6] He would
later abandon his wife, openly declare his love for another woman, Mao
Yanwen, and then, when he had let Ms. Mao slip through his fingers,
bemoan his loss in poetry.

As a result of such public stunts, Wu Mi made himself the frequent
butt of essays, satiric verses, and moralizing cartoons. He even achieved
a kind of international fame when I. A. Richards, in an essay exploring
dangers that the Chinese and the Americans encounter when they begin
to assume that they understand one another, asks his reader to "imagine
a course of lectures on English Literature delivered on the assumption
that any pair of male and female characters left by a novelist alone
together must be supposed to misconduct themselves. The well-known

Anglo-Saxon prudery explains why the novelist does not indicate this." Such a course of lectures, he continued, "were given annually by a Chinese Professor of English Literature who ranked as a scholar in Chinese among the most eminent there are.[7] That scholar is certainly Wu Mi, whom Richards met during his first visiting professorship at Tsinghua National University in 1929-1930.

Dressed in long gowns and old-fashioned jackets, Wu Mi was the very type of the refined Confucian scholar, "who, in class sang the praises of America's 'new humanism' but outside of class, if we can trust the words with which he denounced his decadent bourgeois past in 1952 . . . tried to pursue various ladies, some of them my students, but always without success."[8] In all these ill-sorted tendencies, he was presumably following models he had learned from literature. And while he did not exhaust the possibilities, he was one version of the modern Chinese humanist, picking his difficult path toward a modern Chinese culture.

Winter too would live to feel the sting of his own contradictions. Like Wu Mi, he was capable of a moral clarity that often set him apart from those who allowed themselves, unchecked and unquestioning, to be driven by the turbulent energy of events. But Winter's flamboyance, homosexuality, and assertive moral iconoclasm, like Wu's, sometimes delivered him into the hands of his enemies.

*   *   *

Though he was too green to take a position in the controversies that raged over China's efforts to modernize and at the same time to preserve her native culture, Winter learned through Wu some of the intensity of this struggle. He arrived in China at a time of tremendous intellectual ferment. Indeed, Wen-I-to's championship of progressive politics and modern verse helped attract him in the first place, in somewhat the same way that later Westerners visited Mao's China with "red stars in their eyes." To many, it seemed that China could shape her own destiny simply by choosing the correct idea or ideology to steer by. Nothing was unthinkable, intellectual sects were everywhere. Wu Mi, we have seen, had wedded himself to Babbitt's New Humanism, a conservative cultural ideology that had much in common with Confucianism. Others—most prominently the Columbia University-trained philosopher Hu Shih—were involved with the New Tide, which identified itself and was identified by some of its Western admirers with the European

Enlightenment scarcely more than a century earlier. But these were merely two among dozens of similar movements that were drawing young intellectuals to their sides.

The intensity behind this intellectual moment had been triggered by a series of international humiliations, beginning with the intrusion into China of the Western powers in the early half of the nineteenth century—the very subject that Winter's student in Evanston had written about. China's defeat at the hands of the Japanese in 1895 had newly shocked the Chinese, who had always considered themselves the dominant culture, Japan the parasitic imitator. This display of Japan's new military might showed the Chinese that, in the unfolding world of modern power, Japan had not only displaced its mentor, but had accomplished quickly and efficiently the modernization that China had yet to begin. A result of China's defeat at the hands of the Japanese was a frantic attempt to catch up, triggered by a series of edicts issued by the young Qing emperor during the famous Hundred Days of Reform in 1898. The edicts ranged through an array of fundamental social issues— education, medicine, the army and navy, inventions, study abroad, agriculture, the penal code. But they created nothing more than the political chaos that led to a coup d'état by the Manchu empress dowager, Tz'u-hsi, who brought all reform to a screeching halt.

The Revolution of 1911, which a dozen years later nominally established China as a republic, in fact succeeded only in putting an end to the Qing Dynasty. Sun Yat-sen eloquently spoke to the issue of China's powerlessness in the modern world when he described how she was "being carved up by her enemies like a ripe watermelon." As Winter had learned back in Evanston, China entered World War I on the side of the Allies in the hope that she might elicit the sympathy and help of the European nations in winning back territories held by Germany since the 1890s. As an ally, China gave what she had to give: manpower to serve as stevedores and porters in Europe. But the Treaty of Versailles confirmed that the West was far from ready to deal honorably with powerless China; instead of restoring to her the territory the Germans had seized, the treaty transferred it from Germany to Japan, compounding the humiliation.

Out of these bitter experiences, those who still hoped to preserve China as a nation, and especially young intellectuals, united around at least one common purpose, the purpose of nationalism, expressed in a slogan to which all parties could subscribe: "To save a state that is perishing and to find a way of [preserving the nation]." The new energy, strong enough to provide China with the faith that she could get moving, was issued from the May Fourth Movement, which begun on that date in 1919 as a demonstration to protest China's treatment at the Paris Peace Conference. Within a year, however, it had developed into a national movement for cultural and political awakening.

The broader movement undertook the reexamination of issues ranging from language and literary reforms to attacks on the Confucian idea of the family. It also inspired the educated elite to intensify efforts to gain a mass hearing for their radical views. This new generation of intellectuals emerged with a new confidence from their early efforts to spread their ideas through street lectures. They had successfully employed critical reason as a tool with which they roused their less-enlightened contemporaries, as Mao and his cadres more successfully would do in the still distant civil war between the Guomindang and the Communists. Ancient ideas and ancient social structures, like the system of Confucian power relations that prevailed in the family, had been revealed to many as archaic and insupportable.

A year after the events of 1919, Luo Jialun, one of the leaders of the student demonstration and also a founder of the New Tide Society, wrote that the glory of May Fourth lay in shaking China out of its prolonged backwardness:

> Before, we Chinese students had claimed to be able to smash heaven with our words and aimed to overturn the earth with our pens . . . . Only this time [during the May Fourth Movement] did we begin to struggle with the forces of darkness with our bare fists . . . . China before the May Fourth movement was a nation gasping for breath. After the May Fourth movement, it is a more vital, lively nation. The glory of the May Fourth movement lies precisely in getting China to move.[9]

This was the stirring, mythic idea that emerged from the events of 1919: that the movement had gotten China to move, thus to break totally and irrevocably with the past.

The important philosopher of this period was Hu Shi ("Hu the Fit"), a name he adopted to convey his faith in social Darwinism. Hu had established the basis of language reform as a means to liberating the Chinese mind from its conventional patterns, and thus releasing a new power in the use of the native tongue.[10] It was he also who had spelt out the implications of radical disbelief as a cure to China's ills, suggesting that by moving from the old, blind enslavement to received ideas to a critical attitude, China could achieve—and here he quoted Nietzsche—"a transvaluation of all values."[11] He was part of the new galaxy of contending schools that gathered around the writings of Bergson, Nietzsche, Schopenhauer, Kant, Hegel, around positivism, even around phenomenology. Strangely enough, as late as 1921, when the Communist Party of China was founded, Marxism was still relatively little known in China, and by no means a significant force in the war of opposing schools.

World War I, with its large-scale slaughter not of professional soldiers but of ordinary men, caused the moral prestige of Europe to suffer badly in China. But it did not lessen interest in Western ideas. Shortly before Winter's arrival in China, Bertrand Russell, Teilhard de Chardin, and John Dewey, among others, had traveled and lectured in China by invitation. To the ascending, younger members of China's intellectual establishment, they seemed representative of the best the West had to offer.

Not everything that the visitors had to offer was what intellectuals like Hu Shih wanted to hear. Russell and Teilhard were disappointed to find in China in the 1920s "a rush toward the same modernity that they hoped to leave behind in Europe." But John Dewey, although suspicious of the hasty tone of the manifestos of that moment, was more positive in his response. As Vera Schwarcz observes, Dewey was "less eager to find relief from the pressures of Western modernity in an idealized image of an harmonious, traditional China," and thus "he was able to note, even if critically, the promises of the incipient Chinese enlightenment." In an essay he published in *Asia* magazine, Dewey wrote in 1921:

> The movement is still for the most part a feeling rather than an idea. It is also accompanied by the extravagances and confusions, the undigested medley of wisdom and nonsense that inevitably mark so ambitious a movement in its early stages . . . . One could easily hold up the whole movement to ridicule, as less than half-baked, as an uncritical, more or less hysterical mixture of unrelated ideas and miscellaneous pieces of Western science and thought . . . . And yet, the new culture movement provides one of the firmest bases of hope for the future of China.[12]

Unlike Russell, with his Laurencian dreams of a primitive utopia, Dewey stroked China the right way. He represented the West for the young Chinese as they could best understand it: pragmatic, engaged, confident of change—the precise remedy for their own debilitating ancient adage that "knowing is easy, action hard." And, especially, he represented an idea of education as the very agency of change.

Dewey's emphasis on making new people, on making each department of learning clear and simple from the beginning, and on a universal educational system designed to make each child fit to earn his living and contribute to the life of the community—all this excited Chinese liberals, telling them what they most wanted to hear. And all this provided the context for Robert Winter's teaching, for he too was a Westerner who might have in his power the knowledge and understanding that young Chinese intellectuals needed in order to transform their nation by making it fit to survive. As events would prove, though his own academic credentials were negligible, Winter would exert a deeper, more sustained, influence on China than did better known people like Dewey. Naturally, since he experienced the culture from a much more intimate vantage point than the philosopher's, he would also be more deeply impressed.

An aspect of what impressed Winter was that, in the midst of these whirling forces that urged China to become "modern," there was something counter, the residual force of a civilization that had evolved along a certain line for five thousand years and was not likely to transform itself in an eyeblink. Winter's apprehension of such home truths came to him through personal experiences that he recorded in parable form. In these early days in Nanking, for instance, he lived in a large, complicated Chinese household, which included his landlord and his family, servants, and other tenants like himself, who rented rooms. Above Winter lived a young scholar who had studied in America and who liked to talk with him. The young man, Tu Kung-sun, had been born into a poor family in the province of Kiangsi (Jiangxi), five hundred miles to the southwest of Nanking. As a schoolboy, Tu had shown such brilliant promise that his family borrowed money to send him to Tsinghua College in Peking, at that time a kind of preparatory school that trained some of China's best and brightest for study in the United States. Wen Yiduo had studied there before coming to Chicago. Studying night and day, Tu Kung-sun won the recommendations of his instructors, thence a scholarship to an American university and eventually a doctor's degree in history, though by then he had ruined his health by working so hard.

Just before he sailed for America, his parents, who were old, had arranged a marriage for him so that they would have someone to help about the house. When Tu Kung-sun returned to China after five years, he refused to be bound by a custom that now struck him as medieval and that, as he learned in the States, all civilized countries abhorred. His work at National Southeastern University was also strange and distressing to him. He found it most difficult to adjust to Chinese ways after so many years abroad. "He wanted to help his country to emerge from its political chaos, but how was he to begin?"

He never had a chance to find out. Within weeks after he began his work at the university, his lungs hemorrhaged. Refusing to have a doctor because of the expense, he tried to resume his teaching after a few days. But within a week, he was unable to get out of bed. Without his knowledge, the university telegraphed to his wife, five hundred miles away, in their hometown in Kiangsi. She came, riding day and night, covering the overland journey in a little over a week, and nursed him through his last days. Winter remembered her "a little mouse-like creature who had put on enormous shoes with cotton in the toes to please her modern husband," and who slept in the same bed with the man she had never lived with when he was well.

Beyond pleasing, Tu died soon after, on a bitterly cold day in a room without fire and with no furniture but the white-curtained bed in the corner. When Tu Kung-sun died, Winter remembered, his wife

> was pinned into hastily improvised garments of unbleached muslin, and she sat on the floor, keening shrilly, night and day. On the third day a man arrived in our courtyard carrying two large baskets of lime on a pole. In order that he might not steal a handful on the way a design had been printed in black on the surface of the lime before he started. For five hours the man sat on his haunches besides the baskets, for the coffin had not yet arrived. Late in the afternoon the preparations began. Kung-sun's bedclothes were put into the coffin first. Then his body followed, covered with a piece of cotton cloth. Although he had a fur-lined garment, it was not used, for it might encourage his soul to be reborn as an animal. The lime was wrapped in paper and packed around his body. During the process paper money was thrown into the air and firecrackers were set off until the lid was safely nailed down. The coffin

was slung on the shoulders of two stout coolies and the widow followed on foot, wailing louder than ever. The coffin was deposited in a temple until the widow could take it back to the family burial ground five hundred miles away. Unfortunately, she had no money. She no longer belonged to her own family and her husband's family was all dead. What was to become of her? No one could answer that. In any case she would have to mourn for one hundred days in white, for a year in part white, for one year in gray, and for one year in black.[13]

All that Winter could remember about her after her husband's death was that

for some days, in the dead of the night, when the hi-hi-hi-ho of the carry coolies had almost ceased, when even the barking of the dogs had died away, at the time when spirits who have no sons walk abroad, Mrs. Tu would bring out the Big Ben alarm clock which her husband had brought back from America, wind it carefully, set it for intermittent, and let it run its course. After that I would prepare myself for sleep.[14]

After such privileged glimpses, Winter was under no delusions about the obstacles that stood against China's movement into the modern as some had imagined it.

*　　*　　*

But other of his experiences he took in with awe and a kind of delight. When he was a very old man, near death himself, Winter still remembered gratefully how Wu Mi had honored him to the point of allowing Wu's wife to sit at the table for meals with the two men, a thing that normally was never done in the case of guests outside the family. At work and at leisure, the two men spent much time together and confided their inmost hearts, even as they shared with one another the precious gifts of their respective cultures. Once, in a story both intimate and didactic, Wu told Winter an odd story about his childhood. When he was six years old, his grandmother took him to a dinner party. As Winter remembered the story some twenty years later:

The hostess selected choice bits with her chopsticks and put them on his plate. Of course he would hardly dare to take anything himself. There was one particular food that he disliked. Suddenly the hostess put some of it on his plate. Of course he had to eat it. He did so without a world of protest and with no change of expression except for a momentary glance at his grandmother out of the tail of his eye. The dinner ended and they went home. He went to bed as usual. When everybody was asleep, his grandmother came into the room where he was sleeping, pulled down the covers, and gave him a severe beating with a leather strap. She did not say a word and he did not make any outcry. He understood perfectly what the punishment was for. It was never referred to again.[15]

The question of how Chinese people feel was always fascinating to Winter. In this case, the boy Wu Mi was being taught that mere personal feeling must never violate decorum, that one must regulate one's feelings in accord with the larger harmonies. Winter later came to understand Chinese serenity in the light of the late Confucian thinker Hsün Tzu, a moral realist who taught that we cannot abolish desires nor should we wish to. Our aim should rather be to choose wisely among our desires, "selecting for gratification those which 'pay,' those which do not stand in the way of too many other gratifications." Such a philosophy of emotions especially appealed to him because it so closely resembled the one that the literary critic and "moral scientist" I. A. Richards would set forward in 1927 (the same year that he met Winter) when he argued that "the most valuable states of mind are those which involve the widest and most comprehensive coordination of activities and the least curtailment, conflict, starvation and restriction."[16]

Winter understood that such emotional utilitarianism could be as hard to maintain as it was to achieve. As he explained to John Blofeld a decade later, though "some sort of laugh or smile is the normal Chinese response to misfortune," a breaking point is reached where propriety, the Book of Rites, and all are thrown to the winds," and the Tajen, the would-be superior man, finds himself as much at the mercy of his feelings as any other guy."[17] Then mixed human nature showed itself in Chinese people as baldly as in all others.

All in all, his new world was kind of playground for his heart/mind. Everywhere he turned was alive with lessons and with symbols. Outside his window one day, he heard the sounds of students playing football. Looking out, he saw "delicate, consumptive youths dressed in long silk gowns lifting their skirts daintily as they kicked the ball—but usually the air—and between kicks, languidly waving elegant fans inscribed with Tang poems."[18] One could hardly imagine an image more expressive than this one of the precarious balance of China's youth at that moment—the languid, androgynous boys and their efforts at vigorous activity. Though by his own account he had stopped writing poetry long before he met Wen Yiduo in Chicago, Winter never lost the poet's way of discovery through images.

Another sound, constant, that he heard over his garden wall when he awakened and that put him to sleep at night, was the cry of the carry coolies: "Hi! ho! Hi-a-ho! Hi! Ho! Hi-a-ho!" Years later, Winter told David Finklestein and Beverley Hooper that he did not consider himself a Communist, or for that matter "as a political animal," but that as early as the 1920s, it did seem to him "that the Communists had something to offer the Chinese people."[19] The carry coolies whom he heard through his window and saw in the streets owned nothing but "the rag about their waist," and their song, "which kept time with their steps, was both a protest and a warning to the passer-by." Even children, even dogs and cats, Winter observed, "know when we have been unjust to them. Dare we assume, then, that the lowest of these coolies was not aware, in one form or another," of the abject futility of his existence? Winter could not. Instead, he quoted an unidentified philosopher who says that from the moment one becomes so aware, "his individual experience ceases to be adequate, and he endeavors to project himself beyond it by creating ideal worlds of semblance, Utopias of other time and place in which all has been, may be, or will be well."[20]

The '20s, though without much encouragement from history, was China's utopian era. Early in that era, and again late, when "some of the fury of the warlords had died down, all of these Utopias were dragged out from library shelves into the open." Winter heard Ts'ai Yuan-pei, the chancellor of Peking University, in his eloquent speeches and articles, throw together a glorious "eight-precious-pudding," made up of "the philosopher kings of China, the Garden of Eden, the City of God, Plato, More, and Rousseau. Dante, Shelley, Ibsen, Wilde, Tolstoy, Russell, John Dewey, eugenics, free-verse, free-love, fraternity, everything could be found there, in an atmosphere uncritical, perhaps, but oh so gloriously alive."[21] What distinguishes Winter's response from that of his more purely philosophical colleagues was that he understood the place of the carry coolie in the midst of this heady atmosphere.

His capacity to learn from experience, even unpleasant experience, helps account for why Bob Winter was able to survive in China as long as he did. Like so many Westerners before and after him, he never got used to the crowds, a phenomenon especially menacing to the occidental, who never fails to draw them. Whenever he went into the streets of Nanking, Winter "was jostled by these crowds, all dressed alike, and moving forward with no words of excuse." No one considered excuses necessary in the case of any inconvenience one might cause to another when one was caught in a crowd. This Winter discovered when he tried in vain to apologize to a man whom he caused to spill his soup when he bumped against him.

Sometimes, "hoping to get a moment's breathing space from this welter of humanity," Winter would cut down a side street or go into a temple, but wherever he went, crowds, sometimes of children, would spring up out of the ground. Even when he tried to find a corner where he "could relieve nature" in private, "a dozen children would crowd shamelessly about to peer most indiscreetly and then comment even more indiscreetly."

"The American imagination," Winter observed, "sees leprosy in these crowds, to say nothing of scabies, and smallpox, and a host of other unpleasant things." But once, when desperate and in a fit of temper, he shouted at the crowds to leave him in peace, to give him some air, and they did fade away, Winter was ashamed to find "on their faces no trace of anger or resentment, only surprise." He especially noted one coolie, "naked but for a pair of torn and faded cotton drawers, [who] moved away with dignity, making a pretense of never having seen me, so as to spare his feelings and my own."[22]

Only once in Nanking was he ever actually baited in the streets. This happened in May 1925, as Winter remembered, but it must have been early June, a few days after an "incident" in Shanghai in which some students were shot by the British police had put all China in an uproar. On this day Winter had walked into town from his home in the outskirts. Later, ready to return, he got into a rickshaw and gave the rickshaw man his address. When the man remained standing without picking up the shafts, Winter repeated the address. He did this several times, thinking that the man was deaf or didn't understand the name of the street. By this time a crowd of about two hundred people had gathered about them. Then the rickshaw man turned to Winter, "squared his shoulders, and said in a loud voice and in a tone of withering contempt, 'I wouldn't pull one of you dirty foreigners if you gave me ten million dollars.'"[23] For

Winter the episode was no more than the inconvenience of having to walk home when he had intended to ride. But it serves as forewarning of how, with rising force, history would infringe on his private life.

The episode in Shanghai that triggered this event came to be known as the May Thirtieth Incident. On that day in 1925, Chinese demonstrators, most of them students, protested the killing of a Chinese worker by a Japanese foreman in a Japanese-owned textile factory. When they thronged in front of a police station in the international settlement, the British officer in charge gave the order to open fire. The resulting carnage left eleven of the demonstrators killed and scores wounded. It provoked a surge of anti-imperialist feeling that expressed itself in widespread strikes and boycotts and that made the student movement more militant. A short-lived newspaper, the *Public Truth Daily*, was even founded for the purpose of spreading the suppressed news of what quickly became known as the May Thirtieth Movement.[24]

In commemoration of the May Thirtieth Incident, the poet Zhu Ziqing wrote and published "The Song of Blood," in which he declared that history had now become synonymous with violence. Now there was no place left, either in the Chinese soil or mind, where one could hide from "the hand, the eyes, the mask of blood." One result of the May Thirtieth Incident was that some May Fourth veterans like Zhu Ziqing now began to lose their faith in critical reason and to turn down revolutionary paths. Most of them, however, held their ground.[25] This meant that while Winter could still discourse on Western thought and art to receptive ears, even among students who had not become outright revolutionaries, the days of Confucian piety were coming to an end.

Winter's own first experience with the Chinese student movement (in an episode that foreshadows Red Guard behavior under Mao) occurred that same spring, when Hu Kan-fu, widely perceived as incompetent, was appointed by the Chinese government as president of Southeastern University, where Winter taught. (In his diary, Winter calls him variously "Hu Kan-fu" and Hu Tung-fu.) The appointment had been made against the wishes of most of the faculty and the students and was followed by protests that grew louder and louder, "especially after it was learned that he had bribed the Nanking post office to send him all letters addressed to members of the university so that he could learn who was opposed and be prepared to dismiss them when he took office."

One night, without ceremony, Hu, with the help of his brother, head of one of the university's science departments, installed himself in the president's office, took possession of the seal, and prepared notices that he had posted that morning announcing that he was now invested as president. When the students saw the notices, they marched to his office. At first, they simply shouted through the Western-style door, whose upper half was a pane of crinkly glass, that he leave the campus immediately. When he refused, they broke the glass and entered the office, where they found him crouching under his desk.

By this time, thousands of students had massed. Forming a line, they passed him one by one, each spitting in Hu Kan-fu's face, till the saliva actually ran down his body and made a stream across the floor. At about this time the vice president called for Winter and asked him, as a neutral observer, to see that the students were not causing any physical damage to Hu Kan-fu.

Winter performed that service and was present when Hu Kan-fu got up and said, "We give up." The students, after having Hu and his brother sign their resignations, called in a foreign doctor, who examined the two men, stripped for the purpose, and signed a statement that they had suffered no injury except for a slight scratch on Hu Kan-fu's face. The brothers were then clothed and led to an open carriage. As it "passed through the main gate of the university, two enormous pails of liquid human manure were poured over their heads." They were then driven to the railway station and put on the train in that condition.

Winter would tell this story years later, to illustrate that the Chinese student movement was "one of the brightest and most admirable factors in China during her transition period." While others might respond to the students as "extremists," Winter's view was that they had been compelled by bad government to act as they did. Rarely, he concluded, had he "seen a situation handled more methodically or more effectively."[26]

Though some were unpleasant, Winter's ordinary experiences in Nanking had for him a richness and depth he hadn't been able to find in his native land. Once, years after he had left Nanking for Peking, he came upon a book he had owned, a copy of Montaigne, in a bookstall, where the Japanese who had stolen it—along with other belongings Winter had been forced to leave in his house when he left Peking in 1939—had sold it. Though Winter could not afford to buy it back, he took the book down again to gaze at the seal he had imprinted on the title page, and as he looked at the "delicate tracery which said, 'Gentle Virtue His Book,'" his mind went still further back to when he first came to China—as it had recently formed "a tiresome habit of doing." He thought of Lou

Kuang-lai, who in Nanking gave him the Chinese name meaning "Gentle Virtue" and first taught him to write it. His description gives us a sense of the patience and care with which he practiced aspects of Mandarin culture. And he remembered how he practiced, first, hesitantly, taking up his ink stick, "carved intricately with a design representing the four classes of society in ancient China—the scholar, the farmer, the fisherman, and the laborer"—each design "delicately illuminated with green, blue, silver, and gold." Each time he took the ink stick up, he hesitated, knowing that "eventually the stick would be worn down and the design would be lost."

At last he would moisten his stick and prepare to rub it into his inkstone, but here he had to pause again. The inkstone was velvet to the touch. On one side it was embellished with the carved shape of a temple bell, above which stood "the name of a famous lady of the seventeenth century under whose direction it was made." On the other side, a landscape in low relief was carved with such preciosity that Winter had to smile.

Finally, with his bamboo brush he made three strokes that were three drops of water. Then with three more strokes, he drew a box to represent the kind that prisoners who had been sentenced to starve to death were put into. Next to the box with two strokes, Winter drew a man, and under the box, with five strokes, a bowl of rice. With this, his family name was complete. He had made the character that means "gentle" or "compassion" because it represents "the act of giving water and food to a starving man."

Stroke by stroke, Winter would compose his Chinese identity, back in the early days, when the act of writing his name was fresh as water. Under the character for "compassion" now he drew again a man, this time adding a stroke above his head that showed him moving forward. Now with two strokes, Winter drew a cross that represented "the five points of the compass, East, West, North, South, and Center." Then with five strokes, he drew an eye, with one, a carpenter's square, and under that with four strokes a heart (mind). So his given name was finished. It showed "a man moving forward, and no matter in what direction he goes, he keeps his eye and his mind ('heart') as straight as the carpenter's rule." So Winter was transliterated to "Gentle Virtue."[27]

To write his Chinese name back in those early times must have been for Winter a kind of crossing over, a conversion to a potential identity in the form of a man who, moving forward in whatever direction, always kept his mind/heart "as straight as a carpenter's rule." He took seriously the opportunity Chinese philosophy offered him to become the Tajen, the superior man, and that path required that he read his own experience in a correct and profitable way. One text he chose for guidance and copied as a kind of epigraph to the section of his diary in which he recalls how he learned to write his name is a verse from the Tao Te Ching that reads:

The Sage

Puts himself in the background; but is always to the fore.
Remains outside; but is always there.
Is it not just because he does not strive for any personal end
That all his personal ends are fulfilled?

In principle, Winter never wavered from such principles, though his dramatic personality often drove him into the center of things.

*   *   *

Nanking had been enjoying relative tranquility at the time Winter arrived, but this did not last long. In the late summer of 1923, the city began to prepare for the expected attack by Chang Tso-lin, the warlord of Manchuria, whose intention to drive out Ch'i Hsieh-yuan, the warlord of Kiangsu, had long been known. Four months before the attack began, the city was placed under martial law, which included a curfew which began at sunset.

It was during this period, Winter said, that he "began to love the Chinese people through the person of a guard on duty down the street from my house." Winter had been visiting a friend and, lost in talk as usual, he realized that night had come on without his knowing it,

> so I stayed on with the idea that I might as well be shot for a wolf as a sheep. It was after ten o'clock when I started home and at a cross-roads I was challenged fiercely by this guard, who put the point of his bayonet uncomfortably near my stomach and shouted, "Give the pass-word!" I didn't have the pass-word. In fact, I could only remember the pass-word of two days before, which I gave him in a tone that clearly lacked conviction. "That's not the pass-word for today," he said sternly, and then, a little less sternly, "Today's pass-word is so-and-so!" "So it is," I replied smiling, and went on home.[28]

During the four months when the city awaited the northern army, it was "in a state of utmost confusion." While peasants poured into the city for protection, "those who could afford transportation were pouring out." These latter "ran in and out of their houses dragging trunks after them . . . ." Then, when the trunks had been piled up "mountain high," the people "climbed to the precarious top, had the babies handed up and dashed off to the railway station." Soon, the city was emptied of rich and important people. Winter, being neither, stayed home.

But his landlord, who had a different estimate of the American, provided Winter with an early lesson in the complicated uses of extraterritorial immunity. Hastily tearing off his own name plate from the front door, the landlord "hung up a board five feet long on which he had written, 'This is the Official Residence of Gentle Virtue, Previous Begotten from the Great United States of America." Then, after dragging his trunks, filled with furs and curios, under Winter's bed, along with revolvers and ammunition, the landlord sat in Winter's room most of the time, along with his three concubines, who stayed busy at their embroidery.

Then the army arrived and for three days streamed into the city. Peeping out through the crack in the front door, Winter saw the "endless line of Peking carts, each drawn by five mules, one between the shafts, one beside the cart, and three far ahead attached by ropes." And in each cart, on top of the baggage, "strange to us southerners," sat four or five northern soldiers, stranger still, "with flat copper-colored faces under high hats of sable or squirrel fur. Each held his rifle ready for action, for the army which preceded them was pulling out as they came in. Day and night the cars rumbled by, but there was never a word spoken."[29]

Once they had taken the city, the northern soldiers carried out only what the Chinese called "a small looting," robbing the large shops before burning them to the ground but leaving most of the private houses more or less intact. Not everyone got off as lightly as Winter's landlord, however. After hiding in his house for four days, Winter cautiously opened the door when he heard weeping in the street. The widow who occupied the house next to his sat in the mud before her door, "her hair, always before so immaculately oiled and smoothed," was now disheveled. She held in her hand a box of face powder which she was eating, apparently in an effort to poison herself, and then allowing to run down her chin in a froth. Meanwhile she was keening in long descending chromatic scales, "We are an old established family. We have lived in the same house for a hundred years." The soldiers, she went on, had broken into the rooms of her female servants last night. They stole her thirty dollar gold hair-pin. They raped her sixteen-year-old daughter. "We are an old established family," she kept wailing. And the neighbors, peering from their own front doors, said to one another sadly, "She has gone mad. They stole her gold hairpin. They raped her daughter. What will become of China?"[30]

I can hear her lament in my mind's ear even as I write, because as I write PLA soldiers of the infamous Twenty-Seventh Army have gunned down unarmed citizens on the main avenue of Peking, and in the alleyways, and in their homes. Again survivors, in their rage and grief, are wondering, "What will become of China?"

For Winter, who would have so many opportunities to explore it, the Chinese reaction to disaster was a central theme for inquiry. Wu Mi had shown him that, because in China "every child is taught never to let his face betray what his heart feels, complete abandonment to one's emotions becomes almost impossible. Every gesture is symbolic, and there is almost always a certain amount of histrionics mixed with displays of feeling."

That, at least, is the perspective from which he read the widow's behavior. "The first duty of every woman," Winter observed, "is to comb her hair in the morning, and coolie women doing the hardest manual labor observe this ritual until they go off the edge and become beggars. Then they deliberately dishevel their hair." That the widow woman is performing this act should not be interpreted as "faking."

> The disheveling of the hair and the frothing of the mouth were symbolic manifestations of the aesthetic attitude, which is spontaneous in all Chinese people, even of the lowest class. There is no more reason to object to this woman's acting or to assume that her feeling was not genuine than to declare that an actress can have no real feeling or sympathy for the part which she is portraying. This aesthetic attitude has, of course, nothing to do with the question of whether the Chinese are or are not capable of producing works of art."[31]

Things soon settled down in the city, and the rich and important people returned, "perched on their baggage." The university opened again, and eventually the teachers got their back salary. "Then another army swept in from the east, and the whole thing had to be gone through again." In the sigh of the people, Winter heard the words of Shakespeare's Thersites: "Still wars and lechery; nothing else holds fashion: a burning devil take them!" I don't think that Winter went to China in order to suffer or to drink more deeply of weariness and pity. But even during his first days in Nanking, he couldn't help but learn that suffering is fundamental to Chinese experience, and, as his friend William Empson put it, to "learn a style from a despair."[32]

Where suffering is unavoidable, what shall we make of it? Winter took up this question in a diary entry dated January 1, 1924-January 1, 1947:

> What remains when I have driven away the swarms of ghosts from these twenty-three years? Weariness and pity. Not, I hope, a mere thoughtless heaving of the solar plexus, but something, perhaps, more like what the Buddhists call the Great Compassion, which sees where the roots and the cure of all this suffering are to be found. "When he is weary of these things, he becomes free of desire. When he is empty of desire, he becomes free. When he is free he knows that he is free."[33]

But when, after two years in Nanking, Winter accompanied Wu Mi to Peking, he had not yet achieved such freedom of desire. It was fortunate that he had not. His new university, Tsinghua, would prove to be the place where intellectual veterans of the May Fourth Movement would gather strength and forge a new community of ideas and hope.

CHAPTER THREE:
TSINGHUA

Winter's appointment to Tsinghua might seem to have been made in heaven, but in fact it was made in Chicago. Back there, as we've seen, Wen had written to Lian Shi Qiu in China about the brilliant charm of his new American friend, then added that the American "couldn't be in the States any longer and wants to come to China."[1] Wen asked Lian to use his influence with Tsinghua President Cao (to whom Wen had also written), to help arrange an appointment for Winter. By employing his own network of personal and impersonal relations, through the established social custom of *kuan-hsi*, Wen had made a place for his American friend in a university that had just come into existence.

Winter would later be involved in actions against Japanese invaders and was a staunch adherent to a kind of humanistic radicalism; he was not, as he often insisted, a political man. Yet he landed at Tsinghua at a time when it was a rough sea of clashing political views in which Wen was one of the helmsmen. Winter thus had little contact with him. He taught Shakespeare and other Western classics against the din of clashing ideas about China's future.

* * *

Like all things Chinese, Tsinghua was riven with contradictions from the time of its founding. In an era of strong antireligious sentiment, many of its science faculty were recruited by the YMCA, which remained which remained active on the campus.[2] In an age of broiling nationalism and anti-Western sentiment, Tsinghua was instituted on the foundation of a gift of nearly US$12 million from the American government, though the gift was less open handed than might appear. In 1901, the United States had received $25 million from the Chinese as indemnity for the damage done to American persons and property during the Boxer Rebellion. While the American share was only a small part of the $350 million in total indemnities (an exorbitant sum that, incidentally, crippled the Chinese government) responsible American officials recognized it as excessive. The American contribution was to be used for educating Chinese in the U.S. By 1929, 1,268 Boxer indemnity scholars had been sent to the States under the program, and many of them, like Wen, were among the nation's most promising.

From the start, it was clear that for the program to work, students would have to be provided special training to ready them for study in America, and it was to that end that Tsinghua was instituted. The fact that its budget—the staggering sum of $400,00 assured annual income—was independent of the vagaries of warlord regimes gave it a special kind of energy from the start, a befitted part of the vanguard for the forging of China's brighter future. This new model of what the engaged scholar had a right to demand of the state, though many times bloodied, proved vital enough to survive as late as June 3-4, 1989, when it was bloodied once again.

China had labored to reform her ancient system of education throughout the last third of the nineteenth century, but relatively little had come of these attempts. One problem was that even during the brief period when the "Boy Emperor" was persuaded that a particular reform was desirable, there were never enough trained teachers to bring the reform about. Such educational reforms as did go through at first were narrowly pragmatic, kindled by the need to strengthen the country to resist foreign invasion and to provide the political and economic training necessary to officials in the new republican government that the country seemed to be straining toward.

In the 1880s, reform-minded scholar Zhang Zhidong worked out a formula that still has its appeal to the inner circle of China's leaders determined to ensure China's cultural identity even as they adopt Western technical and economic models. Zhang's suggestion was simple enough: Chinese learning as the goal, Western learning as the means (*zhongxue wei ti, xixue wei yong*). Of course, it did not take long for reformers to discover that—as Vera Schwartz remarked—"embedded in Western 'means'—that is to say, in technological experts—were distinctive goals that were inimical to the fundamental values of Chinese, or more precisely, Confucian, civilization."[3]

Even more dramatically inimical was the notion that education might provide a student with the training necessary to govern his own life rather than to enter a specific profession. This notion, of relatively recent Western origin, finds neat expression in Kant's "What is Enlightenment?"—a question that Kant answers thus:

> Enlightenment is man's emergence from his self-inflicted immaturity. Immaturity is the incapacity to use one's own understanding without the guidance of another. This immaturity is self-inflicted if its cause is not a lack of understanding but a lack of courage to use understanding without the guidance of another . . . . *Sapere aude!* Dare to know! Be guided by your understanding! This is the watchword of enlightenment![4]

In a Chinese context, such an idea, as Schwarcz viewed it, demands that one cut through the bonds of feudalistic thought—specifically, to sever the three Confucian cords that bind sons to fathers, wives to husbands, and ministers to rulers. Such aims require a new and truly revolutionary faculty of what the Chinese would call the heart/mind—a grounding in the skepticism that lies at the root of modern science.

Tsinghua College became a principal conduit through which these new ideas flowed into the mainstream of Chinese thought. If in the latter part of the nineteenth century Chinese students went to the West in order to learn technical languages and skills, now they went to study the "new learning" in all its branches, often with the aim of becoming teachers who could disseminate modern ideas and thus move China toward her necessary revolution. In the first eighteen years of its existence, about 1,300 men and women went from Tsinghua to America, pilgrims to the Mecca of enlightened modernism.

Some would experience disenchantment. Wen, for example, declared in an essay: "On the basis of my own ten years of study, I conclude that American culture is not worthy of our assimilation." America "brags about its material, economic, and practical success," he went on, "but it is mediocre, shallow, vain, impulsive, and extravagant."[5] That view corresponded exactly with Robert Winter's.

Yet whatever Wen may have thought of American culture, young Wen, idealistic, and bewildered on the grand scale that only can occur when a dying ancient culture and a vigorous modern one make deep contact with one another in a fresh and vital mind, compounded his dilemma by invoking for Eastern civilization the Western apostrophe he had discovered in Wordsworth's sonnet, "London 1802":

> Oh, raise us up, return to us again,
> And give us manners, virtue, freedom, and power.

So for all his disillusionment with America, Wen's evocation of Wordsworth suggests his craving for a rejuvenated world culture that rose from a union of East and West, though his uneasiness wasn't put to rest by his visit to America. In 1925, just returned from his studies there, Wen was a co-author of a manifesto issued by the Great River Society, a literary society that he had helped organize in New York. "Unenlightened education," these "returned students" declared, leaves an evil influence worse than that of lack of education, but Westernized education is still worse than unenlightened education.

> It is true that nowadays among the students who have studied abroad there are many who were supported by Western missions . . . . But in reality these educated students with their Westernized habits, speech, writing, views, and thought, are the very ones to imperil China's future because they have forgotten their cultural origins . . . . There is more than one way to carry out cultural aggression. Under the pretext of returning the indemnity funds, certain foreign powers have sought to control the educational and publishing enterprises in China.

Yet the Great River Society's manifesto simply underlines the dilemma from which China even today has not managed to disentangle itself: in order to change, China requires the bringing in of new ideas from outside, but such ideas always carry with them the potential of obliterating that which is essentially Chinese.

Less directly, the manifesto underlines another unpleasant truth. American benevolence toward China has rarely been disinterested. Just as the missionaries brought to China their own proselytizing agendas that did not vitiate the value of their teaching, so did secular agencies. When the American Congress appropriated funds to bring Chinese students to America to study, as, later, when the Rockefeller Foundation determined to launch its own education efforts in China, it was never far from anyone's mind that whatever else such efforts might accomplish they provided a way of influencing and perhaps winning the friendship of the minds that would shape their nation's future. As the president of the University of Illinois wrote to Teddy Roosevelt in 1910 about Tsinghua: "This type of operation is more useful than an army."[6] While none of this seems to have diminished Winter's popularity in the early years of his teaching, later, after he had been affiliated with the Rockefeller Foundation, it would become a serious mark against him among the Communists who now ran Peking University, where he taught at the end of the Civil War.

*   *   *

When Winter arrived there in 1925, Tsinghua had begun to move toward a new balance that would eventually placate some of its critics. In its inception, the staffing of the school had reflected China's abject dependence on American scholars to train her own. But now the staff was predominantly Chinese (although as late as 1937 two-thirds of them had been trained in the U.S.). And, as E-Tu Zen Sun puts it in *The Cambridge History*, those Chinese "who elected to embark upon the task of creating a system of higher education clung firmly to the classical tradition that the scholar is not a mere technical expert but must think like a statesman on behalf of the whole society, rulers and people alike."[7] All this made for a heady atmosphere for a Western scholar like Winter, who already embraced Matthew Arnold's idea of the man of letters as disinterested critic of his own society—a function that also corresponded with the traditional Chinese notion that drew poets to the courts of emperors—until their disinterestedness displeased.

*   *   *

Even as Tsinghua was reverting to Chinese hands, there remained a small Western colony, most of them teachers of Western languages and literature. For Winter, it must have provided an island of tranquility. The head of the English Department was E. K. Smith, who had been part of the group that founded Tsinghua in 1910, and who remained at his post until Tsinghua reverted to the Chinese and he moved to Yenching College, a missionary school. It was Winter's strange destiny to live here for some time among missionaries and others who included the Westernized J. Wong-Quincey, and Arthur Pollard-Urquhart and R. D. Jameson, both of whom would later work with Winter as part of the Orthological Institute of China, about which more later. Smith's daughter, Janet, who spent her first eight years at Tsinghua, was gifted with a splendid memory and allowed me to see Winter's comfortable among people more genteel than himself.[8]

Inside the university gate "were some imposing Western-style buildings housing the administration, classrooms" and an auditorium that "made a half-hearted attempt at looking like the Parthenon." Dormitories and the infirmary stood off to one side. The Smiths, along with the rest of the Western teachers, lived on the campus in faculty housing that "was a short walk beyond the classroom buildings, against the back wall of the university." Here stood "eight one-story, grey brick, Western-style, duplex buildings on two adjoining sides of a square, with a tennis court and a park area and another man-made hill filling the rest of the square." Winter lived in this compound for several years before taking a house in the city.

The Smith children (besides Janet, there were Dorothea and Ernest) spent a good deal of time in the house that belonged first to Paddy Malone, who had "two lively boys," and then to the Wong-Quinceys, who had two somewhat less lively daughters. They called Malone Uncle Paddy, because he had been part of the group that had come to China with their father in 1910 to start Tsinghua.

Wong-Quincey was a Chinese urchin adopted by General Gordon and given a British education. More Chinese than English, Wong-Quincey in fact did not know Chinese very well. He could be seen almost any day dressed in bow tie, a natty tweed jacket of English cut, plus fours, and high woolen stockings—all this crowned with a light-colored fedora. I have seen a picture of him that stands as a frontispiece to a book on big game hunting that he wrote. He is dressed in hunting garb, carrying a heavy gauge rifle at parade rest, his right foot firmly planted on the corpse of a large tiger. Wong-Quincey was also a dramatist, still remembered by some of his former students as having had produced in New Haven a play he wrote when he was a member of George Baker's famous workshop at Yale. The play was called *She Stoops to Compromise*.

Other members of the Tsinghua Western community included R. D. Jameson, who lived at Tsinghua with his wife, Dorothy, and his son, Michael. In the picture I have seen of him, Jameson is dapper and wonderfully alert in double-breasted tweeds (though his son Michael, now a classicist at Stanford, tells me that "dapper" was not his father's characteristic state). Jameson would later leave Tsinghua for Kunming, where he founded the Orthological Institute of China, of which more later.

There also was Arthur Pollard-Urquhart, who, like Jameson and Winter, would later work with the Orthological Society of China, launched by I. A. Richards. Pollard, the only bachelor in this compound besides Winter, was Scottish and came from a distinguished old family. Slim, tall, gray and elegant, he had at one time been a tutor to the sons of the king of Italy. These brilliantly unconventional bachelors were exotics in this still-distinctly missionarial atmosphere, but Janet's sister Dorothea remembers Winter and Pollard as her favorite uncles during her childhood. I assume from the obvious intimacy of the relationship between these two "uncles" and from Winter's sexual proclivities that theirs was a gay relationship,[9] but they were among Mrs. Smith's best friends and joined the Smith family on Christmas, New Year's, and Thanksgiving, as on other occasions when, from the perspective of the Smiths, a single person might be thought to miss his own family.

Winter and Mrs. Smith recognized one another at once as kindred spirits—two odd birds. She was born in China, daughter to the well-known missionary Chauncey Goodrich. She had refused to speak English at all until, at the age of nine, she was brought to America, where she was laughed at in school for answering questions in Chinese. Though her American classmates failed to appreciate the fact, her Chinese was elegant, the Chinese of the court. She had been a friend of Prince Tsai T'ao (or Pu Ju) and interpreted for him at embassy dinners when he was invited.

Already, two of Winter's favorite pastimes were evident. He loved animals, and while in faculty housing, he kept a cat whom he managed to toilet train by getting it to pee not in a litter box but in the toilet—though when the cat was angry with him, it would pee in Winter's bed. On the brighter side, a great swimmer, Winter managed not only to put in a swimming pool but for a while avoided paying for the water until the authorities caught up with him.[10]

Mrs. Smith was interested in the arts and in Chinese antiquities and fine furniture, interests which her husband, of a more abstract and philosophical bent, did not share. She was a high-spirited woman who delighted in the blending in Winter of sensitivity with his courage to speak his mind and perhaps even in his characteristic irreverence, which must have proved something of a relief from the company of her admirable but more conventional husband. So Winter's brilliant gossip often held her glued to the back fence, and Janet remembers that "whenever he and Mother were in conversation and I approached, their voices would drop to almost a whisper and I had the feeling of observing two conspirators." She remembers them standing against the backdrop of Winter's gorgeous irises, talking and gossiping. Winter had a lively (and sometimes inventive) talent for gossip. Richards's widow, Dorothy Gaylord, told me over the phone that Winter didn't care whom his wit hurt, and that "he wouldn't come to other people's rescue who needed it."[11] But anecdotal evidence indicates that she was wrong.

E. K. Smith may have been made uneasy by his wife's friendship with the eccentric bachelors, but, as his daughter Dorothea reflects, he "refrained from enlightening my mother . . . because he thought mother's friendship with them was harmless enough and because they supplied her with an artistic companionship that my father, who was more of a philosopher and intellectual, did not give her. Daddy was courteous to the two men but never had the common creative ground to stand on that mother" had with them.

That creative ground had its odd eruptions. Dorothea recalls that Winter "once borrowed the toothbrush of a guest visiting him and during one night of high artistic endeavors, painted upon a king-sized sheet, three disciples of Buddha from a small illustration he found in the *Encyclopedia Britannica*. For many years, these three lovely figures, painted in muted colors, like an old fresco, hung on the wall of the Smiths' dining room.

Winter had been graced with a strong and passionate mind. He matched that with a strong and vigorous body. Well into his nineties, Winter "was a great swimmer." During the summer spent in this Western colony, he sometimes visited the Smiths for several weeks at their seaside cottage in Beidahe. "Mother used to have fits worrying about him," Dorothea writes,

> for he would swim out into the Pacific Ocean and stay in the water alone for hours at a time, a mile out at sea, happily floating, meditating and smoking. Meanwhile, mother spent the time pacing our front porch, trying to catch a glimpse of [Bob], pleading with whomever happened to pass by to take a glimpse in her strong binoculars to see if [Bob] was "still out there."

Bob, as the Smiths knew him, reciprocated such concern by taking his avuncular responsibilities seriously. The year after Dorothea Rhodes graduated from Tungehow, the missionary boarding school, she was invited to a dance at the Peking Hotel by a man with a notorious reputation. As Janet remembers it, her mother, unconventional as always, "let her go, as she said she must learn to handle herself in the world. Bob happened to be at the same dance, and was so appalled by the situation that he didn't take another drink all evening so that he could keep an eye on Dor. (I gather he really lived it up in those days.)"

*　　*　　*

I have a blurred reproduction of a formal photograph taken in 1927 of the faculty and staff of the Western Languages Department at Tsinghua. They stand in front of a handsome Chinese building, grouped on the portico against a row of latticed windows. Framing them are two columns, to which have been affixed, in the traditional manner, parallel couplets, in which each character of the one couplet is mirrored by the corresponding character of the other. One knows from the number of characters that the windows, the couplets, and the men are facing south, the auspicious direction, toward which the grandfather in the traditional household, or the emperor in his palace, would also face.

The couplet on the western pillar cannot be read in the copy I am looking at; too many characters are blurred. But the Taoist text on the right, crudely translated (as any Chinese poem must be) reads: "Outside the door, the mountains endure. Spring, Summer, Autumn, Winter. Thousands of changes: a realm that is not the realm of men." The men framed by the couplets were scholars of the East and the West or whom such words signified, scholars who had had glimpses of the vastness of the realm and knew that their small enterprise was a part of a larger one not their own. But they were also men who, gossiping in the courtyard, lived private lives. Finally, by virtue of their residence in China, they had all seen their share of trouble and violence and had become sufficiently Chinese to expect the even flow of existence to be ruffled periodically by the winds of war.

*　　*　　*

Janet Rhodes remembers a period when her father carried "some sort of firearm" and "the faculty men were taking turns patrolling the university at night." And she describes very vividly "the really dramatic night" when

> a train full of explosives belonging to one warlord was set on fire by men fighting for another warlord. Rather than having it explode in Peking, the locomotive gave the train a good push and it came to a stop next to our house with just a wall between us. We were awakened by the rat-a-tat of a carful of bullets going off, during which time I believe my mother was holding my father's leg while he stood on a ladder propped against the wall and tried to see what was going on. This was even more difficult than it sounds for there was a row of broken glass cemented to the top of the wall, which was the in-thing for walls at that time. Presently the fire reached a carful of hand grenades and it became obvious that we had better go elsewhere. So servants and children were marshalled for an expedition to the auditorium. The faithful Te She T'ou carried the Precious Only Son, and we were always amused looking back to remember how he carried him on his shoulders so that he served as very good protection for Ta She T'ou himself. The explosions became enormous and lit up the sky, but I don't remember being afraid. The auditorium was jammed with students. I remember being impressed that most of them had blankets over their under clothes. It was decided to go on to Chinese Faculty friends, the Hos, across the campus, where we spent the rest of the night. After that one of our amusements was to pick up bomb fragments all around our house.

But whatever such explosions may have meant to children, to their elders they reinforced a lesson they would have reason to learn well: violence and education walked hand in hand through Chinese groves of academe.

*   *   *

"The scope of all speculation is the performance of some action, or thing to be done." So said Hobbes. Yet it is in the East, in China, in the years immediately following the May Fourth Incident, that faith in that proposition ran highest. Even to a foreigner like Winter, to be at the heart of an intellectual marketplace where ideas mattered as intensely as they did at Tsinghua must have been intoxicating when it was not terrifying.

Just a year before Winter moved north from Nanking to Peking, the already-heady intellectual ferment in China was made headier by a two-volume collection of essays on the meanings of science for the new China. The words "Science and Democracy" had been a kind of slogan of the May Fourth Movement, for whom "science" meant both empowerment that would prevent new imperialistic humiliations for China in the future and the kind of skeptical, disinterested inquiry that Chinese intellectuals began to see as essential to their own pursuit of truth. But now the editor of the new collection declared:

> During the last thirty years there is one term which has reached the seat of supreme majesty in the country. Whether men understand it or not, whether they belong to the conservative party or the reform party, they all dare not publicly reveal an attitude of contempt towards it. The term is "Science." Whether this almost universal worship is of value or not is another question. The least we can say is that since the change came in China no one who can be counted a forward-looking person dared decry "Science" until about 1921 Liang Ch'i-ch'ao did so in his *Diary of Reactions on My Trip to Europe.* Then for the first time in China formal notice was served on Science that it was bankrupt.[12]

Liang Ch'i-ch'ao had long been the most vigorous and popular Chinese proponent of the theory that the radical deficiencies of both the West and the East could be corrected only by blending the strengths of each.[13] Now, in his *Reflections on a European Journey*, Liang reported on the malaise that he found had settled over European intellectuals after the war. The war, he argued, was an expression of the rationalism (or science) that "had destroyed all spiritual values by reducing man to a materialistically determined part of nature. If people are just biological mechanisms, functioning according to invariable physical laws," he went on to ask, then "how can there be any responsibility for good or

evil?" The war expressed for him the inevitably negative answer to that
question.

But Liang's conclusion was hopeful. The war had caused "the
majority of the people's philosophy of life to undergo a change.
European intellectuals had awakened to the faults of their previous
faith in the 'omnipotence of science' and unending material progress
through unbridled competition." Having discovered, according to Liang
Ch'io'ch'ao, that Chinese culture contained humanistic ideals similar to
their own, the Europeans would now rely more and more on Eastern
spirituality to correct Western materialism. As E. R. Hughes reflects,
"The controversy is illuminating, not because it points to a disbelief in
science as helping to make human happiness, but because it shows the
nature of the reaction against the dictatorship of science in human affairs.
There is the revolt of the humanist against the mechanization of life."[14]

Interestingly, Winter himself, deeply enough instructed by Western
literature since the Romantic period, had come to a similar conclusion
about the limits of reason back in his senior year at Wabash College,
when he closed an essay on Thackeray with these words:

> In these days of the scientific method some advocates of the old
> school have almost feared that art might be extinguished; what
> should be a mean has become an end and the novel approaches
> a scientific treatise on the genus Homo. But this will work out
> its own destruction in the end. Knowledge is necessary but it
> must be kept subordinate; the artist's function is to see and feel;
> not to miss the slightest shade or line of what he sees about
> him, but to give it to us as his eyes see it, as his heart feels it,
> but not merely as his mind knows it.[15]

And years later he would copy these words from I. A. Richards's
Science and Poetry: "To live reasonably is not to live by reason alone—
the mistake is easy, and, if carried far, disastrous—but to live in a way of
which reason, a clear full sense of the whole situation, would approve."

But Richards's formula assumes a stable world in which a clear sense
of the situation might lead to appropriate response. What happens when
that subjective luxury is erased by events and history is out of control?
What happens when mind no longer has any bearing on event, and the
heart's only bearing is anguish and rage? Gradually, China was being
swept into the same spiritual malaise that Liang Ch'io'ch'ao had seen as

afflicting Europe. For some, appeared that the spiritual revolution that had given the May Fourth intellectuals hope had been proven a mere "lie" by subsequent events.

In the spring of 1925, when Japanese and Western soldiers put down strikes against foreign concessions by killing more than sixty students and other demonstrators. They did not, however, quench the rising antiforeign fever. Winter experienced that fever when a rickshaw man told him, "I wouldn't pull one of you dirty foreigners if you gave me ten million dollars."[16] The slaughter also helped to make the student movement itself more militant, if more sober.

As the poet Zhu Ziqing had said in his poem, history had become synonymous with violence. There was no place left now, either in the Chinese soil or in the mind, where one could hide from "the hand, the eyes, the mask of blood." History had become synonymous with violence. In the Tiananmen Square demonstrations on May 4, 1919, no one had been killed. Now all was changed utterly.[17]

Less than a year later, on March 18, 1926, another incident occurred that deepened the anguish of blood. When the warlord Feng Yuxiang mined the harbor of Tianjin in order to prevent his rival, Zhang Zuolin, from making a landing, and the Japanese ordered the harbor cleared because it interfered with trade in what they considered to be their sphere of influence, the students again rallied on Tiananmen. Organized jointly by representatives of the Communist Party and the Guomindang, they demanded of "the chief executive" (the title General Feng had given to his own representative in Peking, in the absence of an elected president) that they reject the Japanese ultimatum. The reply was a burst of gunfire that killed forty-seven of the marchers, most of them students, on the spot.[18]

Wen Yiduo, who returned to China in 1925 and who had been teaching at Wu Han University, to which he had been attracted by the fine new buildings and good salaries, was in Peking at the time of the shootings. Although Wen had opposed previous student demonstrations, he wrote and published a poem on the occasion, after a long period of silence. The new poem was called simply "The Gate of Heavenly Peace," and it described the slaughter of the students from the perspective of a rickshaw man. He also wrote a long essay in which he declared that the dead students who had died on March 18 "were not just patriots, they were the grandest of poems." He thus reluctantly, annunciated the founding of a new school, the literature of blood.[19]

China's greatest writer of vernacular prose, Lu Xun, responded too. He had been warning his radical students for more than a year that something like this might happen and that when it did, the teachers would disappear and so would most of the students, leaving only a few scapegoats behind for the slaughter. They might think that they would "kindle a fire in men's hearts and create a blaze which may revive the nation. But if men refuse to be kindled, sparks can only burn themselves out, just as paper images and carriages burn out on the street during funerals."[20]

Now, on the same day that Wen's essay appeared, on April 1, Lu Xun expressed his own personal feelings about the deaths not merely of an anonymous group but, especially, of two of his own students, including "the smiling, gentle Liu Hezhen," who had been drawn to his writings:

> I did not see this, but I hear that Liu Hezhen went forward gaily. Of course it was only a petition, and no one with any conscience could imagine a trap. But then she was shot before Government House, shot from behind, and the bullet pierced her lung and heart. A mortal wound, but she did not die immediately. When Zhang Jingshu, who was with them, tried to lift her up, she, too, was pierced by four shots, one from a pistol, and fell. And when Yang Dezhun, who was with them, tried to lift her up, she, too, was shot: the bullet entered her left shoulder and came out to the right of her heart, and she also fell. She was able to sit up, but a soldier clubbed her savagely over her head and her breast, so she died . . . .

> Time flows eternally on: the streets are peaceful again, for a few lives count for nothing in China. At most, they give good-natured idlers something to talk about, or provide malicious idlers with material for "rumors." As for any deeper significance, I think there is very little; for this was only an unarmed demonstration. The history of mankind's battle forward through bloodshed is like the formation of coal, where a great deal of wood is needed to produce a small amount of coal. But demonstrations do not serve any purpose, especially unarmed ones . . . .

Since blood was shed, however, the affair will naturally make itself more felt. At least it will permeate the hearts of the kinsmen, teachers, friends, and lovers of the dead. And even if with the flight of time the bloodstains fade, the image of a gentle girl who was always smiling will live on forever amid the vague sorrow . . . . And this is quite enough.[21]

In such ways the often-violent history of the time left its thumbprint on the "non-political Winter, in a mild omen of worse impacts to come. What made the May Thirtieth incident so especially terrible is that this time the murderers were not Englishmen, not Japanese, not Sikhs. This time it was Chinese soldiers gunning down Chinese youth. That was why Lu Xun wrote in his diary, on the day of the slaughter, that this was the "darkest day since the founding of the Republic."[22] Yet darker days were coming.

From 1922 to 1927, China's Nationalist Party, the Guomindang, and the Chinese Communist Party (CCP) combined forces in order more effectively to challenge their mutual enemies, foreign imperialism, and domestic warlords. They had even worked out a strategy that allowed members of the CCP to join the Guomindang without losing their prior affiliation. For the moment, the pressure on intellectuals to affiliate themselves with one or the other side died down. Both parties appeared to be pursuing the same revolution.

Then, in Shanghai on April 12, 1927, members of Shanghai's Green Gang, masked and wearing uniforms marked by the character *gong* (worker), attacked labor union headquarters and "arrested" some three hundred union leaders. The next day, a crowd of workers, more than one hundred thousand strong, marched through the working class district of Shanghai, and then to the headquarters of the local Guomindang commander, which they fired upon without warning. According to one witness who recalled the confused terror of the moment:

Lead spouted into the thick crowd from both sides. Men, women, and children dropped screaming into the mud. The crowd broke into mad flight. The soldiers kept firing into the backs of the fleeing demonstrators. From the adjacent alleyways, the attackers fell upon the crowd, swinging bayonets, rifle butts, and broad-swords.[23]

Contemporary accounts estimated the dead at five thousand. This violent schism was the end of the united front and the beginning of the white terror—a manhunt that would continue for the better part of the decade.

The effect of the white terror on progressive intellectuals who lived through it was terrible. Vera Schwarcz quotes one of them, Zhu Ziqing, who was at the time a professor at Tsinghua, a student of classical Chinese poetry:

> Living in Beijing, I am remote from the turmoil of these times. Still, I feel its intimidating influence. I am unsure of the nature of the threat, but I cannot get rid of the feeling of dread . . . . Often, I am overcome with this feeling of being pressured, beleaguered. Although I personally have no reason for total panic, I feel increasingly so. It leaves me scared, stupefied . . . . At present, the course of revolution is all confused. Even the meaning of the word "revolution" seems totally lost. And yet, class struggle is getting more and more bitter. To carry out attacks [on behalf of the bourgeoisie] and to struggle against the proletariat is inconceivable . . . . To speak on their behalf [as would proponents of the new revolutionary literature] is equally impossible for someone like me.[24]

Even Lu Xun, who could be steely nerved, sank into doubt whether anything could be done to "save the children" as he had urged in his first vernacular short story, "Diary of a Madman," almost ten years earlier. Now, as Vera Schwarcz writes, Lu Xun, who was being accused by some "of having infused youth with the false hope that enlightened thought could make a decisive contribution to revolution in China," confessed "the powerlessness of critical reason in the face of terror":

> I am terrified, and it's a kind of terror I have never experienced before . . . . My dreams have been shattered. Up till now I have always been optimistic . . . . I used to see myself as attacking society, but all that was beside the point. Society did not even know that I was attacking it. If I had realized that, I would long be dead without a place to be buried . . . . What I have said was as ineffective as an arrow aimed into the sea. I feel I shall perhaps have nothing to say from now on.[25]

China's intellectuals had enjoyed a brilliant moment of purposefulness. Now, in the collapse of their dream of enlightenment through a culture that had no regard for class, they fell back into a terrible sense of their own impotence and irrelevance. To make matters worse, Communist propaganda teams in the countryside, as if in anticipation of Mao's Cultural Revolution, were stirring the peasants with the slogan "Down with the Intellectual Class," identifying the intellectuals with all those who in the bad old days had demanded much and given nothing.[26]

Afraid and disillusioned with their own hubristic notion that by the force of reason they were in a position to steer and even to redeem history, intellectuals had begun to lose their sense of self-identity. Zhu Ziqing, once a fervid believer in the power of culture to bring light and still determined to defend it against the political claims of both sides, felt dismay: "They are destroying our finest possession: culture," he wrote. "We damn them . . . . But our words show that we are using our criteria to determine value, and our criteria are rooted in our class-consciousness . . . . Our curses and our rage are merely ours."[27]

*   *   *

As Winter's story develops, we see ever more plainly that, like Zhu Ziqing and many other intellectuals of the time, he would be left increasingly to his curses and rage. But sometimes he felt obliged to act. I was told by a Norwegian scholar-gypsy named Tölef, he more than once stood in the front ranks of demonstrating students to protect them from being fired upon—foreigners being considered impropitious targets, lest outside powers intervene in Chinese internal affairs as they had often done in the past.

What China was suffering in this rising tide of barbarity was not confined to China. Witness Yeats:

> The night can sweat with terror as before
> We pieced our thoughts into philosophy,
> And planned to bring the world under a rule,
> Who are but weasels fighting in a hole.
>
> He who can read the signs nor sink unmanned
> Into the half-deceit of some intoxicant
> From shallow wits; who knows no work can stand,
> Whether health, wealth or peace of mind were spent
> On master-work of intellect or hand,

No honour leave its mighty monument,
Has but one comfort left: all triumph would
But break his ghostly attitude.[28]

The collapse of culture under the onslaught of violence was a world event that affected Yeats much as it affected other Western and Chinese intellectuals contemporary with him. Violence was in the saddle and riding mankind. And almost as dismaying, the dream that art could continue to provide a beacon and refuge against historical forces was dying. Now Yeats would describe art's high creations as "pretty toys," ("We too had many pretty toys when young") while T. S. Eliot saw it as "fragments" we have shorn against our ruin.

How one goes on after such a chastening is a question of existential importance. As Camus said, the central question of philosophy is the question of suicide, and all value questions finally can be reduced to this. One way that wounded people avert suicide is by keeping on, in the palest hope that things will get better, or alternatively, by wanting less, hoping less, willing less, expecting less. In China, that often proves to be the only way open.

For Winter too, hauling in sail was necessarily the order of the day. That is, in the late '20s he did pretty much as the majority of his colleagues did—though he could act with courage when need be, he otherwise kept his head low, glad that he still had the privilege of teaching and of living and observing with his usual intensity. I remember talking to a distinguished Chinese academic in the winter of 1986, just a day or two after the wave of student demonstrations that had been sweeping the country for months had reached Beijing. It was obvious that some crisis was near at hand, and I was very excited at being there, on the spot, where history was being made. His response to my excitement, and to my own jejune dreams of freedom, was an enormous weariness. All I want, he told me, is to be left alone and to be allowed a little time for this (he gestured toward his books) and for this (he gestured toward the desk where he wrote).

Historical violence notwithstanding, Winter's cultural life was quite full. With Wu Mi, in the late '20s he designed the curricula of a program in Western studies, a kind of great books course synthesized from Wu Mi's academic experience at Harvard and Winter's at Chicago.

At Peking University, Zhou Zuoren had taught a history of European literature since 1919.[29] Now Tsinghua would offer one, and Winter's electric teaching would be central to the program. Whether he was teaching Browning or Shakespeare or Dante and Gide, he created scholars. In some cases, as in a famous advanced French course he taught at Tsinghua, four of the five members went on to be professors, including one who tried to introduce Gide into Chinese for the first time and another who succeed in introducing Molière. He also loved to teach Baudelaire and Browning,[30] both of whom gave him opportunities to employ his genius for reciting poetry, which was one of his ways of teaching.

As always, Winter continued to find time for theater and the contrivance of bibelots. Harold Shadick arrived at Yenching University and became a near neighbor and friend of Winter's, as well as of Jameson and Pollard-Urquhart, through the regular theatrical performances Shadick staged through the Yenching dramatic club. Shadick remembers Winter as a remarkable man in whose company life was always interesting, and he was surprised to learn, as he finally did in 1986, that Winter was sixteen years his senior. (Winter's youthful appearance, which he preserved until close to the end, was part of his legend.) By his own account, Shadick gained much from Winter. He had previously been enslaved to a "more austere regime," and Winter and Jameson and Pollard-Urquhart contributed much to his "broader humanization."

Shadick especially remembers how "Bob Winter's many talents were frequently drawn on" by the drama club. Once Winter appeared as a snooping detective in a farce by Wong-Quincey. But his performance was not confined to acting. For a play called *Minnikin and Mannikin*, "the action called for a Dresden-china clock in scale with the figures. Bob Winter produced the most marvelous rococo confection some eight feet high, a conversation piece much appreciated when the play was repeated at a club in the city of Peking."

As Shadick recalls, "Bob seemed able to do anything requiring knowledge and skill and do it better than most." One season, he astonished everyone "with the most magnificent border of annuals and biennials," which he grew from seeds and bulbs sent from America. Brilliant gardening was just one of Winter's many skills. As Janet Rhodes remembered her mother and Winter talking against a bank of gorgeous irises, Shadick remembers a new giant aquilegia hybrid that Winter started indoors and then planted "out in a long strip of land along a campus road, turning it into a showpiece worthy of a botanical garden."

Years later, after the Japanese occupied North China in 1937, causing national universities like Tsinghua to migrate to Southwest China, a Chinese colleague asked Winter to try to preserve his rare collection of iris plants. In Shadick's account, his trust was not misplaced. Winter somehow became the proprietor of a large garden, or rather private park, in the southwest corner of the northern city of Peking, put in his charge by an owner who had left the Japanese-controlled region. The hundreds of irises were then lifted from Tsinghua Yuan, transported to the city and replanted in labeled rows.

Shadick remembers an enjoyable day with Winter in this garden. "It was the ideal setting to find him in. There was a large serpentine lake, at this time dry. There was a zoological garden which included foxes. The house was an elegant bungalow featuring a bathroom with a black marble pool set into the floor. After lunch Bob tried to refresh my little knowledge of Chinese chess."

To those who saw Winter occasionally, "it was easy to get the impression of an aesthete insulated from the sterner issues of life." But much later, in 1939 or early 1940, Shadick had a chance to see that the aesthete was only one of Winter's many personae. Shadick was going into Peking when his bus was stopped at the city gate checkpoint. While the checking was going on, Winter pulled up on his motorbike. The Japanese guards examined his pass and waved him on, but instead of making a quick getaway, he chose to intervene where a Chinese was being roughly handled. This required great conviction and courage. "Our bus moved on and I don't know how Bob fared. He could have had a very rough time. It was a rare foreigner who would dare to challenge Japanese guards in those days."[31]

But back in 1927, when China's more idealist academics had become disillusioned to the point of despair and when others were doing what they could to live from day to day as pleasantly as they could, a Westerner would arrive in Peking who profoundly changed Winter's life. I. A. Richards had recently decided, rather like Marx, that instead of describing the world he would prefer to change it. So he came, bristling with the very hopes that for most of the Chinese had sunk under a hail of bullets.

CHAPTER FOUR:

I. A. RICHARDS AND THE OIC (1923-1937)[1]

Ivor and Dorothea Richards came to China in the winter of 1927 as part of the spectacular honeymoon that Richards had helped finance by writing a piece for the *Atlantic* called "The Lure of High Mountaineering." The Richardses were married in Honolulu. From there, they went to Japan, where Ivor lectured at Kansai University in Osaka. In midwinter, they sailed to Peking. Harsh North China winters didn't deter them. The stayed for several months, "saw everything and ran around everywhere."

Mountaineering was to Richards what swimming was to Winter. Ebullient spirits draw nourishment from the exhilarations of the body. Richards had taken to mountain climbing as an undergraduate, in a characteristic response to a second bout of the tuberculosis that he had first come down with at the age of fourteen. Later, he met his future wife, Dorothy Eleanor Pilley (who preferred the name Dorothea) in the Welsh mountains in 1917, where he discovered that she was as passionate a mountaineer and rock climber as himself.

A marriage grounded on the peaks led to intimacies of an uncommon kind. In *Climbing Days*, a book that has been called "a classic of mountaineering literature," Dorothea recounted how, in a tricky moment in the Alps, she joined I. A. on "a nook the size of a dinner plate, with one handhold! It needs some experience for two people to stow themselves in such a place with comfort. The contortions of the human body are, fortunately, easier to perform than to describe." A climbing companion came upon them there "with a broad smile and an '*Ah, les amoureux!*' as he spied [them] clinging together to [their] joint and solitary hold."[2]

Dorothea described Richards's particular genius as a mountaineer with loving objectivity: Richards was loose limbed, she said, and he liked "using footholds near his chin . . . . Analytic and scientific by disposition, he would sit at the top of a pitch and give me the most extraordinarily detailed instructions as to the precise movements which would bring me up with the least stress and strain. He was in fact of the cautious-controlled type *in excelsis*, tentative in his movements and always seemed able to come back without difficulty from any position, however experimental!—a sign of conscious, deliberate planning of the balance."[3] Prudence balanced with risk, tentativeness with controlled will, and a genius for *reculer pour mieux sauter*—these were also elements of Richards's intellectual life. When the moment was right, he leapt across a void.

Those winter months in Peking were happy ones for the Richardses. Although Ivor was only thirty-four when he first came to China, Winter told me that he was always at the center of any group he entered: "Richards was the soul of the thing everywhere."[4] Gifted with extraordinary clarity of mind, a passion for literature, a high but beautifully modulated voice, and a powerful faith in our human capacity to become more than we are, he was a teacher whose classes, like Winter's, overflowed into the streets, where students listened through windows.

When he arrived in China, Richards was already famous author. He had published *The Meaning of Meaning* (which enjoys the dubious distinction of being perhaps the most popular book on semantics ever written), which he coauthored with C. K. Ogden; *The Principles of Literary Criticism*, in which he began the task of inventing the critical mode that would govern the Anglo-American literary establishment for some four decades, and author as well of *Science and Poetry,* in which he would brilliantly state the case for poetry as an integrating force in an analytic, scientific age. Soon, with the publication of *Practical Criticism,* he completed the task he had begun with *Principles*: in the words of Basil Wiley, with this book Richards supplied literary criticism "with a vocabulary which has become currency for so long that its origin is often forgotten."[5] Equally important, no one, except perhaps Richards's long-term friend T. S. Eliot, did more to establish the agenda for modernism in Western departments of English.

Given Richards's intellectual temperament, it seems inevitable that this quintessential modernist should have come to China. As John Russo remarks, Richards's "intellectual map is crisscrossed by oppositions:

empiricism and idealism, science and poetry; strictly controlled expository language and the untranslatable ambiguousness of poetic modes . . . . theory and practice; East and West."[6] Richards was drawn to China in the same way he was drawn to all contraries. Like William Blake, he knew that "opposition is true friendship."

*   *   *

When the Richards first came to Peking, "seeing and doing everything there was to see and do," Peking was still, in John Blofeld's phrase, the "city of luminous splendour" that had witnessed the rise and fall of five dynasties. Superficially, it was unchanged over its millennia. Chinese scholars (and their Western counterparts) still awakened to wipe the Gobi dust from their mahogany desks, carved brush holders and embossed inkstones before sitting down to brood over the thoughts of the masters, just as men of letters had been doing for many centuries. All this endured, despite the violence seething around it.

Yet at the same time, "violently and reluctantly, Peking [here another contrary of the kind dear to the future-minded Richards] was also stirring from an ancient sleep."[7] At the university, he met and befriended the philosopher, Hu Shi, the disciple of John Dewey and major spokesman for the view that China's salvation must come from the West. Practicing what he preached, when he was not traveling in Europe, Hu preferred to spend his time in the company of Western and Westernized intellectuals.

Despite the contacts he made at Peking University, Richards found himself more at home at dynamic, progressive-minded, and Westernized Tsinghua, which was about to experience a renaissance of its own with the appointment of Luo Jialun, a former May Fourth activist, as its new president. At the same time, it was shedding the parochial mission implicit in its American orientation, and about to be incorporated into the system of national institutions of public learning. Before long, Tsinghua would become China's most important center of liberal learning. Indeed, during the 1930s, Vera Schwarcz writes, "The spirit of intellectual inquiry at [Tsinghua] was much freer than at the officious and by now quite reactionary Peking University."[8]

It was also at Tsinghua that Richards met a group of Western intellectuals who had preceded him in attempting to bridge the chasm between East and West—most notably, three relative veterans of the Western teaching staff: R. D. Jameson, Arthur Pollard-Urquhart, and

Robert Winter. At this time, Richards couldn't have foreseen that he was on the brink of an adventure that would put to a test his best skills as equilibrist or that, against a career made up of what often seemed flawless moves from one peak to the next, he was about to be tripped up by history or by his own hubris. Least of all could he see that late in his life he would "eat bitterness" and curse his most ambitious project by calling Basic English "the perpetual poison of my existence."[9]

But for now, these new Western friends gave him the what's what of the Chinese university system, educational reform, the status of programs in Western languages and literature, and some sense of the violent political tensions that had flared up in the universities over the past decade. Not only did he learn from them the necessary background for the establishment of Basic English in China, but they would also provide him the staff he needed to launch his project. Pollard-Urquhart and Winter were charming and cultivated men with his own passion for language and literature. Jameson was less flamboyant than the others, but, unlike them, he had excellent diplomatic skills and had already become a kind of unofficial dean of English studies in China.

Jameson also had the most solid academic credentials of the three. Before coming to the East, Jameson had published several books under the nom de plume Raimon de Loi, and during Richards's first and second visits to Peking, he was completing a five-volume *A Short History of European Literature* and working on *Three Lectures on Chinese Folklore.* He was deeply interested in *The Meaning of Meaning,* of which he had written an important review when the book came out four years earlier. He also had a pioneer spirit and a restlessness to attempt new boundaries that Richards found congenial. John Fairbank, who met Jameson in 1932, remembered him as "a man with a funny goatee and glasses, an enormous grin and charming manners" as well as "an infectious laugh and enthusiastic interests in Basic English, folklore, and English literature."[10]

The more worldly Pollard-Urquhart, amused and amusing, had also written literary history. Though he was less of an idealist than Jameson, ironically, it was he, who would sacrifice most for the cause of Basic English. But Ivor and Dorothea spent most of their time with Winter, who had published nothing, and who, temperamentally, was actively skeptical of great schemes and high-soaring hopes. Winter's brilliance and indefatigability as a grammarian (I was told that he once carried a year-long debate correspondence with Richards's friend C.

K. Ogden about whether the comma went inside or outside quotation marks) appealed to the linguist in Richards, and Winter's brilliance as a storyteller fascinated the Richardses as it fascinated almost everyone he met.

Though Winter had only been in China for four years when the Richardses first met him, he already seemed the thing itself, the acclimatized Westerner, fit initiator for the novice. As Dorothea put it in a letter to me, Winter taught the Richards "much of the old culture." His knowledge of China, she added, "was deep, varied, and witty." He was also, even at this early date, an established character in this environment of vivid characters: very popular with his students, a noted teacher, he "could keep any party going with his shrewd stories."

Winter had also acquired a kind of street knowledge that made a deep impression on the Richards. "These were the days when rickshaw coolies still wore pigtails and white socks and ran the 14 miles from Tsinghua to Peking and returned in all weathers and at great speed. [Winter] had a reputation for knowing the coolies' most uninhibited forms of swearing well beyond the average foreigners' range." (Winter's genius for invective in a number of vernaculars would save his life at least once, but it also caused grief to some of his Chinese friends, for whom his brilliantly articulate expressions of an often-fiery temper were less than amusing.)

The Richardses found so much in Peking to fascinate and charm them that, after spending scarcely two years back in Cambridge, they returned happily in the autumn of 1929. Ivor would spend three terms teaching English literature, writing a book called *Mencius on Mind,* and promoting the cause of Basic English, an international language that his friend C. K. Ogden had just finished inventing back in Cambridge. Dorothea learned the Chinese language (which, unlike her husband, she came to speak moderately well), and, on weekends, climbed with Ivor in the nearby Western Hills.

Richards's experiences teaching in Peking deepened his affection for the place and for the people. Though China was again on the verge of political chaos—as she had been continually throughout most of the twentieth century—Richards was impressed with the stalwartness of the "black-haired people, the sons of Han, that stable, humane, non-violent, mutually respectful, custom-ruled, law-abiding, frugal society showing one how human beings can live safely together under conditions of daunting hardship and impoverishment. It was a deep lesson in what matters."[11]

Richards later came to see other, less attractive facets of the Chinese character, but he would not cease to be fascinated with it. Oddly, his lifelong interest in Coleridge, which flowered in his study of *Coleridge on Imagination*, first published in 1935, provided an underpinning for that fascination. He had come to share Coleridge's aversion to the human shrunken to its mere rational capacities and preoccupation with scientific knowledge, which, according to the Romantic view shared by Richards, had diminished our capacity for other kinds of knowing.

But Richards also believed that the defects of our own philosophical and psychological methods might be corrected if we were able to imagine "other purposes than our own and other structures for the thought that serves them." An ability to read Mencius in his own terms would be a step in that direction. With the considerable help of three Yenching professors (Richards didn't read Chinese), he took up the study of Mencius and concluded that the Chinese psyche lacks our sharp dividing line between nature and human nature, concepts which are both encompassed in Mencius's word *hsing*. In short, Mencius's psychology lacked a dualistic bent of mind that our psychology considers universal—"namely cognitive contemplation interested only in what a thing is, in itself, apart from any use or moral significance that it may have."[12] So dictates Western dualism.

Western and Eastern thought, Richards argued, represent two sides of the human mind, and it would become an ultimate aim of what critic Geoffrey Hartman calls Richards's "dream of communication"[13] that these two agencies be made responsive to one another and coactive, thus generating a third sort of mind (Coleridge called it a *tertium aliquid*, which is imagination itself) in which the capacity to reflect and the capacity to analyze, simulate, and project worked hand in hand. In this, Richards found support in those contemporary Chinese thinkers who similarly had been urging that China's cure, and perhaps the West's as well, lay in this kind of contemplative cultural merging.

The practical extension of these ideas was a language system developed by C. K. Ogden after he and Richards completed *The Meaning of Meaning* in 1921. While Ogden and Richards were writing that book (which between themselves they called *The Beading of Beading* because they had so many heavy colds during the period of the writing), they had their best fun, Richards recalled, on chapter 6, on definition. "In the course of this we realized that a relatively small number of words could, theoretically and within describable limits of exactitude, deputize for the rest of the Dictionary."[14]

Armed with Jeremy Bentham's writings on language and his own long-standing interest in universal languages, Ogden went off to select the words and provide a comparably simplified syntax. The job took him ten years. When he was done, he labeled his new language Basic English ("'Basic' was then an almost unused word," Richards remarked), and Ogden and Richards were ready to launch their project.

Basic requires only 850 words, six hundred of them names, four hundred "fictions" (or abstractions) two hundred "picturable things that can be pointed to," 150 qualities (or adjectives), fifty of them opposites, and the rest "operators"—verbs, prepositions, directions, the glue of language. Not only did Ogden manage to reduce our four thousand common verbs to eighteen, but he also compressed the entire vocabulary, plus the grammatical rules necessary to govern it, to "a list able to be printed on one side of a bit of business notepaper."

The immediate success, even the glamour, of Basic English was spectacular. To provide a shining example of the power of this system, James Joyce (in collaboration with Ogden, Richards, and Ogden's assistant Ms. L. W. Lockhart) translated sections of *Finnegan's Wake* (a text using a vocabulary of 850,000 words) into Basic, with its vocabulary of 850. In the spring of 1932, luminaries such as George Bernard Shaw, H. G. Wells, John Dewey, Kemp Malone, Julian Huxley, Paul Robeson, along with a steadily growing list of supporters from Russia, East Europe, and Japan, put their names under a manifesto that read:

> The undersigned are convinced of the urgentness for an international auxiliary, but are unable to accept, as satisfactory for the purpose, any artificially constructed system. They feel that some form of simplified English, such as Basic offers, will meet that demand. They would therefore welcome any provision for its practical application, especially for Commercial and Radio requirements, and the establishment of closer relations with the people of Africa and the East.[15]

It was the sort of document that, given the cultural éclat of the signatories, would catch the world's eye.

By 1934, Ogden, having claimed volunteer representatives in thirty countries, announced that "the future will be largely determined by the speed with which English can be acquired in the Far East; and an extensive research program on the adaptation of Basic to the needs of the Eastern learner will be completed in 1935."[16]

One eye that the movement caught early was that of David Stevens, the newly appointed head of the Rockefeller Foundation's Humanities Division. From 1922-1932, while he worked to develop Basic, Ogden had invested $150,000, money he had secured partly from loans, partly from gifts from sympathetic persons "who had faith in the project and realized its value for international understanding" and partly from his own services gratuitously given.[17] The Foundation has been invested in China ever since the refund of Boxer Rebellion indemnities had been used to found Tsinghua University.[18] In January 1933, the Rockefeller Foundation began to support the work of the Orthological Institute, as Ogden called the agency that he constructed around Basic. In July of that year, the Foundation funded a conference on Basic English held in New York for Chinese and Japanese delegates to a staff meeting of the Institute of Pacific Relations. Both Ogden and Richards (who in general hated conferences) were there to present the new program, which was a resounding success. Arthur Hummel, at the time chief of the Library of Congress Division of Orientalia, wrote to Stevens to thank him for the conference, and to express his "regret that during the ten years in which I taught English, in both China and Japan, the principles underlying Basic were unknown, and that I had no chance to apply them."[19]

The work of Ogden and Richards dovetailed with the globalist idealism that was a principal motive to Stevens, as to other intellectual activists during the decades following the Great War. "Nationalism cannot resist the force of powerful intellectual curiosities that carry individuals beyond all borders to common sources of knowledge," Stevens wrote in 1933, in a statement that was to be the starting point of the Rockefeller Foundation's interest in modern languages. Raymond B. Fosdick, trustee of the Foundation at the time and president from 1936-1948, would later reflect on that commitment:

> In a world whose ties are increasingly interwoven and inter-related, it is not enough to have the barriers of language breached by only a handful of cloistered scholars. If cultural interests are to be given a wider currency, and if the imperative need of mutual under-standing between races is to be met, something must be done to break down the insularity created by ignorance of other languages.[20]

Naturally, Rockefeller Foundation officers also saw in Basic important practical merits. They viewed it a way of facilitating their larger mission of standardizing scientific methodology throughout the world. Given the urgent need on the part of the Chinese to gain access to Western science and given the inefficiency of their own ancient language for that purpose, the Basic project, at this initial stage, must have seemed heaven sent.

But the Foundation was also caught up by the sweep of Ogden's and Richards's world federalist vision. As early as 1926, in their preface to the second edition of *The Meaning of Meaning,* the two had called for "an Institute of Linguistic Research with headquarters in Geneva, New York, and Peking." The purpose of such an institute, Richards made explicit some years later, during a time of renewed world war, when he wrote that "A common medium of communication between peoples rather than between governments" had become an evident necessity.[21]

At the same time, such a common language "neither can nor should be imposed by one nation or group of nations upon others. It must come into use freely, as a general convenience, under the urge of the everyday motives of mankind," and "no one in learning the world language must have excuse for even the least shadow of a feeling that he is submitting to an alien influence or being brought under the power of other groups." To guard against that danger, we must "conceive a world language in a truly planetary spirit—as a universal medium, not as an extension of the sphere of influence of some one pressure group." Indeed, the learner's very desire to learn and use this common language should symbolize "his participation in the common human political effort, a sign that he recognizes the claim upon him of the world community—beyond that of his regional, racial, or cultural group." Richards believed that only so could the spread of a world language "be linked with the greatest of the unused sources of power—man's new need, corresponding to his new knowledge, for a loyalty larger than any he has yet known."[22]

In April 1936, with the support of David Stevens of the Rockefeller Foundation, Richards returned to China in April 1936. By then the newly entitled movement Orthological Institute of China was being directed by R. D. Jameson, aided by Winter and Pollard-Urquhart, was already three years old and flourishing. In a report that he wrote in March, 1935, on "the present position of Basic in China," Jameson stated the aims of the Institute: "to devise ways of teaching to students in Middle Schools and Colleges an English which will be of use to them and at the same time save them two years of word learning with the thought that these years can be put on more profitable work" and "to present the material in such a way that an analytical—as opposed to the temperamental Chinese synthetic—habit of thought will be acquired."[23]

To implement the first aim, Jameson and his coworkers were considering practical questions such as: the order in which Basic words have to be presented, which Chinese linguistic habits can be most readily exploited in the learning of Basic, and how much "grammatical notation as rules" is needed to teach learners to read, speak and write English. As to the more abstract second objective, its accomplishment was essential, Jameson observed, "in solving the problem of Sino-Occidental communication as well as in attempting to adapt Western scientific methods to Chinese needs." But providing the Chinese with an analytic language involved "not a transformation in the Chinese way of thinking, but rather the attempt to make available to the Chinese the logical or analytical habit of thought which has been the cause of much of our own progress in the sciences." Without this, knowledge of the mechanics of Western scientific procedure and an ability to parrot Western terms could be of no value. The trick of the thing was our habit "of analyzing complexes into their elements and reconstructing the elements into general principles."[24]

That was the habit that Jameson wished to graft onto the Chinese mentality. Previous failures to do this and blindness on the part of both Chinese and Westerners to the fact that "though they may use the same verbal symbols in speaking each other's language, these symbols refer to entirely different fields of discourse" accounted for the slight success of attempts to rebuild "China's rural and social structures along Western lines."[25]

Though Jameson had in mind no less a goal than to establish Basic as an instrument of reorganizing China along modern Western lines, at this time he was working with a staff consisting of only a Chinese clerk and a worker on fellowship. Yet despite the size of its staff, the Institute had made remarkable strides, and indeed, Jameson feared that the movement was taking hold too fast, beyond the efforts by him and his coworkers to keep pace. Besides preparing teaching texts, bringing to heel a company that had been pirating Ogden's books and helping to establish a Western Language Association of China whose members were Chinese teachers of Western languages sympathetic to Basic, Jameson had won the support of Dean Hung Shen, head of the English Department of the National Shantung University, Tsingtao. A former cinema director and a distinguished writer, Hung was at work on three one-act plays in

Basic. Another enthusiast, Chao Yuan Jen, head of the Department of Linguistics at the Academia Sinica, had "just brought out an excellent set of 12 phonograph records in basic." Chao had been appointed by the Philological Society of China "to be the Ogden of China" and had just completed an article in Basic English on "Basic Chinese."

Other well-placed Chinese scholars had identified themselves with the new movement. Shen Yu-ting, professor of philosophy at Tsinghua, was following up on Richards's pioneer work with a complete translation of Mencius and planned to use "the Basic method of tracing ambiguities and outlining the configurations of Mencius' thought." And there was also work afoot by Professor Shui Tien-tung, "one of our field representatives," and Mrs. Dorothy Kemp, who would eventually become Jameson's wife, to produce Basic versions of "Good Stories from Greece and Rome" and the first part of *Gulliver's Travels*.

Finally, Basic was making inroads into the university and secondary school teaching of English. Basic English would be used as part of the freshman reading course in the National Tsinghua University in the following year, and the Orthological Institute had been asked to provide a Basic course for a summer school to be held in the National Shantung University in 1937.

In addition to all this, Tyler, an expert in Basic and a former assistant to Ogden, was in China in 1935 representing the Institute of Pacific Relations. She'd made contact with the Minister of Education, T. C. Kung, and learned of his dissatisfaction with the present situation in English teaching and his desire for advice as to how that teaching could be better accomplished. Tyler was able to interest him in the possibilities of Basic and went back to the States to work for Columbia Broadcasting System in order to acquire the practical knowledge of broadcasting methods that would help her promote its use in radio.

In sum, though Jameson and his staff could not keep up with the demands on them, they had reason to feel sanguine about the future of the movement: "The enthusiasm and controversies of 1933 have given way before a realization that we are neither an emotion nor a fad but that we are offering a reasoned approach to an important question."[26]

Two months later, Jameson confidently predicted that by 1938 the Institute would be in a position "to take over a *hsien* [county] where in the middle schools we can work out the techniques for making Basic part of the national program." (That hope would in part materialize in Yunnan province more or less on schedule, though facilitated by the odd means of the Japanese occupation of Peking in 1937, which forced the major northern universities to move to Kunming.) By 1938, or earlier, Jameson also expected that an arrangement could be made whereby he would be lent to the Ministry of Education in an advisory capacity, thus, in effect, serving as the provincial minister of education in matters related to the teaching of English.

At Jameson's request, Richards returned to China in the spring of 1936 to help dispel a rising opposition to Basic that he felt at the university. To some Chinese professors, Basic seemed a kind of baby talk, intellectually demeaning to the user.[27] At the same time, with the approval of the Ministry of Education, Jameson had scheduled a summer program for one hundred Chinese teachers, and Richards as well as Jameson thought it desirable that he use this opportunity to test the method. This meant also that Richards would expose himself to some of the practical difficulties with which such regular field workers as Jameson were already familiar.

Thus, in June, he grumbled in a letter to Stevens about "the half-baked state of most Chinese Middle-School teachers and teachers-to-be." He blamed it on bad method: how could students jaded by years of staring at "'typical errors' and lists of incorrectness" help but be weary and incapable of either thinking or writing with language so acquired? Richards also found reason to complain about some of his Chinese assistants: keeping them "on the boil is no light business," he told Stevens. "Less than a certain constant supply of energy from the West—and nothing happens." [28]

As if all this were not bad enough, the amorphic resistance at Tsinghua was beginning to make itself felt in subtle and potentially harmful political maneuvers. For instance, Jameson's contract with Tsinghua had been held up, and there had been some concern that a faction at Tsinghua might use Jameson's outside work with Basic as a reason for putting him out of the English Department. Richards's sketch of "the extravagant complexity of the internal politics of a Chinese university" is especially vivid:

> Jealousies, ancient feuds, pressures from influential persons with a friend who would like a professorship, and a long bad history of sinecurism, absentee [tenure], plural livings, and many less easily imagined factors come in. All complicated by *opera bouffé* interventions from students who make patriotism

an excuse for refusing to sit for examinations, while demanding
their degrees, and who manhandle timorous professors.[29]

Richards had sunk a long way from the exultation of a month ago
when he had told Stevens's assistant John Marshall, "You would be green
with envy if you knew how easy it is to make a difference to teaching
here."[30] But he remained intrepid. His staff had found a small core—Ms.
Tam, Wang, and Chen—of excellent teachers, and for the rest, Richards
and his colleagues had concluded, "we must put into our Readers and
teacher's handbooks even more than we had proposed. Almost nothing
can be left to the common sense or initiative of a middle school teacher."[31]

The Institute's Chinese staff was expanded that summer to include,
besides Mr. Liu, Professor C. W. Luh, Professor Shui, Ms. Tam, and
Professor Chao, all of whom had helped conduct the summer training
session for teachers from all over the country that the minister's
committee had assigned to the Institute. But Jameson had also recruited
two new American workers, whom both he and Richards anticipated
would make a lot of difference to the overall program.

One of these was Jameson's old colleague, E. K. Smith, whom
Jameson described as "one of the most experienced and best elementary
English teachers in China," who would be helpful in "giving suggestions
and in shroffing the lessons as they are worked out by the Institute." (To
"shroff" was a favorite verb of Jameson's; in China and throughout the
Far East, it signified the testing of coins in order to separate the base from
the genuine.) Richards would later describe Smith as "one of the most
successful of the senior Missionary-type American teachers." His role
would be that of "detached outside critic." The other American appointee
was Robert Winter.

Jameson and Richards had considered the possibility of bringing over
a trained "Basicist," who would be concerned only with translation and
editing." By finding on the spot a person so fitted for the job, they had
saved time and expense, Jameson wrote in his proposed budget for May
1, 1936, to June 30, 1937. Winter, he added,

> probably has had better training in linguistics than any
> other teacher in China. His knowledge of languages and of
> grammatical principles, etc., is exceptional and will be most
> useful in our preparation of texts as well as in the editing
> and translation. His knowledge of the Chinese language and

psychology of the Chinese will also be extremely helpful. We feel that the $200 a month we have budgeted for him is low for what he will be contributing and in the event of a future program we would hope to raise this sum quite substantially.[32]

Later that summer, Richards described Winter as "a great increase to our strength . . . an excessively gifted man who seems to have almost been waiting for Basic to give him his proper work to do. He will be our linguistic conscience—much as Ms. Lockhart is Ogden's in London—and much more."[33] For Winter, whether or not the appointment felt like a conversion experience, it provided him a supplementary salary of $200 monthly—a very substantial improvement of his standard of living—and allowed him, while he continued to teach at Tsinghua, to do something else that he was very experienced at: the preparation of texts for the teaching of English.

*　　*　　*

The Richardses remained in Peking through the hot summer (though Richards had earlier said that "July and August are, for me, wiped out by the heat"), Richards preparing for a second summer training program, this one at Shi Ta, the chief teachers training college in North China. Richards, as usual, worked well into the night, and that obliged him to move at an inopportune time. In the midst of all this, the Richards had had to move. They had been living in a little house in Ta Yan Yi Pin Hutung, just five minutes on a bicycle through the lanes to the Institute. While this situation allowed them an intimate perspective on Chinese folkways in the streets, Richards was beginning to find that intimacy a little oppressive. At 2:00 a.m. on a summer night, while he was catching up with his correspondence, the soup sellers were still "wandering through the streets calling their wares so that the opium smokers could have their late meal after waking." Then there was the night watchman, clacking his stick "to scare the thieves out of his path." Added to the soup sellers' cries and the watchman's clackings, there was also the problem of "three quarrelsome neighbours only three yards away, and an especially vociferous stream of hawkers passing by whenever the neighbours are eating or resting." All this Richards could hear through his paper window.[34] By late July, such distractions had driven the Richards "out of our little house." The new one, formerly occupied by Osbert Sitwell, was retired and roomy and had only the Brazilian ambassador as neighbor. That gentleman, apparently, turned out to be satisfactory. The Richardses remained in their new house until December, when they headed back to the West by way of the Trans-Siberian railroad.[35]

Richards knew that China was especially volatile at this moment. Just a few days before, he and Dorothea left Peking. Chiang Kai-shek was made prisoner by his own officers, who hoped to compel him to renew the united front with the Communists and to fight their common enemy, the Japanese invaders in Manchuria. But such affairs did not disturb Richards's equilibrium. He enjoyed a kind of beatific faith in the capacity of Basic to ride such storms. "The new Chinese convulsion," he wrote to John Marshall, "won't affect our Chinese doings seriously, and . . . even if Chiang Kai-shek is done for, the Ministry of Education will remain much as it is. Changes in China are never as big as they seem to be from a distance."[36] No doubt, he intended to allay fears back in New York and to ensure the continued funding of his project. But he also believed genuinely that Basic somehow transcended all national interests, and thus enjoyed a kind of special protection. This would prove a naive dream.

*   *   *

Robert Winter too was living out the last phase of a dream of his own, in the city that, though only for a short time more, would continue to be enchanted. For this while, Peking was a city full of trees, and if you stood on Coal Hill, at the edge of the Forbidden City, the city below seemed to be built in a forest. The junipers in the imperial parks filled the air with a soothing fragrance, the restaurants were prepared to satisfy the most exacting tastes, and the curio shops were filled with paintings and jades well within the budgets even of Westerners on fixed income, like Winter, whose own furniture collection was sufficiently discriminating to win photographs in George Kates's classic volume on Chinese furniture.[37]

In the Forbidden City, one could still see intact the imperial collection of art treasures, brought to its final perfection in the middle Ching, much of it to be carted off to Taiwan at the end of the Chinese civil war. In the paintings of the Tang, Sung, Yuan, Ming, and Ching Periods, the living spirit of China was still vivid in the landscapes, the mountains, the myriad shadows of supple bamboo, and in the collections of ancient calligraphy.

The Orientalist John Blofeld met Robert Winter (Blofeld calls him "Professor Luton") at about this time, through a friend of his who was attending Winter's class in European literature for second-year students.[38] Luton was trying to make them appreciate Proust. "We are most of us so fond of him that we forgive him things which would otherwise cause a riot," Blofeld's friend—he calls him "Chu"—remarks. For instance, "Last week, in class, he cursed the whole Chinese race. He said we lived only for our bellies, that we have combed earth and sky and sea for everything remotely edible, and that we should long ago have become cannibals if human flesh happened to be more delicious than pork! Some of my classmates were so angry that they walked out of the lecture room."

But when Winter "realized how we felt, he apologized very pleasantly and soon won our sympathy. He told us he had twice taken a lot of trouble to grow some rare flowers from seeds especially ordered in America. Each time, as soon as the buds opened, one of his neighbors (so he says) sent a child over the wall to pull of the heads. He believes they were taken away to be cooked." Chu admitted that Winter might be correct: "Plenty of flowers make delicious eating. You must have tasted fish or chicken dishes sprinkled with lightly fried chrysanthemum petals."

Blofeld was eager to meet the irascible but lovable American, and a few days later he and Chu found themselves in the neighborhood of the old elephant stables walking down a lane between "high windowless walls, broken at intervals by ornamental roofs overhanging copper-hinged gates of chipped and fading lacquer." Inside the outer gate to Winter's house, they found their way along a stone-flagged path. "The main building, which surprisingly had no courtyard and faced east instead of south, must at one time have formed part of a larger complex of buildings. Western-style flowerbeds and lawns contrasting with formal arrangements of glazed pots containing flowers or ornamental shrubs bore witness to the owner's West-East tastes." Blofeld found the overall effect charming, though to Chu's Peking-formed mind the lack of symmetrical arrangement looked untidy.

Blofeld had been prepared by the gossip he had heard about Winter "for some degree of eccentricity," but he was far from ready for what came next. "A heavily built, bearded American came stalking out, a finger to his lips, making ostentatious rather than effective efforts to tiptoe silently, and carrying in his left hand a freshly severed dog's tail, raw and bloody at the end." Blofeld thought that Winter's "recent loss of his cherished flowers" might have driven the American mad, but his young Manchu companion, who had known L for a long time, "showed no change of expression, even when the Professor gestured excitedly to prevent him from introducing and rebuking him with a burst of shushing noises, explaining that Wu Kuan-T'ien, the greatest master of the seven-stringed lute, much beloved of the ancients but rarely played in modern times, was inside.

So the three men entered the house, where Winter, after disposing of the bloody tail, led them to an inner room where "seven scholarly-looking old gentlemen dressed in gowns of dark-coloured silk suitable to autumn—deep shades of blue, grey and bronze," were seated around a thin old man leaning over the lute lying on a low pearwood table in front of him.

It took Blofeld a moment to realize that the old man "was engaged in plucking from it the sweetest sounds imaginable, for the silken strings gave forth notes softer than the buzzing of a single bee!" The melody "was woven of sighs and murmurs, the tinkle of jade ornaments, the wind in the pine-trees, the whispering flight of pigeons. It was ancient and remote, like ghostly music echoing faintly through the silence of a haunted grove, yet not so much melancholy as sweetly solemn with now and then a hint of gentle gaiety."

When it was over, Winter made the introductions. "He was a man transformed—a man now as calm, affable, dignified and ceremonious as his Chinese guests." Yet Blofeld found in his well-meant imitation of the Chinese manner was "a discernible element of the grotesque." Gestures "admirably suited to pale, delicately formed men in silken gowns are less becoming in a large, red-faced, bearded Westerner, especially as, lacking a gown, he cannot perform suitably low bows without an O-shaped space appearing between his trouser legs!"

After the other guests had left, Blofeld and Winter chatted. Chu had gone home alone, suddenly overwhelmed by the recent death of his brother, though when he first reported it to Blofeld, he had giggled. Winter explained Chu's behavior at some length. Chu must have argued, the American said, "that you are not, as yet, an intimate friend, so he ought not to burden you with his personal grief. His giggling is less surprising than his not having told you earlier. You've noticed, haven't you, that some sort of laugh or smile is the normal Chinese response to misfortune; it goes with shock, fear, embarrassment and sometimes with anger."

But what of Chu's sudden bursting into tears just moments after the giggle? "You didn't find that strange, did you?" The Chinese feel what we feel, perhaps more intensely. If they appear not to, this is because propriety is so important to them. "All their actions are governed by it—up to when they reach breaking point." But "beyond that—well, the youngsters especially have no more control than you or I. Less, maybe, because their emotions have been bottled up until something bursts inside them. When that happens, the Book of Rites is forgotten and the Tajen, the would-be superior man, finds himself as much at the mercy of his feelings as any other guy."

They went to lunch in Winter's dining room, "lighted by windows intricately latticed to form the pattern known as 'cracked ice.'" Blofeld had been in China long enough to recognize that the furniture, "built of darkly gleaming wood with simple functional lines," was genuine Ming. There were only four pictures in the room, "a set of black and white landscapes depicting the four seasons," which Blofeld recognized from the brushstrokes (as well as by "the silken mountings yellowed with age") as the work of some antique master." On the other hand, the food, though served on fine porcelain plates with an apple-green glaze, was so uncompromisingly Western that Winter felt it necessary to explain that though he loved Chinese food, he could not eat it every day. Blofeld would have to make do with ox-tail soup and grilled fish Blofeld managed, Chinese style, to repress his suspicion that the bloody dog's tail he saw upon his arrival might have been the main ingredient of the soup.

Then, after lunch, followed by "coffee on a terrace set about with pots of pink and white oleanders, sitting in the sun away from the hibiscus-shadowed trellis," Winter took him to "a corner of the garden, secluded by a thick-set row of flourishing camelia-trees," where they came to another terrace, this one surrounded on three sides by cages and barred enclosures.

Here was Winter's menagerie, a dozen varieties of animals together with a much larger number of birds, including peacocks. Blofeld particularly remembered (as did most of those who visited Winter at this time) "some evil-looking civet cats glaring at us banefully as they paced up and down their cage, and a pair of hideous grey monkeys chattering with glee and stretching their paws through the bars of their cage to welcome their master." Then to the left of this they came to an enclosure that towered over the rest, "its heavy iron bars covered with fine wire netting." Inside paced three gray-furred animals that Blofeld took to be "undersized and unfriendly Alsatians of impure stock."

Winter quickly corrected him. Hadn't he seen wolves before? "No? Well, these fine fellows, captured somewhere in the Manchurian forests, were "fierce enough to welcome a chance to bite your throat out." Though they know Winter and his "number one boy," Lao Liu, so well, they never went in to feed them without taking a whip. "And now," Winter added, with a proper dramatic pause, he would explain to Blofeld what had happened just a little before the music started, just before Blofeld arrived.

Lao Liu had opened the padlock and gone in to feed them as usual. Then, "while he was still in the cage, after distributing a basket of raw meat, he went over to that trough there to turn on the water tap." In front of it, "he saw lying on the ground a tail—a freshly bitten-off tail with blood staining the earth close to the severed end." His first reaction was to stare at each of Winter's three wolves, looking for injuries, but, as Blofeld could see, their tails were all in place. That only deepened the mystery, "since even if some fool of a dog should have rubbed against the cage in an effort to be friendly, the mesh was too small to let them get hold of his tail."

The final explanation provided by Lao Liu was so odd that Winter thought Blofeld would "find it easier to believe the goddamned thing grew there of itself!" At the bottom of Winter's garden was a fox tower, where some of Winter's "more ignorant neighbors came most mornings to burn incense."

This particular tower was "not dedicated to the *huliching*, a sinister and deadly sort of fox spirit, but to a *huhsien*, a male fox credited with the power of turning himself into the form of an old man . . . . fond of creating insoluble mysteries and of perpetrating those stupid practical jokes all *huhsien* seem to enjoy." It was this spirit, Lao Liu had explained, and now Winter explained to Blofeld, that had played the prank that so startled Blofeld as he had first entered Winter's world.

Blofeld wondered whether Winter actually believed such stories. "I suppose," the American reflected, "when you have spent years and years in a city where even the papers report such things as factually as an outbreak of measles, you do begin to wonder." Had Blofeld seen in the paper last week "that column about a burglar who climbed a tree in full view of the policemen chasing him and then, turning into a small brown fox, disappeared among the leaves? They were afraid to shoot, for fear it would come back and haunt them."

Naturally, Blofeld came back often to chat with the American professor. Clown and connoisseur, zookeeper and folklorist, Oriental sage and American guy, Winter was above all a man who loved the dramatic, and who knew how to make it part of his life. On another occasion, he told Blofeld a chilling tale about a student of his who died of tuberculosis, which his fellows explained had been aggravated by the boy's "uncontrolled indulgence with a lovely but mysterious prostitute." Winter soon learned, however, that the popular belief held the prostitute to be a huliching, who had gradually drained the boy's strength. Though the boy eventually recognized her for what she was, he could not escape. In Winter's words: "You know what they say about a huliching. She is irresistible. A guy who has once tasted her embrace is beyond saving." Even when the victim realizes that death his near, he cannot bring himself to save himself or ask help from others. "Every day you think: 'Tonight I'll go to her for the last time and, tomorrow, take the first train to Nanking—anywhere that's a hell of a distance away.' But you never go. It's always tomorrow and tomorrow, until, sucked dry to the last drop of energy, you stagger or are carried home to death."

At the end of Winter's story, Blofeld found himself shivering. Winter, "in relating this gruesome story, had passed from smiling matter-of-factness to a grisly solemnity. No longer a raconteur striving for effect, he had become a man powerfully moved by his own words. I was glad when, of his own accord, he decided that one such story was enough and turned to pleasanter things."

On a day devoted to pleasanter things, Winter took Blofeld to "the House of Springtime Congratulations," Winter was a familiar figure at the house, and here Blofeld depicts him as a Shriner on convention. "I like to have fun with a girl without having to mess around with a couple of hundred rules of can-do and can't do," he told Blofeld. "That's what you'll like about Golden Cicada. I've taught her a thing or two, as you'll see. She's a honey."

Indeed, Golden Cicada greeted him brazenly, rushing forward with a scream and throwing her arms around his neck—as he had taught her— and gave him long kisses, which he obviously relished. Blofeld could only conclude that since Winter, despite his many years in China, "still retained an affection for the frankly bawdy prostitutes of his own country, these girls, having divined his tastes, were willing to indulge them." That is, in his presence, they abandoned the refinement they had learned as flower girls.

That side of Winter, though it must often have been witnessed, has been rarely recorded. More familiar is the picture of him Blofeld paints in describing a party given for him some years later when he was about to depart from China. After a dinner that included deep drinking of the good *Shaohsing huang chiu*, the guests began playing wine games. Blofeld suggested that they play a game involving composition of extemporary poems at speed, the toastmaster producing the opening line at random, then three other players composing second, third, and fourth lines in turn, each suitable in terms of content, rhythm and rhyme, and each delivered within a set time limit. A player who hesitates or fails must down three cupfuls of wine as penalty.

One of the players suggested that Winter set the first line since "his Chinese is better than ours." To this compliment, which the Chinese often pay to foreigners though it is seldom if ever deserved, Winter quickly replied: "Thank you, thank you, Chang Taifu. Your praise is more kind than accurate. A stupid fellow like myself is bound to find it embarrassing. Allow me to decline the honour." So Winter, by answering gracefully, in idiomatic Pekingese, "was allowed to escape a task too difficult for a foreigner at such short notice."[39]

It was in recollection of scenes like this that Blofeld, like so many other Westerners who knew the graces of Peking in those days, could say:

> For me the joy remains,
> Unchanging and unchanged![40]

Blofeld's memories, unlike Winter's, remained unspoiled by the events that once again proved no joy remains unchanged.

CHAPTER FIVE:
WAR AND THE OIC

For all the power of his intellect, Richards was also tuned in to his heart's dictates. In early February 1937, he wrote to David Stevens, who had become the Rockefeller Foundation's point man on the Orthological Institute Project:

> We are enjoying the birdcalls and scents of Magdalene garden while we may. A rose was still flaunting a week ago and now there is a golden carpet of aconites under the trees. A strange deeply peaceful life it might be. I often wonder what itch makes me want to jiggle [joggle?] about the world interfering with other people. Why, in our time, should Auden, say, in writing the line, Leisurely reading the masters in their rock garden intend it to be a scornful description (I think, of Bridges)? My rock garden has grown about half an inch of moss since I last saw it. I find I'm really much more attached to Cambridge than to China. However, I want to go there!"[1]

But he knew perfectly well what drew him from his peaceful garden. In an afterthought written down the left-hand margin of his letter, he asked Stevens: "Do you recall Political Godwin's resolution: 'The remainder of my time I determined to devote to the pursuit of such attainments as are afforded me the most promise to tender me useful'! I wrote it up over my door, in fun, 20 years ago. It seems to be having its revenge."

Richards had several reasons for believing that he could be useful in China at that moment. For one, he had been working with Ogden again, finding the collaboration as easy and pleasant as it had been nineteen years ago when they were writing *The Meaning of Meaning*. While Richards helped Ogden see what the special school problems and the special Chinese problems were, Ogden, with the help of his able coworkers Lockhart and Graham ("tremendous workers—about 40 Chinese power each!"), was making good progress with the Basic dictionary and collateral school-reading material needed in China. With the help of these new materials and his discussions with Ogden, Richards could return to Peking "to do more and better work in training people to teach."

In retracing the intricate path Richards followed in order to launch this pet (though by no means his *only*) project, we observe the workings of Richards's particular genius tendering himself useful. He did this by being where he needed to be at the time he was most needed, by persuading both American and Chinese officials to support him and by having an appetite for detail framed by the very grand vision of world peace and harmony. That he failed in the end would be history's fault, not his.

Richards was particularly eager to put Ogden's stuff into a report to the Ministry of Education, whom he hoped to persuade to contribute a share of the support of the Institute. (An important measure of the success of the project would be for it to become independent of Rockefeller Foundation support and, of course, for the Chinese government thus to acknowledge its efficacy.) He felt that Ogden was a poor expounder of his own theories, and no one in Peking, not even Jameson, could put them forth them with Richards's brilliant authority. To shape a report that would be "a permanent guiding document for Chinese education," Richards would have to be there, on the spot, "with the actual people who are carrying it out at present, as it were, in the room."[2]

Good news he had received from Jameson made Richards uneasy and fanned still higher his desire to return to China. At their winter meeting, Jameson had cabled, the Western Language Association had passed a resolution "requesting the Ministry of Education to allocate a special area for a three-year experiment to be conducted by the Institute." Richards was glad to learn that in response to the resolution Jameson was "treading warily." The Institute didn't have the staff necessary to carry out so ambitious a project. Besides, fully initiated into the nuances of academic intrigue on several continents, Richards feared that the resolution itself might be a subtle trap. After all, it was proposed by F. T. Ching Chen

Futian, head of Freshman Composition at Tsinghua. Sensing the low esteem in which Ching was held by Richards and Jameson, Richards suspected that Ching urged the resolution as a means of bringing their project down around their ears by involving them in an enterprise beyond their present powers.[3] It's astonishing that, despite such political scheming, the many other projects he was involved in, and the imminent Japanese invasion, Richards's enthusiasm for the project would remain unflagging and committed.

Richards left Cambridge in March, and in the States busied himself with conferences arranged by John Marshall of the Rockefeller Foundation. Working his way West, he found people all across the country who were interested in his work and guided by his principles and practices. These visits played an important part in consolidating his influence in American universities. Then, in May, he sailed west out of Seattle.

For all the risks implicit in the situation he was returning to, Richards was excited by the possibilities of the moment. Letters from the Ministry of Education that had been coming in showed that "they are hoping for a lot from us." He now was convinced that the Institute, despite the shortage of trained teachers, was nearly ready to provide it. A central task remained the report that the Institute was preparing for the ministry that hoped could be "a permanent guiding document for Chinese education." It was particularly to get that report done that Richards was again sailing to China, for this was the document through which Richards and his coworkers would provide the superstructure for all secondary-school English teaching in China and eventually for university teaching as well.[4]

As he wrote to David Stevens about these matters from shipboard, it must have seemed to Richards that after so long and painstaking a preparation he could almost touch the goal he had been laboring toward. As he would define it some thirty-five years later, that goal was "(1) to do something to ease, in time, the task set the Chinese people and the Western people of understanding better one another's positions for living, and (2) by the same means help forward and speed up a supply of persons more competent to meet what was clearly going to be the ever more taxing problems of our planet."[5] Now, at least the solid beginning of that task was at hand, and with it the realization of what Richards had come to recognize as his lifework.

*   *   *

Late in the spring of 1937, it was "raining and blissfully cool still." When it warmed to the torrid Peking summer, Richards and Dorothea planned to move into some cool retreat, where he could draft "the big report." In the meantime, long interested in exploiting the potential of the rapidly developing communications media for the purposes of education, he was looking at radio as a means of supplementary instruction in Basic. He and Jameson were enthusiastic about bringing Charlotte Tyler back to Peking from her job at the Columbia Broadcasting Company.[6] Marshall thought that she could be available in a year or sooner.

Toward the end of June, the last piece of the project seemed to fall into place. Richards presented his case before a committee convened in Nanking by Wang Shih-chieh, the minister of education, who presided. Committee members included, besides Richards and R. D. Jameson, George Yeh (Yeh Kung-ch'ao), who, after a brilliant undergraduate and postgraduate career at Amherst (where his linguistic and poetic talents attracted the attention of Robert Frost) and in Cambridge, England, where he took an MA degree in Indo-European linguistics, returned to China, quickly to earn a reputation as an outstanding scholar and provocative teacher. His admirers knew him as "the Dr. Johnson of China." Other members of the committee included C. W. Luh, Chao Chao-hsiung, Shui Tien-tung, Chao Yuan-jen, Wu Fuheng and other persons directly or indirectly in close touch with the work of the OIC (Orthological Institute of China).[7]

Predictably, the committee approved thirty-three resolutions that in effect endorsed Richards's program for training middle school teachers in Basic as the first step of a nationwide experiment. Richards wired to Dorothea, who had remained in Peking: *Have everything I want. Something must be wrong.*[8]

What was wrong became apparent two weeks after the meeting, on the night of July 7, 1937, when shots were exchanged between Japanese and Chinese troops at Luykuochiao, Marco Polo Bridge, near Peking. Though the Japanese insisted that this was merely an incident, not the beginning of war, history snickered. The Sino-Japanese War would continue until August 14, 1945, only to be followed by four additional years of civil war. Richards's dream of a common language that could be "the instrument of purposes transcending those of any nation or group of present nations," and that "must be identified with a world view which values nations only as they contribute to a world aim" was, for all practical purposes, drowned in a sea of blood.

To me, the history of the Orthological Institute of China encapsulates the drowning of culture throughout the world in waves of almost continuous violence. Projects begun as steps toward fulfillment of a dream of peace now,[9] as we look backward, seem almost unforgivably naïve, and one can argue that even this project was tainted by Anglo imperialism. But the taint shouldn't obliterate the essence of the dream, which was hope, when it was still possible to hope, that human beings could get along with one another.

To the three human beings who were enjoying the evening after a hot day in Peking on July 26, the death of dreams must have seemed remote. As the Richards dined with Robert Winter in his house in the West City, "far from most foreigners' haunts," as Dorothea Richards described it in a letter to me, the shots fired on July 7 seemed a passing thing. They were snug a house made legendary by virtue of the beauty of its garden (Winter specialized in "startling tall, multicolored iris") and of the exotic collection of animals he kept—"there was a parrot somewhere, I think, and a cageful of wolves which he loved handling."[10]

I see the moment as a kind of photo of the last moment when the years were still fat. The interior of the house was rich with the objects Winter loved collecting. His furniture was made up of museum pieces. There was an exquisite game table with sunken recesses for counters and board; a ch'in cho, or lute table, very simple and tranquil; a large wooden k'ang, or daybed, almost ten feet long, once used to accommodate two opium smokers reclining on it at full length; and a smaller couch, or large chair, of the kind that was used by Ch'ing emperors as they sat enjoying nature from a pavilion of a palace garden such as those that not so long ago had been cultivated in the Western Hills, not far from Winter's home.[11]

In the daytime, Winter's dining room was lighted by windows intricately latticed in the pattern known as "cracked ice," and the only pictures, as John Blofeld recorded, were a set of black and white landscapes depicting the four seasons—the works of an antique master.[12] In such a setting, with Richards's recent triumph casting its own light on the room, and Winter beguiling his friends with gossip and lore, spirits ran high.

Then, Dorothea recalled, "quite unexpectedly, the Japanese attacked and as I remember bullets started flying around. Clearly it was important to lie flat, where we were, as soon as possible, which is what we did." They were pinned down there until the next morning, Mrs. Richards remembered, but through what must have been a long night, "Bob remained a cool and cordial host." On the next day, following bombardment by planes and artillery, the Japanese prepared to occupy the city.

A month later, Richards's response to this catastrophe was similar to Winter's. Coolly enough, he proposed to David Stevens "that we economize drastically, conserve our best workers and the resources already granted to us, concentrate on the texts which will implement the Ministerial Committee's resolutions and so prepare for the post-war reconstruction period." Indeed, Professor Shui had persuaded him that the war might prove a blessing in disguise because the people in the ministry might find it "a heaven-sent chance to do fundamental work—since the squabbles between university dignitaries, and such like things, which usually distract them, are suspended."[13]

For the present, Richards admitted, the local situation in Peking was "horrid." During the first few days after the Japanese began their occupation of the city, airplanes swooped over the housetops not more than fifty feet up, "and gun fire (of all sizes) [was] audible nightly." But not even such horror shows broke his cheeriness: in the midst of such conditions, he added, there was nothing much to do "but write a Primer of English on a new model and try to believe in a future which will redeem the time."[14]

Richards's unflagging optimism can be heartbreaking. The "scents of Magdalene garden" must never have seemed more remote. He and Dorothea had been "rather unlucky" personally. Their life savings of about $5,000 gold had been placed in fixed deposit in a Chinese bank, and now they couldn't get it out. "We fear it is gone for good. I always plan to retire at 50 and settle down in a cottage somewhere to do some real work at leisure on fundamental linguistic problems—so this is a blow. However, so many people have been blown to bits lately near here that while one has life and limb and freedom one can't complain."

In September, when Peking had capitulated and things quieted down, Ivor and Dorothy left Peking for the south, below the fighting line (though a good part of the way they were scarcely a step ahead of it), and traveled with "a party half made up of gunmen, necessary for protection against bandits or "Trotskyites"). Though mountain climbing was as always an important part of his itinerary, Richards was also searching out the abundant "disengaged talent" that would be free down there and looking for a new place to carry on the work away from "our new rulers," with whom Jameson, unlike himself, according to Richards, was "admirably fitted" to come to terms.

Years later, Selskar Gunn, a Rockefeller official in charge of overseeing projects in the Far East, told Jameson that Richards was no good friend. That would seem to be the case, for in his August letter to Stevens, Richards, himself a genius at adjusting his sails to the wind, quoted against Jameson these lines of Byron:

> Well, well, the world must turn upon its axis,
> And all mankind turn with it, heads or tails
> And live and die, make love and pay our taxes,
> And as the veering wind shift, shift our sails.

He then added: "It is necessary but, for the time being, I should do it badly."[15] Yet it was Richards, not Jameson, who convinced himself, with what seems stunningly narrowly self-serving vision, that if the Japanese did seize control of China, the Orthological Institute would continue to function and "our work might thus find a new channel into Japan."[16]

Whatever Richards thought might be useful for Jameson to do, Jameson had other plans. In a wire that arrived in Kunming on the day after the Richards did, he told Richards that he was liquidating the Orthological Institute of China headquarters in Peking and would move as soon as possible—by early November, he hoped—to Changsha, capital of Hunan (where Mao had once taught at Normal School Number 1). Barbara Tuchman has described how tens of thousands of evacuated civilians were already being moved there "in boats and junks or overland in trucks and handcarts," as were "trainloads of half-starved, tattered war orphans gathered up from the battle zones by a women's committee organized by Madame Chiang."[17] The major northeastern universities too—Tsinghua, as well as National Peking and Nankai Universities—first evacuated to Changsha before moving to Kunming. Jameson headed there to be with the faculty of his university.

But Changsha proved too vulnerable a haven and was soon bombed by the Japanese. Before long, many—including Jameson and his wife—who had sought refuge there resumed their flight, this time on the long, difficult overland trek through the mountains to Kunming, part of which (blessedly for those lucky enough to ride precariously on the high, swaying load of a truck) was over a main motor route. While the female students and the faculty of Tsinghua University were allowed to make the journey to Kunming by train, the male students from Tsinghua

University and two other Peking universities were led on this march by a scholar of Chinese literature, Wen Yiduo.

Jameson and his wife stayed in Kunming for about a year. As she recalls: "We knew that this country [the U.S.] was going to get into the war, and we thought you ought to be in your own country during war. The Institute wasn't doing anything, and we didn't want to take salary for doing nothing. And we thought that in this country people didn't know what was going on."[18]

But before they left, Jameson had confirmed the support of T. C. Kung, the commissioner of education for Yunnan Province, whom Charlotte Tyler back in 1935 had convinced of the powers of Basic as a teaching instrument. On March 20, 1938, Kung requested the Institute to "undertake formal cooperation with the educational authorities in the province for the teaching of Middle School English." He also indicated that eventually his government would take over the Institute, something that the Rockefeller Foundation especially desired, since their interest was in setting in motion programs whose effectiveness would quickly make them independent of Foundation support.

While all this was going on, and while Winter remained in Peking, the Richardses traveled through the southwest, having met with Richards's friend and disciple, William Empson, who accompanied them for a while. Empson was already famous for *Seven Types of Ambiguity*, the book he wrote as his thesis at Cambridge under Richards's supervision. In addition to being an already-famous literary critic, Empson was a prominent modernist poet, whose lean lines had become a model for the next generation of Anglo-American poets. He had come to China to serve as visiting professor at Peking National University and to work with the Institute. (Richards considered Empson "quite one of the best Basic experts there are," though Empson himself later would say modestly that when he translated some of the essays of JBS Haldane into Basic, "a good deal of correcting my verbal usages had to be done in the office.") Empson traveled with the Richards until mid-October, as far as Indochina, through some of the wilder parts of Kweichow and Yunnan provinces, and was "a bit startled to find [Ivor] so well known and esteemed in places which seemed to me remote." Not even in China's remote southwest would Richards fall out of contact with his work and the people whose support he needed. But with Peking University closed down, Empson was at loose ends, and after traveling with the Richards, he returned to England in mid-October. In 1939, he returned to

Kunming to teach at Lianda, the university in exile, for a year, in which he suffered bitter wartime conditions with the students and other staff. Alcohol seems to have helped him through. Empson's former roommate at Lianda told me that he awoke one morning worried to find Empson missing, until he found him sleeping under his bed.[19]

One of Richards's purposes on the journey was to show the newly published *First Reader* to the chief members of the Secondary School English Committee, now relocated in Kunming. (Winter was essentially a cowriter on this project, though his work went unacknowledged.) Through the *Reader* he hoped to present the Western way of thought simultaneously with the language. So the readings themselves provided basic information about Western logic, science, hygiene, and other matters. Soon, for the *Second Reader*, Richards would have William Empson writing essays in Basic about fundamental Western concepts such as "system"—with material that would later lead to Richards's *Basic Rules of Logic*. Had history cooperated, such a program might have accomplished much. As John Fairbank remarked to Alger Hiss several years later: "The amazing thing is that ideas are as easy to bring here as airplanes. Yet an idea program for China has been delayed and frustrated by lack of imagination in the proper places."[20]

Once Richards had finished his business in Kunming, he and Dorothea turned to their pleasure. They sought out Joseph F. Rock, the Austro-American botanist and explorer who lived from 1932 to 1949 in the Lijiang Valley, where he studied the Naxi people about whom he wrote in his eccentric classic *The Ancient Na-khi Kingdom of Southwest China*—a book that Ezra Pound would get hold of in 1956, when he was locked up in St. Elizabeth's Hospital and extrapolated from Rock's book an upland paradise he then celebrated in his "Cantos":

> And Over Li Chiang, the snow range is turquoise
> Rock's world that he saved us for memory
> a thin trace in high air.[21]

(Coincidentally, it was the same high air that Robert Winter would breathe before his wartime adventures were over.)

From Rock, the Richardses obtained directions into the Himalayas, where they intended to climb the 18,700 feet Ha-pa Shan ("Snow Mountain"). It was of this ascent that Dorothea reported to her brother: "If it hadn't been for 100 m.p.h gale it would have been an easy snow peak. As it was we had quite a struggle but reached the summit without frostbite."[22]

* * *

Before the war broke out, Jameson had made a persuasive case to the Rockefeller Foundation for renewing their support of the Institute. Later, in the summer of 1938, when Jameson was working for Archibald MacLeish in the Library of Congress and Richards on a new appointment to Harvard, the two went to New York to discuss with the Foundation the future implications of their work in China. Persuaded that the accomplishments of the OIC were already solid, and that, as Jameson argued, the war in China "had not greatly reduced opportunities for progressive work," the Foundation renewed their support with an appropriation of $29,000 to cover expenses during the period of April 1, 1937, to June 30, 1939. (The total Foundation appropriation to the project from the initial allocation of $15,000 appropriated in February 1936 to the final allocation of $20,000 granted in October 1947 to help support Winter's work at the reestablished Tsinghua, ran to $101,550, which, though not a major allocation by Rockefeller Foundation standards, was no small potatoes.)

The new allocation was to support the Foundation's recently established work in Kunming, now under the direction of Arthur L. Pollard-Urquhart. Pollard-Urquhart, like Jameson, had gone to Kunming in 1938, as did the Chinese associates Shui, Wu Fuheng, and Chao. Here a new office of the Institute was opened, now called, to reflect the intentions of the Yunnan education minister, the Provincial English College, and despite the chaos of war, the work *did* go on.

* * *

In the midst of all this motion, Winter had remained in Peking. Though the Japanese quickly closed down, Winter kept himself busy editing the *First Reader* and helping to compose the second. For a man of such flamboyant temperament, Winter had an extraordinary capacity for taking pains. His editorial notes and corrections for the *First Reader* run to fifteen pages, single spaced, and range in scope from his observation that on page 4, the "Last word 'bottle' requires a comma after it, so does next bottle on top of p. 5," to such more ruminative notes as this:

> it seems possible that the sustained chorus of praise for
> electrical gadgets might seem a bit depressing, now that [in

China] the gadgets are further off than ever. If you could take the trouble, I think that taking out one or two of the electrical articles (the ones about the farm perhaps are likely to be the most remote) in favour of more general, applied science, would give more of the feeling that they were learning something real all the time.[23]

But not all his energies went into editorial matters. Winter would remain in occupied Peking for nearly three years, living a complicated and sometimes dangerous life that came back to haunt him twenty years later. But even when he was a very old man often no longer lucid, and long after Mao's Red Guard used some of his espionage acts against him, Winter remained proud of that chapter of his life. Sometimes when he talked to me, he imagined that he was still back at Tsinghua, trying to protect the nightmare campus from the soldiers who had displaced its proper inhabitants. Back then, he began to carry a pistol.

CHAPTER SIX:
PROTECTING TSINGHUA

It was Robert Winter's destiny more than it was Richards's to live with historical events that sicken hope. He remained in the trenches, more and more naked to violence. Richards had another world. China for him was always an interlude between projects at Cambridge or Harvard or on the road elsewhere at the behest of the Rockefeller Foundation. But Winter had no other world. China had become his only home.

Why Winter remained in Peking at his post in Japanese-occupied Tsinghua University after most of his colleagues fled to Kunming to start a free university in the south needs some explaining. The university had necessarily left behind, along with her buildings, equipment and such of her books as could not be transported, largely by foot and pack animals and a "few wheezy trucks." Her human elements, the knowledge and spirit embodied in living women and men, moved by stages, first to Changsha and then to Kunming, where academic operations resumed, though straitened. While many of their elders found transportation, the students, led by Wen Yiduo, moved like a foot army, each trekking unit preceded by a communications squad, a foraging section, and a police section; the rear, as Theodore White and Annalee Jacoby describe it in *Thunder Out of China*, was "brought up by pack animals carrying rice and wheat cakes and by a few wheezing trucks crawling along unimproved roads."[1]

Winter remained amid the abandoned buildings and remaining equipment, fighting hopeless battles to preserve them from the Japanese, who purposefully made front lines of the universities, showing their contempt for Chinese moral opinion by bombing to rubble famous Nankai University in Tianjin. The bombing was part of their policy to destroy China's major universities. Besides Nankai, the primary targets were the other three great northern universities—Peking National, Yenching, and, of course, Tsinghua. Ironically, the Japanese shared with Richards and Winter a strong belief in the powers of education, which they aimed to obliterate.

At Tsinghua, they stabled their horses in the gymnasium and converted another academic building into a brothel. But these were minor outrages. The particular targets of the occupying armies were the university's scientific and technical resources. These were valuable plunder, and at the same time, by stripping the Chinese permanently of these resources, the Japanese were guaranteeing the future weakness of their enemy by denying to her the humane and technical knowledge she would need to rebuild. White and Jacoby tell how, before they were done, the Japanese would seize all the university's laboratory equipment, sending what they could use back to Japan and smashing the rest.[2]

These were the circumstances in October 1937, when Winter decided to remain at Tsinghua at the university's request. As a citizen of a neutral country, he had been selected to serve as a kind of caretaker against the Japanese. Having agreed to serve, Winter took his task perfectly seriously. Of course, he had no real authority or power that the Japanese recognized, and his posture would have seemed quixotic in a man without Winter's strength of ego or less skilled at the arts of extraterritorial privilege.

Winter's first skirmish with the Japanese began on Friday, October 8, when for the fourth time Japanese soldiers "visited" Tsinghua and "removed truckloads of university property." He went at once to C. H. Pi, the university's remaining Chinese spokesman, to decide on a course of action. Pi, like all other Chinese university officials, had been prevented from accompanying the soldiers as they entered university buildings, but he gave Winter a summary of the events together with a list of the property stolen, so far as he was able to determine.[3] Once he had that report, Winter acted. He was muscular and stood over six feet tall, therefore he towered over Japanese soldiers and officers. Add to this his genius for translating rage, whether righteous or not, into eloquent invective, we see that he was ready to defend the dicey principle that an occupying army should be governed by law.

His effort didn't begin auspiciously. He called on a Mr. Mori of the Japanese Science Library and was sent on a wild-goose chase. Winter had been told that Mori was chairman of the Committee on Cultural

Relations, and thus a man who might be open to a civilized appeal. It turned out that a Mr. Hashigawa and not Mr. Mori was the person who held that position, but Mori was happy to talk the matter over with Hashigawa on the phone. Winter agreed to this, but, unable to reach Mr. Hashigawa, Mori spoke to a Mr. Takeda, who, like Hashigawa [I take to be one person the man whom in two different parts of the report Winter spells as "Hashikawa" and "Hashigawa"], was an advisor to the Peking Peace Preservation Committee, about which more in a moment.

Mr. Takeda proved less obliging than Mr. Mori had been. In fact, as it turned out, he had authorized all four visits. Further, he did not believe that the report Pi had given to Winter was accurate, "or that the soldiers had committed the misdemeanors of which they were accused." In any case, since Mr. Pi was in charge of the university, Takeda insisted that he would receive the report only from him.

Winter was in a weak position. He was being permitted to report the university's grievance only by telephone and through the intermediary of a third person since he did not carry sufficient rank to deal directly with Mr. Takeda. Further, he had to concede that since neither Mr. Pi nor any other Chinese official of the university were allowed to accompany the soldiers on their raids, Pi's report might be less than accurate.

But Winter, who had had a decade-and-a-half experience in the Orient, had resources in this kind of confrontation. Now he presented himself in a threefold official role. First, he had been appointed by Mr. Pi to present Pi's report to the Peace Preservation Committee, whose Japanese and Chinese members had ostensibly been assigned to do at Tsinghua what their name suggested. Second, he was a senior member of the university staff, many of whose members had already gone into exile. And, finally, he was an American citizen who held himself responsible to his government for "a report as to the manner in which buildings and equipment donated to China by the American Government, with the strict stipulation that they be used for educational purposes, were actually being used." All in all, he improvised an impressive formal posture. It would have been pointless to confront the Japanese officials as an isolated individual without giving the appearance of firm institutional and even possible diplomatic support.

But for all Winter's chutzpah,[4] the Japanese must never have doubted that they would get away with their pillage. The United States, hardly eager for confrontation, was unlikely to question them or protest, and the Chinese were powerless to do so. So now the game took a new turn.

Mr. Mori advised Winter to wait until the Peace Preservation Committee had delivered the results of their investigation. He also asked Winter to notify Mr. Pi on behalf of Mr. Takeda that within a few days "responsible authorities would occupy the Tsinghua campus, and that there would be no further question as to whether any acts committed there were officially authorized." Winter left Mori's office with the understanding (wishful, it turned out) that Mori's statement meant there would be no more thefts.

Winter's adeptness at such skirmishes served him well even before he visited Mori, when he delivered copies of the list of stolen materials to Mr. Lockhart of the American embassy, Mr. Shima of the Japanese embassy, and Mr. Fisher of the United Press. In addition, he had submitted his complete report in Chinese to one of the officers of the Peace Preservation Committee, who had promised to take the matter up at once upon receipt of the report. Although he did not mention this to Mori or the committee, Winter had also sent a copy of the complete report to the Rockefeller Foundation. All in all, for a man who had no actual power, he did a splendid job of fabricating what he lacked and playing his essentially weak game with admirable patience and care.

In the course of "visits" that occurred on the third, fourth, sixth, and seventh of October, along with the one on the eighth, Japanese troops took from the scientific and technical departments of the university not only books and laboratory instruments, but even the keys to the buildings and laboratories themselves. On the less formal level, individual soldiers had even taken "personal things such as watches, pictures and stationery." On one raid, military police had even beaten two servants of the Electrical Engineering Department.

In the face of all this, Winter submitted to the Peace Preservation Committee Mr. Pi's summary of the raids and his list of stolen items under a cover letter to the committee. In the letter, he argued that the key questions of policy to be established by the committee were these:

1) Is it the policy of the Peace Preservation Committee to maintain Tsinghua intact as an institution of higher education for Chinese?

2) If this is in the affirmative, I will be pleased to receive a statement of the reasons which led the Peace Preservation Committee to authorize persons who are not members of Tsinghua to remove property from the University.

3) If the Peace Preservation Committee has granted and is
   granting permission for the removal of any property,
   what is the extent and duration of the authorization;
   what is this property to be used for, and, in the case the
   property is damaged, who will be responsible for proper
   compensation?

Winter must have had a pretty good idea how the Japanese would
answer these questions if they were to answer honestly, but he was wise
enough to leave the questions open. After they had established a puppet
government in northern China, the Japanese had also established these
Peace Preservation Committees for the purpose of protecting aliens from
interference by the occupying armies and preserving the status quo. But
the Chinese discovered at the first preliminary meeting of the committee
not only that they were underrepresented on it, but that ten important
resolutions were read and adopted "without any form of discussion."

The Japanese continued to insist that they were defending China
from the Communistic menace against which she had grown too weak
to protect herself. These invaders wanted it believed that actions taken by
the PPCs, which included a token Chinese member, were actions by the
Chinese themselves. One of those actions, as it directly affected Tsinghua,
was to transform that proud institution, the central agency of China's
modern education, into a school of physical education.

For his next move in this elaborate chess game, Winter's simply took
the committee at face value by assuming that it would be as shocked as
he was by the rapine. After naming in both Western letters and Japanese
characters the military officers in charge of the raiding parties, Winter
disingenuously recommended to the committee that in the future at
least "the names of the persons who are to be held responsible" be given
in advance to the Chinese authorities of Tsinghua and that "a properly
appointed member of Tsinghua's Committee for the Preservation
of Grounds and Property [accompany] the members of the Peace
Preservation Committee and officers of the Japanese army whenever
they enter buildings for the purpose of removing property." This policy
would allow an autonomous university official at least to stand witness.
Winter also wanted the keys returned ("It is obviously very difficult for
the Tsinghua Committee on which I serve to function if we do not have
the keys to the property we are to preserve"), and he wanted the name
of the officers in charge of billeting so that there would be someone to

complain to about unauthorized persons occupying university property He would welcome an early response on these points in order "to avoid misunderstandings in the future." The Japanese would see the necessity for doing so, he felt, since "it is clear that any American associated with Tsinghua has as his duty to do all he can for any institution established through the generosity of the American Government, and to report to his government as to what is happening." What Winter was asking was from one point of view moderate and perfectly reasonable. From another, it was outrageously quixotic.

My own fascination with the details of this episode arises from what it illustrates about *praxis*—that is, how, in dire circumstances, an act of resistance can be mounted by a resistor with sufficient cunning, perseverance, and simple courage. In Winter's case, his genius in such directions could go back to a childhood spent in a house of women who completely spoiled him and allowed his wishes to be their commands. To me, Winter's resistance to the Japanese was heroic in its almost classical meld of perseverance, clearness of purpose, and refusal to be daunted even by apparently insurmountable obstacles.

When three days after his letter to the committee he hadn't received an answer, Winter wrote another letter, this time to Mr. F. Shima, third secretary of the Japanese embassy in Peking, to whom on October 8 he delivered a copy of the summary of the raids and list of stolen property. He wanted Shima's prompt attention to the fact that on Tuesday, October 12, while Winter was on the campus to witness it, "about six officers and twenty-five soldiers—who had arrived for the purpose of selecting quarters for the billeting of the troops that the Peace Preservation Committee were sending to guard the University"—had stolen more university equipment.

Years later, Winter would write that he had been born in an age of terrorism and would die in an age of terrorism. Terrorism is merely a way of obtaining by force or threat of force what one cannot obtain by law. (The word has its origin in the actions of the French revolutionary government during the Reign of Terror.) Thus the Japanese assaults against the Chinese universities were acts of terrorism, plain and simple.

Whatever doubts on that score Winter may have entertained earlier, all doubt was removed on the twelfth, when a platoon of soldiers and officers arrived at Tsinghua to select quarters for the billeting of troops who were to be sent to "guard" the university. While one of their officers was speaking with a member of the Tsinghua Committee for the

Preservation of Grounds and Property (apparently Winter himself), "the other officers and soldiers ordered the servants of Tsinghua University to unlock all the doors of the first and second courts." Winter knew that many of the rooms in these courts had university property stored in them, so he insisted on accompanying the soldiers.

In one of these rooms, he found three soldiers "throwing things about in their search for valuables." Though they had already put some of the smaller things ("a cigarette case, a bronze ink holder, and ink stone, some old coins, among other things") in their pockets, Winter "ordered them"—his choice of verb tells us much about his special capacity for grace under pressure—to replace the things and leave the room. When they had obeyed, he locked the door behind them and reported the incident to an officer, who was sufficiently concerned with face to reprimand the soldiers in Winter's presence. But even while the scolding was going on, Winter saw that other soldiers were trying the doors and windows of the locked Engineering buildings, which he knew to contain very valuable property.

Winter had visited Shima on Friday, the eighth, and had been assured that "Japanese soldiers were well disciplined and would not commit such acts." On the same day, Takeda had told him that there would be no further occasion to worry about loss of Tsinghua property because well-disciplined soldiers would be quartered there to stand guard against theft or damage. Now Winter wished to call to Shima's attention that "the very soldiers sent for this purpose were the ones guilty of such misdemeanours."

Predictably, Winter's efforts to preserve university property—a ten-day frenzy of reports and conferences, confrontations on the scene of the crime, and visits to Japanese officials—came to nothing. But he had managed to speak out in such a way as to make inescapably clear that the Japanese were acting barbarically. Under the circumstances, he could do no more, and given his temperament, he could do no less. This would not be the last time that he would show painstaking courage in the cause of simple justice or assert a moral order in circumstances that would seem to deny the possibility of one.

*   *   *

Winter remained in occupied Peking until August 1940, using the old capital as a base of operations. Even before occupation, the city had begun to lose its charm because of invasions of Japanese businessmen and busloads of Japanese schoolchildren on excursion. Now Peking was unequivocally an occupied city, and those locals who had not been able to leave looked sullenly on the occupying armies. Writing in late December,1937, the editor of an important journal, the *T'ien Hsia Monthly*, reminded the Japanese that the only peace acceptable to the Chinese would be peace in terms of Article 1 of the recently drawn Nine-Power Treaty, which resulted from a conference in Brussels. This article assured that the Japanese would respect "the sovereignty, the independence, and the territorial and administrative integrity of China" and that they would "provide the fullest and most unembarrassed opportunity to China to develop and maintain for herself an effective and stable government."

But to residents of Peking, it was all too clear that the Japanese had no intention of adhering to these or any other of the four items of the article. For instance, they had encouraged the establishment of drugstores in which opium and smoking equipment could be purchased. Japanese enterprises were rapidly replacing or simply engulfing their Chinese predecessors. The very atmosphere of the city was becoming Japanese. Everywhere one could see the Rising Star shining in flags overhead. The shop signs and advertisements were more and more often in Japanese, and the rickshaw pullers were so used to Japanese customers that a Chinese who employed one was likely to be mistaken for a Japanese. Many of the markets, cabarets, and cafes were in bounds only to Japanese troops.

Still more seriously, both the Chinese and the foreign press in Peking were entirely in the hands of the Japanese. Now anyone who wished to learn of the victories of Chinese armies would have to read the Peking and Tientsin *Times* or *North China Star*, both out of Tianjin. In the papers that were readily available to the Pekingese, one found only headlines like "Nippon Imperial Soldiers Push Southwest," or "Hopei People Contented under Japanese Jurisdiction."

Despite all this, outwardly the Japanese were living in the midst of a peace and order and prosperity of their own making. With some success, they were wooing foreign correspondents by spending large sums for their entertainment and providing them with airplane transportation, military interviews, and hotel accommodations. And to the Chinese journalists, they were giving free exhibitions, movies, and drinks.

But these bold pioneer efforts at public relations, though they may have bought some temporary sympathy from the foreign press, accomplished little in the way of creating that peaceful and orderly city of which Japanese propaganda boasted. In truth, the "Japanese militarists" lived in a state of fear. "Why not," asked a writer in the independent *China Weekly Review* in September 1938, "when the Chinese guerillas are constantly harassing them all around the city, derailing trains, disrupting communications, attacking stations, filtering [through] the city gates?"

Japanese propaganda had held that, among their other benevolent aims, the Japanese were taking steps at "educational reform." The reality behind these reforms was Tsinghua, a university without students, its laboratories and libraries plundered, its walks echoing with the boots of the soldiers billeted there. Indeed, as Barbara Tuchman observed, everywhere in the city that one might go, one saw Japanese infantry and cavalry drilling to the accompaniment of shrill bugling. (The officers rode on horses too big for them, which they could mount only with the help of orderlies, who then trotted behind them should they need further boosts.) Official cars flaunting the flag of the Rising Sun sped through the old city streets.[5]

The city occupied, most of the Chinese who remained were silent with impotent rage. The Japanese had a way of entering houses without warning and with the brutal tactlessness of all armies of occupation. Though they gaped at the beauty and ancient greatness of Peking, everywhere they went, they felt the force of local hatred, and as the war went on, they knew that they might be murdered at any time. Were they not under constant threat of attack from the guerilla armies in the nearby Western Hills?

Naturally under such circumstances, the future of English language teaching in the occupied (and for that matter, even the unoccupied) territories of China had become problematic. By February of 1938, all the schools in Peking were required to teach Japanese, and Richards, back in China again, was in Tientsin, looking into the possibilities of moving the Institute's northern headquarters there. Two of the younger men of the Orthological Institute of China staff had been successful at teaching beginners in Basic at the Hautes Études Jesuit College in Tientsin, using the primer. Now Richards was ready to bring Chao Chao-hsiung down from Peking to teach in an expanded program at the Hautes Études.[6]

On February 6, Winter took the two-and-a-half hour ride in an unheated coach to meet Richards and discuss his future, but before the ride was over, he had developed a sore throat and high fever (he had been susceptible to chest ailments since he came down with flu during the epidemic of 1917), and Richards feared that he had scarlet fever. But although Winter spent four days in the hospital, his ailment turned out to be no worse than a very bad throat. Between him and Richards, nothing definite was decided.[7]

Winter's old friend and colleague Arthur Pollard-Urquhart was already in Kunming carrying on with Basic affairs, but things were not getting on very well there. His work during February 1938—so he wrote to David Stevens—was held up "by air raid precautions, two false alarms and one actual raid." After the first aborted raid on February 21, the city schools had been immediately evacuated to the temples of outlying villages. Pollard-Urquhart was trying gamely to establish his program in these newly relocated schools, but so far he had found only one—the Yun Jui Middle School—where the principal was actively receptive and the students sufficiently advanced and mature.

In the meantime, he was trying to make contact with the middle school teachers now dispersed all over the countryside. He had managed to gather twenty of them at a reception he held on Saturday, the twenty-fourth. These twenty, "who represented the more intelligent of the teachers," agreed to come in for regular instructional meetings that would begin on the following Saturday," but Pollard-Urquhart feared that continued meetings would prove unlikely under present conditions.

The single air raid that he had so far experienced occurred a month before, but it had made a deep impression on Pollard-Urquhart. The Japanese had concentrated their attack on the buildings of the Kunming Normal School, where Tsinghua University in exile had rented dormitories and mess halls for students and professors. Some of the students and university servants had been killed, and there were heavy casualties among the people living in the neighboring street.[8]

Now the city life was disorganized. Each morning at eight o'clock, most of the population poured out through the Kunming city gates and did not return until after twelve o'clock. (The Japanese had won a reputation for regularity.) The city was so small that a raid on one quarter was dangerous to all. Under such conditions, Pollard-Urquhart naturally wondered whether it might not "be necessary for us to move from the city to some other place."

Back in Peking, Winter continued to have a different sort of bad time. Scarcely more than a month after his sore throat, he'd begun to experience sharp kidney pains. He went to the hospital where the doctors quickly got him ready for an operation (which they'd informed him would be "painful as hell"). The doctors had already filled him with dope when they told him to empty his bladder, and as he tried to do so, he experienced terrific pain. Then the stone fell out—about the size of a pea, but three cornered. The doctors, relieved, burst into laughter and sent Winter home. He was able to have lunch with Richards, who was back in the city, a couple of days later.[9]

For all his physical ailments, Winter suffered from a more serious affliction. It began to appear that his occupation was gone. Neither at the university nor at the old Orthological Institute headquarters in Peking was there any chance for him to continue teaching. Although the Rockefeller Foundation, at Richards's urging, had increased Winter's salary from $200 local currency monthly to U.S. $150,[10] that fat salary was assured only till the end of the year, and for all Richards's optimism, it was still much in doubt whether there would be anything further for Winter to do once he had finished writing *The Second Book of English*. True, he was now in complete charge of the OIC office in Peking, but it was hardly a bustling office. In the fitful light of the war, the Rockefeller Foundation seemed at the point of closing down its operation in China.

Though Winter left no record behind of his mood at this time, it must have been similar to what George N. Kates felt when he came to what he spoke of "the end of my adventure." For a good while after the Japanese occupation of Peking, Kates said in *The Years That Were Fat*, the Westerner living there remained untouched and unharmed. Nevertheless, "he did live more and more like a man who, although physically comfortable knows that he has a fatal disease, clawing even at the moment in the dark at his vitals. Mutely I began to say farewell to many gentle pleasures, sensing that each time might become the last."[11]

Unlike Kates, Winter remained in China, but for him too something was ended, probably irrecoverably. The richly cultivated life of the Westerner in Peking, lived and experienced by a privileged group of expatriates that included Kates, Harold Acton, John Blofeld, and Edwin Bachaus ("the hermit of Peking") had come to an end as all good things must. Whoever remained in China now would be obliged to live on other terms than aesthetic ones.

So now, the routines of his peacetime life shattered irrevocably, Winter began to employ his energies in opposition to the forces that shattered them. He was known during this period as a man willing to put himself out for his colleagues and friends. He helped them to smuggle money past Japanese officials; he helped them to get out of the occupied city. Legend has it that he smuggled guns to Communist forces outside the city and that once, when the military police came through his train coach to check baggage, Winter, with his foot, shoved a carton of guns under the seat of the Japanese officer sleeping beside him, and so escaped inspection.[12]

I remember a conversation I had with a Chinese professor in 1984, when I was first becoming fascinated with Robert Winter. He had been sketching a few of the episodes that make up the Winter myth, and I'd remarked: "Ah, he took risks." "Yes," my visitor said, "he was a man who took all the risks."

In late 1938 or early 1939, a new adventure began for Winter, and I tell it at length because nearly twenty years later, it came back as part of the charges leveled against Winter by the Chinese Communists. The episode began when one of his colleagues in the Tsinghua Philosophy Department brought to Winter's room a woman named Hsiung Ting. At that time, Hsiung was Mrs. Feng; later she became the wife of the writer Robert Payne, who came to China in 1941 and remained until 1946. Besides being a woman of storied beauty, Hsiung Ting, better known as Rose Hsiung, was the daughter of Hsiung Hsi-ling, prime minister of China during World War I. This beautiful and willful woman had grown up in a vast palace on the Shih Fu Ma Tachieh, where she was the playmate of the boy emperor Pu Yi and spectator to the traditional ceremonies that still went on in the Forbidden City long after the Manchu Dynasty had theoretically been toppled by the 1911 Revolution. In Payne's phrase, "She grew up among brocades, and became weary of them."[13]

Rose's thirteen-year-old daughter, Mary, according to Payne's *China Diaries,* gained fame or notoriety in the late thirties by assassinating a Chinese quisling in a movie theater in Tianjin, then joining her classmates in a corner store where they all ate ice cream to celebrate. The movie was *Gunga Din,* and at the height of a battle scene, the cinema filled with the din of machine gun fire, she shot her man in the back of the head. Guomindang officials later feted Mary in Chungking, and she stayed in the house of Tai Li, the head of the secret police, himself a connoisseur of assassinations. Though she later became a Communist, after Liberation, someone remembered her associations with the Guomindang and she was sentenced to an indeterminate term of hard labor. By the time she was released, she was prematurely aged and dying of tuberculosis.

The young Mary seems to have learned her taste her taste for steely nerved resistance from her mother, who was also an adventuress and a patriot, actively engaged in anti-Japanese resistance. At their first meeting, Rose Hsiung was introduced to Winter simply as a person working against the Japanese, a person who needed the help of a foreigner to accomplish her work, but Winter must certainly have recognized her. In any case, he agreed at once to be her man. There the matter rested until, some days later, Hsiung returned to Winter's room, this time to ask him to transfer a codebook ("of the greatest value and importance") from the British to the French concession of Tianjin.

At this point, Winter had some reason to believe that he was working for the Communists. In the course of establishing her bona fides, Hsiung Ting told him that she was buying guns from Japanese renegades and turning them over to Chinese guerillas, a job at which she was being helped by an Englishman named Price. But before the adventure was over, Winter had to suspect that he had, unawares, been recruited as an agent for the Guomindang.

Whomever he thought he was working for in those relatively innocent early days of the anti-Japanese war, twenty years later he would look back ruefully at his political naiveté at this time: "I must have been very stupid politically," he reflected. Before the Japanese attack, he had refused the prospect of a post as an advisor with the Nanking government (so-called because the Nationalists had their capital there), an opportunity offered him by Chiang Ting-fu, a professor of modern history in Tsinghua University, who was for many years Winter's neighbor. Winter had refused, he said, "because of the attitude of the Chinese government toward the Communists." But after the attack by the Japanese, he allowed himself to believe that "all China would be united against the Japanese and forget their differences."[14] That dream was widely dreamed in China during the first years of the war. For an action to be anti-Japanese at the time seemed enough, regardless of who was sponsoring it. Chiang Kai-shek and his forces had not yet fallen into the reckless abuse of the Chinese peasantry, which, more than anything else, brought about their downfall.

So it began. Following instructions, Winter took the train to Tianjin, where, in a hotel in the British concession, he was given the notebook. Now he had only to transport it into the French concession. What made the job tricky is that on the way to the French concession, he would have to pass over the French bridge, where the Japanese would certainly search and possibly strip him. Getting past that obstacle was what made the game interesting.

Winter's scheme to deceive the Japanese was at once witty, dramatic and practical. At a pharmacy, he purchased bottles of iodine and mercurochrome and a roll of gauze bandage. Back in his room, he wrapped the codebook around his penis, and then, in his words, "bandaged the whole thing with gauze soaked and spotted with the red and yellow medicines." When he got to the bridge, the Japanese did have him take down his trousers but they did not, he recalled, "interfere with the bandage."

Winter worked with Hsiung Ting on one further mission, this time in an adventure that twenty years later would become the ground of Communist charges against him. In the summer of 1938, some months before Hsiung's first visit, Winter met Delewa Gegen, living Buddha of Uliassutai, Outer Mongolia. Emily Hahn later met this Buddha in Hong Kong through Winter.[15] In *China to Me*, she remembers "Bob's Buddha" as "a man between fifty and sixty, with charming manners and a pock-marked face." Winter himself, in his own words a "fanatical atheist" long interested in "the queer superstitions of Lamaism," was delighted with his new companion. He and Delewa Gegen had long conversations about esoteric Buddhism, and the living Buddha took a great liking to Winter, whom he considered the best friend he had.[16]

During one of their talks, the Living Buddha told Winter that "the Japanese were trying to make use of him" and that he wished to escape to Tibet, his spiritual home and, as Emily Hahn has it, "a place he knew well, although in his present incarnation, he had never been there. By capturing the Buddha and returning him to Uliassutai, the Japanese hoped to lend an air of legitimacy to their presence in Outer Mongolia. Winter, who had already had experience in smuggling friends and colleagues out of the occupied city, said that he would help to prevent that from happening.

So when he returned from Tientsin after successfully having delivered the codebook, Winter made a plan for the escape of the Living Buddha that involved tampering with his passport, a job that the dexterous Winter carried out with skill and alacrity. Hsiung Ting thought that Winter would be of more use to her if he had the backing of the Chinese government, then at Chungking, and suggested that he go there. Since the living Buddha also wished to stop in Chungking on his way to Tibet, in order, as Emily Hahn recalled, "to assure the Generalissimo of his preference for Chinese rather than Japanese," the two schemes coincided, and Winter agreed to Hsiung Ting's proposal. He would visit Chungking, after first getting the Living Buddha to Hong Kong. After that, the Buddha could journey, by way of India, to Tibet and safety.

The affair began smoothly enough. Winter and the Living Buddha traveled separately to Shanghai, he by boat from Tangku (a port town near Tianjin), the Buddha by train in disguise. Winter's voyage was uneventful, but it became interesting when Winter discovered that one of his fellow passengers as far as Wei Hai Wei was Chou En-lai's younger brother, who revealed himself to Winter as traveling to the guerillas in Shantung.

In Shanghai, Winter met the Living Buddha and traveled with him to Hong Kong. They had some trouble at the border, however. For one thing, the Buddha, although willing to discard his robes for the occasion, insisted on dressing in the obligatory shade of yellow, which left him decked out in yellow tweeds and, in Emily Hahn's words, "a yellow plush hat something like a Homburg." It was hardly the appropriate costume for a man who wished to move incognito. To make matters worse, the living Buddha was unable to produce a vaccination certificate, but, as Emily Hahn recalls, he was finally let through when he pointed to his pock-marked face and asked, "Isn't this enough?") Safely in Hong Kong, the two men took rooms at the Liu Kuo (Luk Kuok) Hotel.

At this point, the story grows a little confused. As Winter told it to his Communist interrogators in 1959, he had not discussed his own plans with the Buddha, whom Winter assumed intended to travel directly south from Hong Kong on his way to India. But upon learning that Winter planned to fly to Chungking from Hong Kong, the Buddha decided to come along and stay there for a few days. He had a message for Chiang Kai-shek, he now told Winter.

There is no evidence that Winter knew any earlier than this of the Buddha's intention to visit Chungking. But he had good reason to distance himself from this part of the plan when he later recounted it to the Chinese interrogators, since the trip proved a disaster for the Buddha and a triumph for the Guomindang. But in the end, the two oddly matched friends flew together to Chungking, where they were to be met at the airport by a man who told them they were to go to Hollington Tong's house before going anywhere else. Tong (Tung Hsien-huang), a man almost exactly Winter's age, had studied in the States at the newly founded University of Missouri School of Journalism. He then worked as a reporter on several American papers, including the New York Times, before he returned to China in 1913, for a brilliant career in journalism and in government service. When Winter met him in 1938, he was already a skilled publicist for the Guomindang cause. Later, it would be through his efforts that such important Americans as the publisher Henry R. Luce would be drawn to active sympathy for Chiang Kai-shek, and from April 1956-September 1958, after already serving as ambassador to Japan, he became ambassador to the U.S. Tong was thus a principal conduit between the Guomindang and the United States, and twenty years later, Winter's connection with Tong, however tangential, would be a cause for suspicion to the unforgiving Communists.

Shortly after they were led into Tong's house, Winter and the Buddha were separated, and Winter was taken to an old-fashioned hotel, where he was visited by a young man who called himself Hsieh. They chatted for a while. Hsieh told him about his hatred for the Japanese, and he thanked Winter for the things he had done against them. Finally, he asked Winter to wait for a few days, when he would get further instructions.

Winter was never a man for sitting around, and to make matters worse, he had nothing to read. So without waiting for Hsieh's return, he moved to the Chungking Hostel, where there were a lot of foreigners living and he could find both books and companionship. There he met Corin Bernfield, an English girl who later killed herself after being captured by the Japanese, and Emily Hahn, who was in Chunking writing a book about the Song sisters. Together with the two women, Winter went to look up the living Buddha at the Meng-Tsang Wei Yuan Hui and ask him to dinner. Ms. Hahn remembers, as she told me on the telephone, that the dinner was a picnic at which the living Buddha entertained the others by singing Mongolian cowboy songs.

A few days after that happy event, Winter was visited by two men who thanked him for what he had done against the Japanese and told him to wait. The man whom Winter took to be the superior in rank was short and rather thin and had a red face. Winter thought that he might be Tai Li, who had helped Chiang Kai-shek rise by organizing the gangs and secret societies in Shanghai. Since that successful effort, Tai had been at Chiang's side as a kind of intelligence officer. Later he became head of a force of one hundred thousand secret police agents. Many of them, as John Fairbank records in his memoir *Chinabound*, over the objections of the embassy, General Stillwell, the Office of Strategic Services (OSS) and the State Department, trained and armed by the U.S. Navy. Whoever they were, these visitors also departed without giving Winter instructions more specific than that he was to wait.

A day or two later, Winter was visited by Hollington Tong himself. Tong told him that the living Buddha wished to give Chiang an important message, and that Winter was to be present when he did. Till then, Tong added, Winter was to wait. But while Winter was waiting for this important meeting, young Hsieh returned and asked him to dinner. The two men walked till they came to a house that was just opposite to Chiang Kai-shek's house and went in through a little door. One of the people present was the short, red-faced man who still did not introduce himself but whom Winter took to be Tai Li.

Again the conversation dwelled for a while on Winter's anti-Japanese activities, and then the short man Winter took for Tai Li asked Winter if he thought that it would be possible to operate a radio transmitter in his house in Peking. Winter told him that it would be, and he was then introduced to a young man who would operate the radio but would pretend to be his servant.

Financial arrangements were also discussed. Winter was instructed to open an account in a Shanghai bank on his way back to Peking. Whatever expenses he incurred for building the transmitter, for his travel, and for the young man's travel and wages would be deposited in that account. There was no mention of Winter's receiving any remuneration. Neither, as it turned out, was a cent of the expense money ever deposited.

To this point, as Winter later told the tale to his Communist interrogators, arrangements had proceeded smoothly enough. But now the short man began to talk about the Communists. Under no circumstances was Winter to make confidences to them; indeed, he was to have nothing to do with them. Winter now objected. He reminded the short man that Hsiung Ting had said "she was buying guns from the Japanese traitors and turning them over to the guerrillas and that the guerrillas must be communists." The short man didn't respond, but Winter went on to say that his only purpose was "to protect China against the Japanese," and he didn't care what kind of Chinese he helped so long as he was doing this. On that dissonant note, the dinner ended and Winter went back to his hotel.

A few days later Winter was again visited by Hsieh, who told him that he must return to Peking but that he was first to be present when the living Buddha had his interview with Chiang Kai-shek. Hsieh also proposed a peculiar scheme. Winter knew a young American woman,

Geraldine Skinner, whose Chinese name was Su Ping Hsin. She was the daughter of missionaries, but she was now living on her own in China. Hsieh proposed that upon Winter's return to Peking, Tai Li's agents would murder this woman in such circumstances that it would appear that the Japanese had killed her. Then, according to the scheme, Winter would present himself as a witness to the murder and would testify against the Japanese. In this way, the United States would be drawn into the war. Winter laughed the scheme away. They were crazy, he told Hsieh. "The Japanese might kill any number of Su Ping Hsin's without having any effect on American policy."[17]

Hollington Tong then took Winter and the Living Buddha in a car to Chiang's house. Soon after they arrived, Chiang entered the room where they were waiting, and immediately thanked Winter for his services against the Japanese, a gratitude that of course had already been abundantly expressed by Chiang's agents. Then Chiang turned to the Living Buddha and asked him what his message was. It turned out to be this: the Mongol Prince Te Wang, held under a kind of house arrest by the Japanese, wished to escape to Chungking. He had asked the Living Buddha to tell Chiang personally that on a certain day and hour and place the prince and some members of his family would be waiting. Chiang was to send a plane to pick them up and take them to Chungking.

Without replying, Chiang left the room, and Winter never found out (or at least, never recorded) whether he acted on the prince's request. Winter himself shortly afterward returned to Peking. The living Buddha would remain in Chungking, where he'd been asked to stay a bit longer as a guest. Emily Hahn was able to visit him there once, and though "he was sitting comfortably in a large room overlooking a hanging garden," he was bored and a little fretful. "I have nothing to do all day," he said, "but chant the Sutras."

It was only in 1949 when the Living Buddha came to visit him at Tsinghua that Winter learned that the Buddha had been held as prisoner in Chungking throughout the war. The Buddha told him also that although his life as Buddha had been a good life, "not as stormy as some of my former incarnations," conditions being what they were, he wondered if he "shouldn't look for a different job." He gave Winter an embroidered woolen coat that the person who described it to me said was the most beautiful needlework he had ever seen. But when I looked for it in Winter's big Chinese wardrobe, it was gone, and Winter remembered nothing about it.

The story does not quite end here. When Winter got back to Peking in the spring of 1939, he followed his instructions and asked a man named Bok (whose father was German and his mother Cantonese) to build a radio transmitter for him. Bok, of course, was not to tell the Japanese. Some time after Winter had paid for the transmitter and gotten it home, the young man who was to operate it arrived. But by now Winter had realized that he did not like the people in Chungking, nor, since they had paid him nothing, even for his expenses, did he feel under any obligation to them. So he let the young man stay in his house for a week or so, then gave him money for his train ticket and sent him off, without his ever having made use of the transmitter.

Getting rid of a powerful radio transmitter for which he had no use and which would prove embarrassing if it was discovered by the Japanese proved more difficult than getting rid of the young man. Winter was not allowed by the Japanese to call taxis. So a Frenchwoman, a friend of his named Wu-Morey, who belonged to the same resistance organization as Rose Hsiung's daughter, got a man named Pei Wenzhong[18] (he was the discoverer of the Peking Man's skull) to pick Winter up in a taxi and help him to get the radio to Wu-Morey's house. From there, they moved it to the house of E. K. Smith, the Yenching University English professor who had for a short time been involved in the OIC project. Smith waited until nightfall and then took the radio to Michael Lindsay. And Lindsay delivered it to the guerillas in the Western Hills. So the radio that Winter had purchased at the behest of the Guomindang ended up in Communist hands, after all.

Emily Hahn, who liked Winter, said that he was "an exhibitionist and would sell his grandmother if the transaction would make a good story. Or rather, he wouldn't bother to sell her; he would merely say he had done it and make a better story than the truth out of the old lady." My own view is that Winter, like Huck, "told the truth, mainly." To the extent that the story was true, it suggests also that it would have taken a far more prudent man than Winter to see his way safely through the maze of plots and counterplots to which he exposed himself when he said yes to the living Buddha and to Rose Hsiung.

Winter said to me once, with pained concern, that he thought he might once have worked for the enemy without knowing it. He must have had in mind this story of his first visit to Chungking. It was the subject of exercises in self-criticism he was later compelled to conduct. Many Chinese, though few Westerners, would live to see acts they had believed patriotic at the time listed in bills of particulars drawn up against them by the Chinese Communist government. At least some of these people, and Winter appears to be one of them, were guilty of nothing worse than taking seriously the pledge of the Guomindang to work cooperatively with the Communist Party of China against the Japanese. It must have been difficult sometimes to remember that not one but two wars were going on, one of them civil.

CHAPTER SEVEN:

THE WAY TO KUNMING

During the three years he spent in Japanese-occupied Peking, it was impossible for a man like Winter to do what Richards and the Rockefeller Foundation expected of him—that is, protected as an American, to go on with the task of establishing a system of language teaching to deepen communication between East and West, at a time when that possibility was deteriorating rapidly. What they least wanted was for him to act in any way that might compromise the neutrality of the Foundation itself and thus destroy their capacity to act in the Far East.

But that is just what he did. Winter's partisan actions had become the talk of Peking. He had attempted to keep the Living Buddha out of Japanese hands, lest they use him to legitimize their presence in Mongolia. He had smuggled a codebook out of Japanese-occupied territory into the hands of resistance forces. He had even helped some of his students to escape into unoccupied territory, in some cases working together with his friend Wu Han, the historian who would later become a vice mayor of Peking. As one of those former students recalls: "In 1939 I went to Kunming. I went by boat from Tianjin to Hong Kong. Then to Vietnam and into Kunming. Of course, the Japanese were here [in Peking] already and it was rather difficult to get away. I had some American money and Winter carried it on board to me [past the Japanese sentry]. And he gave it to the bursar for me, so that I could take the money with me." He did such things for many students.[1]

Winter also served as a courier and messenger to the guerillas in the Western Hills, carrying to them not only communiqués but also sometimes radios and, as I touched on earlier, possibly guns. His hatred of injustice and oppression, as well as his addiction to dramatic situations, especially when spiced with danger and enlarged by an historical frame, made him a natural for his role in the resistance. But he was certainly not alone in his actions and his assumptions that whatever could strengthen the Chinese resistance and damage the Japanese hold on the country was worth doing. American professors at Yenching University, similarly protected from Japanese retribution by the cloak of extraterritoriality, performed similar services against the Japanese, services that worried some officers of the Rockefeller Foundation and that endangered his position with them.

Inevitably, the time came—in the late summer of 1940—when Winter was at last obliged to leave Peking for Kunming in the southwest. Ironically, he was driven by pressures both from the Japanese and from the Rockefeller Foundation. As to the Japanese, though Winter's American citizenship was a strong shield, each confrontation with the Japanese tested that strength. A man who sticks his neck out can't count on being safe anywhere, and certainly not in an occupied country. The Japanese had an eye on Winter. They were probably monitoring his mail, and if he pushed them hard enough, they were prepared to do worse. He was already pushing them hard.

Yet it is not certain that even these pressures would have been sufficient to send him south if the Rockefeller Foundation hadn't hinted their own disapproval of his current activities. The Foundation had for some time expected Winter to move down to Kunming with Pollard-Urquhart. There in the southwest provincial capital was the site of the only ongoing activity in Basic language training. Further, Kunming was by this time the site of his university, now part of the Southwest Associated University (Lianda). Professionally speaking, it was where Winter belonged.[2]

But Kunming held few charms for Winter, despite the sweet plateau climate that makes it known as Spring City, or the classic portals or archways that ran along its main streets and so sharply reminded some of the exiled students of their academic home up north that they dubbed Kunming *Hsiao Pei Ping* ("Little Pei Ping"). At the same time, it was to Kunming that in imperial times an emperor's enemy might be sent into forced exile, in part because of its distance from Peking and the near impossibility of direct journey between the two cities, in part because it stands at an outer boarder of empire, beyond which lurk the minority peoples who, from a Chinese perspective, are barbarians.

Besides his prejudice against returning to the provinces after having worked his way into the metropolis, Winter had lived in Kunming from January through March 1940 and had not liked it very much. He left abruptly at the end of March, ostensibly because he heard that the Japanese were trying to get his house and garden in Peking. But he was also looking for such an excuse.

Winter's friend Pollard-Urquhart, in a letter to David Stevens, regretted his departure. He saw his old friend as "very much the brains of the Concern," and had "looked forward to his help in the important work of getting on with the Senior Middle School Books"—that is, the classroom testing of the *Second Basic Reader* that Winter was writing in collaboration with Shui Tien-tung, who, along with Chao Hsui Chao and Wu Fuheng, had come down to Kunming to work with Pollard-Urquhart. But, Pollard-Urquhart had added a bit lamely out of loyalty to his friend, there was not much for Winter to do in Kunming, and besides, Winter had agreed to complete the textbook while he was away.[3]

M. C. Balfour, a Rockefeller Foundation field officer who was making it his business to track Winter's movements, took a dimmer view of Winter's return to Peking, maintaining in his letter to Stevens that Winter had simply become "fed-up with the backwoods of Yunnan and yearned for the more pleasant surroundings of Peking, which is understandable." But if Balfour found Winter's preference for "pleasant surroundings" understandable, he had still more trouble with Winter's activities in these surroundings. Regarding Winter's claim to have written letters to the Foundation that were not delivered, Balfour remarked to David Stevens, a bit priggishly, that "we have no difficulty with legitimate mail between Shanghai and Peking, and censorship is limited mostly to parties under observation."

Winter's own reports early that summer about his labors in the Foundation's behalf had been enthusiastic: he had persuaded three principal schools in Peking (Yenching, Catholic University, and the Marist brothers, all of them Western-sponsored) to adopt Basic texts for their elementary English classes. He was also busy trying to get a new edition of the *First Reader* printed. That last labor, he said, was what kept him in Peking past the time that he was expected to move south. But Balfour tossed aside these claims as factitious efforts on Winter's part to gain extended support from the Foundation, as well as permission to remain a little longer in Peking.[4]

In late August and early September, Balfour himself visited Peking, shortly after Winter left, and pressed his investigation. J. Leighton

Stuart, then president of Yenching University (one of the three that Winter claimed he was working with) and a future ambassador to China, informed Balfour flatly that "we are not at present using any Basic English books or specifically Basic methods," though the Yenching English Department would be glad to if they could obtain the texts and the teachers. (What it required to get books from the printer, we will see in a moment.)

But there was something that bothered Balfour more than Winter's failure to get the books through the printer in time to provide them to Yenching. When Balfour asked Stuart ("whom you may know as a thoroughly reliable and conservative person") about Winter's activities in Peking, "the reply was 'that is what most of us in Peking are wondering.'" Indeed, the general reaction to Balfour's inquiries, he told Stevens, "was surprise to learn that [Winter] was still connected with the Basic English studies or any Foundation supported project." It was Stuart who told him that Winter was helping the guerillas, which, he added, embarrassed members of the British embassy with whom Winter associated. So also, Balfour insisted, it must embarrass the Rockefeller Foundation: "Since the Orthological Institute is supported entirely by the Foundation," wrote Balfour, Winter "is literally an employee of the Foundation, and it seems to me that it would be extremely unwise if this connection be continued."[5]

There was another point of view, of course, and Winter had expressed it to Stevens more than a year earlier, when he foresaw the problems implicit in his anti-Japanese activities: "Personally, I look at the Institute as a small item involved in much larger issues, and I hope you will not think me sentimental if I refer to the pathos of a situation in which the Chinese are clutching at any encouragement sympathetic Americans are willing to give them in hundreds of ways, outside of the work of the Institute, as they hear so many of their hopes of the last few years crashing about their ears."[6] This was exactly the point of view that troubled Balfour, who also thought that if Winter's mail to Stevens was being delayed, this was because the Nationalists suspected him of helping the Communists.

As it happened, independent of Balfour's recommendation, Stevens had decided to write Winter out of the Orthological Institute of China budget—on the same grounds laid out by Balfour. In early September, Stevens was visited in New York by Robert Drummond, a friend of Winter's (who later would join him in Kunming as director of the American Red Cross there). Drummond reported with what appears to have been naive enthusiasm that as of July 1, when he himself left China, Winter "was busy on very interesting assignments that cannot be summed up in a brief note except that they are not related to the projects of English teaching." To Stevens, this meant the Foundation was not responsible for his livelihood.

Winter summed up his own view of the matter in an exercise in self-criticism that he wrote nearly twenty years later, in 1959, when Communist suspicions about his activities had come to a point. Because he was known to be "very pro-Chinese," he told his accusers, he served the Foundation as window dressing. But their true attitude became clear, he said, when Drummond visited "some Rockefeller people" in New York and "told them that I was working heroically against the Japanese." Drummond "innocently thought that they would be pleased," Winter went on. But in fact "they immediately wrote to Pollard-Urquhart in Kunming dismissing me from my post."[7]

Winter did not learn that he had been fired until he arrived in Kunming. The news was particularly stunning in the light of the difficulties that he experienced in getting there and in working to complete a task that remained for him in Peking. In mid-August, Winter had gone by train to Tianjin, just a few hours south of Peking, to pick up two hundred copies of the *Basic Reader* that the printer finally had ready for him. Winter intended to bring them back to Peking, where he could have them loaded on a boat for Hong Kong and eventual transportation to Kunming.

When Winter got to Tianjin, the city was under the blockade the Japanese had imposed early in the previous June. In this they were simply putting into practice the policy they had declared back in November 1938: that the Open Door was no longer a principle that governed their economic conduct in Asia. Now they had more or less closed down the foreign concessions, and movement in the city meant passing through barriers and checkpoints.[8]

But in that late summer when Winter pulled in, the Japanese were merely part of the city's woes. On top of everything else, Tianjin had experienced a catastrophic flood, and now much of the city was under "four to eighteen feet of water," with the Japanese controlling the barricades from boats." Winter managed to engage a boat of his own without much trouble, and then set out to move it from the British concession where he had begun into the old city where the printer had his shop. This he managed, though only after straining his Japanese "far past the breaking point," and having "to pull the one about the USA and the Japanese being the best of friends."

But the flood had hit old city especially hard, and as Winter described it the boat ride was a nightmare reminiscent of Hemingway's account of the quai at Smyrna:

> We went on through a fantastic and horrible Venice in which the ridgepoles of all the houses were straddled by thousands of starving people too far gone to beg for food and water. It was like the scene in *Snow White and the Seven Dwarfs* where Snow White saw only eyes in the water. As they died they fell off and floated in the water. Sometimes we met a family floating on a coffin. All the coffins from years back of which the wood was not entirely rotten floated to the surface and formed the only refuge for this dying population. Something like 10,000 bodies were collected with hooks and towed to points outside the city. It was impossible to burn them until weeks later when the water went down.

Winter found the printer, half crazy, in the upper floor of his shop, which Winter entered from his moored boat by means of a ladder. The two hundred books were then lowered into the boat and Winter got back to the British concession triumphant—though prematurely. That afternoon he started by boat to the railway station, the books packed in a crate that took three men to lift. It was still pouring, so on the way he stopped at Whiteaway's and bought a raincoat, without noticing that it was a British Army trench coat. This turned out to be a major error (assuming that Winter might otherwise have managed to conceal his distinctly British appearance) since, while the local Japanese military authorities had directly challenged the British and French in Tianjin, they were leaning over backward to avoid offending American citizens in the hope that the United States would not join the British in drastic action.

Trouble began when, near the barrier outside the station, a Japanese sentry stopped Winter's rickshaw and ordered Winter out. When he asked permission for his load to be carried up to the barrier where it would be inspected, the sentry, seeing his raincoat, instead of answering, hit him in the chest. Winter had admired the mysterious serenity shown by his friend C[9] in the face of his own adversities. Indeed, it was that kind of Taoist balance, unshaken even by the worst provocations of grief or rage, that Winter especially admired in many of his Chinese friends. He thought that it proceeded from "a sort of balance, which leaves the Chinese inwardly free to maintain an independence of thought and feeling," even when the feeling was very much alive. Yet for all his admiration, Winter did not have an iota of this capacity himself. When the Japanese sentry hit him, he was so angry that he "hit him back, hoping that he would kill me and force my government to wake up, although I remember that it flashed through my mind at the time that I was probably not important enough to produce such an effect. He hit me again and I hit him again. At this he struck his bayonet twice into my stomach hard enough to hurt but without serious damage to my anatomy." Winter pushed the sentry aside and ran the three hundred feet to the barricade, where, because he was recognized as an American, he got an apology. But the officer who apologized refused to accompany him back to the first sentry for fear of causing the sentry to lose face.

So Winter, ready for a fight, his books still on the wrong side of the barricade, returned to the sentry. Here, over the sentry's protests, he managed to stop an Italian who was driving through, explained his situation, and got some coolies to load the books into the Italian's car. But when Winter got to the station, although "there were crowds of Japanese putting their chairs and tables and oleanders into the baggage car for Peiping," his load was refused, over his protests that he would report the incident to the embassy.

In a defiant, purposeful rage, he returned to the city to look for small suitcases to purchase, and after three hours, he had managed to collect the five he needed. He then went back to the station and retrieved his book load, which he had transported back to the Italian restaurant where he had left the suitcases. Here, he distributed his books into the suitcases and then started again for the station, arriving in time for another train for Peiping. Outside the coach, Winter stopped passengers who were boarding the train until he found three who would take one suitcase each aboard with them. He carried two himself, as well as a pair of rubber boots thrown over his shoulder.

At about midnight, he arrived in Peiping and tried in vain to get a cab. The cars were stopping only for Japanese. Finally, he went back into the station, rounded up porters, and with their help walked the books to the American embassy only a mile or so away. There, under the watchful eye of the embassy guard, he left the books in the middle of the street until he could recover them the next morning.

A few days later, in order to get his trip to Kunming under way he had only to add these books to the nearly four thousand he was transporting from the OIC library, and to get them onto the boat for Hong Kong. This required "even more patience," he remarked to the Richards. But of course it was not patience that kept Winter going through ordeals like these. It was a will as dogged as it was fiery—the will of a man accustomed to having his way and ready and able to fight for it when it was not granted to him at once.

*   *   *

Two months after his arrival in Kunming, Winter reported little of his journey there, except that after his previous adventures, Kunming, "with nothing more serious than air raid alarms," seemed a very delightful Florence-Seville sort of a place by contrast." In fact, as his colleague T. T. Shui would later tell Stevens, it took Winter the better part of those two months to recover his health after the journey.

The two-week truck ride was a saga of bombed out bridges, rails torn up, and interminable official delays (the Rangoon authorities kept him waiting for a month for his landing permit). Winter catalogued the ordeal vividly in a letter he wrote to the Richards just two weeks after he arrived. He had been fourteen days on the Burma Road, he said,

> fighting every inch of the way against drivers who tried to steal my baggage, black-water fever, the fatigue that came from the constant loading and unloading without the help of coolies, the long waits by bombed bridges, living on tea and fly-specked cakes, with a serious lumbago got by sleeping on the ground at the top of mountains nine thousand feet high, the tiresome suspicions of soldiers and officials, and the strain of bracing myself from dawn to sunset—and sometimes half the night— to keep my head from striking the roof of the truck.[10]

Winter, as we know, was ready to exaggerate for the sake of a good story, and his statement that he saw "five trucks a day plunge over the precipice or lying at the foot after they had plunged" may have been such an exaggeration. In any case, his personal suffering dimmed when, in Lashio, Burma, more than three hundred miles upriver from Rangoon as the crow flies, where the seven-hundred-mile, single-lane Burma Road had its southern terminus, Winter learned of Pollard-Urquhart's death (just as, some six years later, as he stopped in a village tavern on his way back to Kunming from the Tibetan border, he would learn of the political assassination of Wen Yiduo).

Pollard-Urquhart's was a peculiar death, the result of an accident in a time of war, when the thresholds of life are enfeebled and low. As Winter pieced the story together through conversations with T. T. Shui, the British consul, Pollard-Urquhart's brother-in-law H. Prideaux-Brune, and others, it began on October 2 with the sounding of the air raid alarm. At the first warning wail, "the entire population of the city" ran for the gates to take protection in the wooded hills half an hour away. Ordinarily the alarm gave the necessary half-hour warning. But on this day, the planes came in only ten minutes after the first warning, and the scene was a bedlam. People ran through the narrow east gate with valuables on their heads, in a throng of old women, opium smokers, cripples, students with packages of books, housewives half crippled by bound feet, clutching such valuables as a clock to their bosom, along with cars and trucks.[11] Pollard-Urquhart was knocked down by one of the trucks, and he got a bad cut on his left knee. After the raid, his wound was dressed by a doctor named Craddock, who told him to come back in a few days. But there seemed to be no complications, and Pollard-Urquhart failed to return.

For more than a week he went about as usual, "sitting in the hills during the day time and teaching in the afternoon and evening." Then, on the twelfth, he went with a friend to help him dig possessions out of his house that had been destroyed in the morning's raid. Pollard-Urquhart complained at the time of a pulled muscle, which he thought he'd got on the previous day by running up a hill for cover. The next day he felt pain all over his body and was unable to go to the bathroom unassisted. Since he was now obviously unable to get out of the city when the Japanese planes hit next, his brother-in-law, Prideaux-Brune, the British counsel in Kunming, drove him to Lo Tzu, a place about seventy-five kilometers west of the city.

Prideaux-Brune returned to Kunming the next morning to look for Dr. Craddock, but he was unsuccessful. The doctor had refused a Shanghai truck driver admission to his hospital on the ground that the driver was drunk, and a crowd of drivers had attacked the hospital. One doctor was carried off and beaten. Craddock had managed to hide and was still hidden when Prideaux-Brune came looking for him.

Late the next day, almost two weeks after Pollard-Urquhart was injured, Prideaux-Brune finally found Craddock, who returned with him on the following morning to Lo Tzu, prepared to amputate Pollard-Urquhart's leg. But when they arrived, they found that Pollard-Urquhart had died of gangrene on the previous evening. He was twenty-five. His friends wrapped him in a bolt of Mongol cloth, they arranged for him to be buried there in Lo Tzu.

A few days later, a service was held for Pollard-Urquhart in Kunming at the Southwest Associated University. T. T. Shui had wished to have a Chinese funeral and send scrolls, but a man named F. T. Ching, Winter reported bitterly, collected a preacher somewhere and a girl student who gargled "Nearer My God to Thee." After that ceremony, Prideaux-Brune asked "Polly's" friends to come and select souvenirs from among the belongings. Winter, who had not yet come down with the sciatica that developed from his lumbago, went, and took a book. But there, in his friend's nearly empty house, he had a bad moment, remembering "The Apparitions," one of Yeats's last poems: "Fifteen apparitions have I seen; / The worst a coat upon a coat-hanger."[12]

Arthur Pollard-Urquhart was a gifted and charming man. He had written a literary history, *Great European Novels and Novelists*, for the use of Chinese students, and he was, as Kung Tsu-chih, the Yunnan Minister of Education, put it (in a statement for the bronze memorial put up for Pollard-Urquhart) one whose teaching "was conducted in a spirit of gentle, untiring persuasion." I. A. Richards remembered him as "the oldest of all our friends in China." Robert Winter and Pollard-Urquhart had been longtime neighbors as well as close friends at Tsinghua University. They had come to China in the same year. They had looked forward to being reunited again, even in the increasingly dim prospects of Kunming.

Now, despite his own resistance to the move and despite the obstacles that he had had to overcome, Winter was in Kunming without his companion, and there he remained for the better part of the next six years. Had he known what awaited him, one wonders if Winter would still have chosen to remain in China. I suppose that he would. For a variety of reasons, moral, intellectual, and temperamental, he had burned his bridges behind him. Then, hardly a week after he had heard in Lashio of Pollard-Urquhart's death, he arrived in Kunming only to learn, from "a somewhat ambiguous letter from Richards," that his connection with the OIC had been cut by the Rockefeller Foundation.[13] That intimation was confirmed by a cable he received from Balfour on November 11, more than a month later.

To make matters still more confused, Pollard-Urquhart had died between the time when Stevens decided to exclude Winter's salary from the new budget—he had been persuaded only at the last moment to allow the OIC to continue operations for another year—and the time of Winter's arrival in Kunming. It would be December 6 before the matter got altogether disentangled.

But on November 4, 1940, Richards wrote to Winter to tell him that within a day or two he would receive a cable from Balfour inviting him "to take over Pollard's position as responsible head of the work—under the condition that the Basic Program and your activities as its Director be confined to Yunnan and South West China," where there were no guerillas—that is, Communist forces. Richards, speaking for the Foundation, feared that further political activities would compromise Winter's position and thus endanger future funding for the OIC.[14]

With his red marking pencil, Winter put an exclamation point against those last two sentences, but he also marked with a double line in the margin Richards's closing sentence: "I'm very sure that if you join Shui in the teaching, the results will be all that human powers under these conditions can achieve." So when, on November 14, Balfour transferred to Kunming a cable from Stevens offering Winter an appointment as head of the OIC there, Winter's mind was presumably already made up. A few days later, Prideaux-Brune sent to Balfour a wire that read: "Winter accepts appointment and gives desired assurance."[15]

Balfour was traveling to Manila when he picked up Prideaux-Brune's cable in Hong Kong, and it was not until December 17 that he sent to Stevens a letter confirming Winter's acceptance. It must have been hard for him to do so. In his letter to Stevens, Balfour let Stevens know that as far as he was concerned, the letter of explanation Winter had sent to him on November 11 was "a matter of self-justification." Although Balfour "had not considered it useful to enter into any discussion about the past" with Winter, despite Winter's explanation, he considered Winter's stay in Peking from April to August 1940 was either for Winter's personal pleasure or in the performance of duties most definitely not in the interests of the Rockefeller Foundation.[16] Winter defended himself, a bit circuitously, by saying that at the time he didn't know that he still had a job.

*   *   *

Although Winter's new appointment was made over the recommendations of Balfour and, initially of Stevens, he was not without supporters. Pollard-Urquhart himself had wired in September that Winter was indispensable for the Institute's present work.[17] On November 12, Shui had echoed Pollard-Urquhart's words and added that in the light of Pollard-Urquhart's untimely death, there should no longer be any question on the point of Winter's indispensability: "I can assure you that with Mr. Winter in charge, the O.I.C. will be able to fulfill its promises and render great service to the cause of education in China." Finally, Richards had talked the matter over with Wu Fuheng, who was now at Harvard studying in the school of education. Wu agreed that "Pollard's death made it extremely desirable to get Winter to take over his classes in the Teacher's School." Besides, Richards added, "You know how high I rank his powers in that line and in 1939 he did manage the financial side of the project with great care. It is simpler now and he could be entirely relied on to do it well. Pollard took it over because business came easily to him."[18]

On November 2, after meeting with Richards in Cambridge, Massachusetts, Stevens had written in his diary:

> English in China to Richards seems entirely dependent next year on use of Winter. He accepts all the criticism that is made of Winter's diversity of interest. He strongly urges that a message be sent to Balfour, backing Winter for work on the plan until summer only in Yunnan and completely on this one problem. The prestige of Winter, as one of the outstanding teachers of Tsinghua, is greater than that of any other man in this field of work. Undoubtedly, he would have more influence now in Yunnan than anyone who could be sent or secured from an American college in China.[19]

So Winter was rehired, despite Balfour's suspicions. If the project were to go on, the Rockefeller Foundation had no other choice.

Chapter Eight:

University Under Seige

When Winter arrived in Kunming at eleven o'clock at night on November 8, 1940, covered with road dust, he looked like a clay statue, eager for the amenities of the Hotel du Lac. (Two years earlier, on the last day of 1938, it was here that Generals Stillwell and Chennault had sat, talking over a long dinner, their bitter quarrels still in the future.) But Winter found the hotel closed, its windows blown out in a raid two weeks before. Finally managing to rouse the small boy who had been left in charge, Winter bullied him into letting him sleep "in a room full of broken glass and feathers from the damaged mattress."[1] On the next afternoon, he found Prideaux-Brune just as he returned from the hills, and Prideaux-Brune wired to Balfour to tell him that Winter had arrived. Balfour's answer arrived promptly on the following day: "Winter's connections with Institute officially ended September stop Welcome suggestions Winter or Shui future of Institute."[2]

On the fifteenth, a cable Stevens had wired through Balfour arrived in response to one he had received from Prideaux-Brune pleading Winter's case. Stevens wrote: "I approve Richards' recommendation of Winter to carry on English project provided you get assurance complete exclusion all other activities."[3] Prideaux-Brune and Winter had been separated for several days by air raids, so Prideaux-Brune sent this wire to him, with a cover letter urging: "May I hope that you will regard the condition as arising from misunderstanding, and fall in with their proposal—for Arthur's and Richards' sake, and everyone else's?"[4]

Winter fell in. But while the question of his employment was now more or less closed, his life did not turn carefree. A "violent sciatica" that had developed from his lumbago slowed his movements, and a week after he arrived in Kunming, he fell behind the crowd that poured through the east gate during an air raid and never got as far as the wooded hills. Instead, when the planes came in, Winter was sitting in a wet rice field where he had to remain "while the planes dived at the crowd throwing hand-grenades, killing two students." The pilots were apparently out of machine gun ammunition, and their marksmanship with the grenades was very poor, fortunately for Winter and most of the rest. As it was, Winter suffered no harm, except that the all-clear didn't sound for another six hours, so that he was cold and drenched. By the next day he couldn't move without agony, but the always-kind Prideaux-Brune sent him his hot water bottle ("a thing which is not available in Kunming"), which made him feel much better.

On January 15, Winter sent off to Balfour the financial report for the quarter July-September 1940 and worked on the report for the second quarter, which he hoped to send off on the following day. He had typed the first and part of the second of these reports (left incomplete at the time of Pollard-Urquhart's death) as he lay in a cemetery among tombs to dodge shrapnel "and with several degrees of fever from the local typhus, which I presumably got from the bite of a rat while I was asleep." A friend of his had remarked that "there is no time here now to be old, ill, or to die."⁵

It was the reliable Prideaux-Brune again who made it possible for Winter to type at all. Thieves had broken into his room, split open the trunks with crowbars, and stolen his portable Hermes—this, he added ruefully, on the only day when he had not carried the typewriter with him. (The thieves also got the rest of his personal things, only two months after he had struggled with the trunks over the Burma Road. These belongings he would recover in February, only to have them bombed almost immediately after he got them back.) Prideaux-Brune lent him a typewriter from the consulate, but it was heavy, and Balfour would have to laugh, Winter said, "if you saw my servant and me running with it for two or three miles when the siren blows." He dressed in odds and ends of secondhand clothing given to him by friends.

An air raid on January 5 had flattened everything from the Institute's school to the American consulate, and though Winter knew that this was "child's play compared with what is happening in Europe," for a "tenderfoot" like himself, it was not pleasant "to see stupefied women sitting like watch dogs in the craters where their families had blown up." Winter's sense of horror (and occasionally his self-pity) breathe through these early letters and reports from Kunming. He was learning how to suffer passively—a difficult role for him.

Winter speaks at some length of the hardships and horror of life of Lianda and rarely of its intellectual pleasures. Yet there must have been many. Though Winter never made close friends at Lianda, or anywhere else, here he enjoyed the company of many of the best minds in China, including the economist, Chen Deison, a man whom he admired greatly. Chen had been his next-door neighbor at Tsinghua and though they had no common academic interests, they had talked often back in Peiping. Back there, Chen had admired his garden and, later, when for a while Winter shifted his taste from plants to animals, Chen also admired the array of pet wild things that Winter kept, including his wild monkey, whose sometimes aggressive temper people saw as a kind of analogue to Winter's own flashes of temper.

Chen remembered that at Lianda everyone liked Winter: "We all thought him a nice chap." But then he added:

> One thing about him is that Bob never had a very close friend. He used to go around with Polly [Pollard-Urquhart], but I don't think they were close friends. That's the reason why he is so lonesome now. There were quite a few American and English teachers at Tsinghua, but he never developed close friendship with them. Not with Chinese either. He had many students, of course, but I wouldn't say he had any close friends in the student body. [6]

*   *   *

The barrage of telegrams, sometimes at cross-purposes, that Winter kept receiving from the Foundation must have piled their own anxiety on the anxiety of the raids. Further, the Institute was hanging on by a hair. Yet Winter's second quarter report, covering October 1, 1940, to December 31, 1940, contained some upbeat news concerning the well-being of the project, if not of its staff. The Yunnan Commission of Education had officially authorized the Institute to administer an English-training school for which the commission contracted to provide the buildings and furniture as well as the running expenses (exclusive of salaries). This was in keeping with the Rockefeller Foundation's hopes of transferring responsibility for the Institute to the Chinese, and it encouraged the Foundation to continue to provide salaries for the Institute staff, however minimally, despite the otherwise discouraging situation. T. T. Shui translated the contract and sent it to Balfour. Other forms of recognition from the Chinese government were forthcoming. In mid-January 1941, Winter and (posthumously) Pollard-Urquhart had been awarded certificates from Chunking conferring on them the Second Class Order of Merit for over fifteen years service to Chinese education.[7]

When he wrote to tell Winter that he had been "reappointed," Richards had advised him to avoid arousing resentment in his Chinese colleagues by allowing too great a discrepancy between Chinese and Western salaries. (Such economies would also make a good impression on the Foundation officers, who, had it not been for the complicating factor of Winter, were inclined to drop the project.) Winter not only complied by reducing his own salary by 20 percent, but he then went several steps further. Pollard-Urquhart had been holding expenditures to 44 percent, despite the soaring inflation rate. Winter proposed to hold them to 37 percent of the original budget for the third and fourth quarters. That would mean that by June, he would have spent less than half of the annual fund. He was under great pressure to economize. Only with the help of previously unspent funds would he be allowed to go on for another year after the June deadline.

But these economies had been achieved at serious sacrifice. Pollard-Urquhart had slashed printing by 100 percent, travel by 90 percent, foreign salaries by 50 percent, running expenses by 42 percent, and Chinese salaries by 18 percent. Winter's comments on these figures succinctly suggest the absurdist drama in which he played. For example, the small amount left to the travel budget, he said, was irreducible: it represented "the expenditure of our teachers who are now obliged to take a train at six o'clock in the morning, and then walk or ride a donkey for five miles to meet their classes in the evacuated schools."

There was tight-lipped drama also in his comment on the running expenses, which included "such unusual items as a large bill for radiograms in connection with Mr. Pollard-Urquhart's death." Winter would have promised a considerable reduction in the running expenses, "if the raids had not become more destructive lately."

Against one economy, however, he drew the line. He was reluctant to reduce Chinese salaries further. In fact, he believed, as Pollard-Urquhart had, that raises were imperative. The faculty of the Southwest Joint University—Winter was still one of their number, although inactive at this point—had gotten substantial "cost of living" raises and in addition received a rice allowance which amounted to about 10 percent. (That would hardly make their lives opulent. John Fairbank would observe that by late 1942, the purchasing power of the Chinese dollar had shrunk to 1 percent of what it had been in 1937 and that "Students and faculties survived mainly because the government rice allowances gave them something to eat, roughly on the standard of concentration camps.") But Winter's staff had neither received the raises nor the rice allowance. Raises were necessary then, not only because Pollard-Urquhart had promised them, but because otherwise the staff would starve without them.

In order to cut his own salary by 20 percent, Winter had to sign away "the margin of funds which would have made it possible to get out of Kunming in a serious emergency." But perhaps that was no great loss, since it is hard to imagine what, by Kunming standards, would constitute an emergency worse than what had already occurred. The school was destroyed by air raids on January 29, 1941 ("27 planes, 50 bombs, 600 houses destroyed, about 200 casualties"). That might seem serious enough, but since Winter had been living at the school "in order to see that things were done properly," he had also lost all his personal belongings again. (The loss amounted to about one year's salary, Kunming prices.) The school had been destroyed, but the loss to the Institute, he reported assuringly, "was not great" since the bombing took place during the New Year recess and no students were killed. Neither would they lose time from classes because Chinese workmen had "promised to clear the debris from the two class-rooms which were left standing before our scheduled date of reopening." As if this were not good news enough, Winter also expected the commissioner of education, Mr. Kung, who had honored their contract so far, "to pay for the work of clearing and reconstruction."

Winter's apparent optimism is best understood in the context of a quality of the Oriental character he admired and sometimes rose to. Once, at the start of his visit to the U.S. in 1943, he saw that quality in the great bust of the Trimurti on the island of Elephanta. The triple figure is said to represent the three aspects of Shiva: creation, protection, and destruction—a balance often incomprehensible to Western eyes. This is the balance he saw in his friend C, who calmly met enormous pressure from the Nationalist government (the pressure included the assassination of several of his friends, including Winter's friend, Wen Yiduo). In both the statue and the man, he saw a balancing of contraries that resulted in the energy the Chinese call *ch'i*, or life-spirit, of which Chuang Tzu said: "Store it within; make of it a well-spring, flood-like, even and level. Make a very store-pool of ch'i." Though he could complain bitterly of his lot, Winter too could sometimes embody that spirit.[8]

Kung's had promised to support the OIC to the tune of about $12 a month, but he made the promise in 1942, before the air raids began. Now the raids came in three or four times a week, the city could offer no resistance, and Kung no longer had funds. For the while, Winter and his staff camped in their old office space. From here, they could "get a view of the beautiful Kunming sky through the ceiling since the last raid." The commissioner had provided that space to Winter and his staff as temporary living quarters, and he also helped the Institute "to obtain the use of two other schools to move into when the ones we are now occupying are bombed." Since the schools had evacuated and moved to neighboring villages and temples, such space was easily available.

Thus the fortunes of the Orthological Institute in Kunming balanced on a hair. Before Winter returned to Kunming, the school had lost half of its students, some promising to return. But so far, only two had come back. Winter took some comfort in the fact that twenty-five others had registered for the entrance examination. He anticipated that at least twenty of these would arrive at the eleventh hour. As he saw it, the Chinese tend not to act before it is necessary. Given the kinds of pressures they lived under, that was not surprising. Their confidence in anything so abstract as a future had been badly strained over the ages. So Winter expected the enrollment to come up to something like the original number by the time the next fall semester began, and he promised to run the school through the summer so that the new students would be at speed with the old by September. Such talk gave heart to Richards, no doubt, and may have placated people at the Rockefeller Foundation, but much of it was wishful thinking, made more intense by the fact that without the Rockefeller Foundation funds, Winter's own already-harried existence would get much worse. For the time, while the future of the project certainly looked dim, no one could doubt the spirit of both Winter and the handful of students to go on. He gave Balfour a detailed account of how he and the students had dug through the rubble of their school in search of important documents (including an earlier version of this report, which "was one of the things . . . we failed to find"), using their fingers until they were able to borrow a shovel.

When, toward the end of the Sino-Japanese war, Guomindang soldiers killed four students, Winter confronted the GMD general. Though R. D. Jameson's widow told me that Winter didn't put himself out for other people, he took great risks in protecting students, and sometimes colleagues, by hiding them and helping them to get to areas held by the Communists. Such acts won him a reputation as "a brave progressive friend"—though after Liberation that reputation did little to protect him against harassment by the Red Guard.[9]

The Institute lost buildings, papers, and students but retained some kind of working relationship with all but one of the schools that had been cooperating with them at the beginning of the academic year, and the Provincial College of Education in the neighboring province of Szechuan was urging the Institute to establish a Department of English there. Under their present system, the president and the head of the English Department of that school feared that "the wretched and hopeless plight of English in our colleges and middle schools" would encourage influential educators to abolish English teaching in all middle schools and this would result in the eventual loss of "a valuable medium of knowledge and culture" and the return to "another age of the closed door and ignorance."

Although the Institute's "program of rigid economy" prevented them from responding to the provincial college's petition for staff to teach Basic, Winter could only offer advice and copies of texts that the Szechuan officials would have to print themselves. There were other shakily encouraging prospects nearer to home, when Dr. Huang Zijian, dean of the College of Education at the Southwestern Associated University (Lianda) called on Winter to express his sincere desire for cooperation with the OIC.

*   *   *

Naturally, Winter's extraordinary report produced mixed effects on those at a distance from the combat zone. But the unquenchable Richards kept spirits at the home office from flagging. He more or less persuaded John Marshall that, under most difficult conditions, Winter continued to do the work he was being paid for. Marshall agreed that the OIC work should be extended until January 1942, drawing on money remaining from the last previous grant.[10]

Later in March, Richards told Winter that he was confident the $9,600 remaining in the fund could be used to extend the Institute's franchise until June 1942. "By then, but it is unwise to develop any hopes in these days, it may be possible—in view of the fact that China is becoming a sort of Anglo-American ally—to get some financial aid toward the reconstruction of English teaching in China." He asked that Winter continue to feed him material with which to make arguments for the Institute's extension.

For Richards's purpose, even Winter's misfortunes became grist for the mill. "We are full of concern for your wretched bad luck in having your things bombed just as you got them back," his letter of March 19 opens. "That and your other adventures make horrible reading—but they help very much to make the picture for us here. You can be sure that everyone understands how remarkable it is that you and the Institute are carrying on at all."[11]

What was at stake here, Richards argued, went far beyond his self-interest. Back in March 1939, he had written to Stevens from Magdalene College that

> in spite of, but indeed, partly too, because of the extraordinary difficulties of the time in China, I would like to make the strongest plea I can for a continuation of the work. It is not merely that I personally want to stand by China (or rather, by the intelligence of the Chinese child) at this turning point when it is being so deliberately threatened. I believe that a technical intervention here can have momentous consequences for the life of the East later, and that time lost now may matter immensely.

As Empson once remarked about Richards's Benthamite morality, "The idea of making a calculation to secure the greatest happiness for the greatest number is perhaps inherently absurd, but it seems the only picture we can offer." For Richards, the OIC was an element of that greatest good. To see it defeated was to see the defeat of mind by the barbarism of war.

So Winter's bald images of the continuing nightmare in Kunming became, in Richards's alembic, images of the spirit's carrying on in the face of adversity. Of course, there were images coming out of Kunming that could not easily be so transformed. For example, when he was still in Peking, Winter, who sometimes took perverse delight in shocking the real tenderfeet, told his sister Elizabeth that Pollard-Urquhart said,

"The most unpleasant thing he knows is walking on human flesh and having a human hand roll out of your sheets as you pull them up around your chin."[12] But whatever dab of sensationalism with which Winter sometimes colored them, his pictures of extreme horror constituted a kind of witness. He was giving voice to suffering that would otherwise be wordless, and in this, he was embarking on a new avocation.

*   *   *

As to Richards, his hope, arguably *any* hope, was perhaps naive. He wished to see his nearly completed Basic version of Plato's *Republic* translated into Chinese, for instance, because, he told Stevens, he intended "to send it to Mme. Chiang (with the Basic New Testament when it appears) . . . to enlist that lady's interest in Basic as an agency of moral reconstruction." But in fact the moral reconstruction the Wellesley-educated Mme. Chiang had helped institute through the New Life Movement was a thinly disguised effort to use Confucianism, as well as Christianity, to implant in the Chinese people the spirit of mobilization under strong leadership—a spirit that Mao also would inculcate.

Yet however dimly one views his hope of bringing Mme. Chiang (and through her, her cruelly illustrious husband) around through the use of plain versions of Plato and the New Testament—later he would also try Plato on the Communists—Richards had other grounds for attaching great significance to the survival of Basic in China. In a letter forwarded to him by Winter, Richards had heard from Liu Shih-mu, the head of the English Department of the Szechuan Provincial College of Education. Liu had argued that the success or failure of Basic in China "does not mean only the success or failure of a theory; it means the life or death of the English language in Chinese schools." If the quality of English teaching continued to deteriorate, Liu went on, English would simply "be wiped out from the curriculum, at first in junior middle schools, then in senior middle schools and finally in colleges . . . . By the loss of such a link, such a medium of culture and of mutual understanding we should lose much, and the Anglo-Saxons should lose much too."[13]

Liu appears to have read his *Mencius on Mind*; he certainly had some imagination for the reciprocally noetic-healing advantages Richards foresaw in intimate communications between East and West. But Liu had also read his Confucius, and the close of his long and carefully reasoned appeal for help (though it contains its own little chirrup of self-interest) ends on a high note indeed. "In the last place," he wrote, though his college would be very glad to have the cooperation of the Institute, he does not expect it. He had talked to Winter in Kunming and reported that, as a result of Winter's description of conditions at the Institute,

> I have to give up my long-cherished hope for lost, though with some regret. I can only hope that some day in the future when I should be still in a position to do something, I might be of service to you and work out our faith to a success. But at present, I shall feel quite satisfied, like a Chinese with a Confucian ideal of living, with the fact that I have done my utmost for a noble purpose—the propagation of a truth— though without success in the end.

> Similarly, others also who, whatever their sympathy with Richards's dream, were more influenced by the realities. A month after Richards's meeting with Marshall, Balfour, from Manila, reported a recent meeting with Winter in Kweiyang. Balfour had for the time left behind his earlier irritation with Winter, who he now said was carrying on the work "with devotion" despite the extreme difficulty of the conditions. But it was his "frank opinion that there seems to be a doubtful prospect of permanence for the Orthological Institute in Yunnan Province"[14]—an opinion that Jameson had reached two years earlier when he decided that he could do no more real work through the Institute in China.

In the same letter to Richards in which he challenged Balfour's "frank opinion," Winter remarked that "In addition to many minor raids, we have had two 'total' bombings this month." The last of these total bombings was "a nasty piece of work," he went on. Because there was only a quarter of an hour's warning, the streets were strewn with killed and wounded. More than five thousand people lost their homes." In the earlier saturation bombing, "Polly's rooms and the last of his possessions were destroyed."

Winter's description of recent raids could hardly help Richards's arguments for the Institute's extension. Instead, with its peculiar melding of literature and reality, it makes a different kind of argument. Winter depicts this contemporary reality in the bleakest modernist terms: it is fragmented, it is the city of hell, to which we descend, like Odysseus, or Dante, or John Webster, or T. S. Eliot. It is "terrible," like the world of Hopkins's "terrible sonnets." As in some extreme metaphor of Charles Ives, we hear in it strains of our own "Battle Hymn of the Republic." But above all, it carries the feel of the thing as registered in a man unable to protect himself by feeling nothing at all. I quote Winter's account in its entirety. It isn't great literature, but it has stunning evocative power, and it reminds us of the degree to which Winter invented himself and interpreted the world around him through the lens of poems he loved.

> Ridiculous the waste sad time
> Stretching before and after.[15]

> Kunming lies beneath me, laid out, like Florence, by an artist-god. Above the slow swell of the roof-tiles, the gate-towers are riding quietly at anchor. Thin lines of eucalyptus and cypress trees wander in the distance along the devious dykes. Beyond, suave mountains shut us safely within the radiant cup. A hawk turns lazily in the blue sky. Oh! virgin, vivacious, and beautiful today![16]

> Shrilly, the siren screams its warning and then dies away with a petulant grunt. Soldiers, sauntering home from the hunt with a handsome yellow dog slung from a pole over their shoulders, drop their quarry and start to run. In a second the street is surging like the angry Salween. We are carried on the current to a city gate. A fierce struggle there. Then the stream fans out into the fields.

> A more hysterical but shorter shriek of the siren. The "urgent"! Figures dart aimlessly about the fields. They hold a handful of grass over their heads, or put up umbrellas, or go, hunched and limping, looking for a hole. Some, in a nightmare, are conscious of the danger, but unable to move.

> A distant humming like a swarm of bees. A solemn stillness settles down over the gay spring morning. We crouch in a huddle in the muddy ditch, avoiding speech. Brown peasant

women press for consolation against the one who can mutter the mysterious words, their tense fingers telling invisible beads. Like Geryons, polluting the whole world, the shining beasts come swimming, slowly, slowly, wheel and descend . . . . But already we hear the whistling, the hideous roaring . . . . The ground shakes as the city shoots into the sky in an opalescent cloud . . . . Falling towers Jerusalem Athens Alexandria Vienna London Unreal . . .[17]

After a time, cautious heads are lifted here and there.

The smouldering sun has beaten, beaten, all day long, belching its heat over the wilting fields. The blood slackens in the heat. The sweltering air presses all thought and feeling down into the scum-green marsh. Our cells become a mush as in the pupa of a moth. What metamorphosis can come from emotional death in a ditch? . . . I think we are in rats' alley where the dead men lost their bones . . . . My son, how did you come down to the cloudy West, and you alive? It is hard for the living to see this place . . . . A decayed hole among the mountains . . . .[18]

The "all-clear" sounds its steady note, as welcome as a cool breeze bringing rain. The crowd streams back in silence to the city.

Our path winds under the cool willows of the lake. The clay bust of a woman, armless and smiling, is leaning against the foot of a tree. Across the road, on a bubbly black pool in the dust, crawling with flies, float white grains of rice. From the centre, a little red hand, an inch long, is pointing at the sky. Cover her face . . . . Why do they make the cheap boxes so narrow? It doesn't matter, when there are only bits to be shoveled in, but this naked fat man, whose shoulders are still entire, has to be forced in with the shovel. But surely there is some mistake. More and more dusty pieces of meat are thrown in, till a muffled protest comes through a handkerchief: "A butcher shop!". . . . A car passes, carefully closed against the dust and smells. Inside, a delicate and clean finger is pointing at a collection of dusty rag-dolls, in assorted sizes, down to a foot long, which are being hauled from the ruins by the neck and heaped in the road. Red stuffing shows here and there. Is man no more than this?[19] What vintage has been trampled out here with so terrible a wrath?[20] . . . Before my door a man is kneeling, his bottom high in the air, like an Arab at prayer. His head is gone. They say it is my carpenter . . . . A woman has climbed to the highest point of the ruins of her house, and her face, hot and shining from digging in the tangle of beams and wires, catches the last rays of the low sun. Pitched past pitch of grief.[21]

Depths of suffering in her eyes. Irony, futility on her lips.

The boom of the cannon, sounding nine o'clock, startles a silent city. In the space of a few months, the thousand-year-old ritual of wailing for the dead has gone the way of other luxuries. Only rat's feet over broken glass . . . . Skarfe up the tender eye. Night whelms, whelms, but will not end us! As silent and anonymous as an army of ants, two hundred thousand people, whispering together with dry voices, will ooze over and through the ruins under the starlight all night long. The army of the curious, the army of the five thousand dispossessed today, the army of beggars, picking up bits of wood and wire, the army of pickpockets, the army of rats, brown rats, grey rats, black rats, typhus-bearing, rats will limp their mangy way together in the promiscuous blackness . . . .

"Wipe your hand across your mouth and laugh"[22] while there is still time, for tonight, when you have turned the key in the lock, slipped the ready cartridge back into its clip, blown out the candle, and you sink down, your eyes, the mouth of a bottle suddenly overturned, will go on dripping till you are on your feet again. Your bed a rack, where "thoughts against thoughts in groans grind."[23]

As I've suggested, Winter's heavy use of quotation in this piece suggests how for him literature was a lens through which to see the world. But the particular passages he chooses, including even the references to *King Lear*, are the very earmarks of a terror, the terror deeply embedded in modernist literature in the face of the emptiness left by "the death of God" and by the horrors of WWI—and now, for Winter, by the horror all around him.

*   *   *

Conditions did not improve much through early May 1941, according to the "gloomy" report that Winter sent to Stevens at the end of the month. The city was bombed repeatedly at intervals of only two or three days. The warnings were short and the casualties high. "Sometimes the roads leading out of the city were covered for hours with writhing figures calling for help, who had been bombed or machine-gunned while trying to reach the fields." During April, classes had been held during the preliminary air raid warning—which meant only that enemy scouts were overhead. But during the period of the heavy raids, this practice had to be changed because the students would have vividly in mind images of the writhing figures who had not reached the fields in time during the last raid.[24]

There were also new inconveniences to adjust to, of course. Though the new school was a handsome three-storied modern building about half a mile outside the city, with a fine view of the Western Hills, the authorities had ordered all glass to be removed from the windows, and Kunming is a windy place. "This seemed Spartan to me," Winter observed in his report, "but the students seem to find it luxurious, and they are right to be thankful merely for a roof over their heads in a city where so many people do not have one."

On days when there were alarms, everyone was accustomed to having only one meal and to carrying with them at all times their most important things "so that they will not be destroyed." In Winter's case these were his typewriter, his glasses, a raincoat to put under him in the ditches where he sought shelter from shrapnel, and a briefcase containing the Institute records. Classes were in session from eight to ten in the morning and from three to six in the afternoon since raids before ten and after three were unusual. Everyone on the staff, including Winter, met about twenty-five classes each, so they cannot have had much time to brood.

Indeed, everyone agreed that, despite these conditions, the students had made remarkable progress. "You might suppose that these conditions are very disturbing to our work," Winter told Stevens, "but the surprising thing is that most people, and particularly Chinese, adjust themselves very quickly. Probably the enforced physical exertion and tension leave little room for emotions. I am not able to sleep after a day of horrors, but I have not noticed that the students are affected in the same way. In my case, it may be partly caused by the unaccustomed altitude."[25]

The rains had begun, and this was encouraging because last year, from early May to September, there had been no raids, and everyone was "hoping for a few months of comparative quiet." But that quiet period had not begun yet, and for the moment the rains were an inconvenience because now the irrigation ditches were full of water and there was not much shelter against flying shrapnel.

Force of circumstance required the traditional respect for the dead to be harshly modified, the dead now "to be disposed of as quietly and quickly as possible." There were no funerals, and Winter would not have known of the death of Mr. Pirey, "an old French gentleman who had kept an English school in Kunming for many years," if he had not "happened to pass a group of twenty odd students running out of a gate with a coffin on their shoulders. A small cotton flag on a bamboo stick gave his name in Chinese and said that they were taking his body out for burial."

The good news was Stevens's cable stating that the balance of the present year's fund would be made available for the coming year. Winter and his staff "had been busy making plans with that continuation in view," the thirty newly admitted students proved better than the ones lost in the fall, and despite the air raids, "most people here have a sense of security and confidence in the future." So, at least, he reported to Stevens.[26]

But in a letter to Richards written on the same day as the report, Winter admitted to discouragement. For example, things had not been going so well at the Lianda College of Education as he had hoped. He regretted the absence of George Yeh (chief Communist representative of the executive headquarters—that is, of the command post of Marshall's peacekeeping force), who had been kidnapped by "the Japanese gangsters in Shanghai" and still found it difficult to stand because he had been kicked in his backside "all day for about six weeks." Happily, he'd been ransomed "at the cost of most of his uncle's fortune," but one of the conditions of his release was that he could not come back to Kunming. He was a great loss, Winter said, because "he could always be brought round to some sort of reason."[27] Yet in 1941, prospects for any sort of reason hardly seemed bright either in Kunming or anywhere else in the world.

*   *   *

Wu Fuheng, the codirector of the Institute who had been studying at Harvard, was due back in Kunming in late August. Demands were being made on the Institute that could not be met by their present staff, and Wu's arrival meant stronger prospects of an expanded program. For that reason and others, Winter took keen interest in Wu's return to China. At the end of July 1941, Winter was able to reassure the still-absent Wu that they would probably not have "such a miserable year from bombing" as they had had during the past year, because there would now be some defense. (An American volunteer group [AVG] of fliers, the predecessors of the Flying Tigers, under General Chennault, was expected in the fall.) But the state of the economy was less encouraging. Prices had doubled in the past six weeks, and the only purchasable milk, which was "still made of beans" and smelled of gasoline, had risen in two months from $3.50 to $16.00 per gallon.[28]

Winter sent Wu a long shopping list for himself and Shui. It was primarily composed of book needs, including thirty copies of a Basic "General History" and another thirty of a Basic geography ("if there is such a thing"), fifteen copies of Haldane's *Outlook of Science* (which Empson had rendered into Basic), a small etymological English dictionary, as well as a complete Shakespeare and a complete Shaw. But there were also personal needs. Besides asking for thirty pounds of powdered milk ("the only important item . . . . I have lost over twenty pounds lately from lack of food"), Winter requested such things as a Schick shaver kit, flints for a cigarette lighter, "rubber sheets for repairing tears in clothing by pressing with hot iron," an aerial for an RC 12Q4 (which Wu would have to smuggle in), and "some book with coloured illustrations of modern European painting, which I understand are done very cheaply now."

Though it would not be for long, in the summer of 1941, it was still possible to have things shipped up from Rangoon by commercial carrier, and Winter recommended Steele Brothers, a reliable firm that used Indian drivers. "Don't under any circumstances trust the things to any Chinese," he warned firmly. Further, he urged Wu himself not to attempt the journey by truck convoy:

> I have seen tougher people than you [he presumably refers to himself] have everything stolen from them on the road,

even when they were fighting their way through with a revolver. I would advise you to fly here from Rangoon. I was practically an invalid for more than two months after my trip. All the gangsters of this part of Asia are there and they have turned the road into a sort of wild west show. Of course the Japanese occupation of Saigon may result in fighting over the very route you are expecting to come and might even prevent your crossing the Pacific. My advice applies only to present conditions.

*   *   *

Winter had hoped that the summer of 1941 would be more tranquil than the spring not only because fighter protection was expected with the arrival of General Chennault's volunteer Flying Tigers, but also because the rains would keep the Japanese planes from coming in. Indeed, there was a respite from May 10 until the close of the summer session. But just as the students were beginning their final examinations, there set in "an unexpected stretch of dry weather . . . . which encouraged enemy to vent their spite on us continuously for ten days."

Miraculously, the Institute office stood "unharmed amid acres of desolation." The school also was undamaged "except that the ceilings fell when the neighboring campus of the Southwestern Joint University was bombed." Although at the university a number of students "had arms or legs blown off," the Institute suffered no casualties because the student body was small "and we [were] able to control the students' movements during the raids so as to get maximum safety with minimum loss of time."[29]

Still, the emotional wear and tear was beginning to show. Though the papers (and Winter himself) reported that the bombing of free China had had no effect on the Chinese and that they went about their work as usual, in fact there was "some accumulated shock from repeated air raids. From the moment when the whistling of the released bombs is heard overhead and the time when you awake to find yourself alive, past experiences go galloping through your mind. And each additional experience makes the panorama more complete and more painful."

But the core aims of establishing Basic in China, though not flourishing, were alive. Winter was convinced that the Basic teaching method had been completely vindicated. Indeed, this training must have been a comfort to both students and staff in the midst of the otherwise chaotic conditions. The wall map of the Basic words, a chart designed by Winter to show the combining forms of the Basic vocabulary, hung in all of the classrooms and dormitories, making it possible "to indicate the requirements for a given period with a precision which is greatly appreciated by the students who have suffered from vague and fumbling methods before they came to us. Not only do they learn more English, but such precision has the effect of a much needed discipline in other fields."

I suppose that there was more to it than even that. Ford Madox Ford's Christopher Tietjens (the protagonist of *Parade's End*) murmured to himself in the trenches of WWI George Herbert's "Sweet day, so cool, so calm, so bright, / The bridal of the earth and sky," in order to keep himself a little sane in an insane world. Winter and his students charted the possibilities of the rich English prepositional system with perhaps a similar distractive relief.

There remained much in their world and Winter's that needed soothing, some of it nearly as imperative as the bombs. Winter had spoken in his second quarter report about the necessity of pay raises for his staff. In his summer report, he announced that, in conformity with recent action taken by the authorities of the Southwestern Joint University, he had raised the salaries of his Chinese staff by 25 percent and in addition had granted them "a temporary rice allowance." He sent a copy of the new report to Richards, hoping that his friend would approve of the increase in salaries: "Our people were munching that sort of dog biscuit which the poor eat in China and borrowing right and left. I have started a mess for them, paying for the equipment myself, and I pretend to eat with them, though the stuff served makes me want to vomit." The 25 percent increase in staff salaries involved a budget addition of US$15.42 per month.

Winter's own health was "indecently good" in the late summer of 1941. He ate in restaurants crowded "with Singapore chauffeurs and mechanics in overalls," the new aristocrats of the Burma Road. But many of his friends and old Peking acquaintances fared badly:

> I meet those pretty and sprightly women we used to know
> in Peking prowling in the market in broken shoes and greasy
> dresses for something they can afford to buy. They keep
> their heads down. Phyllis Liang is dying of tuberculosis . . . .

> Prideaux-Brune got to such a state in May that he could hardly
> sign his name. He asked for a two month's leave in Tali and Li
> Chiang. He got back just in time for it to start again. But he is
> looking much better.

(In fact, Phyllis Liang, wife of architect Liang Sicheng, recovered her
health after Liberation and reorganized the cloisonné industry. But
when the Korean War broke out and her daughter went to Korea as a
member of the Chinese army, Adele Rickett told me, Mrs. Liang got
so angry, she up and died. John Fairbank remembers her as "creatively
gifted as a writer, a poet, a woman of great aesthetic sensitivity and broad
intellectual interests, and socially charming.")[30]

By late August , 1941,Winter was impatiently expecting the arrival
in Kunming of OIC codirector Wu Fuheng. He wrote to the American
consulate in Rangoon for the latest information about travel on the
Burma Road and passed his findings on to the Rockefeller Foundation
offices in Manila. He even left detailed instructions for the journey, leg
by leg, in Manila and Rangoon. But only war supplies were supposed to
be carried by air, and he continued to worry about whether or not Wu
would be able to make his way up the Burma Road from Rangoon.

This was about the time when Harry Hopkins, acting for President
Roosevelt, had sent Daniel Arnstein, a New York taxi owner and
transportation expert, to find out "why not a god damn thing was moving
over the Burma Road." Arnstein reported corruption and inefficiency
that he saw no way of correcting except by transferring management
of the road from the Chinese government to a competent person "with
authority" to correct conditions. When the Generalissimo received a
copy of Arnstein's report in Chinese, he was delighted, and offered the
job of managing the road to Arnstein and his two assistants, "as a private
concession at so much percentage per truck." Arnstein declined.

The dismal physical condition of the nine-foot-wide, single-lane road
aside, bureaucratic potholes were enough to stop traffic. For example, in
Kunming, the northern terminus of the road, it took drivers the better
part of a day to pass through the eight custom desks, and there were a
dozen more such checkpoints on the way, issuing local permissions.
On the Chinese-Burma border at Wanting, Arnstein found 250 trucks
waiting anywhere from twenty-four hours to two weeks for clearance.

Even without the problem of multiple authorities, each attempting to
get their share of the squeeze, travel on the Burma Road was not easy.

The Chinese drivers did not practice lubrication, and hundreds of trucks were stranded along the way and cannibalized for parts, which would show up on the black market. At the time when he was expecting Wu, Winter learned that the only way to get a truck up from Burma was to buy a new one in Rangoon (only new trucks on their first trip were at this time allowed on the road), turn it over to the Steele Brothers to drive, and then sell it in Kunming. But he hesitated to take the responsibility for this expensive arrangement without authority from the Foundation.

In late September, Winter still had heard no word of Wu Fuheng (later, president of Shandong University)—who, in fact, had just left the States and would not get as far as Rangoon until November 10. So the timing was considerably off for the meeting that Winter tried to arrange in Rangoon between Wu and Bob Drummond. Drummond, head of the American Red Cross in China, was also on his way to Kunming, and Winter had hoped that the two might be of some help to each other. Perhaps Drummond, as a foreigner, would be allowed to bring in as personal property things that Wu had brought from the States for Winter. The only alternative was to smuggle them in by donkey, but although a system to do this was developing, Winter considered it too complicated and risky. In any case, Winter was not optimistic about Wu's getting in with the things. He had learned that some instruments ordered for the Physics Department of the Academia Sinica had been stuck in Rangoon for almost a year.

While Winter was doing all that he could to expedite the arrival of the comfort-bearing Wu, he was also trying to persuade David Stevens to support the OIC past June 1942, when the present budget expired. His most important arguing point was potentially strong: the Normal College of the Southwest Associated University, or Lianda, had accepted in principle that the Yunnan Provincial English-Training School—now OIC operated—be affiliated with theirs as a special branch for training teachers of English. That would mean that seven hundred first-year students would transfer to the OIC school. Indeed, Winter claimed that the students were already "preparing to move."

In addition, Winter reported, the Yunnan Commissioner of Education, whose own son attended the OIC school, was committed to supporting it to the tune of $1,700 per month, and, in addition, to provide free use of school and office buildings and a subsidy to students amounting to $800 per month. (These allotments were in much deflated Nationalist currency.) It appeared that the Institute was not only maintaining its influence but, given the necessary funds and staff, was in a position to expand it, and at relatively small cost to the Foundation. For the previous fiscal year, the OIC had drawn just a shade over US$3,097, less than a third of their allotment. What Winter wanted to keep the operation alive was simply the unexpended balance (approximately US$3,000) of that previous budget.

Winter was even willing to suggest to Stevens that if the Foundation wished to end his own association with the Institute in June 1942, and thus add his salary to the reserve, Prideaux-Brune might be willing to administer what remained of the fund. He made this plea, he said, because "we have put so much effort into the project in the midst of very trying conditions, that I should not like to see it go under, and because I do not read anything in your last letter which absolutely closes the door against such hope."[31]

But even as Winter was making this appeal to Stevens, Richards was writing to him about "the future of the work of the Institute and your own." Richards's letter was rich with appreciation: "From the moment the War destroyed the North China program, just when it seemed secured in a harvest beyond reasonable hope, you have had to do what you could under appalling conditions to see that some seed was well sown. The tenacity and courage and resource with which Pollard and you, with Shui and Wu, have gone on with the work in Yunnan is something which makes sheltered folk wonder and feel humble."

But the letter's bottom line was that it was now time for Winter to be thinking about his future. "As to your own plans," Richards asked, "Will you, after June, be returning to Tsinghua work, coming back here, or what?" Richards thought that he might have something for Winter at Harvard, but this he would not know definitely "for some months."

Stevens too, in his last letter, had inquired about Winter's own plans for the future. But the fact was that Winter had none. Indeed, under his circumstances, the idea of planning one's life must have seemed a bit comic. The wartime present precluded a future. Winter had had another robbery: "a few thousand dollars' worth of bedding and clothing—not serious like the other one." All that he had come up with in the way of surviving was to hang on to his American connections, and he was uneasy about Stevens's intentions. Just a few days before Richards wrote, Winter had sent him a copy of Stevens's letter with his own reply: "I can't quite make out if he is being pleasant or otherwise, and I should be grateful for your frank opinion if you can get round to it some time. Perhaps living in this bloody place tends to give one persecution mania."

Winter received Richards's letter in November, with just what effect on his paranoia he does not say. But he does allow that he was particularly happy to get it because it was the first communication he had had from Richards since March 19 ("This is not a reproach, but a necessary statement of fact in times like these when letters go astray.") He was also happy to hear from Richards because now he could visit the commissioner—they were expecting a "blitz" in the near future, and when that occurred, the commissioner would seek refuge far into the country and would be hard to see—and convey to him a clear impression of the Foundation's intentions.

What Winter could now report to the commissioner was precisely what Richards's letter had given him to understand: "It seems clear now that the Commissioner will have to take full responsibility after June, 1942, with Shui or with Shui and Wu in charge, if the school is to go on, and that the US $3000 saved will revert to the Foundation at that time." What might not have been previously clear to Richards was that prospects of the school continuing without Winter's continuing with it were dim at best.[32]

The commissioner had requested that the present staff of the Institute "carry the school through three years." Now, with Winter's connection ended and Wu's possibly ended, his request would not be fulfilled; so even if the Foundation decided after all to allow the Institute to use the US$3,000 against next year's budget, the commissioner could not be held to his promise of increased support.

And even if the commissioner decided to give that support, "at a time when teachers are deserting the schools to open shops or to make their fortunes on the Burma Road, I do not see where he will find new ones." Finally, Winter added, he "could not recommend that any accounts be entrusted to Shui," who had taken to gambling and bad debts. Winter closed his letter to Richards by assuring him that he would let him know at once "if there seems to be any hope of the school continuing," but considering Winter's doubts, Richards would not have been holding his breath.

Winter knew his man, and as always, he was fighting tooth and nail for both a principle and his survival. What I find remarkable in this long and sometimes tedious episode is Winter's tenacity and infinite willingness to take pains. I suppose we can charge some of this off to self-interest, but there remains a dogged loyalty to Richards's project. As to Richards, though he might throw Winter to the wolves if he had to, he would do everything in his considerable power to save his friend if that meant to save his project.

Why Winter wished to remain in a city so beleaguered as Kunming is a tangled question that earlier I touched on. The combined agencies of Richards and the Rockefeller Foundation could have found something for him in the States, as they eventually did. Winter himself thought that this required an explanation, and on the same day that he wrote to Richards an official letter about the fate of the Institute, he wrote another personal one to him about why he wished to stay in China.

In the early years, Peking was for him a kind of promised land, a world he found aesthetically pleasing not only because of the beauty and antiquity of its palaces and parks and walls and dwelling places, but because in it everything—landscape, human constructions, intercourse of gesture and speech, even simple actions, like writing—were enhanced by a formal significance that was part of the significance of the whole culture. For a Westerner of Winter's cultivation, to be in China was tantamount to existing within an imaginative construction in which symbols were invested with moral, emotional, and aesthetic power. Where better than in old China was it possible to inhabit Leo Stein's definition of art as nature seen in the light of its formal significance?

And there was more to it than this. Along with a handful of like-minded Westerners, Winter must have felt pioneer's satisfaction of knowing oneself a kind of harbinger, a harbinger of a new consciousness that could cunningly weave together the strands of two alien cultures, and by that interweaving point, toward a third that was to come. For such as these, there was the joy of a world washed fresh by novelty and of the company of artists and intellectuals who shared one's values and pleasures and hopes. In China, Winter enjoyed the ultimate satisfaction of living purposefully as an agent of an historical process and purpose. China was so obviously becoming, and one's teaching was part of that becoming.

Of course, those joys and satisfactions were shattered by war. Now living in China meant contending with occupying armies and the collapse of institutions. It meant witnessing and suffering physical and emotional outrage. It meant seeing one's students and one's friends killed violently or daily sink lower into hunger, endless suffering and travail. It meant the violation of the very fabric of things which makes culture possible and the reduction of human society to the diminished humanity of survival. It meant learning to live with terror. It meant, oddly, experiencing that downward spiritual journey that the Greeks called *nykeia*, and that is so central to Western literature. King Lear, in his forced stripping of himself down to the condition of "poor naked, unaccommodated man," is a prime example.

Given the choice—and, again, Winter enjoyed strong enough connections in America to have a choice—why did he not gladly turn his back on all this and come home to the native land in which he could at least know some physical security, some promise, so certain that it did not even have to be uttered, that his life could not at any moment be snuffed out by some act of sudden brute violence? For that is what he had decided to do, and it was to explain his decision that he wrote this second letter to Richards just a few weeks before America was drawn into the war.[33]

Winter's first reason for remaining in China was that he had been treated there with a courtesy he could not count on in any other part of the world. By joining the OIC in Kunming, he had forfeited both the furlough and pension privileges he had acquired by twelve years active service and two years partial service as the caretaker of Tsinghua property. Yet, though they were under no formal obligation to him, each year the university sent to him a contract offering him the same salary as the president (US$370 a year), which he regularly refused.

What mattered to Winter in this was the quality of Chinese kindness. When he arrived in Kunming just a year before, with $638 in Nationalist currency in his pocket and no position, Tsinghua president Mei invited Winter to live in his house at his expense—an offer Winter did not accept. But he was sure that if he returned to Lianda, "they would find means, in some roundabout Chinese way, of keeping me from starving while saving my face. It is certain that China is the only country where I could count on any such thing, and this knowledge partly compensates for the disadvantages of living here."

Winter's deep appreciation of the justly fabled courtesy of the Chinese, however, only partly accounted for his reluctance to leave Kunming. As he told Richards, there were other reasons, "hard to define and still harder for anyone to understand, why an old man near sixty should not be more appalled at the prospect of ending his days without a bathtub or a good library, or without satisfying his curiosity about his country which he has not seen for eighteen years, than at other things which might befall him." It was here that he remembered Gide's Séquestrée de Poitiers, who, rescued, resisted the room in which she'd been imprisoned for twenty years. What was the source of such an attitude in her—and in him. "Is it conditioning," he wondered.

Or is it some dramatic instinct which makes me fear the dullness of an orderly world? Or is it that on the rough canvas of these lower physical levels one is spared the finicky lines of useless worries at the corners of the mouth and eyes? Or is it mere vanity? My weekly lecture on poetry which I am donating to Lien Ta this year has had to move constantly to larger and larger halls to accommodate the crowds, including large numbers of the teaching staff. Or sheer funk at having fallen eighteen years behind the times and at the effort required to sweep the cobwebs from the brain? Or a secret horror of becoming American in the sense of what one hears over the radio? Or fear that literature would cease to mean as much in more favorable surroundings? Let a T. S. Eliot spend a few months here and he might find that he had a really good reason to get religion. Is it a contagious fatalism?

> God's deep decree
> Bitter would have me taste; my taste was me.

Or, if you like, some brand of mysticism? To save them from their typical cynical detachment, when they came to me for advice I have sent out the best of these young people. They have had their flesh beaten to ribbons, their fingernails pulled out, their testicles twisted off with pincers. Some have been thrown into a pit of starving dogs. Some have come crawling back, unable for the rest of their lives to do anything but beat their heads against the floor and beg for mercy. Some of them you know. You should see Lu Pao Tung's body, and he got off lightly. Leighton Stuart, Pettus, Bradfield, Mac Fisher, we all have their blood on our hands. But after that, to go on sending them out with cyanide in their pockets implies a ruthlessness and a ferocity hard to understand if you have not lived in this country since the war, which is reduced to such a pitch of tragic extremity that the living defenders are literally kept alive with soup brewed from the marrow of their dead fellows' bones. Can one walk out on them after that, before the show is over, no matter how dishonest and callous many of them may be?

Born an alien to his native country, Winter had become a patriotic citizen of the country of suffering. He was ready to claim as fellows such *miserables* as Séquestrée de Poitiers, whose story Gide reported from a true case. The woman, whose name was Mélanie Bastian, was sequestered by her family for about twenty-five years in a windowless room. A brother visited her daily without his conscience bothering him, though she was covered with filth and vermin. The mother and son were later indicted, then released on bail. A commentator on Gide's version of the story said that the story was enough to illustrate an observation Gide had made in *The Counterfeiters*: "All you need is to pile up a number of simple facts to get a whole that is monstrous."

So there it was again. Winter had fallen out of one symbolic whole—traditional Confucian culture—into another. He had sought a meaningful world that only imaginative constructions can provide, but the deep structure of that world had turned out to be not that of a romantic paradise but of a modernist wasteland in which, unlike Mélanie, he chose to be sequestered.

It was not often that Winter provided such privileged glimpses of his own motives. Winter's reference to Gide's story is illuminating in the context of his deep identification with the underdog. He express that attachment first when, a boy of four, he refused to admire his uncle who went out West to fight the Indians. He identified himself back then, as he did now, with those who suffered and were cast away. In Confucian terms, that identity was the undercloak that only occasionally showed through the cloak he presented to the world's eyes. But it was because he wore it that Winter could witness the interior of Chinese suffering.

CHAPTER NINE:
THE END OF THE OIC

In a postscript to the letter in which he stated to Richards his reasons for wishing to remain in China, Winter also voiced his anger and frustration: "I suppose I have sufficiently expressed my surprise and disappointment that we are not to be allowed to use the unexpended balance through 1942-43. This was the chief point in my recent letters, but curiously enough neither you nor Stevens have answered directly." That was in November 1941. In March 1942, Winter still had heard nothing. His letter to Richards in March is again uncharacteristically plaintive: "I was expecting an answer about the time war broke out in the Pacific, but nothing has ever come. I continue to send letters in the hope that something may get through to you."[1]

While Winter waited for news and wondered which if any of his letters had gotten through, Dr. Balfour had visited Kunming twice—in the uncharacteristic role of Winter's supporter. On the second visit, the two men together conferred with the provincial commissioner of education, and "after a few minutes conversation" Kung promised to contribute in support of the school NC $3,000 a month—about twice the 1,700 that he had promised earlier—starting in July. So the Rockefeller Foundation had everything that it wanted. The new allotment from Yunnan would take care of all expenses except such extras as printing—and Winter's salary, which, it was understood, was the Foundation's responsibility. By taking over the basic funding of the OIC school, the commissioner had certified that the project was a success.

Of course, there was still Winter's case. Balfour, shocked to discover that prices in Kunming were double New York prices, promised to wire Stevens a proposal that the school be allowed to use the balance of the fund. Kung promised to send a similar wire. But for all this upbeat busyness, Winter was still hanging. His own financial standing in the community, he mentioned to Richards, was "something like that of our servants in the old Peking Days."

His mood that March was dark. Kunming now enjoyed air protection—with the outbreak of war between the U.S. and Japan, the Flying Tigers had become the USAF China Air Task Force, of which Chennault was again in command—and the Japanese raids had stopped. But there had been little improvement in general conditions. The Burma Road had been cut by the Japanese, and Winter could not see how anything could be gotten into the city "from now on, although they talk of sending supplies from Assam through upper Burma by mule." Nonmilitary supplies of gasoline were already exhausted. This made very bleak the possibility that the city might have to be evacuated.

Winter's old friend Bob Drummond had managed to get to Kunming as head of the American Red Cross there. But on the first day after his arrival, before the raids had stopped, Drummond suffered a Kunming baptism when "he was spattered with the blood of four hundred casualties near a bridge at the East gate but was not hurt." A little later, his leg was broken by a truck. It was not mending well. "Do you think it is possible to die of discouragement?"[2] Winter asked Richards.[3]

From the States, only silence. The Rockefeller Foundation in New York seemed to have forgotten the much-beleaguered Winter. Unable to tell him what he wanted to hear, for the time they were telling him nothing at all. What was there to say, except that, whether or not the OIC continued, Winter would not continue with it? But Winter still clung to some last thread of hope that he might remain in China with Rockefeller Foundation support.

Moving between the two points of view—the Foundation's in New York and Winter's in Kunming—is dizzying. Mail was slow and delivery uncertain. So by the time news arrived at one end, the situation at the other might have—probably had—changed completely. Reading this correspondence one is reminded of our own pioneer days, when a Westering mother like Narcissa Whitman received birth gifts for her child a year after the child had died.

What remained constant is that for much of 1942 and well into 1943 Winter's situation was desperate. Inflation compounded at such precipitous rates that it is difficult to get a fix on prices at a given moment, but in November 1942 Winter told Richards: "We are almost at the breaking point because of prices." A pound of bad tea cost US$50, of coffee, $200, a hat would set one back $500, shoes $1,000. "The most indifferent mechanic in the AEF would turn up his nose at a meal that could be got for less than $200," Winter said, then added: "I feel that I am being extravagant if I pay $20." Powdered milk cost $120 a pound, but despite that, in the university, babies that had been born within the last six months were dying of malnutrition.[4]

So when, in April 1942, Winter received a letter from Stevens that began unblushingly: "This is a word of encouragement at a time when you will doubtless welcome it," the comfort offered was cold. Stevens admired the progress Winter had made "under the greatest difficulties," and he "intended" to have the committee of his trustees "pass upon the recommendation in behalf of the Orthological Institute of China at their meeting on May 20th." If their decision were favorable, he would then see the comptroller about transmitting the funds that remained in the account—US$783.68, after deducting the $1,000 sent to Winter by cable on December 31 (his birthday) in order to keep him afloat.[5] The letter did not, and probably was not intended to, give Winter very much to hang on to.

A month later, word from Richards came through. He had received Winter's November 1941 letters and had answered them, like Stevens, "giving what news and cheer" he could. But his answers had never been delivered, and it was not until May that he could untangle the mess for Winter. When he did, his news and comfort offered no more warmth than Stevens's had. To be sure, like Stevens, Richards offered kind words: Winter's work was "getting recognized as an important contribution etc. to the allied doings by several Gov't Agencies."[6] But although Stevens had long ago agreed to allow the use of the balance of the fund to keep the provincial English-training school in Kunming open until June 1943, Richards had been unable to get him and the board of trustees to expedite that action or even to inform Winter that it had been decided upon.

That spring, Richards was in Burbank working at Walt Disney Productions, where he was "making a Basic teaching film to demonstrate the possibilities." (Over his letter to Winter was the logo of grinning Mickey Mouse, his arms outspread in exuberance and trust). The Disney Studios in Burbank, Richards said, was a nice place to hide in, and the hills looked "amazingly" like the Western Hills outside Peking. Who can imagine what Winter made of the logo? Or, for that matter, of the news that while Richards was in Washington, visiting agencies from which he sought support for new projects and for old, he had bumped into two old comrades-in-arms, Raymond and Dorothy Jameson. Jameson, he said—with perhaps a touch of venom for a former supporter who had turned his back on the Yunnan project because he believed that no work could any longer get done there—was "climbing up very successfully in the Library of Congress—training young librarians in research."[7] Richards's new interest in cartoon teaching films must have seemed to Winter a little bizarre, against his own situation comprised of hunger, disease, and death.

The committee of Rockefeller trustees did meet in mid-May 1943, five days earlier than Stevens had said they would, and they resolved to make available the balance of approximately $1,700 that they estimated would remain on June 30, this to "be used for salary of Mr. Winter and for incidentals." But "incidentals" aside, if and when the money was transferred, it could not last Winter long and was intended only as a stopgap.

By August, Winter had only enough cash on hand to get himself and the staff through to the end of the month. American cigarettes were US$10 a piece, and an electric bulb could go for anything from $300 to $500. The military situation was also precarious, and if things got worse, everyone was prepared "to start walking northeast as there is no gasoline for trucks" (once earlier, in AD 1253, most of the population of Yunnan province had fled on foot, that time to the west and south, from the advancing armies of Kublai Khan). But though the Japanese had penetrated as far as the Salween River, just two hundred miles to the west of Kunming, since they had been there at the Indo-Chinese border for two years, 'there seems to be no reason for alarm.'"[8]

Winter had taken such steps as he could in his own behalf by signing a new contract with Lianda. While he was engaged with the OIC he had, at his own urging, not drawn a salary from the university but instead had delivered a series of lectures on poetry as a kind of donation. But the new salary was only US$52 a month (purchasing power US$13), an amount on which even his Chinese colleagues were unable to keep body and soul alive. Winter was about to expose himself more deeply than before to the starvation and disease that afflicted so many of his Chinese colleagues. He had already sacrificed his comforts by his choice to stay in China. But before the prospect of taking upon himself such suffering as the Chinese endured, even Winter must have quailed.

My account of this period in Kunming emphasizes grim questions of survival to the exclusion of other matters. That is so because of the kinds of documents available to me for this period. Sometimes I have to remind myself that in the midst of the drama, and the ennui, brought on by war and inflation, Winter continued to lead a daily life. An aging man (chronologically, at least) of fifty-five, he walked through these ancient streets crowded with black and white markets and marketeers, with refugees and soldiers of several armies; he ate meals, however bad most of them may have been, saw friends, gave popular lectures, kept up with business, and even read books.

That November, he told Richards that he had seen

> a copy of Empson's poems yesterday (the second volume). Was amused at the apologetic tone in the notes on the Chinese poems . . . . In Bacchus he seems to have gone over the deep edge. The puns which are supposed to produce the opposite effect to the vague imagery of the romantics are often so special to Empson's mind that he comes right back to romantic vagueness by another route. Or am I old fashioned?[9]

Probably, though the letters I have provide scant documentation, he continued the sorts of unromantic pleasures he had shared with John Blofeld in the House of Springtime Congratulations with the prostitutes who could provide entertainments not confined to sex.[10] Even in Kunming, though perhaps in rougher fashion, such pleasures were available. Shortly before his death, Pollard-Urquhart told Empson how dull life had become since his departure:

> I have not done any opium since that time with you, and have been living a blameless existence. I hope to get rid of some of it in Hanoi, and I imagine that as soon as Bob Winter comes here I shall find out the hidden life of Kunming. He has that perverse quality that immediately scents out the wicked quarters, like an old soldier smelling out the places where he can get drunk.

But the times had darkened, and whatever success Winter may still have had in pursuing his pleasures, money remained a concern. In November 1942, he finally received a notice from the Bank of China that US$1,000 had been transferred to them by cable for his account;

but once transferred to the bank, the sum, intended to sustain Winter for seven months, shrunk to $400, which wouldn't last a month. Had the drafts gone directly to him, he could have roof converted them on the black market at almost twice the official rate. Balfour had written in the margin, "A questionable procedure." In the meantime, he had already lived for "at least a fortnight" on the sum he'd obtained for his Wabash Phi Beta Kappa key and would try to live by borrowing or from the sale of (his)_ things since the $400 "is almost of no use." [11]

Back in August, Winter had written to Stevens a long letter full of vivid information about the situation in Kunming.[12] Letters like this made Stevens think that whatever else he had in Winter, he had in him an extraordinarily vivid and dependable reporter on events in Kunming. Stevens had not yet begun to circulate Winter's letters among Rockefeller officials, including Foundation president Raymond B. Fosdick or, for that matter, among State Department officials, such as Charles A. Thomson or Willys R. Peck of the Division of Cultural Relations, but he soon would. Rockefeller officials, like anyone else in these avenues of power, were interested in having getting news they could not find in the newspapers. It helped them plan. For example, accounts like Winter's of the terrible situation of the cream of China's northern intellectuals, now drawn together in Lianda, later encouraged the Foundation to lend aid in their support. For a number of reasons then, the opportunity to have a man in the field who could report back to the home office not just on teaching conditions but on general conditions began to seem attractive.

What Winter's August letter also disclosed is that Kunming had become a refugee center for the whole Chinese population of Burma and West Yunnan, territories now fallen to the Japanese. Some of these people who, in Winter's words, "were dumped on our heads," had walked for months, "eating roots and grasses."

> When Pao Shan [a district capital some 400 miles to the west by road] was bombed two months ago, four thousand people were killed in the space of five minutes and the rest of the population started running in this direction. Refugees who were fortunate enough to get on trucks have told me that the road was so strewn with the dead and the dying that their skulls popped under the tires of the trucks racing along the road. They brought cholera with them. We have reduced the number of cases to about three hundred in Kunming proper, but the

disease is spreading rapidly through the country districts, where there is no control. The streets are lined with refugees offering for sale the last garment which they can decently strip off their emaciated bodies. They are given a small amount of rice each day by the central government. The local government does nothing for them.

Ironically, despite the chaos and squalor that reigned over the city in the late summer of 1942, the presence of the AEF (as Winter old-fashionedly called the American Voluntary Group, now replaced by the American Air Force) protected the people in Kunming, who had not been bombed in more than nine months, but it proved bad luck for the school. The owners of the building that Winter's people were using as a schoolhouse had decided to return to the Kunming and had given the Basic people notice for August 30. Because of this, the commissioner had given them NC$10,000 to repair and rebuild the bombed school in the compound where the Institute had its offices. But the repairs would cost at least $16,000, and Winter was trying—unsuccessfully so far—to raise the difference.

Everything was for sale in Kunming. GIs stood on street corners selling a range of government-issued commodities. It was possible to buy a jeep on these street corners. With several currencies floating about and a flood of modern gadgets breaking into the economy of a previously sleepy provincial town, the opportunities for fast profits were unlimited. Unfortunately, these benefits did not extend to the teachers and students at the university who suffered terribly. Witnesses on this question sometimes disagree, it is true. Though John Fairbank and Winter both reported the dangerous malnutrition of many Lianda professors and their families, Balfour recommended to Foundation president Raymond Fosdick that he "be skeptical of alarming stories that the health of important groups of Chinese educators are suffering." And stoic Chinese with whom I have spoken tend also to take the line that it was not as bad as all that.

In Winter's view, all of the other classes "were profiteering outrageously and nothing is being done to stop them." American troops with American salaries, along with the enormous quantities of military equipment ranging from arms to clothing and food, had completely disoriented the economy of Kunming. But the drunken economy that was benefiting so many was not benefiting scholars and students. Winter did not think "anyone connected with the schools had tasted meat for the last six months." Not only had President Mei of Lianda sent his daughters out to work, but his wife had "disguised herself by using her maiden name and got a place teaching the children of a local official." Unfortunately, she was found out and dismissed, "on the ground that it was not dignified for the wife of the President to teach."[13]

Food prices in August 1942 were ten times what they had been when Winter arrived not two years earlier. So while those intellectuals who remained in Kunming enjoyed a freedom that they could not know anywhere else in the country, they paid a high price for it. And eventually, it would become clear that the Guomindang deliberately kept this intelligentsia in dire straits in the hope that they could thus be more easily controlled.

As for Western civilians, they were pulling out. Professor Hughes, head of the Oxford Chinese Department, had just gone to India for treatment of the stomach condition he had developed "as a result of our diet of rice, red pepper, and tea." Hughes had intended to stay a year but had lasted only a few months. Even Pollard-Urquhart's brother-in-law Prideaux-Brune, who had lived through the worst the Japanese could hurl down, was "unable to stand it any longer and has asked to be transferred to India."

Winter ended this black letter with a grim picture of his state and his staffs:

> I suppose there is no need for me to enlarge upon the difficult conditions under which we are working. We are crowded, underfed; servants, students, and faculty are all mixed up together and we have to climb over ruins to get in and out of the school. "Infinite squalor in a little room!" John Fairbanks [sic] of Harvard, who is now attached to the American Embassy in some cultural relations capacity, has visited our school and something might come from that direction in the course of time. We used to live in terror of the constant bombing. Now I pray for the town to be bombed so that prices will come down. I started this letter on my own typewriter, but got tired of pushing the carriage back and forth by hand, as the spring is broken, and have come over to finish the letter on the school typewriter. A new spring would cost NC$3000![14]

Winter and his friends and colleagues were "almost at the breaking point because of prices . . . . Of course, people of my age can go on almost indefinitely eating any old thing or nothing, but I suppose that there is a limit. And there doesn't seem to be any solution. Everyone who could has cleared out." Winter didn't sound confident that even he could hold out much longer.

But there remained opportunities to take intellectual nourishment. Just before Christmas 1942, Joseph Needham, who would later revolutionize Western understanding of Chinese science and technology, had come to Kunming as a kind of cultural ambassador. Richards had given him a letter of introduction to Winter (Needham, he said, was "one of the most interesting and encyclopedic people there are"), and Needham and Winter became good friends. It was Needham's presence in Kunming that got Winter to thinking about how much better the British represented their culture abroad than we did: they sent men like Needham; we sent GIs. In this he echoed John Fairbanks's similar complaint to the State Department.

But on Christmas Day 1942, his fifty-fifth birthday not a week off, Winter could actually say: "Everything is going well." Through Richards's arranging, the British Embassy had come through with £100, with some hint of more to follow. Winter and his staff had collected from wealthy Yunnanese NC$20,000, with the promise of $30,000 to come. In the light of the contributions coming in it looked as if "the school would be on its feet when I drop out next June."[15]

There were other bright spots and Winter's mood lightened. Wu Fuheng had been asked to take charge of all the English teaching in Yunnan provincial university, and Grace Boynton had written for help in using Basic at Yenching University, though Winter was not in a position to give her anything more than advice. He was excited and pleased that the American ambassador had asked for five Chinese professors to go to America for a year and that the universities had made their selection, of which he clearly approved. (Soon there would be a struggle between Balfour, who recommended that American aid should be targeted primarily to those who now held positions of power in the academy and people such as Fairbank and Winter, who wanted help to go to those scholars who most needed it. Beneath the surface was the debate over whether to support those academics who remained loyal to Chiang Kai-shek's Guomindang and the larger group who, because they did not, were already being subjected to special economic pressures.)

And Winter began to sound like Winter again. He was about to direct a school play, a task that always put him in good humor. He had also resumed gardening and kept animals, including gibbons. This may have been under the influence of R. H. van Gulik, who visited him late in 1942 with a letter of introduction from Richards, and became a close friend. Van Gulik had written about a variety of Oriental subjects. It happened that one of his books was *The Gibbon in China*, which included, attached to its back cover, a forty-five-rpm record of the "Morning calls of a Hylobates Agillis, female, 3 1/2 years old." Van Gulik demonstrated that "for about two thousand years the gibbon played an important role in Chinese art and letters, inspiring great writers and gifted artists to impressive creations." Van Gulik also held that throughout East Asia, the gibbon proved himself a staunch friend and affectionate companion to many grown-ups and to many more children.

Before or after he met Van Gulik, Winter apparently subscribed to that belief, but his gibbon—out of some accident of genes or trauma of upbringing—grew up to be what John Fairbank described as "a fierce biting beast [that] would have to be shot by an intruder."[16] Winter seems to have wanted him that way since he had been much plagued by thieves and intended the gibbon to earn its keep by performing as a watch monkey.

I got a firsthand impression of the biting beast from Bob Drummond's former Chinese secretary. In those days, Winter lived in a bombed-out compound, alone with a woman servant. "Most people would not like to live in that place," my informant told me. "Winter kept a fearful monkey, very big," probably a gibbon. Winter had "brought the monkey to school once, and he got angry. He was very quick to get angry." (As I listened, I thought that it was Winter who got angry; but thinking back, I see that my informant meant the monkey or perhaps both of them. It was popularly understood that there was an identity between the two.) On the occasion in question, Winter, with the ape on his shoulder, had come to a university official to complain about something, and he and the ape had both misbehaved by not remaining tranquil. When they left, the official remarked, "There go two monkeys, the big one with the little one on his shoulder."

Sometimes Winter let the monkey go free during the day. Once, when a Guomindang soldier was about to shoot the gibbon out of a tree, probably for dinner, Winter pulled his pistol and disarmed the soldier. But eventually, the monkey bit a professor badly in the leg, and Winter had to get rid of it. Even he was becoming afraid of it. But he could not find anyone who would take it until finally a Dr. Tang, who lived in the western mountains, said that he would. So Drummond and Winter and the man who told me this story drove out there in a jeep, but the doctor took one look at the monkey and changed his mind. Finally, there was nothing left but to let the monkey off his chain. When Winter returned to the scene a half hour later, the monkey was gone and was never heard of again.

Though for the moment life was stirring in and around Winter, even in such relatively tranquil moments, he could hear the cries of pain that still went up all around him. Skepper and Corin Bernfeld, mutual friends of Richards and Winter who had run the Voice of Democracy in Shanghai before the war started, had tried to escape from Shanghai in the past spring. When the Japanese caught them, they were taken back to prison and terribly beaten. "Skepper was put on the exchange ship half dead. Corin killed herself only ten days before the ship came which would have taken her back to England."[17]

Winter closed the letter with "Christmas greetings to yourself and Dorothea," words that, given their context, must have inspired a hush in the Richards whenever it was that they read them. It was December 1942 when the words were written and mailed. The world was at war, and tidings of comfort and joy were not easy to come by.

*   *   *

In February 1943, the executive committee of the Rockefeller Foundation recommended an appropriation of $7,500 to the Orthological Institute to support its work for the period ending on December 31, 1943. Compared with the budget of $9,600 appropriated for the entire fiscal year of July 1, 1940, to January 30, 1941, part of which was still unspent, this might seem a generous increase, but there had been a fourfold rise in living costs. In recommending the appropriation of the money, the executive committee, despite their enthusiasm for what the Institute had already accomplished, admitted to uncertainty about its actual needs. "As a result of difficulties of communication with China, the officers have no definite statement of the present needs of the work of the Institute."[18]

Three days before the committee passed the allocation proposal, David Stevens wanted to be certain that in granting Winter the $7,500 six-month allotment and the $600 monthly salary, the officers of the committee had considered three points. First, the sum was equivalent to what the State Department provided in salary and maintenance in China for John Fairbank. And Fairbank was a married man. "Winter is there, used to short rations, and single." Second, Stevens wondered how far the money actually would go in Kunming: "The exchange is less significant, I suppose, than the purchasing power of what the $7,500 yields in China. If discounted 100 to 1, to yield $75 U.S., it sounds weird to American ears to say 'go ahead'; but if that sum would feed Winter for six months, the investment is realistic."

Finally, in the draft version of the allocation proposal, Stevens complained,

> The option to bring Winter home is not dealt with unless funds are set up: and for future relations with the Chinese, we should have Winter's advice in detail, given orally, before we set him loose in this country. Obviously to do that much—see him here for our own ends and for his own security—is about the lowest zero in what we should do after Winter's term of work.

John Marshall had written at the top of the document, in the space provided for comments: "I have written DHS [Stevens] that all these points have been covered, and that I quite agree with the decision taken." But when Winter sent a cable asking for "a priority for flying," Balfour replied that the prospect was unlikely.

The allocation of $7,500 was proposed on February 19. Marshall, in New York, cabled to Balfour: "further support Orthological Institute appears futile under present exchange. Only alternative to maintain Winter's support seems to bring him home for consultation if you can arrange." [19] By early March, Balfour, from New Delhi, began to discuss with Winter the question of transportation. It was not quickly resolved. Winter had sent him a cable, stating: "if a new grant should go USA immediately for consultation. Can you help me priority for flying?" But Balfour replied that he considered either prospect unlikely. [20]

While the possibility of flying Winter to the States simmered on the back burner, a kind of countercurrent was stirring. George B. Cressey, head of the American Cultural Relations Program in Kunming, urged the importance of an active cultural relations program in China. Such a program, Cressey urged, was an aspect of "The Good Neighbor policy of giving the best of our culture to others," and as such, that policy "is both a gesture of good will and a means of national security." But there was also another aspect: "In a more selfish sense, Cultural Relations has a second goal, that of equipping us with the vital information and experts needed for international trade, for the education of public opinion, and especially for the conflict which ensues when diplomacy fails and war ensues."[21]

It was part of Cressey's notion that as part of a Cultural Relation program in China, there should regularly be several dozen people from the Department of State in training there. Some would be assigned to intensive language study and the assimilation of Chinese life. Others with slightly less language study might specialize on Chinese universities in order to supply ratings of them in connection with students going abroad. Still, others would have a thorough grasp of natural resources and industrial productivity. The entire range of human affairs is appropriate subject matter. After the initial period of four or five years, some might remain in China while others would return to America and leave the Department of State with the status of reserve officers, to be called when needed. They would then be employed by export houses as university professors, as consultants to the Chinese government, or as cultural attachés. These appointments should become a new type of career men, devoting their life to the understanding of a problem or an area, with alternate residence at home and abroad.

John Fairbank lent his own strong support to the proposed program. Fairbank, who, with his wife, was doing cultural work in China for the State Department, argued (against Balfour's best judgment): "The Chinese themselves will take care of the development of western technology in this country, unless they find that westerners will take care of it for them." What American foundations and agencies could do to be the greatest help to China was "to encourage Chinese social thinking," and a way to do that would be to bring to the States' Chinese candidates for study in the social sciences.[22]

Already by March 1943, the idea of Winter's serving in China as a specialist in the Division of Cultural Relations, whether under the auspices of the Rockefeller Foundation or—an idea John Fairbank has discussed with him in Kunming—under the auspices of the State Department, had been floated. Predictably, Balfour had done what he could to sink it: "In view of Winter's status," he wrote to Marshall, "I doubt if compensation is reasonable on the basis of a specialist from the

Division of Cultural Relations."[23] Winter, after all, enjoyed no academic prestige outside China and the office of the Rockefeller Foundation and Balfour, as we have seen, was a great believer in such credentials.

Winter wanted only to remain in Kunming, but with less precarious support than what the Rockefeller Foundation was willing to provide. Perhaps the State Department support John Fairbank had discussed with him would materialize. There had even been some talk about his working for the U.S. Army, lecturing to the troops about the culture they had been dropped into. But on March 9, 1943, Winter still hung on to the bird in his hand, however scrawny: the surest way to remain in China led through New York. Reviewing the situation for Balfour, he concluded from recent statements by Richards and Stevens "that New York does not wish to let the project go under, but is not willing to pour large sums of money into a place which is suffering from such inflation." Winter's recent reports about funds that he had been able to obtain from the commissioner, from wealthy Yunnanese, and from the British Embassy had led the Foundation to think that by talking the situation over with Winter, they might find a way "to keep things going through the difficult present times with a small expenditure on their part, while waiting for better times to come." Winter thought he could make them see that this was possible, and he requested that Balfour cable them his approval of the trip.[24] Winter had not said directly to Balfour, but he had certainly nonetheless made clear that he hoped the offer to bring him home for consultation implied, sending him back to Kunming regardless of how the consultation went. He was not sure that he would "want to stay in the US indefinitely," and he understood that it was "not possible to get back without giving very good reasons."[25]

There were still other complications in this almost comical situation. Winter was now teaching at the Southwest Associated University (Lianda). If New York approved of the trip, would they want him to start at once in March? Because that would involve his losing several months of teaching, it required that they arrange for his transportation by air. In that way, he could return to Lianda early enough in the summer to make up the lost time. Otherwise, he thought it fairer to finish the semester in seven weeks by doubling lectures "and starting towards the end of April." Winter's sense of obligation to Lianda, which had come up before in reference to the kindness of President Mei, ran deep. He had been with them for eighteen years, and they were very short of teachers. "The money I had received from them since September has made it possible to keep the wolf out, though I have often heard him snarling outside my door."

Even now in a state of anxiety about readjusting after twenty years to what would be virtually a new culture to which he felt no personal attachment, he asked Richards to remind the Foundation "that the amount they would pay for my passage would—added to what I could get from Lien Ta—keep me for another year." A month in the USA might be welcome, he said, after so long an absence, but it would hardly be worth the cost: he would have to sell all his things, including "all his lecture notes, etc."—everything that gave him ballast as a scholar. No, it would be better for him to stay at least six months or a year, "but then my chances of getting back would be smaller all the time."

Underlying it all was also a sour note we have heard before and will hear again: "Judging from the samples which have been sent out here, I might not be very happy there. Recently, the Red Cross has sent out three rather silly girls all the way by air to 'comfort' the soldiers. They have cars, visit and get drunk with anything that has a lot of gold braid on its shoulders, and spend at least US$200 a day on gasoline. In fact, all the Americans here are shrewd in business, and they have good opportunities." Of course he excluded himself from the category "all Americans." Had he been shrewd in business, he would could have afforded the course of sulphathyazole the doctor advised him to take during a recent illness. But the pills cost $50 apiece, and the full course would have cost him $10,000. So he did not take the pills, but he did not die.

As late as April 22, 1943, Winter was still desperately dragging his feet. He told Balfour that he had misgivings about returning to the States. He was still willing to go back, and it might be "better for me to return to the USA," but "for the sake of the project, it would be better sense for me to struggle on here for another year."[26] His argument—especially when we consider that he has now been batting the issues back and forth for the better part of sixteen months—shows high anxiety. As much as he would prefer to stay in Kunming, no alternative funding had materialized, and it seemed more and more unlikely that the Foundation would do anything more for him unless he went to New York:

> I don't know what sum has been allocated for my travel, but I feel that in case I return to China, the amount spent for the round trip would keep me here for about a year. If the project is to be kept up, my long absence would be harmful, as a

number of students have announced their decision to leave the school in case I go away. Moreover, I should have to sell all of my things as there is no way to store them, and I could not replace them on my return. If I am not successful in persuading the Foundation to make any sort of grant, I might not be able to return to China even on my own resources, as I understand permissions are hard to obtain except by persons doing war work. I ought to go to the USA, if only because I have been away so long, but after twenty years here to pull up stakes and go back to stay is a decision that requires some thought.

The prospect of returning to the States seemed more distressing to him than, say, that of being bayoneted in the belly by a Japanese soldier. At the same time, he did not wish to find himself in China without a Western sponsor, and he was determined to avoid that nakedness if he could.

On May 18, John Fairbank's wife, Wilma, entered the act. Herself a scholar who, with her husband, had spent much time working in China, Mrs. Fairbank wrote a cover letter to Stevens with which she included copies of letters from her husband and Winter. She concluded from these letters that "Bob wants very much to remain in Kunming and that his remaining there will continue to support the morale of the academic group with which he is associated at this time, when the Government and various organizations interested in China are spending thousands of dollars to send individuals from this country into China for that very purpose."[27]

The enclosed letter from Winter to John Fairbank, written April 11, 1943, reiterated the now-familiar arguments. Winter supposed that the RF hesitated "to let the project go on the rocks and leave him stranded there" but that at the same time they were "not willing to put money into a place which is suffering from such inflation." If he went back, he thought he might be able to persuade them to keep things going for another year. If that failed, they might make him "a proposition to stay in the States and do something else." In either case, he would be "wasting valuable time" and neglecting his real work, which was in Kunming: "If they don't make a grant, I run the risk of not getting back. I feel that I am best fitted to do the thing that I am now doing, and I don't really want to go home. If I thought that there was any possibility of getting a small subsidy to eke out my salary from Lianda, I should plan to stay here."

It was apropos of this last that he was writing Fairbank. Was there "any possible hope" of his getting a small government subsidy to help him "to carry on here?" It needn't be much, he added, because he lived "on much the same standard" as his Chinese colleagues. But if such a grant proved unlikely, he would "be forced to dispose of all my things and take a lone trip which may be to no purpose." [28]

The excerpt from John Fairbank's letter, dated September 21, 1943, paints a different but equally affecting picture:

> We then found Bob Winter, who is 58 years old and looks as spruce as ever. He has a new suite in a temple which is being rebuilt into a middle school. Wu Fuheng works on English teaching in the school under the provincial commission of education and Bob runs the Orthological Institute in conjunction with it. In air raids his clothes have been completely stolen twice and he now has a pair of monkeys in the yard, one of whom is a fierce biting beast and would have to be shot by an intruder. He has a courtyard full of flowers and a book-case full of books, and knows all the ins and outs of local folklore and gossip. Every Saturday or more often Bob Drummond exercises his recently broken leg by walking in from his Red Cross headquarters on the other edge of town. They both see something of the Tsinghua faculty, who of course esteem Winter; you remember his single-handed defense of the University against the Japs. But aside from them and the consulate, life is pretty lonely. Winter took us to a Chinese restaurant which served delicious food in a hole in the wall place for $90 for the three of us, very cheap. We took him. He is down to a couple of months' savings and has wired Richards for help in straightening out the deal with Rockfound by which Bob thought he would be supported. We both are amazed at his enthusiasm and morale; he is lively in thought and vigorous in comment and a godsend to the Tsinghua group.[29]

It is a wonderful, sunlit picture of a man enduring with admirable spirit.

Stevens was grateful to Mrs. Fairbank for writing, and he invited her to talk the matter over with Charles Thomson, at the time her boss in the State Department Division of Cultural Relations. As for the Foundation's position, Stevens did not see how he could "recommend any term support for the teaching of English in China by aid to training of teachers." But he did believe that Winter could "show how American agencies can work with Chinese agencies, even in these difficult days." Besides, "we should get a great deal of general advice by having him here. It is not a question of aid for one year but aid for a program."[30]

Stevens was interested in following up on the possibility that Winter himself had opened with his letter to Fairbank. Perhaps the State Department could take care of him. "The specific points raised by the Winter letter are whether or not the Division's funds will go to the training of teachers in any general subjects for duty in China and whether they will give help to surveys of advisors with the standing of Winter."

He wrote to Thomson on the same day that he wrote to Mrs. Fairbank, and he got a prompt reply. It seemed to Thomson that "the correspondence arising out of this subject indicates that more frequent consultation between the Division of Cultural Relations and the Foundation in developing their respective programs in China would be profitable." As it happened, the budget for the division's work in China in the fiscal year 1944 was to be decided within the next two or three weeks, and Thomson was apparently willing to write in something for Winter if Stevens could come down soon to talk about it: "If you plan to come to Washington after new funds for the Division's work in China have been allocated, I hope you will find it possible to set aside a time to talk with officers of the Division connected with work in China, with a view to a better mutual acquaintance with the two programs."[31]

A few days later, Stevens sent a memo with letters to Raymond B. Fosdick, president of the Foundation. One of the letters was Winter's April 13, 1943, letter to Richards, which, Stevens felt, "says a good deal and implies much more than I could learn from him" in letter Winter had sent to him.[32] Stevens put up Winter's name with the names of two or three others as men who could work as field officers to help the Rockefeller Foundation develop "a plan of our own" for China—that is, as men able to "define an RF project." Only two of those he names in addition to Winter come up to the mark. Dr. Balfour, one of those rejected, could not, Stevens thought, "cover our substance for either general or scholarly work in China." All that Stevens asked Fosdick directly was that he approve Marshall's sending a note to Winter, reassuring him that the Rockefeller Foundation would care for him if he came home for one year. But Fosdick's comment, penned in at the top of the letter, was: "I think Winter ought to stay in China as he obviously wants to do. He seems like a rare spirit."

By the end of June, Marshall had decided that, although he thought that "it would be immensely useful to have Winter come back, the Foundation ought to take care of him even if he remained in China by allocating to him $2,500 U.S. in China . . . . I guess the choice ought to rest with him."[33] On the very next day, Richards called Marshall. It was his feeling, Richards said, "that since Winter is willing to return to the United States, advantage should be taken of that willingness to bring him back for consultation. There is no question but that Winter has an extraordinary and penetrating knowledge of education in West China."[34]

It happened that Selskar M. Gunn, Balfour's predecessor as the Rockefeller Foundation's man in Shanghai, now with the Department of State, dropped in to see Marshall while Marshall was still talking to Richards. Gunn said "he should certainly like to have Winter in Washington for a period during his stay, because SMG knew that he and others in the State Department could get a great deal from him." Marshall cabled Balfour that the Rockefeller Foundation would do everything possible to ensure Winter's return to China.

Amid all this speculation about what would be best for Winter and how Winter would best serve the purposes of the RF, it turned out that Winter had already taken matters into his own hands. He had just left Delhi for Bombay when Marshall's cable arrived. As usual, regarding Winter's affairs, Balfour was grumpy: "I must advise that he missed a good sailing at Bombay, apparently by choice and due to sight-seeing although he had ample warning and much effort and cables went into effect for him."

The next sailing was indefinite, so Balfour could not say when Winter would get to New York. "In some respects the man is hopeless," he complained. "He will not answer letters, nor has he acknowledged the Rs 1,500 sent to him at his request. I wish you and Mr. Beal luck in trying to get a clear record of the financial position of the previous grant. In Manila we spent more time on his account than all the rest put together."

For me, at least, this extravagantly elongated struggle to come to a decision about Winter's immediate future constitutes a kind of tribute to his standing as a China expert. At the same time, it poignantly reveals Winter's aching loyalty to his Chinese colleagues and to his teaching there despite all obstacles.

CHAPTER TEN:

BACK IN THE USA

Winter left China in July, but he did not disembark at Terminal Island, California, until October 24, 1943. He'd missed what Balfour called "a good sailing at Bombay, apparently by choice to sightsee, although much effort had gone into getting him an earlier booking."[1] Winter was finally footloose after the severe restraints of life in Kunming. While in Bombay waiting for a boat to take him to the States, he got permission from Stevens (Balfour seems to have been unaware of this) to visit the island of Elephanta in the bay. There, in a low temple cut out of solid granite in the seventh century AD, Winter saw the colossal bust of the Trimurti or Hindu Triad—Shiva, Vishnu, and Brahma—and (as we saw earlier) he was powerfully moved by "the life, the refinement, the subtlety, the balance between realism and the ideal conception, which later Indian sculpture did not always keep, the inevitability of every curve of this gigantic power that seem to make the whole island quiver in response."[2]

The Trimurti was a sharp reminder of what he was about to leave behind in Asia—a balance between the "productive, the sustaining, and the transforming," a balance that holds unperturbed even in the face of grief and loss. Winter had seen this harmony over and over again in people like C, "whose intonation and gestures always [kept] in rhythm like Chuang Tzu's cook, but whose just criticism of the government cut like a knife, and who is feared by the Generalissimo." (The Taoist master described a cook whose knife never needed sharpening because he always cut between the bones.) After this visit, Winter was ready to sail to the USA, leaving behind the balance he admired in the Trimurti.

He arrived in New York on November 10, 1943, and at once, the pace quickened. Just as David Stevens and his Humanities Division had resolved to provide no further support to the OIC project, Basic, along with Richards himself, had come into vogue. The *Saturday Review* reported that the War Department was looking at Basic as a possible means of training recruits whose English was limited, and *Life Magazine*, in October 1943, ran an article on Basic that included a picture of Richards framed by a large board of the stick figures he had learned to draw at Disney studios as a visual aid, but the blockbuster came from England. Winston Churchill arrived at Harvard in September to receive an honorary degree and was obliged to give an address, so Richards remembered the fateful affair—"didn't know what to talk about, so he talked about Basic English."

At the time, Churchill's speech seemed a happy accident. As a result of it, the Harvard establishment, in Richards's words, "fell for Winston very heavily." It was the prime minister's endorsement of Basic English that won for Richards an appointment as university professor. But it was also true, as Empson said years later at a memorial service for Richards at Cambridge University, that Churchill's endorsement of Basic proved "the kiss of death."[3]

What happened was that, in a speech to Harvard University on September 6, 1943, Churchill identified Basic as a tool for the construction of what was to be an agreeable postwar world from the Anglo-American viewpoint. He called upon America to continue to stand "shoulder to shoulder" with Britain—not only to march and strive "at this moment, under the fire of the enemy on the fields of war or in the air, but also in those realms of thought which are consecrated to the rights and dignity of man." The two allies would carry on this noble struggle by preserving, after the war was over, the "smooth-running and immensely powerful machinery" of single-minded cooperation they had achieved as wartime allies—that is, by retaining the war machinery itself. They would thus preserve their lives and liberties until they were quite sure that in the place of weapons, they had "something else to put" that would give them "an equally solid guarantee." Already it was beginning to look as if the end of the war would not be the end of the war. And the continuing struggle would be fought in part through linguistic imperialism.

The prime minister, himself an instance of what could be achieved through Anglo-American crossbreeding, recalled how Bismark "observed toward the close of his life that the most potent factor in human society at the end of the nineteenth century was the fact that the British and

American people spoke the same language." Now Churchill urged, as if in realization of that prophecy, the Anglo-American partners must try to spread the common language "even more widely throughout the globe," and, "without seeking selfish advantage over any," possess themselves "of this invaluable amenity and birthright."

The eventual establishment of English as the world language offered, Churchill said, "far better prizes than taking away other people's provinces or land, or grinding them down in exploitation." The empires of the future, he proclaimed, would be "the empires of the mind," and Basic English was the means through which these empires would be established. So it was a special pleasure to be receiving this honor at Harvard University, "which had done more than any other American university to promote the extension of Basic English." And how happy an example of Anglo-American cooperation it was that "the first work on Basic English was written by two Englishmen," Ivor Richards and C. K. Ogden. As high minded as the speech might have sounded to the casual listener, it contained a poisoned bait: Churchill saw the language project in the framework of weapons, and the speech smacked of a new imperialism.[4]

Even as he listened to it, Richards may have felt uneasy about Churchill's speech. A year earlier, in an essay called "Psychopolitics," which he published in the September 1942 issue of *Fortune* magazine, Richards had addressed the same kinds of global questions that Churchill took up at Harvard. But Richards's essay had not offered itself as an ethnocentric credo. Instead, it conjured up a vision of the future ("to make the spirit faint with wonder and delight") that would be our inheritance, Richards maintained, if only the privileged nations learned to love their countries "not for themselves—and certainly not 'right or wrong'—but as regional embodiments or symbols of the common human effort."

> Which do we Americans, British, Dutch, Russians want most: power, wealth, place, etc. for our own group—however splendid its history or its promise—or a decent world community which can and will guarantee for every group and every individual a just equality of opportunity? If we cannot answer this elementary question in psychopolitics, no international machinery will keep us from future wars fought in still more dreadful modes.

Richards genuinely—hindsight would add naively—saw Basic as an instrument of world understanding through which we would eventually transcend narrow nationalistic goals. The prime minister discovered in it the means by which a new ideological colonialism was to come about. Soon, in Fulton, Missouri, where he spelled out the terms of the Cold War, Churchill would variously describe our side as "Christian Civilization" or "the English-speaking peoples." The long-range result of the Harvard address was that Basic English was associated with Anglo-Saxon imperialism. In Richards's words, with Churchill's Harvard speech, everything "went down the drain!"

*   *   *

But for the moment, the darker prospects of Churchill's agenda still somewhat veiled, the Rockefeller Foundation harkened to his call, finding in it a confirmation of their faith in Basic. Just a week after Churchill's speech, John Marshall found in the speech a new reason to get Winter to the U.S., where interest in Basic was now "lively." Stevens saw a visit from Winter as a means of fleshing out the Rockefeller Foundation's skimpy knowledge of China and to help the Foundation shape a program that gave shape to the Foundation's general and scholarly work in China. And Raymond Fosdick, the director of the Foundation, felt that in Winter they had a "rare spirit" whose work in China merited continuing support.

Winter's arrival also stirred in the State Department. A month before Winter returned to the States, Willys R. Peck, special assistant in the Division of Cultural Relations (known familiarly as RC) wrote to David Stevens. Peck was Wilma Fairbank's immediate higher-up in the division, so he already knew something about Winter through her. Now he wanted to let Winter know through Stevens that the officers of the division would appreciate an opportunity "to discuss with him various problem connected with our program in China."[5]

A debate was taking place in the State Department as it had once taken place in the Rockefeller Foundation over the relative importance of cultural exportations as opposed to material and technical aid, and Winter began to look like just the ticket for enacting the agenda of the cultural camp. Early in 1943, John Fairbank had prepared a report for the attention of the political wing of the State Department Far Eastern Section, urging the Cultural Relations program for China to "seek contact at a level above that of Life Magazine." That higher level, he added, "deals with values: Why We Do Things, not How. It is conveyed through the arts, literature, drama, through 'cultural' media. It appeals to the creative people who are seeking new ideas and new art forms, not to the bankers." As an example, he cited the "young Chinese leader in dramatic work, trained at Yale and producing plays in Chunking," who told him that he knew "all about the Russian stage and contemporary Russian life" but that he had "heard nothing of the American stage for two years." Fairbank wanted to know: "What can RC do about this?"[6]

Responding for the Far Eastern Section, Stanley Hornbeck agreed with Fairbank "except as regard the opening paragraph, second sentence—which happens to be, for the moment the most important sentence." Indeed it was. It was the sentence in which Fairbank said that the Cultural Relations program for China suffers because "the policy behind it is inadequate to the occasion." Unless we could export our values with our technology, Fairbank argued, China might accept our technology as Japan had as "the means of opposing us."

Hornbeck could scarcely conceal his contempt for Fairbank's view that humanist values should be an essential part of our lend lease program. "It is not important at this time, comparatively speaking, for us to send to China people who will tell the Chinese about 'the American stage (vide the concluding paragraph of Dr. Fairbank's memo under reference)." What was important was "to send to China materials, instruments, agents, etc. that can and will contribute toward the winning of the war."

This exchange between Fairbank and Hornbeck is an instance of a theme that runs through this narrative. Fairbank, like Richards and Winter, stood with those who wished to send to the East American representatives who represented the richness of our cultural and ethical systems so that these could interact in open arena with their Chinese counterparts. (The British were already doing this. Advocates, such as Fairbank, dreamed of intellectual and cultural communication at the highest levels. Richards went so far as to argue that even Western export of technical thought and vocabulary suffered because the Chinese language and culture wasn't set up to receive them as a result of its tendency to assay new information in terms of how it fit into established traditions of thought. But he was also convinced that Western intellectual fashion, more and more governed by positivist assumptions, could be revivified by a graft of Taoist, Buddhist, and Confucian teaching. As if to prove his point (if not also to make his case more hopeless), the increasingly militarized atmosphere that pervaded both the West and East was not genial to such mind/spirit dreams.

In the meantime, in rooms where large decisions were made, the issue hung fire, at least until Winter returned and State Department people, such as Peck, who sympathized with Fairbank's position, could find in the returned China hand a man who had served and might continue to serve the kind of aims Fairbank described. Two weeks after Winter arrived in New York, Stevens wrote to Charles Thompson, chief of the State Department Division of Cultural Relations, to suggest that Thompson have a talk with Winter alone.[7] In him, Stevens said, Thompson would find "an unusually good informant and possibly a person who could take on heavier responsibilities than he has had as a teacher of his subject." It was beginning to look as if—despite M. C. Balfour's often expressed objections—Winter might return to China in the role of cultural ambassador without portfolio rather as Joseph Needham and E. R. Dodds had been doing, most admirably, in Winter's judgment, for the British.

Certainly, there were ironies in the situation—most saliently, that this expatriated American, who, in a number of ways, including his appearance and his literary tastes, might seem more British than American, should be falling into place as an obvious candidate for the post of American cultural ambassador. Yet when it came to that, what could be more American at the time than for a man of letters to seek his cultural foundations in the productions of other cultures than his own? (Ezra Pound and T. S. Eliot are two obvious examples of highly influential writers who did just that, just as, in a latter generation, Robert Bly, among others, provided the same service.) And when it came to that, if American values continued to be the Lockean values articulated in the great documents that came out of our revolution, where could one find an American who believed in them more single-mindedly than Robert Winter?

$$*\qquad*\qquad*$$

Perhaps the most gnarled issue bearing on Winter's return to America for consultation with the Rockefeller Foundation had to do with the situation of Chinese intellectuals under the Guomindang. Raymond Fosdick himself took particular interest in the question. He had written to Balfour in July 1943 to solicit his views in the matter. There was growing concern "among various groups in this country," Fosdick began, "that the prolongation of the war in China, the continuing increase in the cost of living there and the scarcity of its essential commodities may lead to a dangerous deterioration in the health, morale, and future effectiveness of much of the scholarly and scientific personnel in Free China."[8]

Worse, he continued, some of his sources feared that "we may be facing a 'wholesale liquidation of many of the ablest Chinese educational leaders developed during the past few decades.'" Fosdick had been told by "a very responsible educator, who recently arrived in this country," that Chinese teachers were "now suffering from under-nourishment through lack of a well-balanced diet." The Rockefeller Foundation wished to be of help, but though they had received various suggestions, they did not know what they should do or indeed whether they could or should do anything. Fosdick had enclosed a list of questions soliciting Balfour's views on the general situation as described, the possible effects of deepening inflation on health and morale, what it might cost in the next three years to bring to America for study (and material relief) some of the scholars who would be needed for the period of reconstruction after the war, what portion of them should be "in the medical, natural and social sciences and in the humanities," etc. Perhaps the most loaded of all his questions was: "Would the bringing of such persons to America be liable to misunderstanding?"

The unspoken gist of the matter is that John Fairbank and others had been reporting to the State Department since 1942 on the Guomindang's efforts "toward the regimentation of intellectual life in China" and on the fact that the party met its principal resistance from Western-trained faculty of Tsinghua University, determined "to preserve their freedom of teaching in the American tradition." Fairbank himself had long championed a program that would bring some of these threatened scholars to America for protection. He believed that Western-trained students of the humanities particularly needed the benefit of such a program. "Industrialization in China may very possibly set the [stage] for one of the world's great revolutions. Whether or not violence ultimately occurs, the speed of adjustment will be greater if the balance between the technological and the social studies can be evened up."

In Fairbank's view, that issue, however politically loaded, could no longer be sidestepped:

We Americans cannot expect to see a fuller intellectual life prevail if we do not stand up for it. We cannot expect to benefit the world by exporting science only, any more than it is a benefit to give matches to a baby . . . . If we want the coming generation in China to share in the best that we have to offer, in ideas and standards of conduct, we must personally see to it that they have the opportunity.

The bottom line was that these people, least in favor with their own regime, could be the architects of a democratic Chinese state once the war was over.

In his reply to Fosdick, Balfour was "skeptical of alarming stories that the health of important groups of Chinese educators are suffering, unless there were concrete evidence."[9] Such stories he countered with his own insistence "that the universities in China are not concerned with the war effort." Moreover, people whom he consulted "were unfavorable to an extensive movement abroad of educators" (part of Fairbank's proposal) especially because of "the loss and demoralization to staff and students left behind."

His own notion of relief was "to make grants to senior men through selected institutions to help maintain education standards of the family, limiting such aid to secondary and higher education; indirectly this would aid the family budget and nutrition." These senior men, he explained, would all be outstanding leaders. Indeed, "the idea developed from my many contacts with such leaders." Implicit in Balfour's recommendation was that we support those who enjoyed easy relations with their own government and ignore those critics of the government who most needed and deserved our support. Balfour's opinions, like those of other influential Americans, were cut from Chiang's cloth.

Winter's views on the subject were solicited by the Foundation shortly after he arrived in New York. The report he wrote in response commanded serious attention in the office. David Stevens circulated the draft and final versions of Winter's report to Rockefeller Foundation officers, including Fosdick, with the caution that Winter's views should not be quoted. Winter wanted to keep his "status of independent teacher and investigator," and "any unfavorable comment of his that is carried back to China might damage his status or prevent his readmission."

It is plain why Stevens urged caution. Winter's report left few oxen ungored. At their heart, his remarks were addressed to no less a question than the future of democracy in China. Guomindang China itself was "a frankly avowed Party Dictatorship" which hoped "to attain some day a true republicanism." Because it was an inefficient dictatorship, there remained an overt but "unofficial Opposition . . . represented by the Universities." For some five decades, Winter explained, "the colleges and universities [had] been the centers where liberal thought and democratic ideas [had] been cultivated and from which they [had] been disseminated." Now, however, the Guomindang, in the name of national unity, was tightening the process of control over the universities that had begun in April 1929, at their Third Congress. And though "everybody supports the idea of unity personified by the Generalissimo," Winter argued, "many people in the universities fear that the Party will abuse its power once it has finally become supreme, and they look with increasing admiration at the freedom of American and English universities." Indeed, as they attempted to keep open their own path toward democracy against the increasing pressures of all-devouring nationalism, they looked to the West, and especially to America, for guidance.

In 1943, the stock of Americans in China still stood much higher than it ever had and "much higher than that of any other nation." "But we were doing little to maintain that standing," Winter complained. Not only did our movies represent us "as a nation of gangsters or sentimental idiots," but our ambassadors, the GIs themselves (the only Americans most Chinese saw outside the movies), consisted of "large numbers of ill-mannered, dishonest, and superficial Americans whose activities are only partially controlled by their superior officers." Winter says that he himself did not believe that these people in our movies and our expeditionary forces were really representative of the people of the United States,

> but the average Chinese, although he is a keen observer, has no way of making this distinction. Almost any Chinese has more spiritual discipline, sobriety, and real strength than these people. Democracy is not being presented to the Chinese as a theory of equality of opportunity, but an equality which makes the careless, the undisciplined, and the ignorant equal to the thoughtful, the disciplined, and the well-informed. The "slant-eyes" (U.S. Army equivalent of "Chinese") are being subjected to the evangelization of thousands of missionaries of a new religion—the Religion of a Good Time Twenty-Four

Hours a Day. No one is accepted who is not prosperous, well
dressed, and ready with his fists. The password is "What is your
racket?" Communion is taken as often as a bottle of whiskey
can be obtained. All objections to the doctrine are met with the
answer, "What can China give us that will raise our standard of
living?" It may be taken as a matter of course in America that a
soldier pinches strange girls in the street or tears her picture off
her passport, but such things are actually unheard of among the
Chinese and they are greatly scandalized by them.

Indeed, drunken and violent acts by American servicemen who had been
sent almost perfectly unprepared to a culture they found utterly alien
would prove to be a continuous irritant to the Chinese and a major cause
of eroded goodwill.

But the problem, as Winter saw it, was not simply that we were
poorly represented in China, but also that our efforts at propaganda,
aimed as they were at some American notion of the average citizen,
was wasted on the literate minority whose friendship we ought to be
cultivating. They could only recognize it for what it was: mass-produced
information and propaganda that was produced for distribution to
all countries, with the prayer that it would be understood. What was
needed instead of such propaganda was "close personal contacts with
Americans who have a sense of the Chinese background and a vision of
their possibilities for the future." We needed to "start thinking and acting
at once" not only about the labor and health problems of the Chinese,
"but about the direction which their education is taking, particularly in
the higher levels, which are the ones that count most at this time." This
meant providing books and periodicals that represented us at our best.
"The sending of a few books and periodicals to the intellectuals of China
who are starved physically and intellectually may serve no further purpose
than the injection of morphine given by a doctor to a dying man, but it is
an act which most decent people would hesitate to evade."

Cultural help to China meant also—Balfour's arguments
notwithstanding—a system for exchanging Chinese and American
scholars. The successful visit to Lianda by E. R. Dodds, a professor of
Greek, demonstrated that the Chinese were interested in quality more
than they were interested in specialty. Dodds had recommended to the
British Council that his visit be followed by visits by people like E. M.
Forster, Herbert Read, Lord David Cecil, Professor H. B. Charlton,

and Professor John Crofts. And Needham was making another set of recommendations about scientists. America could be doing likewise.

Winter also wanted to see some sixty to one hundred research students brought to America for study. The Chinese government had, for several years, refused to allow students in the humanities to leave the country. But Winter argued (in behalf of what a later version of Chinese totalitarians would call spiritual pollution), "If, as some people say, there is a danger that the present tendencies in China will produce unthinking regimentation, it may be best counteracted by students in the Humanities."

In order to facilitate the exchange program in both directions, Winter recommended the appointment of a fulltime Sino-American Relations Officer in China to assist in the selection of Chinese visiting fellows and students for American universities. Since Winter himself had provided Stevens with a judicious comment on a panel of outstanding Chinese scholars in the social sciences and humanities proposed by John Fairbank, his own qualifications for such a post were already being recognized.

As to Balfour's arguments that material conditions for intellectuals in China were not so bad, Winter took absolute exception. The American consul in Kunming had estimated that the minimum salary required to keep his clerk alive was US$400 a month, twice the rate that "university authorities claimed was necessary for a Chinese professor and four times the salary of the highest paid professor." Chinese university students, like their teachers, were in dreadful condition. "Acute malnutrition," he said, "made physical exercise dangerous." At least 10 percent of university students were tubercular. No wonder. Most of them wore thin cotton all year round despite Kunming's 6,500-foot altitude. And of course, Chinese universities had suffered tremendous material losses. Where there were classrooms, there were unlikely to be chairs. Students attending Winter's Shakespeare lectures at the Southwest Associated University all stood, each resting his notebook on back of the student in front of him. Universities libraries are "only a miserable fraction of their former" size, and "no effective research in Arts is possible." As a result, there was an "intense desire to renew intellectual relations with western thought and learning."

Winter was familiar with Balfour's view that university students deserved no sympathy because they refused to contribute to the war effort. When Winter had passed through Delhi on the way to America, Balfour had shown him a copy of a report in which Balfour complained that the Chinese intellectuals were not doing enough in the war effort. "American students are doing it," Balfour told Winter. "If we disrupt the lives of half of our one million students, might not China call on 10 to 15% of its economic manpower?"

Winter had ventured to point out to Balfour some of the complexities involved in this question. For one, early in the war, the government had made no effort to spare its technicians and other experts, and the result was that large numbers were killed. Now it was the deliberate policy of the government to spare those who remain for use as instructors in China and to replace those who are lost by sending more students to America than before the war.

For another, as private soldiers, intellectuals would be wasted. Winter would sometimes see in the street "the ghosts of my former students who [had] spent a couple of years in propaganda work in the army until their health broke down." Out of his own office window at 1250 Kuang Hua Kei, he could see the soldiers' open-air mess. In theory, the "enlisted" men received one bowl of rice twice a day, but by the time the last third got to the head of the line, the pot was empty.

> The rest climb trees and eat little birds raw, or birds' eggs, and even have the good luck sometimes to capture a mangy dog which they first beat slowly to death with sticks to make the meat more tender, and then roast in the open air outside my bedroom which is soon filled with the delicious fumes. As they all have scabies and sores caused by undernourishment, a group of them lined up for roll-call seem to be doing a sort of writhing dance all of the time in their efforts to scratch themselves. When they have a wound, they chew up leaves from a tree, mix them with a little earth, and smear the mixture on the wound, as no medicines are available.

But besides all this, the government and freethinking intellectuals were enemies. As to the reports that Fosdick had heard, Winter confirmed them: "While it may be an exaggeration to say that it is the deliberate policy of the Chinese government to starve the intellectuals, that was not far from the case." Winter knew, as anyone who spends time in China can still observe, that the government persecutes the scholars as a cruel mark of respect. It would be unnecessary to persecute them if they were not so potentially powerful, enjoying, on the one hand, the ambiguous status of the ancient system of government by scholars, and, on the other, that conferred by the modern tradition, in which "for the last fifty years the colleges and universities have been the center of liberal thought and democratic ideas." Now the power "to determine the details of the administration and the course of study" had passed slowly to the Ministry of Education, but the still-insecure state continued to fear opposition, especially Communist opposition; and though there was little Communism at this time in the universities, the government tended to mistake any expression of democratic sympathies for it. This meant, ironically, that the very intellectuals most sympathetic with American and Western ideals were the ones most in danger at the hands of the Nationalist government to which we were allied.

*   *   *

The message that Winter brought to New York and Washington was simple enough. He spoke to the plight of China's liberal intellectuals, many of them American trained and committed to American ideals of free inquiry and free expression. He urged that we do what we could to help keep alive in China the practice and principle of liberal education that we had done so much to engender there. What made his appeal problematic is that, as long as the U.S. continued to support the Guomindang, we were joined with the very forces that sought to muffle opposition where it was most articulate—at Lianda University itself. It seems clear in retrospect that he offered very sound advice, but he offered it, unfortunately, when a host of illusions and lies made it difficult for Americans to hear it.

This contradiction glared out of our own war policy, whose ultimate, self-declared aim was the preservation of democracy. But the liberal forces in the Rockefeller Foundation and in the State Department—though they saw the contradiction and its results—could not see clearly what was to be done about it. We could not easily support liberal scholars in China since they opposed the government with which we were allied. Neither could we bring them very easily to America because in so doing, we weakened the liberal presence in China and because such a sign of favor conferred on Chiang Kai-shek's opponents, unless it were conferred with great delicacy, could only alienate Chiang.

Still, though there was no real solution to the dilemma—which would continue to grow worse as long as the Nationalists (Guomindang) remained in power—in New York and in Washington, everyone wanted to talk with the newly arrived American, who enjoyed the inevitable popularity of any astute witness from the field. So Winter had plenty of opportunity to air his views, and though in the pandemonium of New York and Washington Winter longed for the raw simplicity of life in China, he remained for ten months in the States, doing what he could to be useful.

Early in December 1943, having completed his reports for the Foundation, Winter went down to Washington to talk with George Taylor in the Office of War Information. The English-born Taylor, who had arranged his Washington visits, was an old China hand himself before the war had written an important essay on the Taiping Rebellion. Winter also met with Charles Thompson, chief of the State Department Division of Cultural Relations, Willys R. Peck, special assistant in the Division of Cultural Relations, and with Arthur W. Hummel, then chief of the Asiatic Division of the Library of Congress, who shared with Winter not only an abiding fascination with things Chinese, but also a deep-died enthusiasm for Basic English. Unfortunately, if records exist of any of these conversations, I have been unable to pry them loose from FBI files.

Not all of Winter's business in Washington was official. He visited with the Jamesons, whom he had not seen since they left Peking in 1937; and he also spent time with John and Wilma Fairbank, whom he had seen more recently in Kunming. Wilma Fairbank was back in her office at the Division of Cultural Relations. John Fairbank, recently back in Washington from China, was like Winter doing what he could to tell the people back home which way the wind was blowing in China. More bluntly even than Winter, he said that it was blowing toward a revolution that "could not be suppressed by the provocative coercion" of the Guomindang—a prophecy which, before long, when it proved accurate, would have Fairbank, among others, in difficulty with the American Congress.

To the end of his life, Winter remembered another person he visited in Washington—a woman (she may have been Dorothy Jameson) who, after hearing some of his stories about wartime life in Kunming, asked him what he did with his time. He told her that he read a book a day. Back in Kunming more than a year later, he got a wire from her that read: "A book a day." And then sure enough, there began to arrive, and continued to come for more than a year, a book a day.[10]

Another woman, a Mrs. Webster—possibly Nora, the wife of Sir Charles Kingsley Webster, an English China scholar and diplomat who would later help to create the United Nations at the Dumbarton Oaks conference in Washington—provided Winter with a discretionary fund to administer as he saw fit to help the lot of his friends in Kunming.

When he returned to New York, Winter discovered that an old friend had some new plans for him. Richards wanted him to come up to Cambridge for three months of work on the *Pocketbook of Basic* and on an anticipated training center for aeronautical workers. For Winter, who had not yet been assigned a specific role that would take him back to China and who had provided the verbal and written reports that the Rockefeller Foundation wanted from him, a stay at Harvard in the company of the man he admired above all others was attractive.

But the plan ran into a snag. Two prominent Chinese scholars, Chen Fu-tien and Chin Yu-lin [11] were in New York on their way to Harvard to prepare a list of books needed by Lianda to restore their bombed and rebombed library. They were also present at meetings in which Stevens, Richards, and Winter discussed what Winter was to do during the next several months in America. Chen and Chinin thought that he should not be further identified with Basic work and elementary education. They wanted his return to "mean a beginning of direction for all English and humanities work in the Associated Universities." For that to occur, focus had to be shifted away from Winter, the teacher of language and of language teachers, to Winter, the Renaissance man, skilled interpreter of, and spokesman for the texts, scores, images, ideas, and values that constitute Western culture. As we've seen, Basic had always been tainted in the eyes of some Chinese scholars by their suspicion that it was a kind of baby talk, and all agreed—though not without regrets—that the proposed visit to Harvard by Winter was not a good idea.

It had been a long time since Winter could enjoy excellent company in relaxed surroundings. He had known Stevens slightly at the University of Chicago and of course had corresponded heavily with him and John Marshall, but this was the first chance he had had to sit down with them, and he came away with high respect for both the men and their intentions. It was obviously reciprocal. Winter and Marshall had hit it off especially well, and some time after Winter returned to Kunming, Marshall wrote: "Be sure we think of you far oftener than we write. Mary often speaks of the pleasant times we had with you at home, and you are frequently made an unseen witness in such discussions as go on about China here in the office."[12] Years later, under pressure to explain to the Communists his relations with the Rockefeller Foundation, Winter spoke of the pleasant times that he spent with Stevens, Richards, sometimes in the company of Chin Yu-ling, remarking that if the Rockefeller officials had any imperialist ambitions in China, they did not reveal any to him.[13]

Winter was already beginning to take on some of the work that would go with his new position in China—work such as helping to select Chinese scholars especially worthy of American aid. Back in November, John Fairbank, then still in Chunking, had prepared a list of promising and outstanding Chinese scholars from whom a panel of fifteen might be chosen for study in the U.S. He had done so at the request of the American Council of Learned Societies with the support of the Rockefeller Foundation.[14]

Fairbank had been careful to leave the actual selection to eminent Chinese scholars, and the panel was drawn up by a small, informal group, of which Fairbank himself was the only Western member. They came up with a list of eight outstanding and fifteen promising scholars. All of the first group held advanced degrees from Western universities.

Fairbank's report, in the form of a letter to Willys Peck of the RC, was handed over by Stevens to Winter for his comments. In approving of Fairbank' panel, while suggesting some refinements in the overall program, Winter took the opportunity to reiterate what had become for him a kind of credo: What we did for Chinese liberal intellectuals now would pay off for us after the war, because these are the persons who had enjoyed American academic training and who were most sympathetic with liberal academic principles. These were the people who would guide postwar China toward sustained friendship with the U.S.

> A number of the men on the list are outstanding not only for their scholarship but because of their rich personalities and vision—they have not only a sympathetic understanding of both Chinese and Western civilization, but the intellectual capacity to give effective expression to this understanding. We do not know in what direction China will go after the war. If she can be made to believe in a system of collective security there is hope that these people may have a voice in her development. If not, she will certainly exert all her energies to create a strong national state in the shortest possible time, in which the above persons will play little or no part, and after having let some of her most useful men starve to death, fail in the whole scheme. This would be a great disaster for us as well as for China.

This astute analysis would prove prophetic though ineffectual
in the long run.

Early in January 1944, Marshall and Winter in the New York offices
of the Foundation talked over Winter's ideas for beefing up the English
humanities program. It was around this notion that the next stage of
Winter's American sponsorship began to jell. Marshall, after talking
with Winter, reported to Stevens that "a supplement [of 10,000 Chinese
dollars] to Winter's Chinese salary which would bring it to a figure
which he regards as minimum for his livelihood" and that "provision
for a full-time salary of at least 6,000 Chinese dollars a month for an
assistant to Winter, possibly our former fellow, Wu Fuheng," would also
be essential.[15]

In February, while the question of support for a program at Tsinghua
was "still under consideration," Winter was awarded a grant-in-aid of
$250 a month living expenses and $2,500 "for the expense of approved
travel in the United States and toward expense of return travel to
Kunming, China." In addition, he was allowed $500 for the purchase and
transport of books and supplies for use in his work in China. Though
plans for his return to Kunming were well afoot, with David Stevens's
encouragement, Winter took one last look at the prospects of making
a life in America. Stevens arranged for him visits to universities where
he could talk with some of the continent's leading orientalists—among
them, George Kennedy of Yale, Ernest Wilkins of Oberlin, Knight
Bickerstaff of Cornell, and Bishop William Charles White of the Royal
Toronto Museum.

By his own account, Winter was "looking for a job." But whatever
may have come of these visits, nothing did. Although "life in the United
States [was] luxurious and comfortable," Winter later wrote about this
stage of his visit, it was abhorrent to him, "particularly because there
was no purpose in anything one did. The Rockefeller Foundation did
everything they could to keep me there, but I insisted on leaving."[16] The
fact was that Winter had left behind the rich identity he'd created with
the help of his circumstances in China.

While Winter was still on the road, David Stevens, following up on
Marshall's recommendation, wrote to Mei Yiqui, president of Lianda,
asking his advice as to whether "assistance in the development of work
in humanities and particularly English studies would be welcome and
appropriate."[17] (The letter he sent was actually written by Raymond

Fosdick, at Stevens's request, from a draft by Stevens. Stevens wanted to know the range of commitment he was permitted to make, and Fosdick told him: "It seems to me that the statement of the project should be made as simple as possible, and the grant as large as possible.") Now Stevens could state that the program, which would include support for Winter and an assistant, and funds for the purchase of books would cost about US$12,000 for two years beginning on July 1, 1944, The purpose of the program was "assistance in the development of work in humanities." As to the details of the program, Stevens diplomatically invited Mei to work these out. At the close of his letter to President Mei, he hoped that the proposed program, "designed to give some small concrete proof of our desire to cooperate with your country in the field of humanities, may prove useful to you as well as to us." The letter clearly suggested that the arrangement would be of mutual benefit and thus avoided giving offense to Chinese national pride, which would be offended by offers of mere charity. Fosdick seemed to side with the Fairbank-Winter camp in their view that a successful program in the English humanities at Lianda could redound to America's benefit after the war, if the Chinese liberal intellectuals could be sustained in a position from which they could help mold postwar policy.

Scarcely three weeks later, Mei replied that such a grant, if made, would "be most welcome as it will enable us to strengthen our liberal arts departments which have suffered most during the wartime from lack of contact with the outside world and particularly books and journals that have been published in recent years." The university looked forward to Professor Winter's return. When he returned, he would rejoin the Tsinghua faculty "and receive the salary and other allowances as due to one of professorial rank here," but he would still need extra subsidy for his living expenses, and that could be drawn from the Foundation's fund if it were granted.

Pretty much as Stevens had originally proposed it, the deal was closed in June 1944, when F. T. Chen and Chin accepted it formally for Mei: the funds would supplement Winter's salary at a level about twice what he would receive from Lianda and also would subsidize an assistant and give Winter money for the purchase of books and other necessary supplies. The upshot was that Winter would no longer be associated with Basic.

Under this plan, Winter would return to Lianda with enhanced prestige. If previously he had been there as a long-time faculty member and as director of the Orthological Institute—this last, as we have seen, itself a dubious distinction—now he enjoyed the direct support of the Rockefeller Foundation, not as administrator of Richards's project but as the embodiment of his own. He would return to Kunming as the Rockefeller Foundation's man in the Chinese academy.

This point was reiterated by Stevens when he wrote to Willys Peck at the State Department, informing him that one of Stevens's "good friends," Robert Winter, was about to return to his old university but in a broader capacity: "In effect he [would] guide the work of these three institutions in interpreting Western culture through humanistic studies." Although Stevens thought it "quite clear that Mr. Winter [would] gain some values [*sic*] from continuing entirely as a civilian on an educational mission," he also was sure that Peck could be of the greatest help to Winter in his return journey.[18]

With the help of this note to Peck, the rails were greased. In short order, the Passport Division, the War Shipping Administration, and the Army Education Branch, Information & Education Division, were lined up to help arrange the details of Winter's China-bound journey. But there still remained the difficult task of obtaining travel priorities. Present conditions did not bode well for a prompt return; there was a heavy demand for ships and a scarcity of crews. Peck would do what he could, but as he observed to Stevens, who had anticipated the problem: "I suppose it may all be summed up in the imperative demand that the prosecution of the war shall be served first."

Still, other devices were put in motion. Raymond Fosdick wrote a letter to whom it might concern, identifying Winter as a friend of the RF and assuring that "any consideration shown him in the course of this trip would be greatly appreciated by the Foundation." But the sticking point remained how to book a passage to Asia. Unless some military purpose could be assigned to Winter, it would be nearly impossible to get him there. At this point, Peck and Winter seemed to have worked out between them the clinching scheme: Winter would write training manuals in Basic on tank operation and basic medical terms for Chinese troops being trained by Stillwell in India. Winter would then be given passage to India in order to field test the manuals. By September, Peck had succeeded in persuading the War Department that they should provide Winter's transportation "in view of services Mr. Winter is going to perform for the Army in China."

The State Department itself came to Winter's aid by making an exception to its general rule and permitting "the Rockefeller Foundation to ship Mr. Winter's excess baggage and education material in care of the American Consulate General at Calcutta."[19] It appeared that all the parts of this complicated operation were in place. Winter was even assigned a high travel priority.

But there remained one unforeseen hitch: though by September 1944, all arrangements had been made, Winter himself was missing. John S. Dickey, director of the State Department Office of Public Information, wrote to Stevens a bit ruefully on September 7 that his last inquiry "had developed the fact that Mr. Winter had not left, but the Army Education Branch did not know the reason for his delay." It was Bombay all over again.

But Winter did not stay lost for long and managed to board a military transport for India within a day or so of Dickey's letter. He would remain in India until February 5, 1945, when he headed north from Calcutta.

CHAPTER ELEVEN:
VICTORY IN KUNMING

Winter's second visit to India lasted about four months, unpleasant ones by his account. His most vivid impression of the period was "the almost unmitigated grimness of being in and out of hospital." He had spent two months confined there on two occasions, for treatment of an especially unpleasant assortment of ailments that included amoebic dysentery, malignant tertian malaria, and trench mouth. When the doctor in Calcutta finally allowed him to travel, he headed for Kunming, and the change from the hot plains to Kunming's chilly plateau nearly finished him off. A month after he arrived in Kunming, his mood was distinctly bilious, although injections of liver extract and vitamins had somewhat restored his red corpuscles and energy.

Except for his confinements to the hospital, all that he carried away from this second Indian experience was a memory of some boys on a Calcutta street "beating and throwing rocks at a giant Galapagos tortoise which had a very ancient date carved on its shell." The boys were "sweating and exhausted," but the turtle simply pulled its head in when the blows got too bad, "and then, when there was a respite, out came the head again and the slow inevitable movement would begin—like Fate itself." The little drama reminded him of American attempts to control China

He found temporary lodgings in "a garret at the top of the theatre next to the Consulate where theatrical properties were once stored, and now that the broken windows are pasted up, it is quite livable."[1] The theater, which had once been a temple, in fact housed many of Lianda's most distinguished professors (including Chen and Chin, who had also returned from America), although the storeroom above the theater that Winter had discovered was not a room that anyone had previously considered living in.

To visit Winter there, one walked up three flights of stairs. At the top of the stairs, one came to a door scarcely four feet high. Just as one was about to knock "an old yet clear voice" from within called out, "Come in!" Inside, a tall figure drew himself up from his bed. To the students who came to visit him there, his face, though obviously weary, seemed to reflect (as one of them a little breathlessly recorded) "innumerable suns, all sorts of cool or warm rains, a million different faces, every idea that had anything to do with mankind."

Even when I knew him, in his very last years, Winter was revivified by visits. So it was then when he was fifty-eight. Whatever weariness or despair had drawn him to his bed at mid-afternoon, now he rose, utterly attentive to the visitor who had come to talk with him about Henry James. The visitor could not have known what weight of loneliness and despair he was lifting, but now the American listened to his questions and gave him rich response.

The visitor—a student Jin Ti, who would go on to carry out the extraordinary task of translating Joyce's *Ulysses* into Chinese—had never been in one of Winter's classes but had listened to him lecture on poetry from outside the classroom window. Now the old man tirelessly spoke to him, with an enthusiasm the student found very American. Jin Ti had been studying under William Empson, whom he remembered as a great thinker but not a very clear lecturer. Winter, he recalled, "was a great talker, and his explanations were very clear . . . . There's a Chinese expression, 'Go in deep and come out shallow.' Winter was like that, a real philosopher, the kind who could explain his ideas like limpid water."[2]

So they talked, and Winter, from time to time, stroked a Siamese cat, which to the student was an emblem of the American's loneliness. As Jin Ti became more comfortable with the teacher who took him in as a friend, he began to examine the room. The northern and southern walls were made up entirely of windows, as was the upper part of the western wall was all windows as well. The eastern wall was papered white and half covered with gasoline cans that Winter had converted into bookshelves.

"I like this room," Winter told him as he saw the young man looking about. "It was bright," he said, "and the best part . . . is that little balcony there." He gestured to the western wall above Jin Ti's head, but all Jin could see was the row of windows that seemed to be held shut with mosquito netting.

With some impatience, Winter directed the uncertain young man to climb a wooden chest, then mount a table above it, and finally step onto the windowsill, where he released the mosquito netting and stepped out onto "the little balcony made of rough timbers." Beneath him stretched a world of green:

> A vast sea of green foliage and mossy tiles—the Wu Hua hill was a crest of green, crowned by the slender water-tower; the jade green of the Jade Lake was mixed and lost in the general green—bordered with wide yellow fields . . . then, higher up, the transparent blue skies and the graceful floating clouds, shining white and mild lemon yellow. The whole western horizon was occupied by mountains in the form of a sleeping giant, because of whom, so the Kunming people say, no emperor can ever come from the province.

When it was time for Jin Ti to go, Winter, in his customary way, stirred the conversation again: "This room has another great merit," he said. "It is full of sunshine. Nobody ever occupied it before. They all said that it was too hot. The sun is a source of health, yet strange to say, the Chinese don't like the sun. I always remember, when I was in Peiping, people in the bus fought for the shady seats and therefore I could take any seat as full of sunshine as I liked." Then Jin left, walking out backward, as Winter had directed him as more convenient, given the height of the door. His last impression of the teacher "was a face full of smiles, which contained kindness, consolation, and the sense of humor one would need in helpless situations."[3]

John Fairbank, who visited old friends in the theater back in 1942, recalled that it "was of flimsy construction but rent free." As Fairbank sat talking with his friends, "big rats ran over the ceiling paper and almost fell through it, so we discussed getting a cat [the Siamese came later], but a cat would cost $200." Back then, alarmed at the professors' penurious situation, Fairbank wrote: "They are putting up a stout fight but can't go on much longer. You can imagine this situation—the despair, squalor, brave front, mutual support, and gradual weakness of thought and action."[4]

But now three years later, they were still going on. For Winter, there were actually some advantages to his precarious living arrangement. The theater was next door to the American Consulate, and William R. Langdon, the American consul general, was so shocked by Winter's

arrangements that he asked him to have lunch with him daily—a
special favor since previously, Winter had been fighting his way "into
the little restaurants down the street to the tune of NC $1500 a day."
Langdon, whose kindness to Winter kept alive the earlier generosities of
Pollard-Urquhart's brother-in-law, the British consul Prideaux-Brune, had
also allowed Winter to get his mail care of the APO 617 of the American
consulate general since the ordinary mail service had become altogether
unreliable.[5]

At the same time, the runaway inflation rate was now fifteen to
twenty times what it was when Winter left for the States, and students
of Chekiang University (near Kweiyang), for instance, had gone on strike
"because they were getting nothing to eat." Winter did what he could,
using his new funds to loan food and money to needy colleagues, which
was consistent with his new mission. By fall, he had dispensed more than
a quarter million Chinese dollars (including funds provided him by a
Mrs. Webster) "to meet serious emergencies among the faculty."[6]

As a semiofficial cultural ambassador, he also made preparations for
nurturing the spirits of his Chinese students and colleagues. While still in
the States, he had had used $500 the Rockefeller Foundation had allotted
for the purpose to purchase reproductions of paintings, a couple of dozen
albums of phonograph records, a radio and a speaker, as well as a case
of books. These resources, which he had shipped by boat while he flew
to India by military transport, would allow him better to represent the
cultural riches the West has to offer. But in April 1945, almost a year after
he had shipped them, he was still waiting for their delivery. Then when
he finally received word from the American consul general in Calcutta
that his five crates had arrived, he was advised by his old nemesis Balfour
that "there was no provision for their transportation to Kunming."
Winter desperately needed not only the books but also the supplies; even
the cost of a sheet of paper to write a letter on was "beyond all reason."

Human as well as economic forces were conspiring against Winter.
Balfour, who had never been on Winter's wavelength, had now tuned
him out altogether. An entry in Balfour's diary for May 2, 1945, conveys
the tone: "Met W. on two occasions and discussed administration
of Humanities grant and his shipment of four cases still waiting in
Calcutta; some strong words exchanged between us because in financial
and administrative relationship W. is most irresponsible and irrational
person I have had to deal with in China; further, he derides America and
Americans at every opportunity."[7]

Certainly, from the perspective of fiscal responsibility, Winter's case was precarious. As H. M. Gillette, a Rockefeller Foundation officer back in New York, pointed out to Marshall, Winter had already gone over his budget for purchase and transportation of books; and indeed, the $1,800 that Balfour had reported as the cost of shipping the things by air from Calcutta was almost $1,100 more than remained in the grant allotted for getting Winter and his things back to Kunming. To make matters worse, Gillette suspected that the greater part of the shipment was clothing and personal effects. Though neither Gillette nor Balfour said so directly, they obviously suspected that Winter was trying to pull off a swindle. As Gillette put it in a memo to Marshall, "The expenditure of $1800 to ship these things by air seems unnecessary, uneconomical, and probably disproportionate to the need."[8]

In the course of the summer of 1945, David Stevens was drawn into this intensifying tempest in a teacup. A letter to Balfour confirmed Balfour's judgment that the $1,800 fee was exorbitant, but Stevens wished him to be aware that living in Kunming was a heavy burden for Winter. Stevens, who had protected Winter from Balfour's stern disapprobation, again counseled patience. The Rockefeller Foundation had no other person of "quite his tenacity, at least in humanities, doing work in China," and while Winter was "getting all the attention" from the Foundation that they could give "under this small grant," Stevens wanted Balfour to remember that Winter's work was important: "I think . . . that he will come into a good deal of credit for his record during the war and for the footing he has helped put under intelligent teaching of English language and literature."[9]

Always forward looking and optimistic about the future of culture, Stevens was enthusiastic about the pioneering work being done by the Office of War Information. He hoped to see library and information centers created around the world that would have "actual independence of government finally." If such a center were ever to be established in China, Winter, with his books, his pictures, his phonograph records, and his own rich internal culture, would be among its founding fathers.

So went the dreams of peace. But for the present, practical problems, such as keeping peace in the family, had become almost insurmountable. Even as Stevens attempted to placate Balfour, Winter in his turn had become more irritated. His crates had finally arrived in mid-August, and the bill for the lot was only $181.97, which he paid out of his own pocket. But he had accomplished this small triumph only after "some struggle with the forces of obstruction and sabotage in India."[10]

The diplomatic Stevens was puzzled and troubled by this "suggestion of interference" with Winter's plans "by persons in India." While he did not assume "that this necessarily [meant] men in the office of the Rockefeller Foundation at Delhi," he supposed that to be one of the possibilities, so he had reviewed the relevant correspondence. But he could find no "evidence of interference or resistance to practicable proposals." It was he, not Balfour—so he reminded Winter—who had decided that the RF would not "venture to recommend as much as $1,800 for immediate transport of material from India." Indeed, Balfour "would have been glad to have done this in order to clear the shipment." In any case, Stevens thought Winter's accomplishment in getting the material in at so low a cost was good evidence of Winter's skill in negotiation. Naturally, the important element in the affair was not the money, "but the desire of all to help."[11]

Whatever Winter may have done to contribute to the atmosphere of mistrust, he disliked it thoroughly. The American consul in Calcutta had refused to ship the crates until Winter sent him money to cover cartage and storage charges—despite the fact that planes were coming in to Kunming half full at that time. With the help of his friend, the American consul in Kunming, Winter was able to get matters cleared; but by then, the planes were full again because of some military necessity, and that meant a further delay of several months. It was autumn 1945 before the crates finally arrived.

All through these infuriating negotiations Winter had had to listen to Americans shouting "that we were fighting a war," although "they and everybody else knew perfectly well that tons of material were coming in which had nothing to do with the war effort and were not half as important" as Winter's things—excluding his personal effects. That on top of all this, Winter's legitimate request should have been looked upon as if he were trying to put something over was a further annoyance, but the cause of this one, at least, he could understand: "Perhaps it was because so many irregular things were being done that my perfectly legitimate request was looked upon as some sort of 'racket.'"[12]

As to where the fault lay, once he had calmed down in mid-October, Winter blamed himself "for assuming that Dr. Balfour or any American for that matter could take responsibility for charges without knowing beforehand how much they would be." Winter "was simply being Chinese about the whole thing." Any Chinese who knew him would have weighed his character and past record and decided (1) that he wasn't likely to run up unreasonable bills and that (2) he would not incur without authorization costs that he would not be able to pay himself if authorization did not come through.

With his usual genius for apology—a skill he had ample opportunity to develop—Winter explained that his anger had been directed against the whole system that ran through "our State Department and our Army." Everything was entangled in rules; nothing was left to individual good judgment. The result was loss of time, especially serious in emergencies. The British, many of whose ways Winter found superior to those of the Americans, did not operate so; they realized that it was "unrealistic and unimaginative to make such drastic rules which could never be carried out and then yield to pressure and shouting all along the line."

If it was all a tempest in a teapot, it was also evidence, if any was needed, that cultural supplies enjoyed low priorities in time of war, and that whatever faith the Rockefeller Foundation had invested in Winter as a cultural warrior, neither they nor he would find the implementation of that role easy in the atmosphere of war or expectation of war. As John Fairbank put it, events were moving quickly toward the point of no return: "American technology to kill people could be brought into China more quickly than information to improve their lives. Soon the super-technology of the atomic bombs of 1945 would put word-purveyors like myself even further behind. I still wonder if we can ever catch up."[13]

While all this was going on, Winter was teaching full-time at Lianda, offering courses in Dante and in contemporary poetry and preparing to teach a seminar on E. M. Forster's novels if Stevens could send him copies to teach from. Besides, because both the consulate and the U.S. Army disapproved of the presence of civilians who were not "contributing to the war effort," he had volunteered to provide what amounted to fulltime service to the army for the nominal salary of $25 per month. His contributions were in the way of translating and editing, but he also gave orientation talks to both GIs and to Chinese soldiers. Even the army was "beginning to realize that cooperation between people of such different cultures is not easy."[14]

In August 1945, Winter was teaching in a program under State Department auspices, which also included some lectures by Wilma Fairbank, who spent about ten days in Kunming at the time. The program excited Winter at first. It consisted of a series of lectures delivered by Americans to Chinese students and by Chinese to the

American soldiers. The Chinese—and, for the purposes of this exercise, Winter was counted as one of them—lectured on "Chinese Psychology, Family and Village Life, Industrialization in China, Social Welfare, Contemporary History, Chinese Festivals, etc." As for the Americans, their subjects were "American Government and the Party System, the AFL and the CIO, Scientific Research, Clubs, Societies and Voluntary Associations, and . . . Women in American Life."[15] The progressive series was clearly imagined by a person or persons who believed that the task of interpretation between East and West could be, as Richards had long ago imagined, a task between equals.

But this series was offered only once. A month later, Winter was still putting in ten hours a week at the Army's Interpreter's School but now as an English teacher to Chinese translators who were to be prepared in six weeks to communicate in English with Americans. Though he ordinarily enjoyed language teaching, the work at the Interpreter's School wasn't congenial. Just when he had persuaded the authorities to accept material in Basic or near Basic, a group of missionaries had presented an alternative text, which Winter was obliged to use.[16] He thought that Stevens might be interested "in some of the vocabularies" that he was required to teach. The brief list he provided for Stevens included "hit the hay, sack, pin-up girl, Was my face red! Okey-doke, hunky-dory, bitch, cheese it, dirty crack, kick the bucket . . . pimp . . . shoot the works . . . I socked him one . . . roots, chicken, Jane . . . left hook, shoot craps . . . the show stinks . . . hill-billy . . . fairy, homo," etc. Presumably, these "vocabularies" did not come out of the missionaries' text, but Winter did not trouble to make that clear.

The Chinese students at the Interpreters' School were also treated to a cram course in American manners. Here they learned such gems of etiquette as "Don't grab the food; don't be a pig; if you pick something from your mouth like a bone, do it behind your napkin or handkerchief." Winter remarked mordantly that it was "not certain that they can be made refined in so short a time." A program that at once insisted upon American barbarities and denied the possibilities of Chinese civilization did little to sweeten Winter's view of his countrymen.

It also fed his bitterness to see that the English-training school, which had been run by R. D. Jameson, Arthur Pollard-Urquhart, and Winter himself, and which was all that was left of the once proud Orthological Institute of China, was now operating as "practically a British show" under T. T. Shui. Though the total enrollment had dropped down to fewer than a hundred because of his policies, Shui was "doing quite well out of it for himself." When Wilma Fairbank had come through Kunming and visited the school, she and Winter agreed that it no long either needed or deserved "as much attention [as] many other institutions." So it was that the OIC, which had captured the imaginations of so many talented people, British, American, and Chinese, and the attention of the Rockefeller Foundation, disintegrated into little more than just another racket.

Oddly, in this town where nearly everything was becoming a racket, one institution that distinctly was not was Lianda (the association of northern universities in exile), though it was viewed as one by important elements of the Nationalist government. Blessedly for its potential victims, the government was not yet a single voice, but its educational policy, as voiced by the Blue Shirts, the Nationalist fascist wing, was epitomized by the slogan "Nationalize, militarize, productivize."[17]

Nationalization of education meant creating "students possessed of a single-minded love for the nation and a readiness to sacrifice even their lives for it." This required a radical break from tradition, witness Yü Wen-wei: "The children that we educate are the nation's children, not children of the family or clan. The ultimate goal of educational policies must be the nation."

"Militarization" of education meant that future teachers would "train students to be fighters in a great war." Military indoctrination would begin in kindergarten, where children would be given guns and warships for toys and where pictures of battle scenes would be placed on schoolroom walls. Throughout the school years "students would be nurtured in a military environment—with a particular stress on physical development—so that the 'frail and bookish' youth of the past would be replaced by a generation of warriors."[18]

As to "productivization," the Blue Shirts deplored the "long gown" tradition in education. They believed that the schools perpetuated an arrogant and socially useless elite. Under their reform, students would no longer study "dead books" as a means of preparing for government office. "Instead, all students would devote part of their time to manual labor on farms or in factories. The traditional disdain for manual labor and the working classes would in this way be removed, and intellectuals would become producing members of the nation."[19]

To the increasing discomfort of the Guomindang, Lianda, with its commitment to democracy and to liberal education, remained a place where ideas were kept alive against the darkness of war, as if the intellectual heritage represented by the diverse faculty of the associated universities was a national treasure to be preserved for a future that was peaceful. Those who were at Lianda saw themselves as caretakers of the ideas and values, Western and Eastern, that made life human.

At the same time, Lianda provided a forum for the increasingly outspoken criticism of Guomindang policy by China's leading intellectuals. Many of them had learned the heady vigor of free speech in America, and they practiced it now out of loyalty to a tradition they had made their own. Thus at Lianda, an amazing intellectual community had been "forged in the fires of national crisis"—in historian John Israel's phrase.[20]

As Israel tells their story, China's leading intellectuals in exile, their material existence no better sustained than that of the poorest peasant, were faced with the immediate question: "In the midst of death, starvation, suffering, and destruction, how do you justify the pursuit of learning?" Their answer was to create a community of scholars sustained by a hard-earned "balance between the two antithetical conditions necessary for liberal learning: freedom and community—freedom for individuals to think, feel, and explore, and a community to sustain them intellectually, socially, and psychologically."

At Lianda, where so many of the faculty who had studied abroad were now translating their ideas into a Chinese context, there was an inescapable cross-cultural dialectic, and the tension between Chinese and Western cultures was what gave this academic community its coherence. In Israel's words: "To students immersed in English literature, Keynesian economics, or modern physics, the presence of great scholars in the old tradition—conveyors of the national heritage—provided psychological affirmation of their cultural identity even while the Westernized curriculum gave them a sense that they were pioneers on the frontiers of knowledge."[21] That intellectual excitement is one reason—their being Chinese is the other—why former students and professors say little of the suffering and deprivation they experienced there. They talk instead of the exhilaration of freedom—the kind of radical freedom at great price that no university in China has known since—though the events of June 1989, still a taboo topic in China, were an attempt by the students to revive it.

But wherever such brilliant fires burn, there will be those who want only to extinguish them. The Lianda faculty had been kept at sub-subsistence incomes by a simple government policy that held wages at government institutions in all parts of the country at the same level, regardless of local conditions. No provision had been made for the rocketing inflation brought on by American presence in the city. In fact, as John Fairbank, among others, believed, the Nationalists were "bent on the destruction of the [Lianda] faculty."[22]

As it happened, the member of the Lianda faculty who most nearly embodied the university's ideals was also the first Chinese person Winter had known, and the one who introduced him to Chinese manners and who was directly responsible for his coming to China in the first place. This was Wen Yiduo, whom Robert Payne, teaching at Lianda at this time, described as a man who "subtly exercised an intellectual mastery over the Lianda community."[23] Indeed, when in 1946 Lianda's professors prepared to move back north, they chose Wen to compose and carve a commemorative stele with the proud words that celebrate its intellectual and spiritual harmony, along with the ideals of tolerance and free expression. Wen's inscription read: "The five colors blended into a light that grew in brightness; the eight notes played in concert sounded harmonious and peaceful . . . . Within the campus walls it established a model of academic freedom; outside it won acclaim as the bastion of democracy. It spurned the praises of a thousand sycophants for the honest criticism of a lone scholar."[24]

During his first ten years on the Tsinghua faculty, Winter did not see Wen; and even when Wen joined the Tsinghua faculty in the early Thirties, he "was locked up in his study at all times and never appeared at social affairs."[25] Indeed, Wen had never been a man for social affairs. Had the world allowed, he would have confined his attention to the family and his work at revisioning the Chinese classics in the light of modern scholarship. He tried to turn his back on politics, but his moral force and vividness of personality were such that whatever he did was political.

It was the physically slight Wen who had led two hundred of his own students on a long march over mountains from Changsha to Kunming in 1938. It was also he who wrote, as preface to an edition of folk songs that they had collected from the Miao people on the way: "You say these [poems] are primitive and savage. You are right, and that is just what we need today. We've been civilized too long, and now that we have nowhere left to go we shall have to pull out the last and purest card, and release the animal nature that has lain dormant in us for several thousand years, so that we can bite back."[26]

The war against Japan, Wen urged, was his countrymen's final chance to prove their spirit, "a chance that comes once in a thousand years, to let us see whether there still exists in our blood the motive power of the ancient beasts; if not, then we had better admit that as a people we are spiritual eunuchs, and give up trying to survive in this world."[27]

But once in Kunming, though Wen showed great fortitude in coping with the hardships he and his family met there, he found no way to give voice to his patriotism but to carry on his studies of the Tang Dynasty poets and of the social background of such Chinese classics as the *Book of Poetry* and the *Book of Changes*. As for the civil conflict that rose in intensity even as the war against the Japanese moved toward its close, he ignored the violence for as long as he could. But in 1943, Wen was forced into the public arena again. His own sons were almost of an age when they would be conscripted into the Nationalist army, and Wen contemplated the prospect with anguish. The youth of China were already being forced to fight against one another, and Wen could see almost every day strings of Nationalist army conscripts chained together or left to die on the roadside without medicine or food or pay.[28]

One afternoon in April 1944, Wen had taken his eight-year-old daughter and a dozen students to a grassy spot at the edge of town to enjoy the air and talk about poetry. On their way back to the main road, they came across a group of such conscripts. Incensed, Wen said:

> We've got to do something about it. Each time I see these "able-bodied recruits" starved to death at the side of the road it's as if I myself suffered their punishments. Look at them there, tied together, dragged along, driven at gun point, every one of them emaciated to such an extent that their legs are no larger than this.

Here, Wen touched his forefinger to his thumb to show the pitiful thinness of their limbs. "They trudge on, trudge on, and one of them falls to the ground. They trudge on again. Down goes another."[29]

So Wen was reluctantly drawn back into active politics and eventually to participation in the newly formed Democratic League, for whom he helped edit a newspaper. Launched by Nationalists who hoped to establish a democratic alternative to the "expanding Communist influence and Guomindang demoralization," the league enjoyed strong support at Lianda.

Wen was an outspoken anti-Communist. But in his efforts to keep alive the possibility of a third force, he caught the attention of Guomindang secret agents. His friends urged him to go to the U.S. for a while but he refused and instead remained at the increasingly fiery center of the Democratic League. It was all coming about as Wen had anticipated over twenty years ago in a poem that Robert Winter translated:

The lamplight has whitened the walls,
The faithful tables and chairs are as intimate as friends,
There comes from the heaped books the smell of old paper,
My favorite cups look virtuous like virgins,
The baby presses his mouth against his mother's nipples
From somewhere a snore proclaims the health of my eldest son.
O mysterious calm night, O perfect peace,
O voice of gratitude trembling in my throat!
And then once more the sweet damnable curse returns—
Calm night! No, I refuse to accept your bribes.
Who will fill the narrow space between these walls?
My world is larger and includes other worlds:
These walls cannot be separated from the agony of war.
How can you find a way to stop my heart beating?
Better to let my youth [mouth?] be filled with mud and sand
Than to praise one's own happiness and sufferings!
Better let rats dig deep holes in my skull,
Better let worms feed on the pulp of flesh and blood!
Once, did we live only for a cup of bread and for songs,
For the pleasant sound of the pendulum ticking in a calm night.
How did we hear the groans of our neighbors,
How could we see the shadows of the widows and orphans
shivering against the wall,
Twitch of death in trenches, madmen biting their beds,
All these tragic scenes running under the mill of life.
Happiness! I shall not receive your bribes!
My world is not enclosed within these narrow walls.
Listen! The cannon-shot, the god of Death roaring!
O calm night, how can you stop my heart beating?[30]

When Winter returned to Kunming in 1945, he was shocked at Wen's living conditions: "His whole family was crowded into two little rooms, while across the road a man who could not compare with him in scholarship, but who spent a good deal of his time flattering both civil and military officials, occupied a large double house." In his efforts to make ends meet, Wen was sitting up all night carving seals and ruining his eyes in the process. Winter did what he could to help him out. Whenever he bought a sack of flour or sugar, he would share it with Wen. "He lived about two miles across the lake from me and he protested at my carrying the things to him on my back and made me promise that I would let his sixteen year old son come for the things in the future, which I did."[31] In this way, Winter got well acquainted with Wen's eldest son, who, as we shall see, later became his student.

That August, more suddenly than anyone except those who knew about America's terrible new weapon could have anticipated, the Japanese surrendered. But there was little celebration in Kunming. As Winter put it a few days after V-J Day, "The war is supposed to be over, but no thinking person is very much elated in this country."[32] It was not clear when the political situation, transportation, and coal necessary for the coming winter would permit Tsinghua to return to Peking. More disturbing still, the prospect of full-blown civil war, following eight years of resistance to the Japanese, was a bitter pill.

In this letter written four days after V-J Day, Winter confined his remarks largely to the physical debilitation of his colleagues, but there must have been drastic debilitation of morale as well. Everyone knew that the end of one war meant the beginning of another—this new one civil. Lianda prided herself and her singular energy derived from her ability to embrace so wide a range of political and philosophical and aesthetic traditions. Her students too ran the gamut, from impoverished scholars nursing a penny's worth of tea in the teahouses "where they sought refuge from murky dormitories and an overcrowded library, to young men on the make, who used proceeds of smuggling on the Burma road to rent luxury flats for themselves and their girl-friends."[33]

Political loyalties at Lianda ranged from "from the leftist Society of the Masses to the rightwing Three People's Principles Youth corps," and the university also housed an enormous variety of literary societies, dramatic groups, and wall newspaper associations. (Under the tutelage of poet-critic William Empson, there was even a thriving group of young "new critics," many of them also poets working to nurse a modernist Chinese poetry). Lianda's Democracy Wall, where posters and student political opinions were regularly posted, was a special source of pride, "and the institution proudly accepted the accolade as China's 'Bastion of Democracy.'"[34]

Two principles held this radically mixed community together: "First, that China must fight to the finish against the Japanese aggressor. In this national cause there could be neither compromise nor capitulation. Second, that the university must have freedom to set its own course in the academic realm." But now with Japan's defeat, instead of looking forward to the prospects of real peace, the scholars and students of Lianda faced stark reality: with the defeat of the enemy whom he had always considered secondary, Chiang Kai-shek could now concentrate his forces on his real enemy, the Communists. The prospect was of a sustained civil war that only the staunchest supporters of Chiang's Guomindang Party and military apparatus could look forward to. Lianda could expect renewed political and quite possibly military force against them. Moreover, the defeat of the Japanese also meant that the three universities that came together in Lianda, as well as the parts of the Academia Sinica and the Peiping Library that had been relocated for the duration, would now return to their native soil in Peiping, and the Southwest Associated University would be dismantled.[35]

Such bright prospects as there were resided for the most part in the sweet by and by. The university people did look forward to a substantial improvement in living conditions, and the American State Department had offered some help for cultural projects. But no one expected substantial relief in less than a year's time, and Winter observed that for the present the photographs "of people rescued from prisoner of war camps" that had been appearing in the magazines would give "a vivid picture of the way most of the students and professors here look." Many students had committed suicide lately "rather than wait to starve to death."[36] That was the important thing—that people get more to eat. "The Chinese are able to thrive mentally in conditions which we could not endure, but it is not pleasant to see them wasting away physically."[37]

Then Winter went on in a kind of Chinese vein:

> Nothing can be done about that. Only yesterday an important professor in the University, who is already distracted by the narrow margin in which he is living, learned that his wife has tuberculosis. He told me that the doctor told him that at this altitude and in their present circumstances, there is no hope either for her to get well; or for her to be separated from her small children. In the student body, tuberculosis is estimated to be about 25%."

But, as Winter said, nothing could be done about that. It was a disaster that dwarfed the powers of human remedies. Even the surrender of the Japanese to the United States brought little balm.

Winter's life was lightened a little by visits from such old friends as Wilma and John Fairbank and Joseph Needham. He also sometimes enjoyed the company of R. F. Roxby, the British cultural attaché, and the writers Robert Payne and William Empson, both of whom were teaching at Lianda at this time. But though intellectual companionship always meant much to Winter, companionship could do little to mitigate circumstance. The worst expectations of the Lianda community were already beginning to materialize. On October 3, 1945, a fight had broken out between the troops of General Tu Yu-ming, commander of the Guomindang's Kunming garrison, and those of provincial commandant Lung Yun. The Guomindang was consolidating its position, and working for the centralized control of the nation that had always been one of its principal aims. Winter was marooned for four days in the midst of bullets and flying shells ("My garret would be right in the line of fire.") On the fifth day, Winter crept out to search for something to eat. He had a bayonet jabbed at him every twenty feet, and he found all the stores boarded up, but finally he was able to get two eggs through a crack in a door for $400.

The political implications of the clash between the two armies was not lost on the Lianda students and professors. Under the Lung Yun administration, dissident intellectuals had been tolerated. But Kunming's new leaders quickly made clear that that policy would not be continued. Soon the students would be out on strike, in defense of the freedoms that their professors had taught them to value and that for many of them was the meaning of their lives. When professors deplored the strike the students responded with the bitter slogan: "I love my Teacher, but I love Truth Even More." As to the broader conflict between Guomindang and Communists, on October 10, 1945, Chiang and Mao signed an agreement. It was inconclusive and avoided the real issues between them, but for a moment, as Chiang and Mao toasted each other across a Chungking banquet table, people dared to hope that the civil war could be avoided.

By mid-October, Chen Fu-tien was on his way to Peking to see what was left of the university, and President Mei called a meeting at which he would "tell the Tsinghua faculty about the plans for returning to Peking." But no one expected that there would be transportation to take them home before the following spring. Winter's army job had finally wound up, and he had only his eight lectures a week at the university to prepare. But he made use of his recently arrived record collection to gather around him the company that he thrived on.

On Sunday afternoons, students gathered in his house to hear him play Western classics from his collection, and they were there on November 24, 1945, scarcely two months after the Japanese had surrendered, to hear an all-Mozart concert made up of a trio, a quartet, and the G-minor symphony.[38] After the music, his guests stayed to hear the news. Winter had a good radio that could bring in the VOA and BBC. That afternoon, they learned that what they had all dreaded most had happened: full-fledged civil war had broken out in an artillery duel between the Nationalist and Communist armies; the Americans were actively engaged on the side of the Nationalists.

The brief elation they had felt while they listened to Mozart had vanished, and now Winter's students hung their heads. It was not necessary for them to say what they were mourning for: they mourned for their country and also, since they were in the house of an American, for the future of friendship between Americans and Chinese. Perhaps they mourned for themselves as well because some of their fellows had already been arrested or beaten or gunned or grenaded down by the Guomindang, and certainly others would be. One war had ended only to make way for another.

Then Winter transformed this historically terrible moment into an occasion for a piece of teaching. As his students began to leave his house, he called them back and ran to his bookshelf, where he found his copy of Rebecca West's *Black Lamb and Gray Falcon*. He turned to a passage in which, while Ms. West was in a hotel restaurant overlooking the Danube, someone turned on the radio and a Mozart symphony was playing. The music made Rebecca West and her dining partner forget the quarrel they had been having.

Reflecting on what might be the nature of music that can work such powerful healing effects on us, West concluded that Mozart "presents a vision of the world where man is no longer the harassed victim of time but accepts its discipline and establishes a harmony with it." But such a solution depends in part on a technical trick that eliminates the idea of haste from life. Besides, it covers not even a corner of life; and for millions of people who don't like music, its comforts are inaccessible. "How could we hope," asked West, "that [music] would ever bring order and beauty to the whole of that vast and intractable fabric, that sail flapping in the contrary winds of the universe?"

As Winter finished reading the passage, a young woman sitting next to him said: "That sounds like Confucius." That master had also found in music the harmony that is always lacking from our time but for which we continue to hope. Soon, even the blackness of the day yielded to a peculiar lightening as Winter and the students talked, weaving together such consolations of philosophy and art as the West and the East together could contrive. They talked on until a kind of hush fell over them as Winter, still reflecting on the power of music to comfort and inspire, wondered what had happened to the old man who, every evening, across from his house, used to sing of Yao and Shun, the emperors whom Mencius had set up as ideal models for our humanity.

Winter had conjured up a different way of thinking about the power of music. The singer was "a living skeleton and his arms and legs showed like broomsticks through his rags." He accompanied himself on a kind of drum he had made by stretching leather over a length of bamboo. He would wait silently until a crowd had collected around him, then he would strike three majestic notes on his drum and begin. It was astonishing, Winter said, "to watch the faces of the crowd and see the solemn interest they took in the doings of two men who the singer said died 4201 and 4161 years ago." But nobody had seen this singer for a long time. The police had probably long since thrown him on the rubbish heap. Somehow the singer had become an image of Confucius. Both said that in their time there "was in the world no moral social order at all." Yet both said too that there was some hope for all of us and that music brought it out.

I think that this is the way that Winter would like to be remembered: sharing with others his own passion for art as a means of consoling by expanding our perspectives. Winter himself had developed the Chinese capacity to endure the most intense physical and spiritual suffering as if it were, after all, nothing much out of the ordinary. The humiliating life and death of the singer who sang of past nobility, like West's awareness that the magic of Mozart depends in part to a technical trick, is an inescapable feature of a world in which there is "no moral social order at all."

The Chinese people who knew Winter best remembered him as a man who had suffered with them and complained with them and finally complained as powerlessly—a most peculiar, Oriental end for a man who had set out in a Western and even Faustian spirit to seek the wisdom and beauty of the Orient. To learn from China, he finally learned, was to suffer what China had suffered. That is what one of his friends meant when she told me that yes, he was finally like one of us.

CHAPTER TWELVE:

THE STRUGGLE FOR LIBERATION

It's time to say a few words about Winter's diary (November 1945-September 1949), to which I often refer. I first heard about it in Beijing when I was interviewing Winter's old friends and former students in 1984-1985. Several of them told me what a pity it was that the diary had been destroyed during the Cultural Revolution. As it turned out, though certain sections have not turned up, the diary was not exactly lost. One copy had been sitting for nearly forty years in the files of the Rockefeller Foundation archives, where it was marked as Winter's personal property that he would eventually reclaim. Another had remained in China, to surface mysteriously at the moment of Winter's death. This second copy, a carbon of the first, includes a few handwritten revisions and a three-page report on the slaughter of demonstrating students in Kunming. Winter had taken particular pains to get this report to the Rockefeller Foundation offices by clandestine means, but it somehow vanished from their files.[1]

Even in the incomplete form that survived, the historical importance of the diary is apparent. In it, Winter has provided accounts of people, events, and conditions, many of which would otherwise have vanished from memory. Further, the years covered are the critical years of the Chinese civil war, which entered its heated final stage only after the Japanese surrender in September 1945. The diary begins in Kunming just two months after the Japanese surrender. The last entry was written in Peking in September 15, 1949, some nine months after the Nationalist commander in that city surrendered to Communist forces and two weeks before October 1, when Mao stood above the crowd in Tiananmen Square to announce that China itself had been liberated.

Inevitably, the diary sheds light not only on internal Chinese affairs but also on Sino-American relations during the period when, for all practical purposes, such relations came to an end. From the perspective of Chinese Communism, this is the period during which China struggled for "liberation." From an American perspective, it is the period during which we "lost" China. Thus, the events that Winter writes about have been obscured by propaganda wars waged by both American and Chinese cold warriors.

McCarthyism took much of its impetus from the McCarran Committee investigations into the question of who "lost" China. The position of those who believed that China had been lost by American critics of the Nationalist government was summed up in the statement prepared by the Republican minority for the MacArthur hearings in 1951, which saw that loss as the result of

> the terrific impact of the propaganda campaign against the Chinese national government, originated by forces both within and without the United States. The constant attacks upon the leadership of Chiang Kai-shek and the repeated assaults upon the alleged corruption and graft of his associates softened the fiber of Nationalist resistance, especially since many of these attacks originated within a nation which claimed to be aiding and supporting of the Republic of China. It is clear that the defection of a friend is more destructive than the victory of an enemy.[2]

Both in the diary that served also as a vehicle for his reports to the Rockefeller Foundation and in a long letter that he wrote to General Marshall in January 1946, when the general was newly arrived in China, Robert Winter did everything in his power to be part of that "propaganda campaign." Implicit in his position is a view that clarifies as the war moves toward its resolution: that if we can speak of "losing" China, it was the die-hard supporters of the corrupt Chiang Kai-shek, the friends of Senators McCarran and McCarthy, who lost it.

But while Winter's diary is of historical interest, Winter was only incidentally a historian. As he put it in the piece of self-criticism entitled "Relations with the Kuomingtang," his mind remembered "things as pictures or photographs," but he was "not good at remembering figures and dates."[3] More essentially, he was an intellectual democrat and a humanist who saw his role much as the poet Rilke did in a passage that Winter quotes without comment in the diary: The intellectual patiently prepares "in people's hearts those subtle, secret transformations out of which alone will proceed the agreements and unities of a more clarified future."[4] For Winter, the diary was a practical application of these high sentiments. He wrote them not to record history but to help change it in the hope that Rockefeller officers could talk sense to the State Department. Winter had once copied into his diary a line of Hobbes that he had found quoted in I. A. Richards's *Philosophy of Rhetoric*: "The scope of all speculation is the performance of some action, or thing to be done." The diary entries were in that sense a form of action.

Because he wrote the entries under difficult circumstances, often in immediate reaction to the suffering he saw around him, and because he sent them unrevised and largely uncorrected, Winter was modest about their value. To David Stevens, he said of the diary in March 1947 that he didn't write it for any specific purpose:

> The impressions are sincere at the time they are written, but they are inconsistent and they are certainly composed too hastily on the typewriter. Perhaps the relative pronouns go astray from contagion, since there aren't any in Chinese. I hope that they serve occasionally to supplement topical news.[5]

This modest disclaimer did not discourage David Stevens from circulating sections of the diaries that he received to other officers of the Foundation, to RF president Raymond Fosdick. Occasionally, Stevens also passed them on to officials in the U.S. Department of State, for whom Winter's diary sometimes provided the only versions available of events that had strong bearing on American policies in China.

Looking back in September 1959, Winter himself, under pressure from Chinese Communist authorities, reflected on the history and purpose of the diaries. When he became director of the OIC, he said the Rockefeller Foundation expected him "to report to them about the teaching but nothing else." But during the period of the diary, he had taken advantage of his connection "to scold the American government and to warn them of the dangers of following stupid policies." In other words, he voiced to them the convictions of China's intellectual class, his own colleagues and students, as when, on January 12, 1947, he told Stevens that China was "in an uproar," and that the "best elements" in the country were "protesting against an American policy which has supported a moth-eaten regime instead of turning the flit-gun to it."[6]

As he would later emphasize to the Chinese and as he reassured Stevens in that same January letter, Winter was well aware that his work for the Foundation was "not to report on Chinese political developments," and that they were not Stevens's "main interest." But he could not see how plans could be made for "future programs in the field of humanities" unless they took into account "some data on the question of possible disturbance." And who better could provide that data? "I occupy a peculiar position here which enables me to follow these trends better than most Americans who merely go round the circle of cocktail parties for the military like blindfolded donkeys," he told Stevens. "I have felt that it was my duty to inform American official representatives of these trends, including General Marshall himself, who gave me, as far back as a year ago, a polite acknowledgement in these words: 'Thank you for a very clear expression of views regarding this . . . situation . . . . I appreciate your writing as you did and am glad to have the advice in view of your many years of experience in China.'"

Obviously, Winter was suggesting he had reason to expect no less from the Rockefeller Foundation.

Though Winter would tell the Communists that he was merely tolerated by the Rockefeller Foundation as a kind of "window dressing," David Stevens consistently let Winter know how much he valued his diary. As early as January 1946, Stevens asked Winter's permission to select some pages for printing and suggested that Winter "prepare the ms. and possibly make a book."[7] Again, in February 1947, Stevens said: "The prospect ahead is getting better and better for you to produce a book of wartime diary."[8] But in the end, the diary was not published. The pervasive anti-American bias would have made it an impossibly bitter pill for the general reader to swallow, while its criticism of the Nationalists and of the American government for supporting them would have been equally intolerable to American official opinion.

Winter did not change the policies of the American government by describing the brutal results of that policy. But the diary remains a rare example of personal testimony intended, however naively, to influence a government to act more wisely and more humanely. In this respect, as in others, Winter was perhaps acting out not only his role as a Western intellectual, for whom criticism of a government's misdeeds was a right (though perhaps more honored in the breach than the observance) than as representative of the Chinese literati, for whom it was a responsibility.[9]

*   *   *

In earlier times of more local wars, Chinese men of letters, having exhausted their powers of criticism, retired to live like hermits in the mountains. But now there was no place to hide. The age of the solitary scholar was past. Many students and professors at Lianda, such as Winter himself, felt themselves driven to be warriors—not in the armies of Chiang Kai-shek (where death was more likely to come from starvation and abuse and lack of medical care than from wounds at the hands of the enemy) but as soldiers engaged in the struggle to ensure that China might know a future beyond victimization and violence.

V-J Day did not bring that future any closer. To the contrary, Japan's surrender marked the beginning of the now single-minded civil war against the Communists to which Chiang Kai-shek's Nationalists had viewed the anti-Japanese war as a mere prelude. Winter himself, despite everything, had enjoyed a richly satisfying teaching career in China; but the incongruity of teaching, say, the novels of E. M. Forster in an atmosphere of endless warfare, was draining his powers. "I am supposed to be here to interpret Western culture through humanistic studies. I am not sure what the humanities are. I am not sure that if I knew what they are it would be possible to teach them."[10]

Chinese intellectuals had demonstrated astounding willingness to carry on under difficult conditions. At the very outbreak of the Sino-Japanese War, the strongest universities in China had chosen to go into exile rather than to cease operating in the cities of the northeast. And all through the war, despite the shortage of books, quarters, equipment, and nearly everything else except their dedication to preserving their national culture and laying down some foundation for reconstruction once the war had ended, the academic community called Lianda had not only survived but, in the words of John Israel, its historian, had become "the outstanding university in the history of modern Chinese education and probably one of the preeminent centers of learning in the history of world education."

But while Lianda had managed to survive and even flourish as an intellectual community, it had done so at great cost. As early as 1942, John Fairbank had reported that Chinese academics in Kunming, especially the faculty of Tsinghua, many of them American-trained professors, who, in Fairbank's words, "think and speak and teach as we would," were under extreme pressure from the minister of education to think and speak and teach in conformity with Nationalist dogma.[11]

The Nationalist efforts at subjugation were brazenly direct: younger faculty members who joined the Nationalist Party were given special assistance and attention from the wartime Nationalist capital of Chungking; those who did not come around, once they had exhausted their personal resources (which meant selling even their books and clothes), suffered, in Fairbank's words, "continued malnutrition, illness, and eventual demoralization." It was generally understood by Western observers on the scene, including Fairbank and Winter, that these scholars were being deliberately starved to death in an effort by the Guomindang to force their approval of the government. In the long run, unless there was some form of concerted American intervention and relief, Fairbank saw "those faculty members who stand for the American ideal of freedom in teaching" destined to be eliminated by "death, dispersal, or corruption."

The Japanese defeat thus brought no improvement of conditions for China's scholars. In fact, monthly salaries for full professors dropped in September, the first month of peace, from $80,000 to $57,000 Chinese dollars, though Winter estimated the absolute minimum for supporting a man with two children as $300,000 a month. In September 1945, Winter told Stevens that "the pictures of people rescued from prisoner of war camps which have been appearing in the magazines will give you a vivid picture of the way most of the students and professors here look."[12]

Nor was it only starvation that threatened the survival of the intellectual community at Lianda. One of the first sections of the diary that Winter smuggled out of Kunming tells of the suppression and, on December 1, the murder of Kunming students by secret policemen and by soldiers of the local garrison commander, General Kuan Lin-cheng, who was probably being used by Guomindang chairman and acting governor Li Chung-huang or by agents of General Tsung-huang, head of Chiang Kai-shek's secret police.[13]

The immediate occasion for this bloodshed was a demonstration at which the students requested that they "be allowed in practice the freedom of speech which had been granted them in recent edicts; that the civil war be brought to an end; that the American government either withdraw its troops from China or impose conditions on the Chinese government in return" for its cessation of terror. A few nights previous to the actual bloodshed, machine gun fire, aimed in the vicinity of an earlier demonstration and intended as a kind of last warning, had broken a roof tile just over the heads of Winter and a guest who was visiting him in his home. No one was hurt during that shooting. December 1 was the occasion of the second episode, which left three students and a teacher dead and a score of university students lying wounded in Kunming hospitals. (Five days later, according to Winter, ten of the wounded had also died.)[14]

The four who had been killed on the spot, Winter said, were on display in the university auditorium, where they had been laid out by their fellows to perform the tasks that only dead martyrs can perform.[15] Three of them, all men, had been killed with hand grenades. The girl, who had been wounded by one of the grenades, was killed by a soldier who opened her belly with a bayonet."[16] And a month after the episode, an amputated leg cut off a wounded student a month earlier was still lying on a table in the library. The smell was terrible. As Winter remarked, the macabre display showed "deplorably poor taste on the part of the students," but it also registered "the temperature of their emotions, which has reached a pitch far beyond questions of good taste."[17]

This episode marked the beginning of a concerted anti-civil war movement on the part of the students and also of what might be called Winter's political career. Winter's earlier anti-Japanese actions in Peking would not have seemed political to him. He was then, as he later recalled, "in a fever of activity against the Japanese all the time."[18] Perfectly respectable American Methodists were involved in actions similar to the smuggling activities that Winter had carried out at that time. No one but the FBI could conclude, as they later did, that these were "pro-Communist activities." But now matters were different because action involved direct opposition to the Nationalist government, and, increasingly, opposition to his own government as well. But as Winter saw it, he had little choice. A day after the lethal shooting, he wrote:

> I have been deeply moved by this week's occurrences because
> I am tired of the smell of blood in this town; because to me the
> mangled body of a Chinese is just as unpleasant a spectacle
> as the mangled body of an American; because there is no point
> in teaching students who are refused all legitimate means of
> expression; and because these students died asking Americans,
> whom they firmly believed to be their friends, to reconsider
> their present policy, which is clearly one of intervention in their
> domestic affairs.[19]

Five weeks after the incident of December 1, 1945, Winter wrote to General Marshall a letter written, he said, not only because he was "greatly provoked," but also because he was "conceited enough to think" that he "probably understood the precise line of compromise which might succeed at this critical time better than some of those more nearly concerned." He wrote, that is, because he still hoped that the reconciliation between China's two powers—a reconciliation the students had died for—might still be accomplished if Marshall could be brought to understand the issues.[20]

Like most of his colleagues and students, Winter held America responsible for these deaths as accessory after the fact; if it had not been for America's continuing unconditional support, the Nationalists would not have dared to carry out this shooting. And what was at stake for him, most broadly, was the future of Western cultural influence in China. "I am so indignant at this ruthless attempt to tear down everything that I have worked for during the last quarter of a century," he wrote on January 9, 1946, "that if it happens again, I can't guarantee that I won't throw a few bricks myself." His account of the conditions out of which these diaries were born will help explain why Robert Winter steadily and ever more intensely criticized America's staunch support of Chiang Kai-shek. It also explains why he began, at this time, to use the protection he enjoyed as an American citizen to help protect the students whose courage and idealism inspired him.

On December 7, six days after the shooting, on his way out of the university library, he was confronted with a poster that said: "You teachers have trained us to stand up for the right, and now you are abandoning us."[21] Winter was especially sensitive to such a charge. He was a bold man who had always tried to act on the principles that he professed. "It is grotesque, to go on living in a world of frozen thought while such things are happening." He was fortified in that conviction by memories of Yeats and of E. M. Forster, who were among the writers he lived by. Yeats's famous line about the best lacking all conviction seemed unbearably germane. "Can I go on chatting over the teacups," he wondered, "while my friends are being murdered all about me?" The teacup Winter had borrowed from E. M. Forster, whom he quotes at this time in his diary:

> Oh that teacup! To be taken at prayers, at friendship, at love,
> till we are quite sane, efficient, quite experienced, and quite
> useless to God or man. We must drink it, or we shall die.

BUT WE NEED NOT DRINK IT ALWAYS. HERE IS OUR PROBLEM AND OUR SALVATION. There comes a moment—God knows when—at which we can say, "I will experience no longer. I will create. I will be an experience." But to do this we must be both acute and heroic. For it is not easy, after accepting six cups of tea, to throw the seventh in the face of the hostess.[22]

Remembering this passage and Yeats's line about the best lacking all conviction, Winter felt relieved. He knew what he had to do. So accompanied by the writer Robert Payne and by Payne's beautiful and talented wife, Rose Hsiung (Hsuing Ting), whom he had picked up on the way, he went "to slap General Kuan down." Kuan was the local garrison commander whose troops seem to have done the actual shooting.[23]

The famous meeting lasted nearly four hours, with Winter doing most of the talking. He talked in English, thinking it to his advantage to pretend not to know Chinese. Rose Hsiung (Hsiung Ting) with whom he had worked back in Peking in the summer of 1938, served as interpreter. But Winter chose Rose for other reasons as well. The daughter of a former premier of China and a beautiful woman, she would help keep the general off balance. The upshot was that General Kuan, under vigorous cross-examination by his visitors, convinced them that while he had taken some part in the shooting, it was not he who had planned it and that he would do what he could to prevent further incidents.

But as the demonstrations continued and spread, so did the shootings and beatings and arrests spread throughout China—to Wu Han, to Chunking, and, once the universities had returned there, to Peking. And more and more anti-Americanism would be a salient theme of student demonstration. The continuing presence of American troops now that the anti-Japanese war was over was a deepening cause of resentment and outrage. Rapes, pedestrian killings, and injuries by military vehicles driven by Americans, along with America's tenacious support of an increasingly unpopular government, all fed the fires.

But often, less dramatically, the mere presence of the big, well-fed Americans swaggering through the midst of a culture that was all but invisible to them caused daily tensions that could only fester. Winter had a kind of genius for observing and recording such scenes. Speaking to Stevens in the winter of 1947 about the kind of book that he hoped he might write for the purpose of making Chinese and Americans more sensitive to one another, Winter said: "The sort of book I envisage would show on the surface only the flesh (the stories), but the reader should feel that there is a firm psychological, sociological and anthropological skeleton underneath." Or, as he put it in the diary: "So little is needed to evoke a great deal."[24]

So it is that we can sense the depth of Winter's feeling when, in Kunming, on the way to the dentist's office one morning, he saw a beggar, naked except for a few blackened rags about his middle, kneeling on the sidewalk "in an attitude of patient despair." On the sidewalk before him, in "an astonishingly beautiful hand," the man had written four or five hundred characters that told of his education, the exams he had passed, and the positions he had held. A small crowd had gathered around him, moved, and one of them had just put one hundred Chinese dollars into the beggar's bowl when two American soldiers, drawn by the crowd, pushed their way through it, "and unable to understand what was going on, walked over the writing, scuffing the beautiful characters with their shoes. But the beggar didn't raise his head."[25]

CHAPTER THIRTEEN: HOMECOMINGS

On February 19, 1946, the Fourteenth U.S. Army Air Force, under the command of Colonel James L. Jackson, completed their removal from Kunming, leaving behind only a three-man Graves Registration Team whose duty it was to care for the American Military Cemetery where more than eight hundred Americans were buried. Other vestiges of Western influence were vanishing from Kunming as well—the Yunnan Provincial Teachers' Training College, for instance, where the last embers of I. A. Richards's dream of teaching China English through Basic were fading to ash. (Indeed, several people I interviewed told me that Chinese professors in the English department never believed in Basic because it didn't provide enough vocabulary for true expression[1]—in other words, that it had never enjoyed intellectual respectability.)

Although he had remained friendly with Wu Fuheng, the present codirector of the Training College, and in the spring of 1945, at Wu's request, had helped out there for a couple of weeks, Winter never formally renewed his connection with the school after he departed for the U.S. in 1943. The college (like the Basic project at large), which had always lived more by hopes than by accomplishments, managed to wobble along for another three years under the codirection of T. T. Shui and Wu Fuheng. Even after the Rockefeller Foundation, upon Winter's recommendation, ended their support, Richards persuaded the British Council to pick up the slack. But now in early 1946, the British too were ready to let the Training College Basic program die. Percy Roxby, head of the Council in Kunming, had heard from Joseph Needham that Winter had severed his connections with the school because of Shui's gambling habit. In response to a query from Roxby, Winter confirmed Needham's report and thus delivered a deathblow to the Training School.[2]

So although I. A. Richards kept fighting for it almost to the moment of his death some twenty-five years later, his long-held dream of establishing Basic in China was, for all practical purposes, ended, and little had come of it. When Roxby visited the school in the summer of 1945, he was surprised, given the generally favorable reports he had been hearing, that few of the Training School's "products were actually teaching in the Chinese Middle Schools" and that these "did not seem to be of the type that were burning to effect reforms in English teaching."[3]

Now Winter sadly confessed to him that even in the school's heyday, the students admitted by competitive exam were "the sons and daughters of corrupt officials or Generals" and that Winter and his staff "had more than one instance of these students overturning tables and shouting that they would send soldiers in to close the school if they were not given better marks."[4] So whatever Shui's other faults, he was not responsible for the deterioration of the school to "a mere finishing school." The blame for that decline had to be laid at the door of "local conditions." Winter's belated confession raises doubts about his earlier optimistic reports regarding the Yunnan Provincial Teachers' Training College, though those had more to do with possibilities than performance. That mordant fact may also apply to the work of the Orthological Institute in general.

*   *   *

The end of America's and China's war against the Japanese was a time for homecomings. With the ousting of the Japanese, Peking had been restored to Nationalist rule, and people were beginning to think about the dismantling of the Lianda, the university in exile. The moment to make the homeward journey was approaching, and plans were made for the reestablishing of Lianda's constituent northern universities at their old grounds in Tianjin and Peking. Yet for all they had suffered there, no one found it easy to turn away from the wartime university.

Lianda, the Southwest Associated University, had its own alma mater song; its lyrics and, even without music and in translation, give us some clue as to what must have been the complex mood, compounded of hopes realized and hopes brutally trampled:

Ten thousand mile long march,
Farewell to Peiping's palaces of five dynasties;
in Hunan we rested on the slopes of Mt. Heng,

By the waters of the Hsiang,
Then again we moved on.[5]

So went the song (in John Israel's translation), but now, though the Japanese had been defeated, in the winter of 1945-1946, the dream that Peking, Tsinghua, and Nankai Universities would return to their campuses "proud, free and unsullied," as Israel puts it, must have seemed illusory to many. Even home in Peking, intellectuals would still have a grim enemy to face, for the repressive Nationalist army awaited them there.

For all their hopes, everyone knew that a civil war was imminent, more bitter in prospect coming as it would on the heels of the nearly decade-long war with the Japanese. But if Winter considered leaving China for America under this new and especially bitter provocation, he had only to remember the visit he had paid to the States in 1943. The America he had experienced then and the America he and his students experienced now through the presence of the GIs in Kunming, he encapsulated in his diary with the complaint of the poet Rilke: "Now there comes crowding over from America[:] empty indifferent things, pseudo-things, dummy-life . . . . The animated experienced things that share our lives are coming to an end and cannot be replaced."[6]

Winter's experiences with the American military, as I've noted before, had especially soured his feelings for his country. The Americans in Kunming, he and his students observed, "picked up with the worst type of Chinese war profiteer." And now during their preparations for the departure, the American military had destroyed in great bonfires large quantities of equipment and clothing, lest they fall into Communist hands. This dismayed the Chinese, whose "Puritanism," Winter thought "centers about the problem of waste." The Chinese, he explained, "can easily do without things, but once things have been made it is hard for them to conceive of smashing and burning them up."[7] (He witnessed an example of that reluctance one morning in the dentist's office where he had watched an old lady refuse to spit out the mouthwash she'd been given after an extraction. Finally, after the missionary dentist, Sister Kunegond, repeatedly shouted at her not to swallow it, she spewed it into the basin, then said sadly: "Ai ha! what a pity. Why didn't you let me swallow it? It must have cost a lot."[8]

Sexual harassment and attacks on Chinese women by drunken GIs in Kunming and elsewhere had also become intolerable to the Chinese, though they had no choice but to tolerate them. On December 7, the Shanghai newspaper *Shidai Jih Pao*, reporting an incident in which a woman was injured trying to fend of the attack of a GI, observed that "ladies passing by places where American servicemen assemble during the night are always frightened that they might do something against them." The writer hoped that U.S. army authorities would "pay attention to this matter, so as not to let it lead to serious consequences."[9]

Questions of willful vice aside, in Kunming, the American military inadvertently ruffled the feathers of a community that, until the war visited it, had moved at a medieval pace. Winter often spoke of the disturbances caused by American military vehicles on the preindustrial streets. Once he had seen an idiot slave girl—"I don't know what we do with them, but I suppose that we put them out of the way in some very hush-hush fashion. But here they become slaves"—stop in the middle of the street to set down the two great pails of water she was carrying. Suddenly, there appeared "an enormous American truck driven by an equally enormous American soldier." The slave girl, who, Winter imagined, "must not have seen anything more than a great roaring vagueness rushing at her," stopped in her tracks, waved her arms, and screamed. The soldier stopped the truck in time, and then, as he passed her by running up on the narrow sidewalk, "he leaned out of the truck with a surprised look on his face and drawled good-naturedly, 'Why, what's the matter with you, lady?'"[10] In Shanghai, according to a newspaper story Winter translated for his diary in late December, an average of one hundred accidents involving American military vehicles occurred each month.[11]

This was not the kind of meeting between East and West that Winter had wanted and worked for. If he was appalled by the innocent, lumbering violence of GIs in the street, it was even worse when he saw similar callousness even among his cultivated American friends. "The strong doesn't need to know his weak neighbor," he reflected, after a long conversation with Wilma Fairbank. She was then serving embassy officer in charge of cultural relations in Chungking, and they'd discussed the stubborn resistance of the Chinese against what she and the American State Department thought was good for them. What she ought to have done, Winter told her, was "to see what they wanted" and then try to get it for them.[12]

What the Chinese intellectuals most wanted, an economist friend, possibly Chen Daison, told him one afternoon, was that America "state clearly that we would not interfere in a military way," and to warn both Communists and Chunking "that unless they get together at once," we would "withdraw all support for the rehabilitation."[13] And that view also appeared in newspapers, such as the Shanghai *Wen Hui Pao*, which, in late November, had "demanded" that no nation should intervene in China's civil war. "The history of foreign relations of China," their editorial writer said, "is a book of tears and bloodshed of the Chinese people. Our first demand after the victory is to maintain the independence and sovereignty of China regardless of the sacrifice."[14]

But whether such desires were expressed as appeals or demands, the American government showed no inclination to meet them. In the meanwhile, undemanding, ordinary Chinese people took their sufferings in stride. The Chinese, Winter thought, were unburdened by the Western conviction that man in the singular is at the center of everything and that his one little life decides everything. They were also without Western expectations for a richer and better life and without hope that suffering can ever come to a final end. Thus, a Chinese person, if his life presents five evils and five goods, tries to forget the evils and concentrate on the enjoyment of the goods. So now people sat patiently in enormous crowds in the market places, trying to sell their rice bowls, their books, their shoes, their seals, their chopsticks, even their winter clothes, though the month was November—all this to raise money with which to get home after eight years of exile.

Winter too managed to find good in the midst of so much evil. He had told a friend at lunch one day, as, appalled, they watched the vulgar antics of two Nationalist officers and their whores: "But you must admit that it's an exciting period . . . . You have the invasion of the vandals, the sack of Rome, the expulsion of the Goths, the experiments in the use of the colloquial of Dante's time, the great Schism, retreat from Moscow, the romantic period and the industrial revolution, all at the same time."[15]

Sometimes Winter felt like a God, "watching the antics of human beings and knowing beforehand what they are going to do." As Western historical patterns began to imprint on China, Winter, with a kind of Blakean vision, could "sometimes say with considerable assurance what the results will be and give warnings." But he knew that the movement would roll to its conclusion no matter what he said or did.[16]

The movement was rolling, but the times were confused. One day back in November 1945, while he was at the American Red Cross visiting with his friend Robert Drummond, the director, planes had flown over, and two of the Chinese assistants joked about how much happier they were two years ago when the Japanese were bombing them because then they knew how things stood. Now one had only rumors: the Americans were fighting Communist forces in Shanhaikuan; Japanese troops wearing Chinese uniforms had been put into every squad of the Nationalist First Army and filled all "vice posts of platoon commander and above." And Reuters reported that Guomindang generals were preparing to carry out joint operations with American forces to attack areas liberated from the Japanese by the Communist Eighth Route Army.[17]

Perhaps oddly, Winter did not despair of the project that had brought him to China and held him there. To be sure, he found it difficult to carry out his newly assigned job of interpreting Western culture through humanistic studies. But what kept him going was a vague but sustaining feeling that if he made every effort "to expose people he came in contact with" to the things that interested him or that he believed in, there was "some chance that some of them [would] be more decent human beings than they would have been otherwise . . . . The significant effects of our efforts are invisible, incalculable," he reflected; but though such knowledge kept him from absolute despair, he conceded wearily that it "doesn't give one very much to boast of."[18]

At the Southwest Associated University, courage mixed with despair seemed the order of the day. In December, after the murder by soldiers of three of their comrades and a middle-school teacher, the Student Council of Lianda had sent to fifty American universities a brave plea from those who craved freedom to those who enjoyed it: "We, who live in darkness, call to you in sunlight, and we ask for aid. We ask for this urgently, speedily, before our darkness is made perpetual by oppression and we lose the things we hold worthy. If you help us now, you will receive our love forever. If you deny it, a fascist government with 100,000,000 bayonets behind it may rise on the ashes of this war, and we shall be powerless to prevent it."[19]

In the long and judicious letter that he wrote to General Marshall on January 6, 1946, Winter saw both Nationalists and Communists as having "imported methods which are foreign to the traditional humanistic spirit of China," adding that "the eighteenth century writers in the West who are chiefly responsible for our present political philosophy got many of their ideas straight out of China."[20] But now "the Communists place a premium on violence, while the Guomindang leaders do not abhor violence, when and if their antagonists cannot be won over or otherwise disposed of." As to such niceties as freedom of expression or leadership selected by ballot, "both Parties treat public criticism as something subversive; neither is reconciled to the use of the ballot-box. Neither has advanced from the stage of seizing control of political power to the stage of applying that power to constructive purposes."

What Winter proposed to General Marshall was a coalition government whose implementation he had thought through in some detail. Both sides of the coalition would have to agree first to an immediate cessation of hostilities; second, to a foreign policy of friendly cooperation with both the U.S. and the USSR; and third, to a progressive agrarian policy. But a coalition government could be brought about only if America took a firm line with the Guomindang. They would be forced to comply because they could "not stand without our support." The Communists, on the other hand, would agree because they were at a disadvantage.[21] Marshall praised the thoughtfulness of the letter, but as matters turned out, he could not follow the course Winter recommended.

Though Winter struggled to keep hope alive, his nerves were bad—not surprisingly, given the immediate sufferings, the bitter disappointment that one war had ended only to allow another to escalate, and the clouded future prospects. On January 9, he burst into tears when he found that a correspondent to whom he had imagined that he had given offense was in fact not angry with him. On the same day, he mentioned an amputated leg that, for over a month, had been lying on one of the tables in the library. It had belonged to one of the students who had died when soldiers fired into a student antigovernment and anti-American rally a month earlier. The students had left it in the library as an emblem of their pain and rage.[22]

A *Time* magazine story on December 10, 1946, about the return home of Ezra Pound under indictment on nineteen counts of treason, Winter found "too smart-alec" for his taste; but it reminded him that in 1906, Pound had called him "the most civilized person in Crawfordsville, Indiana—perhaps a doubtful compliment now."[23] (He seems not to have noticed that it was also a doubtful compliment then.) If he had other thoughts about this miserable chapter in the life of the teacher who had helped to prepare his mind for the prospect of his own exile, he did not express them in his diary. But it could only have been another bitter weight to see Pound arrive at so abject an apparent end.

*   *   *

For some reason, Winter said nothing either about the funeral procession for the four victims of the December 1 incident, though it took place on March 17, 1946, when he was still in Kunming. He may simply have chosen not to attend, as did most of his Chinese colleagues; but if so, he was practicing an uncharacteristic prudence. After the killing of the students, in the company of Robert Payne and Rose Hsiung, who was then Payne's wife, he had so scathingly harangued General Kuang, whose troops were directly responsible for the attacks on the students, that the general published in a local paper a letter to Chiang Kai-shek in which he declared himself "ill informed about the character of the students and about conditions here," confessed himself unworthy of his position, and requested the general "to punish me to the full extent of the law for the terrible things which I have done in my ignorance."[24] But the bald fact is that the freedom and autonomy that the students had earlier enjoyed at Lianda was, with the end of the war against the Japanese, quickly and violently being beaten down, though dreams of freedom aren't easily extinguished, and what precipitated the December 1 slaughter was a student strike against the imminent civil war.

Now months later, some twelve thousand students and a few professors, adorned with white flowers and black armbands, participated in a funeral march that began in front of the Lianda library, then stretched out for two miles, proceeded into Kunming proper, finally to return to Lianda five hours later. Two of Winter's friends were among the three speakers at the final ceremony. One of them was Wu Han, a historian who specialized in the Ming Period. Wu said: "On the tomb are the four characters, 'Seeds of Democracy.' I think that this place should be made into a Sacred Shrine of Democracy. Historically China has had its sacred places. Soon many friends will leave here. In the future, when a new China, happy and democratic has arrived, we will never forget that in this corner of the southwest, there is a 'Sacred Shrine of Democracy.'"[25] (Some twenty years later, Wu Han would die a victim of the excesses of that New China—at the hands of the Red Guard. And if that irony is not bitter enough, it was the reaction of Communist cadres to Wu Han's historical play, *Hai Jui Dismissed from Office*, in which Mao quite correctly perceived unflattering reference to himself, that helped trigger the Great Proletarian Cultural Revolution.)

The other speaker whose words were recorded was Winter's old friend Wen Yiduo. Before he spoke, Wen, who would not live to see the New China, stood silently for what seemed an eternity. Then he said:

Today, on this spot these four young friends rest in peace. Our road, however, is a long one. A new, democratic China is still remote. Looking below me, I wonder why those participating in the burial ceremony are so few. [Few faculty appeared for the occasion.] Are they afraid? Or are they closing the door and feigning ignorance? I cannot believe that none are moved by feelings of teacher and student, friend and friend, of human compassion? Where have these people gone? I am participating today. What can anybody do to me? Today in front of the dead, I make a promise. Henceforth our direction is toward democracy. We demand that the criminals be punished. Guan Linzheng, Li Zhonguang—let them go to the end of the earth. We will follow them to the end of the earth. If we don't catch them in this generation, the next generation will continue its pursuit. Blood must be repaid in blood.

But it was Wen Yiduo himself who, four months later, would lie in a pool of blood, another victim of Nationalists terrorism. His death was a savage irony against his faith in the inevitable triumph of humane, democratic principles.

*　　*　　*

At the end of spring term, Winter was at loose ends. He spent the day after he turned in his grades examining candidates who would be part of a national slate from whom twenty-five would be selected to study in the U.S. After winding up that and a few other odds and ends, he faced several months with nothing to do "except to work on the problem of getting out of here," and it was a problem that could well take several months to solve.[26]

The original plan for a mass exodus to Peiping involved taking the train to Haiphong, which meant walking a hundred miles where the track was torn up. Unfortunately, the ground would have to be covered on foot, and travelers would have to sleep on malarial ground. Doctors in Kunming estimated that of the four thousand who began the trek, one thousand would contract the disease. So an alternate plan was contrived. Fifteen hundred students and some faculty members would leave Kunming by truck. (There were plenty of trucks but no gasoline, so they would burn alcohol.) They would drive east across the entire width of the country to a town called Wuchow, about 120 miles west of Canton, then proceed down the West River by rowboat until they reached the sea near Macao, where they could get a boat to Canton. From there they would transfer to another boat to Hong Kong and to still another that would get them to Shanghai. By the time they got there, they hoped boat service to Tianjin (which was still connected to Peiping by rail) might be restored, though even that would depend on improvement of the political situation.[27]

So it was that, faced with the two alternatives of a difficult and uncertain journey back to Peping or an extended sojourn in Kunming with those who were ill or too young or too old to make that trip, Winter chose a third. He decided to disappear into the wilds. Shortly before he vanished, he told David Stevens's assistant and his own good friend, John Marshall, "you may not hear from me for some time."

God knows he needed a vacation. He had worked for the American army giving lectures on Chinese culture during the previous summer until after the fall term had begun. And he had not given himself a day off since November—not even a Sunday—since he had begun giving outdoor concerts of recorded classical music complete with lectures for crowds of as many as two hundred people, rain or shine. (In a letter dated July 29, 1986, John Israel told me, in the context of Winter's exhibitionism, that after Liberation, "he would turn his record player up full blast while leaving doors and windows open. This was the only entertainment in town except for a couple of movie theaters, and by March the concerts were being held on the grounds of the American Consulate next door to Winter's house. The concerts began at 2:30 and ran through the afternoon. A typical program was the last, on May 4, which began with Sylvia Marlowe and Sidney Edwards performing the Marcello D Major and ended with the one movement from the Russian Miaskovsky's Symphony No. 21, performed by the Philadelphia Orchestra conducted by Eugene Ormandy.")

For all Winter's efforts to create such little islands of at least an aesthetic harmony, when John Marshall assured him that his last letter gave the impression of sanity, Winter was doubtful. He had begun to experience signs of bad nerves last January and even moments of hallucination. At six o'clock in the morning, back then, a girl student had come to his room to ask his advice about something. Then as she sat at the edge of his bed talking excitedly, she leaned forward and said, in "the low confidential tone that one uses in giving a secret password, 'Hai tei liu hsieh!' (More blood must flow!)"[28]

At that point, the girl's face faded away for Winter, and he remembered a white rabbit he'd kept as a pet in Crawfordsville when he was three. "It was crouching, its ears thrown back, its head up, its pink eyes staring with a sort of ecstasy while a ferret sank its sharp teeth into its throat to drink its blood."

Now months later, the same hallucination had recurred in the classroom when he was reading aloud from Blake's "Auguries of Innocence" and came upon the lines: "Each outcry from the hunted Hare / A fibre from the Brain does tear." He looked up to see in sharp focus the pale face of the same girl staring at him from a sea of a hundred other faces, and again he saw the rabbit and had to turn away to write something on the board in order to regain his balance.[29]

*　　*　　*

Winter's "vacation" started at four o'clock in the morning of May 13, 1946, when he dragged his knapsack and bed roll downstairs and then waited at the front door until he found a passerby who, for the price of two oranges, helped him to carry them to the place where the trucks started.[30] Maybe nothing less than the horror, frustration, and oppression of Kunming could have inspired such a vacation. Yet Winter took such obvious pleasure and showed such an observant eye on this difficult journey through lands rarely seen by outsiders that he makes it seem a genuine lark, and I can't help wondering what heights he might have reached as a cultural anthropologist.

The truck he rode in was already loaded six or eight feet above the floor, and the owners were pushing long boards down between the edge of the truck and the baggage to retain further boxes. When they had loaded crates and boxes up to a height of about fifteen feet from the ground, Winter and the other passengers clambered up, climbing like monkeys by clinging to the ropes until they had reached the top. There they tangled arms and legs together "in a sort of spaghetti-like mass" that they did not expect to unravel until they stopped for breakfast one hundred miles up the road. But just at the top of the pass by which they left the Kunming plain, they were stopped by soldiers for inspection. Everything had to be unpacked, repacked, and then the arms and legs fitted together again like a puzzle. The presence of Nationalist soldiers would be felt everywhere along the road for the next four hundred miles. Where they were not immediately present, beating peasants just to establish their power and ruthlessness over the Yunnanese, they had smeared across the crumbling beauty of ancient buildings the blue suns that were the emblem of the Guomindang.

By May 24, Winter had reached Hsichow, the chief city of the Min Chia tribe, a Mon-Kmer people Winter had met once before in 1940, when he visited Ankor. The Min Chia had no written language, and while their speech sounded to him different from Cambodian, the people had a similar charm. Among the Min Chia, Winter had abruptly entered the healing wilderness that he sought. May 24 was a kind of *Sacre du Printemps* for the tribe. A staid and hardworking people during the year, on this day, they were unrecognizable. The many love songs they had been practicing throughout the year and now performed in a high falsetto staccato reminded Winter of the cries made by his Siamese cat, though hers were legato.

But though Winter's appreciation of their music may have been imperfect, he was unequivocally enthusiastic about the kind of sexual Eden he found among them. He was especially enthusiastic about their marriage ceremony, which involved, after the flowers and flutes and dances of the festival, mating in the evening. If that proved successful, the couple was married. Against this organic ceremony with its songs that cut the air, Winter found the efforts of "the priests of capitalistic Christianity to make marriage a sacrament seem feeble and abortive."

In the sacred statuary of the Min Chia, Winter found further evidence of unfallen sexuality. Their towns were protected from evil influences by great phallic towers that rose from "low hills at strategic points—continuously fertilizing mother nature and assuring strong daughters and mares which can carry unbelievable loads up and down the rocky mountain paths, strong sons who will be able at the age of seventy-five still to run beside their mule caravans thirty-five miles a day on the rocky paths among the clouds."

Though after his return to Kunming, Winter complained to David Stevens that this section of the diary-report would have been "fuller and better written" if he had not been "plunged into a mood of the blackest pessimism" by recent events in Kunming; in fact, there is little evidence of gloom in the text. Instead, Winter sounds like a man who has come out into bright sunshine after a very hard night.

Ten days after his arrival among the Min Chia, Winter moved on to Zhoucheng, where he took up with a family of indigo dyers whose sons ran mule caravans to Likiang near the Tibetan border. About their house were fields of indigo covered with mats about two and a half feet off the ground, "for indigo is afraid of frost and also of the sun."[31] He passed the night of May 27 in their house. The sons spoke a few words of Chinese, and, except that the women and girls came into the room where Winter slept with two of the sons and examined him by the light of bamboo lamps to see how he looked undressed, Winter found their hospitality charming.

Early the next morning, he got up in the dark and helped pack the mules for the five or six day's journey. By the time that the sun came up, they were well on their way; and Winter noticed, presumably from markings on the bales, that the load of cotton thread on the mule in front of his had already been six months on the road from India. Winter's party had been forced to take the difficult east road to avoid "central soldiers," whom his Min Chia friends told him "would seize the mules and give them a beating for good measure." The Min Chia were eagerly awaiting the arrival of the Communists, whom they had heard would be coming soon to help them. They were at first suspicious of Winter as an American until he told them that he did not support Nationalist policy.

This leg of his journey had a variety of charms for the nerve-jangled American. On the morning that they started for Likiang, for instance, they found women sitting along the trail "with great baskets of snow they [had] carried down from the mountains on their backs," and besides these baskets, a bowl of prunes and a jar of cane syrup. They filled a bowl with snow, broke a prune with a chopstick, and stirred it into the snow, then poured some syrup over the top. The confection cost $50, or the price of two cigarettes, and Winter found it delicious.

The first night on the trail, Winter and his party spent at a mule inn in the mountains. One of his traveling companions was the sixteen-year-old son of his Chou Ch'eng host, a boy who stood nearly six feet tall and was half again as heavy as Winter (who weighed 172 at this time, according to an FBI field report). Like the women on the previous night, the boy was curious and crawled over to the pile of straw on which Winter was lying to examine his body for hairs, which were "very surprising to him." Winter made no objection. He felt as pleased about the attention as he did when a dog nibbled his arm for a flea. It was the highest compliment that the boy—or the dog—could pay him.

Winter and the boy talked for an hour before going to sleep, Winter teaching the young man a few words of Chinese, and he singing for Winter snatches of Min Chia love songs (the Min Chia sang the full songs only on one day in the year.) Again, Winter was taken by the power, if not the melodiousness, of these songs, whose effect he likened to "the ruff of the golden pheasant [that] appears throughout the year as a disorderly mass of black and gold feathers, but once or twice a year for a few minutes it is thrown up to one side and becomes a geometrical design of concentric circles which look as if they had been drawn with a compass. The eye of the pheasant is at the center, and it is not surprising that the hen is hypnotized." Whether Winter himself was similarly hypnotized, he doesn't mention. He says nothing of what followed, but given the recent energies of the Min Chia rituals and the urgings of his own sexuality, one may assume.[32]

The food Winter ate on this trip was as exotic as the love songs, if not equally appealing. Still, he found that he could put down a cold salad of sliced raw turnips, walnuts, and red pepper with a few flies, of course, taken with a tablet of sulphaguanadine, and find it quite appetizing. Unlike the Chinese who ate sitting in a circle, the Min Chia ate squatting on their heels in two long parallel lines, and it was "taboo to cross from one side to the other."

Even as he became accustomed to the exotic ways of the Min Chia, Winter caught glimpses of the still more mysterious peoples that lived on their fringes. One night, his party stopped in an inn where five miserable people lay down next to Winter and asked him for medicine for their sores. They spoke a language, one of whose consonants "was like the sound of a mule breaking wind." Nobody "knew where they came from."

The last part of the trail to Likiang was exquisite. The party rode on through the clouds and sometimes "could only see the trunks of pine trees and the grass at [their] feet starred with dwarf anchusa, blue as forget-me-nots, yellow and magenta primroses, purple orchids and lavender daises, down into the valleys through hedges of vivid wild roses."[33] Such sights were an elixir after the violent, dirty streets of war-crazed Kunming.

On June 3, 1946, after the mule train had been a week on the trail, they looked down on the plain of Likiang, rising behind it the snow-covered Jade Dragon mountain, whose steep slopes had been attempted by Swiss experts but which had never been climbed. Here Winter came into the land of a second romantic people, the Naxi, a Tibetan tribe whose legends centered upon this beautiful mountain. (By odd coincidence, Ezra Pound would later discover the Naxis in Joseph Rock's *The Ancient Na-khi Kingdom of Southwest China*. In fact, the upland kingdom became for Pound a version of the terrestrial paradise that he would celebrate in Canto 113 of his epic *Cantos*:

> And over Li Chiang, the snow range is turquoise
> Rock's world that he saved us for memory
>   a thin trace in high air).

To compound the coincidence, Rock himself, a crotchety, strong-minded autodidact who bore some resemblance to Winter, had almost ten years earlier met I. A. Richards and his wife, Dorothea, in Peking and provided them with detailed directions for a six-week climbing expedition in which they followed much the same route as Winter, although, their minds on peaks, they seem to have paid less attention than Winter to tribes. John Paul Russo, Richards's biographer, quotes a letter to his brother in which Richards spoke of Li Chiang as "a lovely little Chinese town, thronged with Tibetans on their way down to fetch tea, etc. Also lots of different tribes Lolo's, Naki's, Miao's, etc."[34]

Winter was fascinated with the Naxi written language, the only extant pictographic script in the world. He made friends here with a Naxi schoolteacher, who gave him one of their books. It was thirteen inches long and three inches wide and read from left to right and top to bottom, like English. He copied five characters into his diary and translated them:

1. Not read (this sign indicates the beginning of a book.)
2. A la muan sher ba t'u dzhi
(Ah! ancient nothing distinct do that time)
Meaning: "In the beginning of time."
3. muan mä du¨ la muan t'u tu dd¨u dzhi
(Heaven and land not come forth that one time)
"Before heaven and earth existed"
4. Bi na la la muan t'u ddu¨ dzhi
(Sun and moon not come forth that one time)
"Before sun and moon existed"
5. Gkur na zaw la muan t'u tu ddu¨ dzhi
(Stars and planets [or comets] not come forth that one time)
"Before the stars and the planets existed"

A day's walk to the east of Likiang, one was among Tibetan people; but here among the Naxis, one met the tangled threads of Indian,

Chinese, and Tibetan cultures. Indeed, Winter found alive in Likiang elements of dynastic traditions that were rapidly dying out in China proper. Every schoolteacher, for example, could paint in the Chinese style, some of them admirably.[35]

But even in Likiang, change had made inroads. Though, as of old, the Naxi women conducted the business of the marketplace while the men stayed at home to do the sewing or look after the children, they no longer dressed in *pulu*, the beautiful woven cloth woven in Lhassa. Now their uniform costume was cotton cloth dyed with indigo, an importation from China.

But despite such innovations, Winter found in the Naxi a version of the noble savage. It was fashionable to laugh at that eighteenth-century dream of a harmonious human state, he conceded, but he had never seen so many beautiful people in one place. The women were strong and clean, though too heroic for Chinese taste. In their turn, the Naxi despised the Chinese and especially the people of Szechuan, whom they referred to always as "the thieving Szechuanese." Among the Naxi themselves, Winter left valuables in his room and never locked the door.

Even the forms of Naxi violence found an admiring witness in Winter. If you bullied or cheated them, he said, they were "quite capable of shooting you and leaving your body on the road." He liked that forthrightness better than the smiling hypocrisy of the West, but on at least one occasion, Naxi forthrightness put him at risk. Three days after he arrived in Likiang, he was walking in the streets when he saw a crowd gathered around a five-year-old girl who had just been taken from the river into which she had fallen.[36] Her parents, kneeling before him, begged him to save her life, and he began to administer artificial respiration.

As he was working over her, the commander of the local militia made a bumptious entrance, demanding names, etc. When Winter told him not to interfere while there was still a chance to save the child's life, the officer got angry, hit Winter on the back of the head, and ran off, only to return a few minutes later "with four rascals from the local government office and a soldier armed with a 45." whom he ordered to shoot Winter. Three times the soldier aimed, Winter laughed, and the soldier returned his pistol to its holster. After the third time, they all went away. Winter does not say what happened to the child.

While the Naxis were capable of violence, they themselves were often its victims. Twice in the two weeks he spent in Likiang, Winter heard "a great wailing when the bodies of men were brought who had been killed in the mountains" by Tibetans in whose caravans they were traveling.[37] When Winter traveled out of Likiang with Tibetan caravans, he took pains not to violate their code, and he often took from his neck the rosary he wore out of some odd nostalgia and told his beads to make the Tibetans "feel at home." The Tibetans, though astonishingly polite, were the cowboys of Asia, fine riders and quick and adept with the rifle.

In the late spring, when Winter arrived, Likiang was full of Tibetans, hundreds of them, waiting for deep summer when they could attempt the three-month journey back to Lhassa. When Winter traveled with them, they carried "sacks of coarsely ground barley, salt, and brick tea." Yak butter they managed to find locally. Except for "an occasional choice bit of putrid meat," their food was simple: *tsompa* and butter tea.[38]

Himself a crafty man, Winter delighted in describing the preparation of the tea. The leaves (ten times as much "as we would use for making ordinary tea") were soaked in water overnight, boiled for from two to four hours, then strained. To the resulting liquid, about the color of "a good undiluted red table wine," salt and yak butter were added, then the mixture was put into a churn made of a palm tree stem and "churned into an emulsion for as long as the muscles of the churner hold out." The resulting drink, which looked like café au lait, he found delicious. Tsompa was made by mixing a little of this tea with roasted oats and yak butter. The resulting paste was then kneaded with the fingers against the side of the bowl, and the lump kneaded a second time in the hands. Pieces were then broken off and eaten. The kneading served a dual purpose, for when water and fire weren't available—as they usually weren't since dung was the only fuel available on the trail—the kneading of the tsompa served as the only way of cleaning the hands.

Though Winter would not be permitted to enter Lhassa, he hoped to get to the mountain town of Chung Tien, some hundred rough miles north of Likiang, where there was a lamasery of over five thousand monks. On the way, he stopped for some days in a lamasery of the red sect.[39] Here he made friends with an old lama who wrote two pairs of scrolls for him on precious paper that came from China and with a pen made from a ten-inch stem of a palm leaf split at the end.

The scrolls, Winter remarked, were "very complimentary" to him. He transcribed them into his notes, copying also the Tibetan words and a couple of the characters. The first scroll described him as a man of extraordinary virtues, who was like the sun arising in a cloudless sky.

In the second, the world lay before him "like a starry sky on a pond of flowering lotus," and he was like a bee who had "gathered all these precious things from everywhere." The old man was impressed by the number of places Winter had been to.

But though he had been promised the assistance of a local chieftain whose daughter he had met in Likiang and though it was only two days away over a range of snow-covered mountains, Winter would never get to Chung Tien. Word had come that three robber cities of the north were preparing to plunder Chung Tien, and though the inhabitants had sent them large sums of money to prevent their coming, Winter decided that it wasn't an opportune time to make a visit. The bandits of the region came in armies of two thousand to five thousand, the men in the front, the women and children behind. "They kill, burn, and loot, and then go back." So Winter and his caravan returned to Likiang, he a bit querulous that he would probably never see Chung Tien or Atuntze, fifty miles farther north, "where the whole caravan is slid across the river on a bamboo cable."[40]

In late June, about a month before he made his way back to Kunming, Winter was sitting in a wine shop, chatting with the proprietress, a Naxi tribeswoman. Inevitably, with the help of a Tibetan interpreter, the conversation turned to how the government cheated and bullied the people. Then the woman told Winter that she had heard how Wen Yiduo had been attacking the government in Kunming, and that he had a large following.[41] She went on to quote from his recent speeches. Winter was delighted to hear news of his friend in this remote place. The young man he had met in Chicago so many lifetimes ago, who was responsible for his coming to China in the first place, had become a national symbol of courage in resistance.

On this trek through the wilder parts of Yunnan, there remained for Winter one more adventure. Because he had incurred the enmity of the local magistrate, uncle to the militia commander who had ordered him shot, Winter was forced to leave Likiang without escort, accompanied only by a student, his servant, a small boy, and a horse. Several hours south of Likiang, though they had just been reassured by militiamen on the route that their way was clear, five men armed with rifles and swords stopped them and declared that they were going to kill them.[42] The bandits then stripped them naked and ordered the student to kneel down so that they could more conveniently cut off his head. At this point Winter, whose quick temper at least sometimes stood him in good stead and who had a flair for picking up the obscenities peculiar to a region, began to curse them. "Their mothers had met an ape in the forest before they were born and . . . they were the result," he yelled. The bandits were so delighted to find a foreigner familiar with their local jokes that they released and his two companions, but only after they had dressed them in Tibetan clothes. (Winter's student companion, mad with fear, tried to drown himself in the river.)

So it was that it was in this garb that Winter traveled the rest of the journey to Kunming with a mule train. On their way, they stopped in Hsichow, a small village in Min Chia territory, where Winter headed for a street kitchen where a man was "frying a sort of doughnut in deep fat" and ordered his lunch. The man asked him where he was coming from, and when he told him that he was coming from Likiang, the man said: "Then you haven't heard the sad news. Wen Yiduo was murdered by the government three days ago before his own door. They say they killed his son too. You must have the privilege of knowing him. It was a sad day for China when that man died."[43]

Winter arrived in Kunming at nine in the evening of July 27, 1946, precariously perched, as he had been when he departed ten weeks earlier, on top of the load on an overloaded truck. Wen, he learned, had been assassinated on his own door step twelve days earlier despite the efforts of his son, who stepped in front of him and took nineteen submachine guns slugs in his intestine—but survived. Winter learned that another member of the liberal Democratic League had also been assassinated, and several others, their lives threatened, had taken refuge in the American Consulate.[44]

The victims of Nationalist terror had been "riddled with bullets from a submachine gun (of the type, so they say, which our navy supplied in enormous quantity to the Gestapo)"[45]—that is, to Chiang Kai-shek's secret police, directed by the much-feared Tai Li. It might not be fair to say that the U.S. was responsible for the murders, he went on, but "it is clear that we could have prevented them—simply by following the very intelligent advice which I gave on January 6th" in a letter to Marshall, a copy of which Marshall had forwarded to David Stevens as part of a report.[46]

Winter still placed hope in certain selections of the American public whose voices, "because we are a sort of a democracy," might still have some effect. As for himself, in a high dramatic style appropriate to the bitter moment, he wished to be put on record: "The men who are being hunted down at this moment are, in my opinion, among the best people in China, they are close personal friends of mine, and I am definitely on the warpath! These men are educators, they are great democrats, and apart from all political consideration, it is my clear duty to defend them."

Not quite three weeks after his return from Likiang, on August 15, 1946, he set off for Shanghai, thence "home" to Peking. He probably suspected, though he could not have known, that the foundations of the Cold War were already firmly in place.

CHAPTER FOURTEEN:
WHO LOST CHINA?

In the summer of 1946, Winter finally flew out of Kunming for Peiping[1] on an American military transport, after leaving four-fifths of his papers behind in order to cut down on weight. He did manage to take with him three volumes of his personal records, dating from 1940 to 1946, though the first of these volumes subsequently disappeared. Among the files he was obliged to leave behind in Kunming were the first fifteen years of "a sort of diary" he had kept since 1925, when he lived in Nanking.

On New Year's Day 1947, the occasion for the first diary entry he wrote after returning to Peking, Winter was in a reflective mood. The previous day was his sixtieth birthday, and this New Year, besides being the first he had spent in Peking since 1940, was his twenty-third in China. Now gazing at that remote past in Nanking in what he called "a Buddhist meditation," he wondered, in an oblique reference to Homer's *Odyssey*, what remained "when I have driven away the ghosts from these twenty-three years?" He hoped this would be "not a mere thoughtless heaving of the solar plexus but something more like what the Buddhists call the Great Compassion, which sees where the roots and the cure for all this suffering are to be found: 'When he is weary of these things, he becomes empty of desire. When he is empty of desire, he becomes free. When he is free he knows that he is free.'"[2] The path of suffering had brought him to a kind of enlightenment.

This side of the Great Compassion few paths to equanimity were still open in China in January 1947. Just a week after Winter wrote his meditation on the vanity of human wishes, a grim new phase of U.S.-China relations began when General George Marshall, recently triumphant as Supreme Allied Commander in the West, announced that his mission in China had failed and that he was returning home. With that announcement, such hopes for peace as were still entertained in China were erased clean. The civil war would go on like a madness. Marshall still hoped that the Nationalists would begin a process of self-reform by bringing members of the liberal opposition into the government, and indeed, Winter had recommended to him a year earlier that the government enlist "new men, familiar with our political system and . . . capable of devising ways by which the leader or leaders of China will be forced to show an attitude of service rather than of ownership in the exercise of their function."[3] But too much blood had been shed, and though, as Winter remarked in his diary, the Guomindang now humbly begged "men whom they were assassinating six months ago to join the government," it was too late. "No decent person would touch the present government with a barge pole."[4]

This failed mission had begun auspiciously enough. Within a month of Marshall's arrival in China, a Political Consultative Conference made up of representatives of the Guomindang, CCP, Democratic League, Youth Party, and nonaffiliated delegates met in Chungking. On the very day the meetings began, "the Committee of Three"—George Marshall, Nationalist general Chang Chi-chung, and Communist general Chou En-lai—agreed that hostilities should stop at once. For a moment, it looked like a strong step toward peace. A cease-fire order was issued by both parties, and with the help of truce teams made up of an American colonel and Nationalist and Communist generals, fighting practically stopped.

But by mid-March, both sides again assumed that their differences would be settled only on the field of battle; and by the spring of 1946, there had been numerous violations of the ceasefire by both sides. Neither Nationalists nor Communists, in sad fact, could find much advantage in a sustained truce. The Guomindang had grown fat on the unflagging stream of funds and supplies that came flowing in from America. Chiang Kai-shek may not have enjoyed the Mandate of Heaven, but the staunch generosity of American support made that seem unnecessary. As John Fairbank puts it, America's divided objective was "to press the Guomindang leaders into reform which would diminish their autocratic power and facilitate internal peace." But to strengthen them, he added, would be as a step toward political stability in East Asia. "We became involved in continuing to build up the Guomindang dictatorship materially at the same time that we tried to get it to tear itself down politically."⁵ As it turned out, the U.S. accomplished only the first of these goals.

The Communists—though General Marshall had found them more cooperative than the Nationalists—were equally intransigent at bottom. They had strong reasons for confidence. Assisted by Guomindang barbarities, they had won the hearts of the people in the countryside. The December 1 incident had done much to drive the intellectual community into their outstretched arms. Finally, the Communists knew that, despite the Nationalist Army's superiority in arms and numbers, the Guomindang as a governing party was hollow and beleaguered.

For most Americans, their own war over, the dynamics of this struggle in China were too remote to be of interest. But for Winter, the fate of liberal democracy was always a local and personal matter. He had staked twenty-three years of his life lost in a dream of China shared by many of his intellectual friends. Now the realization of that dream was more remote than ever. The Nationalist brutality toward his friends and colleagues tipped Winter's sympathies toward the Communists, but as he had told General Marshall in December 1946, when the general had just arrived in China, neither of the forces that were tearing China in two had "advanced from the stage of seizing control of political power to the stage of applying that power to constructive purposes."⁶ Both treated "public criticism as something subversive," and neither was "reconciled to the use of the ballot-box." Both, Winter continued, had inherited their revolutionary practice "not from China, but from the Bolsheviks." Their violent practices and intolerance of criticism he saw as "foreign to the traditional humanistic spirit of China." Both, in short, opposed the spirit of liberal humanism, a spirit Winter believed to be equally native to China as to the West.

Yet it remained true, though only for the moment, that it was the Guomindang and not the Communists who were persecuting liberal intellectuals, who alone understood and desired a government of laws that respected civil liberties and basic freedoms of speech and person. Many of these people, Winter's colleagues and friends, were American trained and had learned their love of democracy from the U.S. But by the winter of 1947, their sympathy with the United States had reached a breaking point. Marshall believed that the U.S. should leave the generalissimo to his fate, but American military transports, in violation of our own declared policy, had flown Guomindang troops to Manchuria so that the Nationalists rather than the Communists could accept the

Japanese surrender of territory. Why, Winter's friends (and of course, Winter himself) wondered, "did the American government continue to support these reactionaries?" Winter reported that his friends "feared that the famous American democracy [was] not intended for export." They feared also that Truman would soon be sending new loans to China under the ruse that the New China was a democracy.

In his farewell statement of January 7, 1947, Marshall had openly declared that there was a "definite liberal group among the Communists" who had "turned to the Communists in disgust at the corruption" in the Guomindang. These were men, Marshall added, "who put the interest of the Chinese people above ruthless measures to establish a Communist ideology in the immediate future."[7] Although five years later, Senator Joseph McCarthy would suggest that this made sense only "if it is read as a propaganda document in behalf of Communist world objectives,"[8] Winter's friends knew that Marshall was correct. They knew also that among those who went over to the Communists were some of the best men and women in China, people who had "spent their lives up to a year ago fighting for American principles" and who had turned to the Communists only after they saw that for their cause "there was no hope of support from America."[9]

Winter closed his summary of the views of his own unaffiliated liberal friends with a prophetic forecast of the broad alliance with the Communists that the liberals would find themselves driven to in 1948 and 1949. "The path of America policy is strewn with lost opportunities," his friends said,

> for you have had your eye on the wrong landmark. The sort of "security" you have hoped for is about as effectual as the Maginot line was. There is a deeper "psychological security" which you have shown little signs of in the last year. As a result of your actions you have gained the hatred of the left wing, the disappointment or contempt of the liberals, and have also, if it is any satisfaction to you, the amused contempt of the reactionaries . . . who have been playing games with you. It's no good President Truman telling us that we are a sovereign nation. If we are then America should not have put her finger into the pie and mussed it up. We feel that you have still not learned your lesson. During the recent students' parades the American army sent many special observers to listen to the Yenan

[Communist] radio to see if the students were being directed by the Communists. This is simply inane, and worthy of the [Guomindang]. But the military mind is always like that.[10]

Student demonstrations had certainly taken a sharp anti-American turn. At a time when many Chinese felt that America was keeping the civil war going by aiding the Guomindang, an episode that occurred on Christmas Eve 1946 brought anti-American feelings to a boil. Coming out of a movie one evening, Shen Ch'ung, a student of Peking University, was assaulted and raped by two American Marines. Such incidents were common enough, but the fact that the girl was a student at China's leading university brought this case to the attention of Peking's leading newspapers. Soon, anti-American demonstrations were breaking out in major cities all over the country.

Winter connected the reaction to the rape to America's "abandonment of strict neutrality and her participation in China's internal strife." The rape was simply "the last straw that breaks the camel's back."[11] There was already "a tendency to lay the blame for all evils in China at the door of Uncle Shylock," he added.[12] "For a year," he told David Stevens,

> the best elements in China have been protesting against an American policy which has supported a moth-eaten regime with millions of dollars worth of assistance instead of turning the flit-gun on it. Whenever they have protested publicly, they have been thrown into jail or massacred. Since they naturally feel that they are worth more to China alive than dead— although some have chosen to be martyrs on the theory that ten will spring up in their place when they fall—they have been lying in wait like spiders for an occasion to demonstrate. It has been impossible for them to communicate with one another by post, and the detectives in the post offices have as the first duty on their list to destroy all communications addressed to General Marshall. Finally, the occasion came.[13]

The occasion was the rape.

Winter had already told General Marshall that in the deep winter months, many students left the universities to join the Communists— Winter supposed because the rivers were frozen at this time, making cross country travel easier. Reflecting on this phenomenon, he cited the views of a graduate student in his department, the head of the San Min Chu I Ch'ing Nien Tuan, (or Nazi Youth, as they were generally known) for Tsinghua University. The young man, who was doing his thesis on Shakespeare and who admired Winter more than anyone else in the world ("please note that not all of my friends are radicals!") came to visit the American often. On the evening before Winter wrote a letter to Burton Fahs of the RF, this young fascist told Winter that "two years ago most of the students thought that the Communists were worse than the government. When they came [back] to Peking a little over a year ago, they thought that the two were about equal." Now he said, "the large majority of the students and the younger teachers are longing for the Communists to take over."[14]

Winter's own political movement was parallel to the students', but like most of his faculty colleagues, he was more skeptical than them. Convinced that the students would be disappointed with the Communists, Winter imagined that things might work out somewhat as they had in England in the time of Cromwell. Then moderate Presbyterians (Democratic League) had found themselves supporting the Independents (Communists) because only the Independents, who had an army, could do anything with an insanely stubborn king. Louis XIV (USA) made things more difficult for them, "but they succeeded in spite of French help. Then they made themselves so tiresome that everybody wanted to get rid of them. The king was restored but the people had gained most of their points and they were so fed up with all the bloodshed that they went in for religious toleration, Locke, liberalism, etc. They had learned the hard way."[15] Who can say that this prophecy might not have proven correct had the Cold War not so quickly provided a continuation of the hot one, if Senator McCarthy had not accused General Marshall himself of having "lost" China, and had American and Chinese troops not found themselves true enemies at last in the battlefields of Korea?

Meanwhile, the catastrophic scenario moved relentlessly toward its climax. During the previous May, Winter reported to Stevens that the government had inflicted 286 casualties among students in the city of Shanghai alone. "By declaring open war on the Communists, it has become even easier to shoot any critic of the government under the label than it was before." Now on the nights of February 15 to 18, Guomindang secret police, whom Winter, like other foreign observers, regularly referred to as Chiang's gestapo, swept through Peking itself, in some areas systematically entering every house. Winter had heard that over 2,400 arrests were admitted; popular estimates were much higher. The police methods were violent: they broke down doors, knocked down victims, and dragged them away. The victims included people like Ms. Yü, "a harmless old maid" who had been assistant to Ida Pruitt[16] in the Social Welfare Department of the PUMC (the Peking Union Medical College—a Rockefeller-founded-and-supported medical facility). Other victims of the raid were PUMC dentists, one of whom was arrested because he had once filled teeth for General Yeh, the chief Communist representative of the Executive Headquarters (that is to say, of the command post of Marshall's peacekeeping force.[17]

Winter was no stranger to terrorism, but these raids, by virtue of their sweep and their programmatic violation of all decencies by a government against its citizens, shocked even him. He was especially revolted by a case in which the wife of the manager of the Sino-American bookshop was arrested. When her husband begged the police not to take her because her two-month-old baby would starve to death, they answered that plenty of Chinese were "dying in the war against the Communists, and that one or two more would not matter."[18] It all reminded Winter of the Irish terrors that Yeats described in "Nineteen Hundred and Nineteen":

> Now days are dragon-ridden, the nightmare
> Rides upon sleep: a drunken soldiery
> Can leave the mother, murdered at her door,
> To crawl in her own blood, and go scot-free;
> The night can sweat with terror as before
> We pieced our thoughts into philosophy,
> And planned to bring the world under a rule,
> Who are but weasels fighting in a hole.

> He who can read the signs nor sink unmanned
> Into the half-deceit of some intoxicant
> From shallow wits; who knows no work can stand,
> Whether health, wealth or peace of mind were spent
> On master-work or intellect or hand,
> No honour leave its might monument,
> Has but one comfort left: all triumph would
> But break his ghostly solitude.

But is there any comfort to be found?
Man is in love and loves what vanishes,
What more is there to say?

In his detailed account of these events, Winter must have felt the tragic despair expressed by Yeats, yet he was also making a desperate case for reason at a moment when his own hopes and that of more than half a century of Chinese reformers were being dashed to the ground. He understood the rising anti-Communist sentiment in the States and the unfortunate American support of the warlord Chiang Kai-shek. And perhaps he faintly hoped that Stevens, through his State Department connections, might be in a position to influence American policy so that it better accorded with the facts. But his hope could only be faint. The polarization of China was in full course, and people dear to him who escaped the military raids had no choice but to take refuge with the Communists, though not out of love of the doctrine. Rather, like himself, they were dismayed by "the lack of judicial security in Communist controlled areas" and by "the confusion of ends and means inherent in the Communist theory." But having lived through the terrors of the raids, they found it easy to sympathize with people who were "too impatient to wait for peaceful methods to bring about desired reforms."[19] They or their parents had overthrown one divine emperor only to gain another who had constructed his own hodgepodge of Eastern and Western philosophy in order to identify his own ends with history's, if not with heaven's. Worse, Chiang Kai-shek had devised carrot-and-stick methods to compel the compliance of his subjects:

> Helpless or stupid citizens who submit or who pretend to submit to thought control are stuffed with American canned goods and vitamin tablets, while those who dare to use the brains that God gave them are starved. If that doesn't cure them, they are beaten. If that is not enough, they are tortured. If that doesn't work, they are shot. Surely it is much more degrading to lived under such a system than under the old regime. They have come to feel as my mother did when I was a child and my older brothers and sisters had the measles. She put me in bed with them so that we would all have the disease together and so get over it sooner.[20]

If Winter can be believed—and nothing he says on this subject is inconsistent with what one finds in such standard sources as Susan Pepper's *China's Civil War*—such accounts as these tell us much about why China went Communist. The intellectuals gave their support to Mao only slowly and even reluctantly, and Mao would never forget their reluctance. He won that support less because of the merits they found in his position than because of the insufferable tactics of the Guomindang. No third option was available.

Further, the Chinese had begun to identify the Americans with their oppressors. American MPs stood by, Winter complained, while the Chinese secret police committed their atrocities. "How encouraging it would be," his Chinese friends would say, "to see an American soldier risk court-martial by resisting Chinese police or soldiers who were committing atrocities. These men are fierce enough in defending their own rights. We always thought in the past that Americans defended these rights on principle." What the Chinese saw instead was "fumbly old colonels with their sadistic wives in the Executive Headquarters, peddling their cases of Parker and Eversharp pens and even electric fans which they tore out of the transports which brought them to China, blandly accepting bribes of rugs and curios from . . . . government officials with the remark that the Chinese are so generous . . . and never seeming to notice that there is a revolution going on."[21]

As an observer of the scene, Winter was in a privileged position. Few Westerners remained on the faculties of Chinese universities. Though at the American-sponsored Yenching University, the leading Christian college in China, there remained about fifteen Americans and one Frenchman, Peking University, which was awaiting the arrival of William Empson from England, had only two Germans. At his own university, Tsinghua, except for a White Russian named Ivan Ivanovich Gaponovich, who had become a Chinese citizen, Winter was the only remaining Westerner.[22]

No wonder that he described with increasing bitterness the systematic obliteration of liberal ideals from Tsinghua's curricula. Winter's work in China had been to help transmit the flower of Western humanistic learning to a new Chinese intelligentsia. He had watched his efforts steadily fall under the shadow of war and the inimical presence of military thinking, whose only value was power. Now the old liberal faith that humans, inherently rational, could resolve their differences through the use of reason rather than force and that freedom of expression and diversity of opinion were indispensable instruments of that rationality—all that had been extinguished in China, ironically, in the very hour when the Axis that opposed these ideals had suffered defeat.

That the expressed liberal policy of his own nation had become entangled in a contradiction simply sharpened the irony: "We would not abandon our ideals of national self-determination and individual freedom for the Chinese people," John Fairbank, himself a close observer of this scene, would write later, "but somehow we could never take action to get these values realized in fact . . . . The result was to encourage in our traditional policy a disconcerting split between humanitarian ideals and strategic realism."[23]

*   *   *

Early in February 1947, Stevens asked Winter whether there was much book buying in Peking for foreign countries.[24] Winter replied that books were about the only cheap thing still to be had in Peking and that the Orientalist John Blofeld, back from Chunking, where he had served in the British Embassy as cultural attaché, had "recently got the entire Buddhist Tripitaka for about US$60."[25] A few days later, Winter stopped at a bookstall in the dingy little market near his house. Here, a copy of Montaigne caught his eye, and he opened it to discover his own seal on the title page. He would have bought it for the seal alone, which was full of memories for him; but cheap as books were, he could not afford to buy back his Montaigne. Instead, he had to satisfy himself with wondering if the Japanese who had taken all his precious books and then apparently sold them had read any of them. If they had read this one, Winter thought, with a humanist's unchastened conviction, "they may have got into trouble, for if anything emerges clearly from the meanderings of Montaigne's mind," it was that "whatever the limitations of reason may be, it is folly to renounce it, since it is the only guide we have."[26] And what to do when reason has been renounced? Winter aspired to follow the Chinese model that allows one to maintain a balance between thought and feeling—a tranquil center, a "well-spring, flood like, even and level . . . a store pool of ch'i," as the Kuan Tzu describes it.[27]

He saw this balance in his friend C, whom secret police had attempted to assassinate that previous July, when they killed Ling Kung-po and Wen Yiduo. After Wen's death, C had refused to take sanctuary in the American Consulate in Kunming (the rest of the intended victims had been given sanctuary there by a vice-consul, who had personally rounded them up in his jeep)—a case where an American *did* act in accord with American ideals. The Guomindang, belatedly, were trying to draw intellectuals like C into their government in order to lend it legitimacy. But when the Guomindang foreign minister visited C, he was kept waiting while C finished a nap, shaved (taking a long time because the blade was dull), dressed (after having his wife restore a missing button from his shirt), and then finally went out to meet his visitor, "who had been waiting in his icy parlour."

C continued to defy Chiang Kai-shek in Peking as he had done earlier in Kunming. Most recently, he had "headed the manifesto signed by thirteen professors in Tsinghua and Peking University in which they condemned the savagery and demanded the release of the victims, with apologies and indemnities from the government." What Winter wanted to know was "the secret power of this man C,"[28] which he associated with the balance of the forces of Vishnu and Shiva that he had seen in the bust of Trimurti on Elephanta.[29] C sat in Winter's "arm chair with downcast eyes and quietly told his story, maintaining the just balance between traditionalism and change," and "between serenity and grim sorrow." C belonged to no party, Winter went on, "but there are thousands in this country who would be proud to die for him"—people in whom is the balance between the complementary functions represented by Vishnu, as animating and preserving principle of being, and Shiva, as the transforming principle. Winter had found a way to take seriously the teachings of the East, so seriously that he recognized in them alternatives of much that we incline to approach through science, for example, psychology and political science. (In this, he was a solitary pioneer in a noetic principle that would later gain strength in the West.)

Winter never claimed such spiritual qualities for his own, except insofar as to recognize them is to claim them. But he loved to be a citizen of a world where it was possible for him to talk to men like C, seated in his own living room. Indeed, it is the friendship of such men that, put in the balance against what one experienced and witnessed of human suffering and human cruelty in China, tips the scale. "When I look back, it seems to me that except for very brief periods the circumstances of my life have been most unsatisfactory, but when I think how many decent people I have known, as for example this man, whose friendship fairly makes the pit of my stomach glow with pleasure, I must say that I have, after all, got at least as much as I deserve from life."[30]

Naturally, the question of whether C's was an untranslatable Oriental power came to Winter's mind. Was there a Western equivalent? In a cold month and a cold historical moment, he reflected on the nature of suffering and endurance, Eastern and Western styles. What he found to put against the Trimurti presented itself to him in the same bookstall where he had found his old Montaigne. Near it, he spied a Japanese edition, on cheap wartime paper, of Beethoven's *Hammerclavier Sonata*. It was a score he knew intimately, and as he leafed through it, it seemed a reflection on the history he was living through, a chart of a place beyond hope where, nonetheless, the spirit can continue to exist.

When he got home, Winter went immediately to look for J. W. N. Sullivan's book on Beethoven, to see what Sullivan had to say about the *Hammerclavier*. What he found was this: the man who wrote this music

> is already a great solitary. He has abated nothing of his courage, but it has become more grim. Suffering, it would appear, has hardened him; never again, one would think, can this man melt. And there is no good humor in the Scherzo. A curiously laconic savagery, with hints of the formidable passion that is expressing itself so abruptly, entirely separate this movement from the frank energy of the earlier Scherzos. The slow movement is the deliberate expression, by a man who knows no reserves, of the cold and immeasurable woe in whose depths, it would seem, nothing that we could call life could endure.[31]

Yet in the Largo that follows a gradual awakening is effected, an awakening "to the blind and desperate energy left in this man when there was no longer any reason to live." That impulse, which "does not contain within itself dramatic contrasts," requires in order to be expressed, according to Sullivan, "a form within which its swiftness and violence can rage unchecked." So Beethoven turns to the fugue, a form that supremely permits a "unidirectional and unhampered . . . flow."

Sullivan points further to a moment of climax in the fugue, an interruption in which

> we are given a glimpse, *dolce* and *cantabile*, of that serene, inhuman eternity that surrounds this blind, furious striving. But it is only a glimpse, a meaningless stare, and we are at

once involved in this headlong rush, this most primitive, fundamental and unconquerable of the impulses that manifest themselves in creatures that have life. The spiritual content of that fugue is the fitting complement to the Adagio, in the sense that nothing else could have survived. And the greatness of Beethoven is shown in the fact that having passed through an experience that left him so little to express he yet expressed so much.[32]

In C's expression of a story and of feelings in which grimness and deep sorrow maintained a kind of balance with an underlying serenity, Winter saw a Chinese equivalent of what Sullivan says is the meaning of the *Hammerclavier*. It may be that in the face of it, we are closer to understanding why Winter chose to remain in China. It was a country in which one had no choice but to confront the tragic vision and make some human accommodation to it. He had chosen it over a country in which serenity is purchased only at the cost of repressing the vision of darkness, deaf to the counsel of its own high art.

CHAPTER FIFTEEN:
WINTER IN THE COLD WAR

When Winter flew out of Kunming for Peking in the summer of 1946, he knew all too well that the exotic delights that men like him and Blofeld had once enjoyed in the city were now faded images from a remote dream of red mansions. What he faced instead was the continuing uncertainty of wartime conditions, the bitter civil war having risen from the ashes of the anti-Japanese War. Rocketing inflation continued to be the salient material problem.[1] During the cold months of 1946-1947 Winter's finances were precarious. He had set January as "the probable limit" of his endurance, and when that time came, he spoke to Stevens about selling out and leaving Peking.[2] But that left the paralyzing question: "Where to?" David Stevens assumed that Winter's talk of leaving Peking was just a way of saying how bad things were for him there. "Every one of us would like to know what you have in mind if you should leave," Stevens wrote in February, "but more than that, what circumstances would give the best plan of your own choice. I still assume that staying where you are is uppermost in your mind, provided you can make the grade on the present salary."[3]

Under present conditions, the Rockefeller Foundation could do little to soothe Winter's long-range anxieties. The very existence of Chinese universities had been precarious for ten years now, and the Foundation was not ready to make any long-range commitment to Tsinghua University. On February 14, Tsinghua president Y. C. Mei sent a wire to the Rockefeller Foundation reporting that the Foundation's last grant of $8,400 was used up,[4] and John Marshall responded with a stipend of $200 a month to supplement Winter's salary.[5] But even that support was on an interim basis as a grant-in-aid. Any further commitment would await a visit to Peking in the spring by Bernard Fahs, David Stevens's assistant director of the Humanities Division. In the meantime, Marshall requested a more detailed report of the use made by the university of the earlier grant than the very sketchy one Mei's cable provided. But the irregular conditions in Peking were not conducive to good bookkeeping, and that report was never delivered.

So once again, Winter's status as the Rockefeller Foundation's cultural attaché without portfolio proved fragile, but, long inured to uncertainty, Winter was happy to get even interim relief.[6] By the time the Foundation approved the new grant-in-aid, he had been reduced to US$10 a month for food.[7] Through all this, Winter sang for his supper by providing practical advice about such matters as the Foundation's efforts to reopen the PUMC (the Rockefeller-sponsored teaching hospital in Peking) and by conveying his sense of the current status of Sino-American relations. For example, General Marshall's recommendation that the liberals take leadership under Chiang "was received with mixed feelings." But the mixture, it turned out, was a mixture of negatives: the report "annoyed the government people, for obvious reasons, seemed unrealistic to the liberals, and seemed very unfair to the left wing because it omitted mention of their main grievance: American help to the Guomindang."[8] As usual, Stevens circulated Winter's letter to other Foundation officers, including President Raymond B. Fosdick, calling their attention to passages in the letter that he thought of particular interest. Because he was able to express externally what Chinese intellectuals could only mutter to themselves, Winter provided frank accounts of informed Chinese opinion unavailable from other sources.

That may be why Burton Fahs[9] returned from his visit to Tsinghua in the spring of 1947, convinced that the Foundation should continue to maintain Winter in China to the tune of $15,000 over five years. Only half of this, Fahs recommended, was to be used for current expenses, the remainder for the purchase of an annuity that would assure Winter "maximum annual return between retirement and death." Otherwise, except for a small sum to support students in the humanities at Tsinghua, a fellowship to bring Chou Chueh-liang, the best student in the university's Foreign Languages Department, to the U.S. or Britain for study and a gift of equipment for the university's theatre program, the Foundation made no long-term commitments.

From a Western perspective, conditions in China made the very concept of a project there absurd. The peace movement had been forced underground by Guomindang terrorism. The assassination of Wen Yiduo, for example, silenced many of his colleagues, as it was intended to. But the rape of the Peita student by American Marines in late 1946 and the growing realization that Chiang Kai-shek, who had promised an early end of the civil war that had proved a pipe dreams, did much to fan the peace movement—now sometimes flying overtly anti-American slogans like "Hands off China"—back into flame. Even while Fahs was in Peking in the spring, Guomindang gendarmes were arresting two thousand civilians in Peiking, three thousand in Tsingtao and Canton.[10]

This time the tactic of mass arrests worked only for a few weeks. Soon, resistance again flared up around the issue of personal liberty in schools. Under the influence of Chen Li-fu, who was simultaneously the minister of education and head of one of Chiang Kai-shek's notorious secret service agencies, Guomindang ideology had pervaded the textbooks. As one anonymous liberal critic made the case:

> Most recently, the parties have all learned that the schools are a source of strength and therefore want to control thought and control the schools. They want to use the students for their own ends and so the schools have become big training camps for the parties . . . . We therefore cry out: get the parties out of the schools; give the schools the freedom to teach; give professors freedom to teach; and give the students the freedom to learn give China the freedom for a new life![11]

Traditionally, in a land that has so deep grained a respect for the scholar, students enjoyed certain political freedoms in China not shared by others. At times, there has even been a kind of boys-will-be-boys attitude toward them, enhanced, no doubt, by the fact that university students were likely to be the sons and daughters of rich and influential families. But most important, students had played a central role during the petulant days of the May Fourth Movement that began in 1919, when they won their stripes as a political force, stripes that have not been torn from them even after Tianamen.[12]

On May Fourth Day 1947, the students acted. All over China, they prepared to parade "against food reduction, against kidnapping, against intellectual persecutions and mass dismissals." Things had gone so far that Chen Li-fu, who admired Hitler, had organized a Youth Corps who, armed with pistols and living on the campus as students, served Chen as spies, and beat students caught reading books that Chen Li-fu considered liberal.

Chiang Kai-shek himself, determined to draw a firm line, met the student parades with bayonets and iron bars, freely wielded against young women and men alike. When the enraged students countered with a series of strikes, Chiang ordered police raids on the campuses themselves. Early in May, these raids swept universities all over China. They came at night and were carried out by armed troops, sometimes carrying rocket launchers and machine guns, and willing enough to use them. In the two weeks from May 20 to June 2, 1947, 923 students and teachers were arrested and more than a thousand were believed to have been killed or injured, some of them by machine guns turned indiscriminately upon an entire student body.[13]

Naturally, there were still those who did what they could to ignore political matters as irrelevant to the real concerns of education. One of them was Hu Shih, the well-known disciple of John Dewey and the president of Peking University, whose only public response to the torture of his own students was a newspaper article in the *Peiping Chronicle* (February 27) in which he declared himself a nonpartisan and deplored criticism of the Chinese government. Hu Shi, once a progressive modernizer, had by this time become a member of the conservative establishment.

Winter, who would soon become active in the student cause, reacted differently. He was especially affected by an experience in the university hospital, where, while he was receiving treatment, the tortured body of a brilliant second-year student of Peking University was carried in on a stretcher. Although the doctors and nurses had been warned that they would be dismissed if the story got out, they rushed in to tell him about the case. "They had the sentimental notion," Winter observed mordantly, "that if I reported the case in the States it would have an effect on American policy." But he "quickly disabused them of the notion that either Wall Street or the military who are running the government had any interest in such matters."

The student, Teng K'e (Susan Pepper calls him Teng T'e)[14] had been tortured by what Winter called "two of the most popular forms of torture this season," called "cold water" and the "tiger's bench," both of them learned from the Japanese. In the first, a hose was forced down the victim's throat and the water turned on. "When the stomach is about to explode, a board is forced on the patient's stomach and a man jumps up and down on it until the water squirts out from one end or the other. Then the hose is applied again. In the second method, the "tiger's bench," the victim is seated on one chair and his feet placed on another. Then bricks are piled on his knees "so that the hinges are bent in the opposite direction from the way nature intended them to bend." In the case of Teng K'e, these tortures went on for ten days without bringing a confession because the young man had nothing to confess.[15]

Winter understood that such tortures were not really meant to be secret. He was familiar with Himmler's 1936 text, *Die Schutztaffel als anti-bolschewistische Kamforganisation*, and he quoted from a passage on page 29: "I know that there are people in Germany who feel sick at the sight of this black coat [the SS uniform]. We can understand that and do not suppose that we are loved by too many people. All who have Germany at heart will and must respect us, but those shall fear us who have a bad conscience toward the Führer and the nation, somewhere and sometime."

There was a technique even in terror, and it was beginning to work even on this aging American, who had seen his share:

> Even a leathery old thing like myself, who has been exposed to every sort of Schrecklichkeit for years, can no longer sleep at night because of this lynching which is going on all the time. It is not the thought of pain that keeps me awake . . . . It is the loss of dignity which has always been the most precious possession of the Chinese, and even more precious now that nothing else is left to them. It is appalling to think of these half-starved boys who, in spite of their solemn preparations and determination, hear suddenly among the barking voices of the torturers the sound of a voice which is not their voice, and which has no connection with them, but which sounds exactly like their own voice, screaming and begging for mercy, as a dog hears with astonishment and terror the rattling and banging of the tin can which some practical joker has tied to its tail.[16]

Naturally, these were not the kinds of matters that President Mei brought up in his correspondence with the Rockefeller Foundation. It is doubtful that anyone but Winter (who, for all his raw exposure to Chinese conditions, still enjoyed a kind of extraterritorial immunity) could have reported them at all. As to Mei, he simply expressed his pleasure over the Foundation's proposal to support Winter for five years. Tsinghua "would like to have Mr. Winter on its faculty as long as he can or wishes to stay with us," he said. In addition, he hoped that, despite Mei's inability to "render a definite account" for the previous grant made to the university, the Foundation might allow annually a fund for the purchase of books for work in the humanities. He still could not send a detailed financial report, he explained, because most of the publisher's from whom the university had ordered books over a year ago had failed to respond and because of the university's move from Kunming last fall.[17]

By fall, Winter's own situation was not much improved. Along with the rest of the faculty, he had lost his summer holidays to the almost incredible grading of fifteen thousand entrance examinations, from which six hundred students were selected for admission. Worse, the Corn Exchange Trust Company in New York had reported that there were no funds in his account. Though Fahs's recommendation was accepted and indeed the sum increased to $20,000, allowing $3,000 a year for Winter plus $1,000 a year for assistance and the purchase of materials, the grant was not approved by the executive committee of the Foundation until October 17. Winter therefore found himself "in the unpleasant position of a person who writes bogus checks and who is faced with a Peking winter without coal." He could not wait much longer before doing something about the situation; if the money had not been deposited or was not going to be, he needed to know at once. He "could survive— barely—in Kunming without coal, but not here."[18]

Other recent RF decisions pertaining to China had also gone less than smoothly. Chou Chueh-liang, for example, was at the University of Chicago, as per Fahs's recommendation; but he had only enough money to last six months, and Winter wished "someone could do something about him." Perhaps the fact that Chou was a poet made support to him sound impractical, Winter said (presumably putting a barb into the well-lettered Stevens), but it did not to him: "All the best writers in China come from the departments of foreign languages in the universities, not from the Chinese departments. And China needs writers."

Though Chou's immediate fate was not so quickly resolved, by the time it got really cold, Stevens had straightened out Winter's banking difficulties. Winter thought the confused state of his finances came about because for about three-and-a half-months during the spring and summer, he had received no mail from the States as the result of what he believed was a politically motivated blackout. During this period, General

Albert C. Wedemeyer was visiting China for the purpose of appraising the "political, economic, psychological, and military situations—current and projected." While this was going on, not only was correspondence with the States discouraged, but the schools were on an especially short rein to discourage contact between Wedemeyer and dissenting students and scholars.[19]

This repressive effort was unsuccessful: Wedemeyer came away with a clear understanding of the Nationalist government's precarious political situation. In fact, in his report to President Truman, the general appraised these matters pretty much as Winter had been doing to the Rockefeller Foundation. For example, Wedemeyer discovered "throughout strife-torn China . . . a passionate longing for peace, an early lasting peace." The Chinese people, he went on, "were nearing final disillusionment with the Nanking regime and were becoming receptive to a radical change on the grounds 'that nothing could be worse than the Guomindang.'" As Forest C. Pogue puts it in his *George C. Marshall: Statesman*: "Coming from a personal friend of China and a supporter of Chiang Kai-shek, Wedemeyer's thunderous charges had a profound influence on Marshall."[20] But on the other side, Marshall also had to contend with demands from the navy secretary Forrestal and army secretary Patterson as well as the joint chiefs of staff for all-out aid to the Nationalists, including American military intervention if necessary.

Despite reports from American generals and expatriate scholars notwithstanding, Chiang Kai-shek showed no signs of growing more flexible. Indeed, according to Winter, the Democratic League ("the only remaining opposition" of which Wen Yiduo was the last bold spokesman) had been eliminated. The Guomindang feared that the next offer of American aid might be contingent upon their broadening the basis of the government, and they wanted to be certain that no organized opposition would be part of that expansion. Further, because the Guomindang had declared open war on the Communists, it had "become even easier to shoot any critic of the government under the label than it was before." A friend of Winter's had been shot under just these circumstances. The man had been the political advisor to the local garrison commander whom Winter knew not to be a Communist. But he had been labeled as such, because, Winter thought, in a report to General Wedemeyer, he had advocated a coalition government.[21]

Winter was also exercised about the political pressures being exerted back home. His Chinese friends admired General Marshall for standing up against such committed anti-Communists and supporters of Chiang Kai-shek as William C. Bullitt, Walter Judd, and Thomas Dewey (who would soon be his party's choice as presidential candidate). But Winter and his friends feared that Marshall, now Secretary of State, might be taken in by Guomindang lies. The facts, he insisted, were that "no reforms will be made, that the elections are a farce (less than 10 percent of the eligible went to the polls), and that there is no prospect of an immediate victory for the Communists." ("Communists" here is almost certainly a slip for "Nationalists." Nationalist generals had for a long while been notorious for prophesying early victory.)

The "elections" to which Winter referred had been held just four days before he wrote, despite the fact that on the ballot were neither Communists nor members of the liberal Democratic League (the Democratic League had in fact been outlawed in October as accessory to the Communist "bandits"). Though the elections were touted as evidence of democratic reform, Winter's view of them was universally shared by the Chinese.

Predictably, not all members of the Rockefeller Foundation approved of the Foundation's continuing support of on-the-scene observers so caustic as Winter. On the top of the filed letter of November 27, 1947, from him to Stevens, one of the RF officers to whom the letter was circulated wrote next to his own initials, "is Winter a Communist?" The Cold War had begun to heat in the Foundation's offices.

Winter's November letter to Stevens in fact bristled with observations that, from the perspective of the dogmas of militant anti-Communism that had already kindled a new "cold" war, looked suspicious. The disrespectful references to Bullitt, Dewey, and Judd, the regretful remarks about the demise of the opposition Democratic League, the insistence that no reforms should be expected on the part of Chiang Kai-shek—any one of these would be enough evidence to damn the expatriate American in the minds and hearts of those who sympathized with Bullitt, Dewey, and Judd, all of them proponents of direct American military intervention as a means of assuring military victory to Chiang Kai-shek.

Nearly as bad in the way of self-damnation, Winter complained that the Protestant missionaries had been caught up in the current anti-Communist hysteria on the part of the Nationalists and had enjoyed an "audience" with the generalissimo and his wife in order to offer their services. But the missionaries were disappointed and "a little hurt," Winter noted wryly, when all they got for their trouble was a haranguing from the Chiangs, who complained that Protestant support so far had been less vigorous than that of the Catholics under Archbishop Yu Pin. ("Someone" had suggested, according to Winter, that the archbishop, who was visiting America, be forced to register as "the agent of a foreign government.") From the missionary perspective, Winter himself was an "un-Christian," the next worst thing to being a Communist, and essentially equivalent to it.

But the topper in the list of provocations that filled this letter must have been Winter's remarks about a tea he had recently attended in honor of Colonel Robert R. McCormick, right-wing proprietor of the *Chicago Tribune.* Winter had apparently remained silent at the tea party, but brooding on his way home over the enthusiastic remarks that "a couple of missionaries" had made to McCormick about the spiritual power of the Guomindang, he thought to himself: "During all these years I have seen no regenerative power in the Generalissimo's New Life Movement, very little indeed in Christianity (Christian theology), but something very much like what one must call a regenerative power in the teachings of the Chinese Communists." He added (in one of his characteristically tepid efforts at prudence) that this idea had been expressed to him recently "by a member of the Chinese secret police, by an administrator who belongs to the CC Clique, and by a Guomindang General, to name only a few."

Diplomatic skills were not among Winter's strengths. To the contrary, bluntness was his calling card. And to persons who had enjoyed a less sustained relationship with him than John Marshall, who, of all the RF officers, seems to have enjoyed him best, or David Stevens, who had known him a long time and who held his powers of mind, heart, and observation in high regard, almost any line of the letter would have been enough to brand Winter as a Communist, unworthy of the Foundation's support. A new chapter was about to open for Winter, one in which his steady loyalty to liberal principles would make him a victim of his own country's declaration of open war on Communists, just as many of his Chinese friends had already fallen victims of theirs, and many American scholars and diplomats would follow.

In fact, neither at this time nor any other was Winter a party member or even active in a Communist cause—unless *we* consider his opposition to the Guomindang and to postwar American military policy in Asia to be support of Communist causes. The Communists themselves, patently, did *not* judge him to be one of theirs when they treated him—in contrast to people like Edgar Snow and Agnes Smedley, for example—as shabbily as they did during the Cultural Liberation. On the American side, not even Burton Fahs (who, in his final letter to Winter, concluded that Winter's international views resulted from his "living in an environment in which all the public sources of information and opinion are controlled and poisoned") believed Winter to be a Communist.[22]

Winter did not have to be a Communist to reach the point that Wedemeyer had reported the Chinese people in general to be nearing: "final disillusionment with the Nanking government" had made him, like them—in Wedemeyer's words—"receptive to a radical change on the grounds that nothing could be worse than the Guomindang." But if Winter was not a Communist, he had certainly become a fellow traveler—if the phrase can be, for this historical moment and place, emptied of the strong disapprobation it carried in the U.S. for so long. Like his fellow intellectuals in China, he had for so long been told that such liberal practices as freedom of expression were synonymous with Communism (or "8th Route banditry") that he may have begun to believe it.

However uneasy individual Foundation officers may have felt about Winter's political loyalties, the Marshall and Wedemeyer reports lent a certain legitimacy to views that would not become subject to wholesale attack until China was "lost" in 1949. For the time being, under no special pressure and reluctant to lose the excellent information and judgment Winter provided on Chinese matters, the Foundation stayed with him. Thus, they were privy to such facts as that Guomindang troops were overextended and vulnerable in Manchuria and that for the last year the Communists had been "coming into the villages around the university at night to do their shopping, while the troops—as thick as flies in this neighborhood—barricaded themselves in their barracks." From Winter they learned that the Communists had even "had a big wedding one night in a village one and a half miles north of the university" and that the Communists themselves welcomed further shipments of munitions to the Chinese governments "as they will get them eventually"—though Winter admitted that such talk might be mere bravado.

Lest anyone miss his gist, Winter closed this long and heavily packed letter of November 1947 to Stevens with a resumé of what he had tried to point out to missionaries:

> that the worst enemies of the Chinese Communists dare
> not accuse them of not being clean; that [the missionaries']

support of the most corrupt administration China has ever known lays them open to the accusation of fearing to lose their property and special privileges; that the question is fundamentally economic, and that the flagrant inequality of possessions naturally leads to revolution; that the government's irresponsibility is essentially un-Christian; that by talking so much about God they seem to be trying to sell a patent-cure-all which may be harmless, but is surely ineffective; and that the part of Christianity which can be, and is, accepted by decent human beings of whatever political colour is the ideal of comradeship [*sic*] and social justice—yes, the classless society with ordered production and racial equality.

The last pellet in that burst of buckshot must have proven especially irritating to the Foundation's more conservative officers. Though in this as in so much else Winter was simply arguing for a legitimate, if neglected, version of the American dream, his repeated identification of Communism with the pure core of Christianity struck some of his readers as a wanton twist of the knife, as he no doubt intended it to.

But for the time being, at least, they did not so strike David Stevens's assistant, Charles Burton Fahs, who was becoming Winter's principal correspondent within the Foundation. Stevens's seventeen-year tenure as head of the Humanities Division was drawing to a close, and he would be succeeded by Fahs, an Orientalist who had served during the war as a research analyst for the OSS and who would later become acting chief of research for the Far Eastern Division of the State Department.

In early March 1948, Fahs expressed his appreciation for Winter's recent "very good letters."[23] He also promised that he would do what he could about Chou Cheh-liang at Chicago, although a question "inevitably" arose about "Mr. Chou's prospects for a position [back in China] in which he could put to use such training as he might receive under a fellowship." Finally, Fahs asked Winter's advice about the qualifications of persons working under Madame Sun Yat-sen and the Chinese Welfare Fund on a program of translations of Western literature into Chinese. In retrospect, there is pathos in these references to a few last feeble attempts at vital cultural relations between the U.S. and China, a project about which I. A. Richards had once harbored such glowing hopes. The real issues lay elsewhere, and Fahs said so. "One of the questions which always arises in connection with discussion of Chinese affairs," he told Winter, "is what the United States might do which would not involve the onus of intervention in Chinese internal affairs but which might at the same time assure some measure of good will and useful contact regardless of the direction in which Chinese internal affairs evolve."

In the winter of 1948, Fahs's question could only have been disingenuous. The real problem was that the United States was in up to its ears in China's internal politics and did not know how to get out. Besides, through much of 1947, secretary of state Marshall had been receiving disastrous reports about the deteriorating situation in China from both General Wedemeyer and Ambassador John Leighton Stuart. Wedemeyer's report was so hot that State Department staff members convinced Marshall to keep it secret until a final policy decision had been made.

Wedemeyer, caught up in the contradiction that no one in Washington seemed able to cut through, recommended more military aid and even the assignment of American military advisers, if necessary, though he ruled out military intervention as contrary to U.S. policy. He made this recommendation of continuing assistance despite the fact that his own report was composed largely of devastating criticism of the weakness and corruption of the Nationalist command. It was growing more and more obvious that the United States had laid hands on a Tar Baby.

Even those American policy makers who would have liked to let go were victims of their own propaganda. For a long time, they had been saying, and in some cases believing, that Chiang Kai-shek was a great and glorious leader, a staunch ally, a warm friend of democracy, and that his wife was the epitome of all that was noble and lovely. That General Stillwell had called the one "Peanut" and the other "Snow White" was not common knowledge.

Stillwell died shortly after the war ended, but not before President Roosevelt had recalled him from China as a result of the general's premature honesty regarding Chiang and the Nationalists. In 1952, Stillwell would be slandered by his old enemy, General Chennault, and Chennault's useful supporter, the journalist Joseph Allsop, who was also a deep-died fan of Chiang. Chennault had the audacity to tell a congressional investigating committee that in July 1945, Stillwell had proposed to divert the Tenth Army, scheduled for the invasion of Japan, to the coast north of Shanghai, "where he would arm 200,000 or 300,000 Communists and lead them south to capture Shanghai."[24] But by that time, one could say anything, so long as it pleased anti-Communists.

Though an early one, Stillwell was but one example among many of the sad fates suffered by persons who tried to tell the truth about China.

Perhaps things would have gone differently if Wedemeyer's report had been made public. Certainly, no one would have found it easy to smear him with the Communist brush. But as it was, all through the fall of 1947 congressional pressure to add China to the list of nations receiving recovery assistance kept growing, as did pressure within congress and without, for direct military intervention. So it was against considerable pressure that Marshall, whose attention was occupied largely with affairs in the European area, decided that American assistance in the way of equipment and ammunition would continue, but that the full-scale American military intervention being urged in some quarters would not be attempted.

Fahs's request for suggestions as to how, without intervening in Chinese internal affairs, the U.S. could act in a way that would assure Chinese goodwill regardless of which Chinese party prevailed was disingenuous and provoking. But as usual, Winter was perfectly willing to say in clear terms what he believed the U.S. ought to do, though he no longer had "the slightest hope of our doing it." In the summer of 1947, he said, when it looked as if the CIO, the AFL, and the Railroad Brotherhoods might be given impetus by the Taft-Hartley Bill to combine into a single union that could exert real pressure for "the defeat of both the isolationists and the Truman Doctrine," he had felt a little hopeful. Maybe now the U.S. might again enjoy a foreign policy not built on the single foundation of anti-Communism. But that hope was now ended.

"There is no use talking about avoiding intervention in Chinese internal affairs," Winter told Fahs. "We have been up to our necks for some time and the recent revelation of the secret contracts for military aid are only a warning of worse to come." As to our assuring "some measure of good will and useful contact," the fruits of our present intervention, he predicted, would be "nothing but growing hatred from all Chinese— and there are 450,000,000 of them—except a handful who are in the Kuomingtang racket."[25]

But that hatred was recent and not yet deep-seated, he continued. All that was needed to wash it away was that we change directions and take "a complete hands off policy"—no more military supplies, American soldiers and military advisers to be withdrawn at once and to wait for the inevitable Communist victory to happen "within the year." In fact, it happened in six months later.

We will never know if amicable relations between the U.S. and China could really have come to pass. But the policy he recommended could not have led to greater disasters than resulted from the courser we followed by supporting Chiang well past the point when the corruption of his regime made his defeat certain. So we lost the possible future he'd envisioned: When the new government was established, we would recognize them, and then provide them with the agricultural supplies and industrial machinery that they needed for recovery and development. The Communists, he was certain, "wouldn't care whether their seeds and industrial machinery came from a capitalist or a socialist state." Rather, we would "soften and tame them with our great resources" and "have a better ally than we shall ever have by following our present policy, which is prolonging the agony of the miserable people of this country, WHO ARE DETERMINED TO GET RID OF THE PRESENT REGIME." As it is, they will never forget their struggle to do that, and "they will teach their children to the third generation to spit when they see an American."

His own position, he went on, was just barely tenable. He was able to maintain it because he was "so old," because the Chinese had known him for so long a time, and because he had completely disassociated himself from the American policy. If he had not done that, his age and his length of service in China would have meant nothing. Already the university community was militantly opposed to "moderates." And the new American aid to the Nationalists would "serve merely as a challenge to the Communists and the middle of the road people" would get weaker and weaker.[26]

Characteristically, Winter closed with an image. Back in 1940, when he had journeyed for two weeks over the Burma Road to Kunming, Chinese engineers in his traveling party would dig out of a crater the nose of an unexploded Japanese bomb, "and each time it had a recent date of the American manufacturer on it." Back then, the United States was still supplying ammunitions to the Japanese, and "We should still be begging the pardon of the Chinese for this," Winter said. But instead "we have started it again," knowing that "these weapons will be used against innocent Chinese. They would be fools if they didn't hate us."

Winter's blunt commentary would have been of little use to politicians, for whom unorthodox assumptions, however true, are a very small part of the data with which they have to grapple. But these remarks could prove valuable to a Foundation that wished to conceive of itself

as disinterested. So as long as the Rockefeller Foundation continued to
solicit his views, it is hard to imagine how Winter could have written
otherwise than he did. He allowed the Foundation officers access to a
point of view that would not have been otherwise accessible, the point
of view of the Chinese themselves—and especially, of those Chinese who
were potential recipients of the Foundation's beneficence.

Just a few days before Winter wrote to Fahs, for example, Harry
Truman held a news conference, reports of which caused students to
come to Winter's house in an endless stream—"nice, decent boys, all
of them, bowing and smiling, but saying such appalling things that
I should not like to repeat them." They were especially perturbed by a
delayed AP dispatch dated February 20 in which, in the same breath,
Secretary Marshall "categorically demanded strictly nonmilitary aid
to China's anti-Communist movement and agreed to continue to sell
China ammunition and air force equipment at bargain rates." When the
students asked him "what this hodge-podge meant," Winter told them:

> It doesn't mean anything. Where did you ever get the idea
> that political statements mean something? If you wrote such
> rubbish in a composition, I would give you exactly zero. It is a
> technicality known as rationalizing, which someone has defined
> as the "self-exculpating which occurs when we feel ourselves, or
> our group, accused of misapprehension or error." Most politics,
> political science, ethics, and so on, are nothing else. This is a
> particularly crude form, but it will probably be swallowed by
> Americans.[27]

When one student concluded that Marshall then was a rascal, Winter
said, sustaining the irony, "No, it's not fair to call him a rascal, for so far
he has been successful. No one who is successful can be called either a
rascal or a criminal. That appears very clearly when one reads history."

Truman himself and, though he knew better, Marshall as his secretary
of state were under pressure from the rising anti-Communist tide that
would soon control American foreign policy. They also had to cope with
key elements in the military establishment who were urging that the U.S.
should defend China at all costs from the Communist victory that looked
ever more possible even to those who refused to see that, by this time, it
was inevitable.

Now on March 11, 1948, Truman had announced (in Winter's words) "that inclusion of Communists in the Chinese government had never been U.S. policy." In a stroke, he had justified the reversal of his statement of December 15, 1945, that "United States support will not extend to influence the course of any Chinese internal strife," and his reaffirmation on December 18, 1946, that the U.S. would not become directly involved in China's internal conflict. He had also alienated, more or less finally, the goodwill of the students, who, as has often been the case in China, were the exponents of the people's general will. As Winter put it in his diary,

> One of these days the Chinese student movement will be recognized as one of the brightest and most admirable factors in China during her transition period. There are two classes who stand far above all others in this country; [sic] the intellectuals and the peasants, and these two classes tend more and more to join hands, as the intellectuals see more and more clearly that the peasants cannot help themselves.[28]

The Truman Doctrine, put forth on March 12, 1948, set the table for the Cold War and America's entry into the Korean conflict. It ignored Marshall's effort in 1946 to implement a plan agreed upon by both Communists and Guomindang to establish a coalition government around a "cabinet responsible to the elected legislature after the British pattern." Marshall's coalition model was strikingly similar to what Winter had proposed in his letter to him, but now that was all bitter history. As Winter anticipated, less than a month after the March 11 press conference, Congress passed the China Aid Act, authorizing US$338 million in economic aid and US$125 million in special grants to the Guomindang government during the fiscal year 1948-1949. As Susan Pepper remarks, everyone who opposed the civil war "condemned such aid as at attempt to prop up an unregenerate Chiang Kai-shek and prolong his battle with the Communists."[29] As Winter, like his students and friends, believed, all hope for peace in China had effectively been sabotaged long since "by Harry Truman and Chiang Kai-shek with George Marshall as a willing instrument of this crime against the Chinese people." So it was that a day after he told Fahs what the U.S. ought to do, Winter told David Stevens: "I have never expected our government to make a moral decision about anything, but I have sometimes hoped that they would make an intelligent one. They will never defeat the Communists."[30]

Even Winter's cultural reportage had become grimly political. He had recently seen the show of 171 woodcuts that was going the round of all Chinese universities. He thought many of them good and some very powerful. "All but about fifteen . . . depicted with a ruthlessness that made me blink the horrors of bad government in China, which has become an obsession with the Chinese."

Although little use was made of Winter's usually acute political analyses, his reflections on more timeless issues fared better. Early that winter, he'd sent to Fahs two pages of comments on Ruth Benedict's *The Chrysanthemum and the Sword*.[31] Fahs then asked Winter's permission to show them to Ruth Benedict, and Winter responded by writing an additional ten pages of comments—as usual, single spaced. Though he apologizes for not having time to give more than a few hours to the notes, he wrote specific comments on more than fifty of her observations—some of them half a page or more long. Like all Westerners, though with deeper experience than most, Winter was fascinated with Chinese psychology and convinced that part of America's troubles in the Orient stemmed from our utter inability to imagine people put together psychologically and spiritually on an entirely different essential basis than our own.

Ms. Benedict had written the book at the request of the OWI as part of an effort "to get social anthropologists and psychologists to understand and explain Japanese motivations." Winter found the book something like the one he had long hoped to write about the Chinese. *The Chrysanthemum and the Sword* was ostensibly about the Japanese, but Winter thought that what she had to say about them provided helpful analogues and contrasts to the character of Chinese as well. Ms. Benedict also, if only inadvertently, helped illuminate the character of the Chinese as against the Japanese. For example, Winter found her discussion on pages 222-23 of Japan as a shame culture rather than a guilt culture perfectly descriptive of the Chinese as well. He found it also true (and important) of the Chinese as of the Japanese that they did not, as we in the West do, think that a good man should "think of what he does for others as frustrating to himself." Oriental people do not, he held, have trouble with Christian missionary teachings about sacrifice.

Benedict's discussion of childhood in Japan he particularly admired and, again, thought germane to China. "In any culture," Benedict wrote, "traditional moral sanctions are transmitted to each new generation, not merely in words but in all the elders' attitudes towards their children, and an outsider can hardly understand any nation's major stakes in life without studying the way children are brought up there." It was Benedict's reflections on child raising that provided a frame for the story Wu Mi had told him about how, because a flicker of his eye revealed that he didn't like the food placed before him, later that night "his grandmother came into the room where he was sleeping, pulled down the covers, and gave him a severe beating with a leather strap. She did not say a word and he did not make any outcry. He understood perfectly what the punishment was for. It was never referred to again."[32]

Winter had often praised and brooded over the Chinese capacity for serenity, an aspect of that would naturally fascinate a man whose own hot temper he was never very successful at controlling. This Chinese virtue, which Winter saw as related to the Chinese incapacity for ennui, he attributed to the fact that the Chinese were "not preparing for an emergency, or for any action, but they let the wind blow through their minds and consider that the resulting state of their mind is its own justification. The Chinese mind is always in a state of alert detachment." In his story of Wu Mi, we get a glimpse of the early training that lies behind such detachment.

And it is interesting, parenthetically, that Wu Mi, at about the time when Winter met him, had become spokesman for the concept of a Chinese "national essence," an element of which, as the modern Confucian Lian Shu-ming formulated it, was a condition of Will not directed forward, as in the West, to conquer the environment and satisfy the primal needs for food, shelter, and procreation, but "sideways to harmonize itself with the environment—to achieve a balance between the demands of the Will itself and the environment." This was the direction toward which Wu Mi's grandmother had so elegantly pointed him. It was the direction in which Winter himself, who so steadily scolded his own culture for its own dense willfulness, wanted to go. But how could so willful a man in so steadily deteriorating an environment hope to make progress toward such an end?

Even in Ruth Benedict's book, for which he had so much admiration, Winter found evidence of the ethnocentricity that had so often annoyed him in his less sophisticated coculturalists. William Empson had pointed out to him, and he agreed, that Benedict's method was weakened by her "neglect of semantics—or rather English semantics." She analyzed the Japanese words with care, but Benedict treated the English words that corresponded with them "rather cavalierly." In this way, she gave the impression that it was "the Japanese who are queer, while the Americans are not, an impression which Miss Benedict, a distinguished anthropologist, could not have intended."[33]

What was "queer," Winter held, was ourselves because we "are something new in the world." The great change came, he went on, with what Richards calls "the neutralization of nature"—the profound upheaval in the history of consciousness that Richards takes up in the fifth chapter of his *Science and Poetry*. The displacement of the "Magical View" that valorizes nature with a scientific/mathematical view that perceives the universe as "a field for the tracing out of ever wider and more general uniformities" was, as Richards showed, a central event of Western consciousness at large. But Winter saw Americans as especially guilty of debunking those patterns of thought that now seemed merely "poetic" or superstitious while preserving for themselves unblinking faith in the validity of their own myths. It was against that context that Winter remarked how General MacArthur had recently reprimanded the editor of a Japanese newspaper for doubting some Christian superstition just after having demanded of the Japanese that they disavow their own superstitions.

A current piece by Jean Paul Sartre in *The Nation* had caught Winter's attention, enforcing as it did his own skepticism about what Sartre calls "a great external apparatus, an implacable machine which one might call the objective spirit of the United States and which over there they call Americanism." Sartre, like Winter himself, saw America as constituted, on the one hand, of an obligatory dream in which everyone believed himself duty bound to participate, and on the other, of a pathetic malaise:

> There are the great myths, the myths of happiness, of progress, of liberty, of triumphant maternity; there is realism and optimism—and then there are the Americans, who, nothing at first, grow up among these colossal statues and find their way as best they can among them. There is the myth of happiness: black-magic slogans warn you to be happy at once; films that "end well" show a life of rosy ease to the exhausted crowds; the language is charged with optimistic and unrestrained expressions—"have a good time," "life is fun," and the like. But there are also [the] people, who, though conventionally happy,

suffer from an obscure malaise to which no name can be given, who are tragic through fear of being so, through that total absence of the tragic in them and around them.[34]

The position Winter wanted to maintain was in a sense quixotic. He identified with traditions like Taoism and Buddhism, which apprehended the individual as a member and manifestation of a single stream of being. These traditions made it possible to bear the tragic actual because they held out no promise of individual happiness except through the acceptance of individual powerlessness. But such traditions had already been undercut everywhere by the industrial hunger at the heart of "modernism," that hunger, which reduces all of nature to material and which assigns to human beings the primary roles of "getting and spending," or, alternatively, transforming and consuming. Industrialism, scientism require at their foundation the divorce of human consciousness from the natural world, and thus the destruction of the fundamental prop the Eastern religions provided.

Ironically, Winter had deliberately attached himself to one of the last cultures in which the old ways remained alive, and he did so at just the time when China was struggling toward her own modernization, a process that would require her to abandon much of the older culture. What I. A. Richards had feared—that the Eastern mind would be devoured by its contact with the Western—was in fact occurring. Persons like Richards and Winter himself, who had hoped for a different kind of contact, were turned out to be powerless in the end.

CHAPTER SIXTEEN:

KEEPERS OF ASHES

In the turbulence of cultural storms, life on the ground followed its own tortuous path. On the top of a high bureau in Winter's bedroom in Peking, waiting for the time when they could safely be returned to the widow, stood an urn in which the ashes of Wen Yiduo were preserved. Always alive to dramatic possibilities, Winter took secret pleasure in the fact that, although the urn stood in plain view, a visitor couldn't examine it unless he stood on top of something in order to reach it[1]

At the time just before Wen's assassination, Winter, armed with a pistol, had stood at Wen's house every night. On the night Wen was killed, according to Tolaf Ås, Winter happened not to be at his post, and he told Ås he felt responsible for Wen's death.[2] Now Wen's ashes had become a relic. To be found with them in one's possession would be to be to identify oneself with the cause of the martyr and thus invite his fate. The ashes came to Winter because, though he loved and admire Wen, he still enjoyed extraterritorial protection.

Winter's ideals—his cranky belief in justice and the rule of law, his opposition to illegal arrests and state violence against the citizenry, his passionate championship of academic and intellectual freedom as cornerstones to the broader freedoms of speech, publication, assembly, and association—had always been American, as was his opposition to one party rule. But they were also principles held by Wen Yiduo and the Democratic League—borrowings from Western liberal democracy that for many Chinese intellectuals were the very pulse of hope because they sustained the possibility of change.

True, as we've seen, Winter believed that Americans, even at home and certainly abroad, honored these principles more in the breach than in the observance—witness the passion of his uncle and his mother for killing Indians, the University of Chicago's policy of discrimination against Blacks and Jews, and his own government's championing of the tyrant Chiang Kai-shek. But Winter's disenchantment with his country for failing to live up to its ideals was in itself a disenchantment peculiarly American—as was the faithfulness with which he continued to live up to them as best he could.

Winter's willingness and his capacity as a foreigner and as a citizen of a country still strongly allied with China to perform an implicitly revolutionary act raises a question. Feeling as he did about American culture in general and American policy in China in particular, should he have renounced his citizenship altogether rather than renewing is passport as he did in 1948 and again in 1974?[3] Sitting in the secure quiet of my study, I am in no position to say. Though his long stay in China was a kind of striptease in which he cast off one after another the layers of protective identity that most foreigners in China enjoyed, he not only held a passport until late in his life, but also stayed in close connection with the American consul, which was reestablished in 1979.

Though I cannot untangle the moral contradictions of Winter's position, I can say that being an American not only protected him but also made him better able to help his Chinese students and colleagues. It also allowed him to offer advice to General Marshall and to send out—by mail and sometimes in the pockets of departing friends—true reports of what he witnessed or had been told about the comportment of China's totalitarian government. Finally, as an American, he could walk into the quarters of a military general and denounce him for permitting his troops to slaughter children and continue, like some of the American Christians at Yenching University, to protect his students back in Peking by hiding them from Chiang's secret police and becoming an agent in a kind of underground railroad that spirited them to the safe Communist capital, Yenan, and to other liberated areas. No Chinese professor could engage in these activities without risking his or her life.

* * *

As Winter kept an urn full of ashes in which the passionate hope for liberal democracy still glowed, Chinese students had become principal keepers of China's living spirit. The students took the risks; they stood together. They were the future a government could not turn its guns against without turning that future against itself. They had been tested—in waves of demonstrations in which they put into practice the principles they had learned in the classroom. Their gallery of martyrs attested to their understanding that the lessons of the classroom were hollow without their practice in the world. Finally, they were often the children of established families; and in turning his guns against them, Chiang Kai-shek was turning them as well against the bourgeoisie who were his natural constituency.

Winter enjoyed the same special connection with his living students as he did with the dead Wen Yiduo. An American and a bachelor, he was cut off from the comforts of family and of ordinary society. Often he was lonely, and it was in the companionship his students provided that he could know such society as he enjoyed. It was with them too that he could practice and test the devices of cultural blending—that is, could create moments in which some essence of Eastern culture could embrace its Western counterpart and conceive, in a transient moment of shared consciousness, a merging of East and West that was alive with the feeling that comes when mutual aliens become communicants.

Regarding the historical moment, he could offer only cold comfort. He told a student in a bath house in Kunming that "if we can't stop [the Nationalists] from shooting . . . Communists and students, we may hope that every shot will make the people who are being shot at more mature and more wise, and that the people who do the shooting will become more trivial and more stupid and more careless every day."[4] In the same letter in which he thus quotes himself, he added: "I write not in a mood of depression but of elation—that the American policy in China is certain to fail."

Winter gladly admitted to David Stevens that he had put his name "to two petitions drawn up by the faculties of Peiping Universities against American statement or acts in China."[5] By doing so, he risked losing his tenuous remaining connection with the Rockefeller Foundation, but in the balance, such a risk was preferable to being "on a false footing" with his friends. As "a point of little importance," Winter also mentioned to Fahs that he'd received no payment from the Foundation in three months, but the fact, he said, was "of little importance measured against the political and military chaos around him, which included the ongoing shooting of his students."

Winter's letters to friends in the Foundation are enormously informative about the day-to-day developments of China's civil war, and he must have had reasonable hope that some of this information was being passed on to the State Department. But he was past hoping that having better information would improve the State Department's policies regarding China. Madame Chiang's glamour and persuasiveness, augmented by William Randolph Hearst's championship of both her husband and of her and her powerful family, the generalissimo and his imposing wife had become nobly heroic figures—which is to say, pure fictions.

*   *   *

For his students, on their part, the American professor was a rare bird indeed. Brilliant and entertaining inside the classroom, outside, he was readily available to them. They came to him with questions about language and Western ideas. They came to discuss literature and to hear music and Winter's analysis of that music, in which he might show the connections between a Beethoven quartet and their situation as beleaguered intellectuals. Sometimes they came to him simply for advice and help. Chinese students were not used to carrying out conversations with professors outside of the classroom or to visiting their professors' homes. They were not used to learning from seasoned adults who were willing and even eager to entertain their questions and ideas to ponder them seriously and to respond. China was still sufficiently Confucian to make the average professor an austere and distant elder. Rare were the teachers, such as Winter or Wen Yiduo himself, who led his own students on the long march from Peking to Kunming and, when they arrived, walked out into the countryside with them, bringing along his little daughter, to sit under a tree and discuss the subtleties of Chinese poetry. And rare were the Westerners who could understand and support them, even stand with them side by side.

*   *   *

Shortly after the terrible raids of February 15-18, 1947, Winter had the students in mind as yet another of those things Chinese that could not be easy for Westerners to understand. "One of these days," he explained, "the Chinese student movement will be recognized as one of the brightest and most admirable factors in China during her transition period." He viewed the students, with the peasants, as one of the two classes that "stand far above all others in this country," and he viewed the two as tending more and more to join hands "as the intellectuals see more and more clearly that the peasants cannot help themselves." Even Mao, who saw the historical energy for revolution coming from the peasants themselves, claimed for himself, an intellectual though a maverick one, the right to lead them.

Jack Belden has shown that though the intellectuals were slow in supporting the CCP and in many cases turned their backs on it, "it was the revolt of many of these intellectuals that hammered the final nail into Chiang Kai-shek's coffin which the bold blows of the peasantry had already hewn into rough shape."[6] They had been driven to that revolt both by the widespread terror practiced by Chiang's "gendarmes and Gestapo" and by the tremendous economic collapse. They felt cornered and turned actively toward the Communists because they "caught in the Communist program a glimmer of hope, a road of escape, a path to the future."[7] Those who remained in Guomindang territory were the only articulate section of the suffering people. For students for whom writs of arrest had been issued, the path to the future led to the liberated areas where they could furnish intellectual leadership to the peasantry. In these ways, they played crucial roles "in both crippling the Guomindang and bolstering the strength of the Communists."[8] And the year 1948 saw a renewed flux of student exiles fleeing Guomindang as ten thousand of their brothers and sisters had done during the anti-Japanese war.

The background to their protests and their actual revolt was not only the political terror accelerating against them but also Nationalist China's unimaginable economic collapse. Hunger and outright starvation were common in the cities, and refugees and landless peasants "crowded into Shanghai and cluttered the alleyways with corpses."[9] Factory workers and rickshaw coolies turned to robbery. Even the industrialists who had supported Chiang were being driven out of business by inflation and Guomindang bureaucracy.

But it was the inflation itself that meant daily devastating demoralization. In Jack Belden's vivid account,

> The deterioration assumed such terrific proportions that the value of Chiang's money dwindled to no more than the paper money burned for the dead. A large paper mill in Kwangtung brought up eight hundred cases of notes ranging from hundred dollars to two thousand dollar bills to use as raw material in the

manufacture of money. The phenomenon of money being used for something else besides money frightened everyone almost to the state of hysteria. Naturally prices bounded upward almost beyond computation.[10]

Whatever difficulty his countrymen at home may have had doing so, Winter understood his students' radical extremism and saw clearly the brutal tactics of Chiang Kai-shek's secret police demonstrated even as Chiang claimed to be working for democratic reform. As usual, Winter felt compelled to interpret these phenomena to the only Americans whose interest and understanding he could hope to hold—the officers of the Rockefeller Foundation. As he so often did, he turned to literature for analogies. The students could be likened to the heroic bandit-rebels of the classic novel, *Shui Hu Chuan*, translated into English by Pearl Buck as *All Men Are Brothers*, but also known as *The Water-Margin*. To Winter, the book was a representation of men who do things that make one's hair stand on end yet who retain our sympathy: "They were made bandits by bad government and if you read the book carefully you will see that there is nothing else for them to do."[11]

Winter wished student political activism to be viewed in the same way. Student "extremism" in China, he said, should not be seen as "mob action."[12] He illustrated the point with another story from his early days in China. In the spring of 1925, as I sketched earlier,[13] Hu Tung-fu was appointed by the Chinese government to be president of Southeastern University in Nanking despite the fact that he enjoyed little support from either the students or the faculty who knew him to be incompetent. They soon discovered him to be corrupt as well when he bribed Nanking post office officials to deliver to him all letters addressed to the members of the university so that he could discover in this way those who opposed him and fire them as soon as he took office.

Because of the opposition against him, Hu was forced to occupy the president's office at night. Here, taking possession of the official seal, he had notices posted, announcing that he was now in charge. In the morning, when they learned that he had actually taken power, the students held a meeting, then marched to his office *en masse*.

The door that stood between them and him was in Western style, the upper half a pane of "crinkly glass." The students called through it, demanding that Hu leave. When he refused, they broke the glass and entered the room to find the newly appointed president cowering under his desk. Again, the students gave Hu warning to leave; again, he refused. So they formed a line, and as each of them passed, they spit in Hu Kan-fu's face, till "the saliva ran down his body and made a stream across the floor."[14]

At this point, Winter, serving his first teaching appointment in China, became an eye witness when he was called in by the vice president and asked to go to the scene to assure that the students were not causing any physical damage to the man. (No Chinese professor could carry out this task because the students might question their neutrality). When Winter arrived, the students politely made way for him, and he stood out of the range of fire and watched till after a few minutes more of this contemptuous treatment, Hu called out, "We give up," crawled out from under the desk, and signed the statement of resignation that the students handed him.

The scrupulous students then called in a foreign doctor who stripped and then carefully examined Hu and his brother (the chairman of one of the science departments who had been in the room throughout the scene). The doctor found no damage except a slight scratch on Hu Kan-fu's face, which he treated with mercurochrome. The deposed president and his brother were then led to a waiting carriage, which they entered—though not before "two enormous pails of liquid human manure were poured over their heads." Then they were driven to the railroad station where they boarded the train in their sorry condition. Far from viewing the student behavior as mob action, Winter had "rarely seen a situation handled more methodically or more effectively."

What was Winter's purpose in recounting this story with all its "revolting details," as he himself called them? For one thing, he wished to make his readers, Americans whose attitudes shaped policies or influenced those who shaped policies, sympathetic with the students. For another, he wished to convey the students' feeling toward the leader whom Americans still supported. Winter sketched the students as a kind of choric moral instrument that, once aroused, is implacable as fate. It was not necessary for him to add that now, as he wrote more than twenty years later, Chiang Kai-shek and his apparatus stood in the place of Hu Tung-fu. The waves of demonstrations taking place as he wrote were expressions of a deep national will. And was that not something new under the sun? "Who says that China hasn't changed," Winter wrote in his diary. "I can remember that in 1923 I once hear outside my window the sound of students playing football. On looking out I saw delicate consumptive youths dressed in long silk gowns lifting their skirts daintily as they kicked the ball—but usually kicking only the air—and, between kicks, languidly waving elegant fans inscribed with Tang poems."[15]

*   *   *

How existentially was the new, more vigorous national will being formed? How can a contemporary Western reader be made to feel the experience that turns civil young people into radical activists? In a journal entry he wrote in February or early March of 1948, Winter sought to make that possible by telling another story, this time, a story about fathers and sons. He had recently read Robert Payne's admiring account of Wen Yiduo in Payne's edition of contemporary Chinese poetry.[16] Payne talked here of the paradox that brought Wen, so devout a student of the Chinese classics, to conclude that China had everything to learn from the West, little from Confucius. He spoke of the transformation of the benign and much-loved "proverbial Chinese scholar" into the "fiery and dramatic speaker, worshipped by the students and justly hated by the reactionary elements in the country for his opposition to a Confucian-ridden system of graft and feudalism." And he spoke finally of how "the murder of the students in December 1945 had made [Wen Yiduo] sick at heart and more than ever determined to oppose the corruption of the government, conscious that in China this was the scholar's traditional task."

For Winter, the major moments of his personal relationship with Wen had been stages of a moral transformation of his own. He had met him in Chicago, where they had talked about verse technique, East and West, and where Wen had provided him with his first exposure to Chinese manners—an exposure that obviously drew Winter toward the nation where such manners were formed.

Then Wen left Chicago suddenly without saying goodbye, finally writing to Winter from Colorado, explaining that he had been obliged to go there to be at the side of his brother, who was dying of tuberculosis. Winter did not see his friend again until Wen Yiduo came to join the Tsinghua faculty in the early '30s, but even then, their meetings were rare, for Wen "was locked up in his study at all times and never appeared at social affairs."[17]

I've spoken earlier about how, after Winter had returned to Kunming from the States in 1945, he saw Wen again and was shocked at the conditions he was living in with his family.[18] They were crowded into two little rooms where the ill and impoverished Wen "was ruining his eyes by sitting up all night carving seals, in addition to doing his other work."[19] Across the road from him in a large double house lived a man "who could not compare with him in scholarship, but who spent a good deal of his time flattering both civil and military officials." Winter occasionally helped out Wen and his family by sharing a sack of flour or sugar with him, hauling the welcome gift the two miles that separated them. But Wen objected to Winter's carrying these things on his back and made him promise to let his sixteen-year-old son come for them in the future, which Winter did; and in that way, he got well acquainted with the son.

On June 18, 1946, Winter was coming down from Likiang when his mule train stopped at a small village where he ordered a fried cake from a street kitchen for lunch. Learning where he had been and where he was headed, the man who was frying the cake said: "Then you haven't heard the sad news. Wen Yiduo was murdered by the government three days ago before his own door. They say they killed his son, too. You must have had the privilege of knowing him. It was a sad day for China when that man died."[20] It was a sad day indeed. Even up in Likiang, Winter had met a Naxi tribeswoman who could recite from Wen's speeches and who reported to Winter that Wen had a large following.[21]

When he finally got back to Kunming on the evening of July 27, Winter learned the details. Wen had been shot outside his own house as he returned from a Democratic League press conference. His teenage son who was at his side tried to protect his father by throwing himself in front of him. The boy received nineteen bullets in the intestine but miraculously survived. "The father's brains were scattered before the door."[22]

In September 1947, Wen's son turned up in Winter's History of English Literature. He wore a dramatically large fur hat and sat in the very middle of the class, obviously trying to attract attention to himself—a fact that Winter didn't like very well. Winter had not spoken with him since Kunming days. Then one morning, he found himself seated next to the boy on a bus to the city. When some Guomindang officers boarded the bus and, because there were no seats, stood in the aisle beside Winter and young Wen, the boy asked his teacher "in a loud unnatural voice: 'What will you do when the Communists take Peking?'" Winter said that he would have to clear out since "they don't like Americans very well." The boy, still speaking at the top of his voice, then made a long speech, "the gist of which was that the Communists would hang and shoot and bury alive all the rascally officials but that they would shower benefits on me." Winter began to see "that the boy was not quite normal. He was itching for martyrdom."

In his telling of this tale, Winter presented himself as initially out of sympathy with the boy. He disapproves of his flamboyant hat, his dramatized taunting of the officers. At the same time, he knows, though he does not state, the connection between the boy's behavior and the savage experience that provoked it. Further, the effect of his richly nuanced tale is to suggest Winter's own conversion toward the "extremism" of the boy himself. In fact, in the end, this is a story of three conversions to "extremism": that of Wen Yiduo, that of his son, and that of Wen's American colleague and friend.

The renewed anger that Winter betrays in letters to Stevens and Fahs during this period has its origin in the death of Wen Yiduo and in his outraged and defiant son. Whatever distance existed between Winter and the suffering around him was rapidly closing in. In part because of America's failure to reconcile her foreign policy with her own principles, his students and the colleagues he most admired were being driven from liberal humanism to Communism as the movement that might bring to realization their political hopes.

One day, a few weeks after the episode on the bus, Winter entered the classroom to see young Wen standing on a desk and haranguing the class. Although the boy stopped and returned to his place as soon as the professor entered, Winter could guess from the expressions on the students' faces that he had been talking about him. Not long after, Winter began to receive visits from people whom he scarcely knew. Life in China, "where there is so much reserve, sharpens one's perceptions until one develops an uncanny power of reading faces," Winter remarked, explaining how he understood these visits to be in some way congratulatory, though no one made clear for what.[23] Finally, Winter was visited by Wu Han, at the time professor of Ming history, later vice mayor of Peking and the occasion for the opening events of the Cultural Revolution.[24] Now Winter learned that Wu had been going through Wen Yiduo's papers (which he later edited), and among them he found a copy of the letter Wen had written about Winter to the president of Tsinghua, urging him to invite the American to China to teach. That letter, in Winter's words, "was full of compliments, most of them quite undeserved," and it was the occasion for the boy's speech to the class and for the unexpected social calls.[25]

Winter's odd posthumous identification with Wen and his having been "mentioned a quarter century earlier by a national hero," had shed "a sort of glory" on him. It also made all the more inevitable Winter's sympathy with the feeling Wen expressed in a poem that, though he wrote it back in the '20s, anticipated his death by rejecting the serenity, insisting that "these walls cannot be separated from the agony of war."[26] Winter had copied the poem into his journal at this point, apparently in his own translation. After it, he wrote simply: "The father was a member of the Democratic League. The son is a Communist. And that is how Communists are made."

*   *   *

Winter also copied into his journal here a commentary written by student number 34119 on George Herbert's poem "The Pulley."[27] It was a forty-minute response to an exercise Winter often assigned: he would write a poem on the board, probably from memory, and then give the students about forty minutes to comment on it. Student 34119 was the nineteen-year-old son of Wen Yiduo. In Winter's words, there was "nothing remarkable about this composition—unless that fact makes it remarkable." Certainly, it does, for the composition is brilliant and in flawless English. Winter was unable to say whether a nineteen American sophomore could write something comparable in response to a poem in Greek or French because it was impossible for him "to imagine what sort of a person an American boy would be if he had been through this boy's experiences."[28]

As to the Chinese boy, the glint in his eye told the professor that "if he had been dragged away for torture, his teeth would never have parted to say the words which would have saved his life. Like his father he would never accept their bribes." There were hundreds of thousands of young Communists like this all over the world, Winter was sure, and "in spite of all the coarse shouting" that he heard "every day from across the Pacific," he couldn't believe that they were "as great a menace to society as, to take a casual example, the head of the American Intelligence Group in Peking, Larry Eshelmann, who has given black eyes to five people in the last month, including Mrs. Empson, because they ventured to disagree with United States foreign policy."[29] Winter could serve his dead friend by protecting his friend's living son. He could also serve him by showing some part of his friend's courage by acting out and thus sustaining the ideals that gave both their lives meaning.

This then was the last turn of the screw. Eshelmann, after all, though real, was also a kind of allegorical figure. He was that aspect of American foreign policy congenial to Tai Li, head of Chiang's Secret Police— commonly called the gestapo by Western observers. It was Eshelmann's kind that, toward the end of the war, shipped, to China from Calcutta, radar and small automatic weapons that went into the hands of Tai Li's operatives after the Japanese surrender—this at a time when the withdrawing American military was methodically smashing with axes and burning useful things, such as typewriters and woolen clothing, lest they fall into the hands of the Communists. Who was America's true representative in China, Winter or Eshelmann?

Reflections like these inspired Winter to write a savage and passionately idealistic prose poem, a kind of ode that celebrates a spirit Winter thought could never die. He called it "A Proposed Subject of Investigation for Arms Manufacturers":

> Take a machine-gun and aim it at the head of an unarmed scholar. (The experiment may be repeated as often as one likes, as the supply of machine-guns and unarmed scholars in inexhaustible. The result of the experiment will always be the same. In [Gerard Manley] Hopkins' words "Flesh fades, and mortal trash fall to the residuary worm." Then turn the spluttering muzzle of the gun against a little scrap of paper on which one of the scholars has written, "Happiness, I shall not receive your bribes!" The result is most curious and unexpected. The machine-gun becomes a gigantic cyclotron with its mechanism reversed. It does not disintegrate the paper. It welds it into a substance harder than diamond, but not a mineral substance, for it can multiply faster than a streptococcus and travel with the speed of light.[30]

The opposing sides in this piece are material and spiritual powers. It is Winter's purpose at this time to preserve his confidence in the ultimate triumph of the spiritual. He was conscious of the pitfalls contained in that word. In one of the early 1948 entries, he asks:

> What do we mean by the "spiritual"? In the West the word has unfortunately become entangled with the supernatural, and it is too often assumed that spiritual values cannot thrive

without that connection. John Dewey and others have pointed out, that is a very cynical view to take of human nature. In materialistic China, people take a more psychological view of the spiritual sense. L. H. Myers [the British novelist and essayist] has caught the point: "It is one of the functions of the spiritual sense to co-ordinate these other senses so that to the persons, circumstances, and events, presented to him in his life experience the truly wise man may respond with perfect taste—which is also perfect wisdom . . . The spiritual sense . . . is the valuator of those other modes of valuing . . . On any particular occasion it decides what elements, if any, of beauty, ludicrousness, pettiness, pathos and so forth enter, and in what degree each enters. In this aspect it is more ordinarily recognized as Taste. But in making these judgments it may also be seen to be Wisdom, for no particular occasion can be judged without reference to the universe as a whole."[31]

He also quotes James Harvey Robinson as coming close to the same idea in *The Mind in the Making* (1921) when he describes a kind of thought that "does not hover about our personal complacencies and humiliations," is not "made up of the homely decisions forced upon us by everyday needs, when we review our little stock of existing information, consult our conventional preferences and obligations, and make a choice of actions," and that finally, "is not the defense of our own cherished beliefs and prejudices just because they are our own." What it is, Robinson tells us, is quite the contrary to these: "it is that peculiar species of thought which leads us to change our mind."[32]

The only true victory for the West would have been for the United States to change its mind and apply its democratic principles to all peoples. Only when Americans can honestly believe that all men are brothers could it begin to experience "that peculiar species of thought which leads us to change our mind." As long as Americans consider other peoples as savages or children, they remain unable to learn from them.

Winter, who, from early on, was fascinated by "the Eastern Mind," reflected often on such intercultural and interspiritual questions. His admiration for the economist C was one such reflection, and this ability to see and take in the existential qualities of Chinese wisdom were among the reasons why he cast his lot with them.[33]

Directly after writing the piece on a subject of investigation for arms manufacturers, he copied out Alfred Einstein's comparison of Wagner and Brahms:

> The greatest tragedy in this—that Wagner was far too much caught up in his century to reap a complete victory over it . . . Wagner wanted to conquer—and had to conquer— and conquer he did. But just because of the power and the violence of his conqueror's will, he afterwards had to lose many of those he captured, chained, enchanted, bound. Brahms, on the contrary, waited till the time came to him. He could afford to wait; he knew the influence of his quiet power . . . . He gathered about him a steadily growing community of followers and, with the passing of time, he caught the masses, too . . . . Brahms was not out to conquer anything., not even the future . . . . Brahms was an heir—heir to a mighty past. Wagner was stimulated almost exclusively by the present, his own present.

Oddly enough, Wagner becomes America, drunk with "the power and violence of [the] conqueror's will." Brahms, on the other hand, is the spirit of humanism, West and East, not out to conquer anything but already "an heir—an heir to a mighty past." And while Wagner, Eisenstein held, was to lose many of his followers because of the violence of his will, Brahms, in his wise passiveness, prevailed at last even over the masses.[34]

If in the troubled spring of 1948 Winter could still respond to Eisenstein's judgment that it is the spirit of Brahms that finally prevails, it was out of faith in the students' dogged defiance of the Guomindang and in their continuing migration to Communist-controlled Yenan. Those who remained in Peking refused to comply with government pressures. University students at Tsinghua and Yenching failed to appear at a pro-government demonstration to which they had been ordered, and those who did show up from Peking University were government agents in disguise.

To retaliate, on the following day, government-paid hooligans inside the city gates waited for the buses in which Tsinghua and Yenching students and professors who had business in the city drove into town from their campuses in the northwest suburbs. The agents took over the buses "and without looking to see who was inside, they declared to the crowds in the streets that the people in the bus were traitors and communists. Then they would drive on a few yards and make their speeches again. Poor Chao Chao-hsiung, Professor of European Drama and formerly a member of the Orthological Institute, was paraded for four hours as a communist before he was allowed to make his escape."[35]

But such violent efforts on the part of the Nationalists were less and less convincing. The tide had turned, and Guomindang violence seemed more and more desperate. China had changed, and the change had now reached even the urban masses. This Winter conveys by a pair of sketches, the first of them called "Village Women (Style of 1923)"[36]:

> I saw three old women sitting in the moonlight before a coffin shop. One of them was sleek and trim. A glossy black wig was neatly pasted to her bald pate and she had the smallest feet in the street. I knew her for the one who carried out my toilet pot. The second was disheveled and grey. When I met here with a mountain of fuel on her back her eyes stared wildly as she balanced the load on her goat-like extremities. The third smoked augustly a pipe four feet long. She always crossed one tiny foot over her knee as she sat before her shop. For her husband was the maker of coffins. I had known all three of them for a long time.
>
> The first one said, "Her conduct was not decorous. To wear a silver pin in her hair while her husband lay in his coffin. One would think her a Manchu woman." The second one said, "It is reported that she took food on the second day, and even sat in a chair. What with her manners and her big feet, it's a wonder she was ever able to marry at all." And the third one said, "To pay only fifteen dollars for the coffin of a husband who had been to countries across the sea, who could read foreign books and write foreign characters. What a disgrace! And she sent out a scornful puff of smoke from her toothless mouth.

He called the other sketch "Village Women (Style of 1948)"[37]:

> At five o'clock in the morning the voices of the two old women came to me through my bedroom window. One of the women

was my servant's wife. Her speech was not very clear, for she has no teeth. She says they all fell out during the occupation as a result of eating peanut shells in place of grain. The other voice was clear and determined. My servant's wife was saying, "you'd better not let The Old Stubborn One catch you taking Mr. Winter's kindling wood. It cost three thousand dollars a pound." (She always calls her husband Lao Chiang. Chiang means pigheaded.) The other voice said pleasantly, "Well, it wouldn't hurt the foreigner to give me a little. How does he expect me to buy it? I'm a stranger here, and I'm out of work." And then, with occasional interruptions from the defender of my property, she explained her position.

My family name is T'ien. I come from Nantsun. We have always lived there. We own thirty-five mou of land. There were seven mouths. My sons were big strong boys who were not afraid of work. Then the government forces came and dragged away the two older ones to fight and it was not so easy. Then the communists came and divided up the land. They gave five mou to each person, so we were not disturbed.

The communist soldiers were good-hearted. They sometimes helped us to get the harvest in. Everybody welcomed them except the two rich families, who were left with the same amount of land that we had. Then the news came that the government soldiers were coming back. The communist soldiers told us to run up into the hills because there was going to be fighting. After a time the government troops left and we went home.

The soldiers had carried off everything they could, but we didn't have much. Then the communists came back and they ordered us all to gather in one place. There we saw the two rich men tied with ropes. An officer asked us was it true that these men stayed behind in the village to welcome the government troops. No one answered. Then they asked us one by one, and some people said that it was true. Then the officer asked if there was any reason why these men should not die, and nobody said anything. Then they took the two rich men and threw them in a hole and shoveled earth over them. That was a terrible sight. I had known these men all my life. Then everything went well for a while.

But one day the government planes came and they dropped fire-bombs and they burned up all our houses. My old man was killed and my daughter-in-law died a few days later. Then the communist soldiers took my other son away to fight and they said that this place was no good to live in any more and that I had better go and look for work. So I came here to wait till the government is defeated and then we will all go back and build a house on our land and all be together.

Then Winter heard his servant's wife say, "Come in and sit down and drink a cup of tea. You must be tired." And their voices died away.

China had changed, except for the recurrent chord: the ground for hope was slight and remote. Winter comforted himself with Rebecca West's belief that humans may change because art may disinfect us and because "History, like the human loins, does not breed true."

In the meantime, atrocities kept accelerating as student resistance to the Nationalist government grew stronger. Chiang Kai-shek tried to cleanse the campuses so thoroughly that no student unrest could be possible during the next academic year. On July 15, 1948, when authorities in Kunming "mobilized more than 200 policeman and gendarmes not to dispel a demonstration but to raid the campus of Yunnan University and Nanching Middle School," the result was that five students were killed, more than one hundred injured, and some twelve hundred arrested—seven hundred of them tortured, and thirty buried alive. None was given a court trial. Elsewhere, though the bloodshed was slighter, the desperate and angry Chiang Kai-shek regime created in 1948 "special tribunals to purge the schools of students the Guomindang spies did not like" and issued writs of arrest for a thousand students throughout the country. By 1948 time, Chiang and Madame Chiang had been on the cover of *Life* magazine three times and of Hearst-edited *Time* magazine half a dozen times. Hearst was an avid champion of Chiang and his glamorous wife, who did so much to add luster to her husband's reputation in America.[38]

After flying out of beleaguered Peiping in January 1949, Hu Shih, a prominent philosopher, disciple of John Dewey, and president of Peking

University, was reported to have told George Yeh, vice minister of Foreign Affairs of the Central Government, that there was really very little to be said for the Guomindang. "The only reason why liberal elements like us still prefer to string along with you people," he told Yeh, "is that under your regime we at least enjoy the freedom of silence."[39] It is no wonder that Winter despised the man who flaunted such a freedom.

CHAPTER SEVENTEEN:

LIBERATION

The defeat of Japan did not mean that normal work at the universities could resume. The last years of Chiang Kai-shek's rule on the mainland were marked by continuing assaults on students and intellectuals. On July 5, 1945, an orderly student protest against an announcement that instead of reopening the schools the Nationalists intended to put them in, the army was met with machine gun fire. Four days later, they protested again to honor those killed in the earlier incident; but this time, the police chief ordered armored cars to be removed and students to be given police protection, and the ten to eleven thousand students were allowed to conduct a memorial service in peace.[1] But such peaceful resolutions were rare.

For their elders too, these were terrible years. On the anniversary of Wen Yiduo's death, two thousand armed soldiers attacked the Nanching Middle School and Yunnan University with machine guns, not only killing 150 and arresting and torturing 1,200, including the president of the Middle School. The list of horrors went on and on, and to make matters worse, Winter states, Claire Chenault's American-sponsored planes bombed two Chinese cities, concentrating on spots where the population was thickest.[2]

Winter faithfully reported such atrocities to his apparent friend, Burton Fahs, who remained politely skeptical. Although Fahs passed on some of Winter's letters to "a few key places," his expectations were low. ("It would indeed be comforting to think," he said, that his efforts would be of any use. And with increasing skepticism, he dismissed the reports that Winter relayed as rumors. As to rumors about America's willing support of Chiang's atrocities, these he loftily dismisses:

> Some of these [rumors] are deliberately propagated, but all of
> them gained a ready currency because of lack of understanding
> of factors that go into policy-making here, particularly the
> fact that a completely rational and consistent foreign policy
> can be achieved, if at all, only under the most full-grown
> dictatorship. If you want the safeguards of good will which go
> with democratic action, you also have to accept some of the
> inconsistencies which result from the fluctuation of democratic
> action.[3]

Winter replied that he didn't think his Chinese friends would accept such
an explanation in the face of atrocities they witnessed and suffered.

But for all Chiang's terrorist efforts to subdue opposition, in the
end, this strategy helped Mao's army by generating active opponents to
the Nationalists and even by swelling Communist armies with bitter
students. To Winter, therefore, news of Communist victories and
desertion by GMD troops was welcome; and by November 1949, it was
clear to him and to reliable American reporters, such as Archibald Steele
(a *New York Times* reporter who won a Polk award for his reporting on
China), that Chiang's game was up. Though Mao's formal victory wasn't
declared until October 1, 1949, almost a year before that, the American
consulate general was urging Americans who wished to avoid present and
imminent hazards to leave on the U.S. Naval vessel available to them on
the naval vessel scheduled to leave Tienjin on November 18.

During the early days of Communist rule, we don't hear Winter
saying, as Wordsworth said of the similar stage of the French Revolution:
"Bliss was it in that dawn to be alive," but he was excited, and the
stimulated by the prospect of a new China and the early stages of
Communist rule in areas where they'd seized control gave him great
hope. Of course, he also suffered the inevitable uncertainties. On the
one hand, he considered his status similar to that of the Japanese in
the U.S. during the war. On the other, he was placed on a prominent
university committee (the Committee of Five) and was encouraged
by the Communist authorities to continue the work in the humanities
sponsored by the Rockefeller Foundation.

Winter remained highly critical of American policy toward the new
government. While many viewed Dean Acheson's White Paper (which
George Kennan thought the greatest state document ever created by the
American government[4]) as too soft on Mao's China,[5] Winter bristled at

the secretary of state's claim that the outcome of the Chinese civil war had been outside the power of the U.S. to change. Winter's view was that by backing Chiang to the amount of three and a half billion dollars (Winter's figure), we prevented a possible compromise between the two parties.[6]

Tough old bird as he was, Winter might not like to be called a romantic; but in having sought to emulate a Mandarin style in old Peiping and in being an agent for Ogden's and Richards's dream of peace, he certainly knew something of the recurrent human hunger for what its citizens could consider a good society. Who can blame him if he hoped, during those early days of Liberation, that the Communists might be the avatars of just that? Certain early changes in how things were done obviously delighted him. For example, when the Communists said they wished to supply the university with food, they insisted that the needs to be estimated not only by the university authorities (whom Winter describes as "a group of Guomindang paralytics") but also by students and workers.[7] "So we had really to wait for the Communists to bring democracy to Tsinghua."[8]

Indeed, even before the Communist victory was complete, cultural exchanges were taking place between Tsinghua students and Communist troops. The students performed plays at Communist headquarters, and truckloads of Communist soldiers gave a brass band performance in the Tsinghua auditorium.[9] Mao's army made every effort to earn the support of the peasants from whom Chiang's troops had raped and stolen. The Communist army, whom Winter saw as "consummate psychologists," accomplished this by *borrowing* food (their own food supplies couldn't keep up with their swift advance) and then returning it with interest.[10] All this meshes with Mao's conviction that he could win the war only with the support of the "masses."

As usual, music was one of Winter's ways of reading the times. In Beethoven's C sharp minor quartet, he heard the conflicted mood of the time—elation coupled with the wisdom to know that revolutionary honeymoons can be short-lived. Frequently, he also talked about opera and band performances by the People's Liberation Army. About an opera (*Hatred of Blood and Tears*) that he missed because he was nursing his cook, he paraphrases Tsinghua's professor of drama, Chao Chao-hsiung, who described it as "a real Elizabethan national, blood-and-thunder play—strong meat for strong men." Of a PLA orchestra performance that Winter *did* hear, he reported that the music wasn't very good, "but it is remarkable that an army can march for hundreds of miles from Manchuria, fighting most of the time, and still carrying cellos on their back."[11] That music should play a part in the Communist program had an impact on Winter, who knew how marginalized the arts were in the West and how remote from politics.

Winter's general enthusiasm for the first stage of the Communist takeover was lively enough to earn him a notice in a news item by George Weller (who subsequently won a Pulitzer) under the title "Reds Hold Office." The story describes Winter as "a sixtyish Shakespearian scholar and bachelor, who has lived more than twenty years in China," and who is "leading pro-Communists on the faculty. He enjoys a $200 monthly subsidy from the Rockefeller Foundation."[12] If the article ever crossed the desk of an officer at the Foundation, it must of caused serious chagrin. Winter himself thought it would have been more accurate to describe him "as riding with the Communist wave rather than as leading the pro-Communists."[13]

Winter had already acknowledged the likelihood of later disillusionment, but for the present, how could he not feel enthusiasm for this first stage of revolutionary power? The PLA had petitioned the students to draw up three principles and eight rules for soldiers that the army would enforce "with the greatest severity."

The principles:

1. Obey your superior.
2. Do not take even a needle or thread from the people.
3. All confiscated property to be pooled for the general good.

(Winter doesn't address the apparent discrepancy between the second and third principle.)

The rules:

1. Speak politely.
2. Do not bargain in buying things.
3. Borrowed things must be returned in perfect condition.
4. Anything destroyed or broken must be replaced.
5. Do not curse or beat anybody.
6. Do not harm the crops.
7. Do not misbehave with women.
8. Treat prisoners kindly.[14]

No doubt, some of these rules must have been "more honored in the breach than the observance," but the order that the army was commanded to observe must have felt like a breath of air after the abuses of the GMD.

Winter remained indefatigable in reproaching "the foolish policies of the Truman administration" and reiterates his belief that this is "a real liberation, a necessary and inevitable revolution and a victory against anxiety, frustration and stagnation."[15] His ongoing connection with the Rockefeller Foundation worsened when he complained publicly about unidentified behavior by an unidentified colleague who was also on the Rockefeller payroll. The behavior was presumably pro-Chiang activities. When Stevens diplomatically reproached him, Winter disingenuously claimed that his various incriminations were meant only to reflect "local feelings." If he had given the impression that any of his acquaintances had blamed the Foundation for funding Chiang supporters, he had been unfair to them.[16] He adds in his defense that another unidentified person had accused him of being an American spy. For the while, the matter was closed, but it left the Foundation uneasy, and years later, the Communists themselves would entertain the suspicion that Winter reported to the Foundation (and thus the State Department) as a paid spy. But more of that later.

In this same letter, Winter sketches the cultural heritage under which he understood the new regime to be operating. He notes the long argument in the West over whether neurosis causes the malfunction of our social and economic institutions or vice versa. Winter see the Communists as "taking no chances" and "attacking the problem from both ends, the socio-economic and the personal." On the one hand, prices are being stabilized after long periods of uncontrolled inflation. On the other, "by a sort of common-sense analysis, or Socratic method, individuals are improved and habits of humanitarianism built up." Such methods "are revolutionary and traditional at once," he continues, quoting the famous historian of Chinese science, Joseph Needham, with whom he had enjoyed a brief friendship back in Kunming: "The Chinese have remained faithful throughout their long history of their philosophy to the belief that man is not to be distinguished from social man, nor social man from nature, and that the very foundations of nature contain something congruent with and favorable to human social order."[17]

In this view, Winter adheres to the vision that he still shared with I. A. Richards and the Romantic poets: that the Western mind, squeezed by the new science, had shrunken to its mere mental capacities and diminished its capacity for other ways of knowing. In such a context, Winter was able to see the new Communist rule as the very synthesis of Western and Eastern mind that was central to Richards's dream and his own.

For a while, Winter's academic position at Tsinghua went on as before. He taught the same courses and had a contract to continue "for another year in the same way." Before long, he was teaching a course in Marxist criticism shaped to Mao's theories, but it didn't win the favor of the authorities.[18] In the late '50s, he was permitted to teach a class of English poetry and Shakespeare to thirteen members of the English department. Professor Wang Shi-ren, who was one of them, said that this was his initiation into English poetry, which he still taught at Peking University at the time I was there.[19]

Not all Winter's friends were intellectuals. He liked to show off his swimming skills in a lake in the grounds of the Summer Palace, reading a newspaper and smoking a cigarette while floating on his back. Some of those he taught to swim or to swim better became his friends[20] and lifelong practitioners of the backstroke, uncommon in China at the time.

Even during especially brutal periods during the Cultural Revolution, he'd swim every day, often the only foreigner among "thirty or forty thousand Red Guards."[21] The crowds would part to let him enter the water, and when he came out, "hundreds rushed to get my towel and rubbed me dry." He seems to have delighted in this, and some of that delight was probably erotic: "You know what delicate hands the Chinese have and how they have to stroke everything in order to understand it. Old scholars used to spend their lives rubbing small jade objects until, after years, they took on a polish which nothing but elbow-grease would give."

In the '60s, after reading Adele Davis's books, he became a king of nutritionists and began eating things, such as bran porridge and fortified milk with powdered yeast, calcium, soy bean flour, orange juice, magnesium. He seemed to have converted few Chinese friends to his newly Spartan cuisine, but he did teach them something about vitamins and prescribe them freely.[22]

Winter no longer cared about the taste of food, Professor Zhou, one of his former colleagues, told me. He would weigh it on a scale to make sure it was precisely balanced nutritionally. He made his own yogurt and depended heavily on his pressure cooker, for which he once wrote to friends in England for replacement gaskets.[23]

Because he was not a Communist and, in his words, was not "particularly revolutionary," his salary (1,300 catties of millet a month) was the highest in the university and more than the mayor of Peiping or the president of the Bank of China received.[24] The reason he received this disproportionate salary is that, as a "petty bourgeois," he was not "expected to make the sacrifices which Communists make." As matters stood, it cost the labor of sixteen workmen to keep him alive, but if he joined the Party his salary would be drastically cut.[25]

During the early months since liberation, he did not call on his friends, lest he somehow endanger them. Nor did he attend meetings unless he was especially invited. But he enjoyed even more visitors than before, by people who wished to assure him that, technicalities aside, he was still considered a member of their community.[26] Further, as we've seen, Winter's opinions were solicited and valued by the Committee of Five, one of the academic ruling bodies. All in all, we might say that at this stage, he was a favored guest of the Liberation. But his unabated criticism of American policy toward China may have given him a false sense of security in relation to the new Chinese government. From the Chinese perspective, his frequently expressed opinion that at a time when the question of who lost China was gaining an ever-more firm grip on American foreign policy, hadn't Winter repeatedly expressed his view that the Chinese see us as "historically determined to continue our insane policy, and then to put the blame on others for our defeat"[27]—a view that he unequivocally shared?

Winter remained as compliant to local Chinese policies as he was disdainful of American ones. When he was asked either to move to other quarters or to remain where he was at higher rent, he complained that the option broke a rule against bachelors occupying single houses. After expressing doubt "whether in a socialist community any moral justifications could be found" for the first option, he requested the committee to assign him to "such a room as [he] would from *all* possible points of view be entitled to."[28]

But such high mindedness suffered an almost comic collapse as his letter continued. Matters of his personal comfort, he said, are out of place, but he wondered whether it was practical for a man of his age, when "his usefulness to the university" becomes the issue "to cross windy court-yards at night to go to the bathroom; whether, after having enjoyed the bourgeois luxury of comparative privacy for over eighty years, I can work efficient with noises coming through thin partitions; or whether, in my opinion, my presence in such crowded quarters would be an embarrassment to others," but these, he adds, "are strictly my problems, and need not concern the committee."[29]

I have to remind myself that earlier in Kunming, Winter had already known what it was to live in cramped quarters, and he was certainly no stranger to the kinds of suffering he shared with many millions of Chinese. Nonetheless, the letter is marked by what in the West looks like disingenuousness but in the East might simply be a polite way of expressing one's desires. Winter continued to live in "one of the best houses on Campus."

Whatever anti-American feeling was general in China at this time, it wasn't directed at Winter. On August 24, he received a note from Ch'I-sun Yeh, chairman of the university council, that enclosed a new contract and requested that he contact the Rockefeller Foundation about whether they would continue to fund his work at Tsinghua.[30]

Winter's university work was twofold. On the one hand, it was his job to translate Western high culture (literature and music, especially) to young Chinese intellectuals. On the other, and very much in keeping with the legacy of the May Fourth movement and "the Chinese Enlightenment," he also translated Western liberal values. In both cases, he worked to transmit what Mathew Arnold, in his essay on "Literature and Science," described as "the best which has been thought and said in the world." Through such knowledge, Arnold held, we come to know the world and ourselves. For a long time, this premise guided the teaching of the liberal arts in the U.S., and vestiges of it still remain in our colleges. With its aid, Arnold argued, we could achieve "disinterestedness," which is the ability to disentangle ourselves from sectarian beliefs and to see things as they are. Such ability serves especially when certain dogmatic notions dominate discussion of a subject—for example, such a subject as American policies in China. With disinterestedness, we can achieve the laser perceptions reflected in the passage Winter quotes in his diary from John Dewey's "Liberalism and Social Action" (1935):

> Any fresh discussion of the issue must recognize the extent to which those who decry the use of violence are themselves willing to resort to violence and are ready to put their will into operation. Their fundamental objective is to [maintain] the economic institution that now exists, and for its maintenance they resort to the use of force that is placed in their hands by

this very institution. They do not need to advocate the use of force; their only need is to employ it."[31]

I raise these points as a way of emphasizing that in holding his views on American-Chinese relations, Winter was not being a crank. He was guided by deep intellectual and cultural traditions deeply rooted in American liberalism and, as it turned out (setting exaggeration and occasional baseless rumors aside), history proved his presumptions to be correct. His lifelong fondness for gossip had grown now into the skills of an able reporter—well-connected, avid after detail, and able to synthesize. Obviously, he wasn't disinterested, but his biases rested on long and tortuous experience under Chiang's regime.

Further, a year later, when John Marshall interviewed I. A. Richards upon his return from a six-month visit to China while on sabbatical from Harvard, he heard a view of the new Chinese army very close to Winter's. While Richards was far too diplomatic to criticize American policy, he found the soldiers, men and woman, to be "well behaved, quiet, and apparently always engage in serious pursuits. You would see, for example, a group in which one member was reading to the others. Its officers wear no insignia, there is no saluting, and it is very much a people's army in the Trotsky tradition."

Richards also found the city, which he'd known since 1926, "more orderly and better governed than ever before." The wild inflation and graft that had characterized Chiang's rule was over: "Strict currency control is bringing prices down, and not once could Richards find any intimation of the graft that was formerly so pervasive." Marshall concluded that, given Richards's disdain for Communist doctrine, this report was "that of detached dispassionate, and, on the whole, well qualified observer."[32]

A couple of weeks later, Richards called Charles Balfour at the Foundation about other matters, including Bob Winter. He thought that Winter's expressed fury against American policy "left of the regime," to his eyes, "were in part a defense mechanism of trying to prove that he was not an enemy alien." Winter was still living in his excellent house and reported that the acting university dean was willing that he continue receiving assistance from the Rockefeller Foundation but that the university would make no formal request. Balfour told him, with some relief, I imagine, that under such circumstances, the Foundation could not make payments "since the original grant was to the University, not to Winter.[33]

*

For Winter, less dispassionate than Richards, the spirit of liberation was heady. Winter wasn't a poet—not in any strict sense, at least, though he wrote occasional translations, including a few poems by Wen Yiduo, and poems and translations when he was young. But to understand him we must see that he thought like a poet, sometimes unrestrained by strict logic, choosing instead associative thought patterns. For example, in his diary he finds a way to define the spirit of the moment through etymology. Thus:

"*Etymologies*: To liberate. Chieh3-fang4
Chieh3. Explain, unloose, liberate, send
Chieh-ch'uan-hsia. Launch a boat.
Chieh-hen. Mediate between hatreds.
Chieh-k'o. Quench thirst.
Chieh-meng. Interpret a dream
Chieh-tsui. Atone by apology.
Chieh-tu. Antiseptic.
Feng4. Release, let go, put.
Fang-chen. Distribute relief.
Fang-ch'i. Let off steam!

Winter has made a lively little poem from these etymologies, a poem called "To Liberate." And in the passage that follows, he likens the discipline of the Communists to that of the Benedictine monks as described in Aldous Huxley's *Ends and Means* and their meetings to Quaker meetings.

The first moments of any successful liberation are ripe with possibility, and one of the possibilities of Liberation, as both John Fairbank and Winter observed, was social integration through revised folk and communal art. Woodcuts, for example, had been part of Chinese culture since the early Tang Dynasty, but now the Communists made them a vital propaganda instrument. In the words of John Fairbank, quoted by Winter in his diary, "Since all things must be done with the materials at hand the Communist cultural movement has stressed the development of pictorial art in the form of the woodcut, which can be cheaply reproduced by woodblock printing for mass distribution."[34]

Especially interesting to Winter was a dance form called *yangko*, a Communist adaptation of a dance created by farmers in the Song dynasty. John Fairbanks describes the modern form as

> an all-talking-singing-dancing poor-man's opera which uses simply rhythms, folk tunes, a very simple chain dance step, propaganda stories, and the subject matter of everyday life to provide entertainment which indoctrinates as it liberates. Getting the common man to express himself in public in country dancing and choral singing is part of the social integration of the individual in the group." [35]

Winter was enthusiastic about these folk operas, which sometimes celebrated battle lust and lust for a plentiful harvest in a single song. [36] In some of them, a blood frenzy prevails:

Projecting
Bones,
Gutted
Flesh
Carries the weight
Of the Nation's
Madness
And the nation's
Roaring!

In such poetry, Winter found "no half-notes, no delicate arpeggios: each sentence is simple, powerful, deadly serious. These short, steady sentences move with the sound of drums: they penetrate into the ears and beat with your heart-beats. You may say that it is not poetry, but if you do, it is because your ears are habituated to lute-strings and have become too delicate." [37]

Winter seems to have plentiful time on his hands to reflect on the spirit of Liberation, finding analogies in everything from Pueblo kiva dances to the dance of Shiva the destroyer and finding supporting quotations everywhere. For instance, this passage from John Dewey's *Liberalism and Social Action*: "Liberalism must now become more radical, meaning by 'radical' perception of the necessity of thorough-going changes in the set-up of institutions and corresponding activity to bring the changes to pass . . . . Today, any liberalism which is not also radicalism is irrelevant and doomed."[38]

I've been tracing Winter's diary musings as he tried to make sense of the dramatically new world that now surrounded him. But at the same time, despite the fact that he hadn't been receiving his salary, he remained the Rockefeller Foundation's (and less directly, the State Department's) cultural ambassador to China. In September 1949, he presented to John Marshall an account of the position of the humanities in the New China his outline based on the confirmation by a gathering of artists and writers of a speech on literature and art that Mao had delivered back in May 1942.[39] He headed his summary by emphasizing the somewhat contradictory role he and other members of the humanities department were now to play. On the one hand, they would be left to plan their own courses, but now "the leaders" would view their work from a Maoist perspective. That perspective, in outline, would be as follows:

1. Both the role of art "among social institutions . . . and its relationship to ethics would now be as important as the analysis of beauty.

2. Art reflects reality, which is largely social. The artist's consciousness "is not merely a psychological symptom of some subjective view."

3. Literature reflects "the struggle of the people's tendency against the ideology and domination of slavery, against religious sterility, against cruelty, against insolence and suavity."

4. Lenin, among others, pointed to the contradictions Tolstoy was caught in when he wrote about social classes. Winter puts a sharper point to such analysis to illustrate the dangers implicit for writers with imperfect knowledge of culture and class. In Tolstoy, he finds, on the one hand, "an artist of genius who not only paints incomparable pictures of Russian life, but who contributes works of the first order to world literature. On the other hand, a landowner wearing the martyr's crown in the name of Christ." On the one hand, Tolstoy's "extraordinarily powerful, direct and sincere protest against social lies and hypocrisies." On the other, a worn-out hysterical sniveler called the Russian intellectual who, publicly beating his breast, cries: "I am

bad, I am vile, but I am striving after moral self-perfection:
I no longer eat meat, and I now live on rice cutlets." So
Winter practices the viewing of literary work from a
Marxist perspective.

5. Our sense of beauty varies with the mastery of mankind
   over nature. "Man, in changing nature, changes his own
   nature as well." This truncated premise would seem to
   refer both to the new Marxist aesthetic and to the Maoist
   intention of remaking human individuals in the spirit of
   the Liberation.

6. Form cannot be separated from content. "Art forms do not
   develop haphazardly, but in relation to that with which
   they are dealing and which they are reflecting."

7. The political value of art has less to do with the artist's
   consciously held political view of the author than with "the
   extent to which reality is actually reflected as it lives and
   moves in the subject matter." Thus though Balzac wrote as
   a royalist and a Catholic and Tolstoy as a man striving after
   spiritual perfection, their work has great political value,
   which "consists primarily in the fidelity with which they
   reflect the complex reality in and through which politics
   moves."

8. "Photographic realism or naturalism is as bad as a utopian
   romanticism! Its defect is the inability to see and render the
   way in which things are moving . . . . It has no faith in the
   future.

In the way of a footnote to Marshall, Winter adds that he didn't have to
read Marx and Lenin to come to these insights. "I discovered most of this
for myself many years ago."

The young man who went to China almost thirty years ago could
hardly have imagined what he would learn in the following years or the
radical transformations he would pass through as China herself radically
changed. But one constant was that Winter loved the streets and the
people he met and talked with. He was notorious for his mastery of
profanity he'd learned from rickshaw men. Now the PLA soldiers were
his tutors, and what they taught was a compassion that reached across
borders. On the way back from a shop where he'd bought cakes, he fell
in with two soldiers—"the typically Spartan which one sees everywhere

now, whose combination of Puritanical hardness and gentleness is so surprising." When he told them he was an American, but sympathetic with their cause," each of them put an arm around his shoulder and begged him not to get hurt by the attacks on American policy that were already current.[40] He liked Agnes Smedley's description of the Chinese Communist Army as "a thinking army." His experience at teaching American soldiers in Kunming taught him that "any lecturer who tried to get them to think was immediately suppressed."

In February 1949, David Stevens wrote to him to remind him that during 1948, the $3,000 had been paid to him in full and that he had been getting good reports of the work he was doing. The bad news was that the Foundation had received no request from the university for any payment for 1949. [41] On the following month, Winter got a letter from R. P. Burden, with the International Health Division of the Foundation, urging Winter to write a book about his years in China. Burden was also the person who had spoken highly to Stevens about Winter's work.[42] In June, the skeptical Burden asked Winter to describe the status of his work in the humanities, so as to justify a grant to supplement Winter's meager teaching salary should Tsinghua request one.[43]

In the beginning, the study of Western literature seemed safely ensconced at Tsinghua. Winter taught an introduction to English poetry to second year students; Shakespeare, required of fourth year students; and a seminar in literary theory required of "The entire staff of the Western Language and Literature Department" as well as fourth year and graduate students. Such offerings, Winter observed to Fahs, "probably [make] me one of the most influential foreigners in China in cultural matters." For the while (and it turned out to be a short while), Winter considered his ongoing work as "no small personal triumph over the damage US policy has done to me and to the things I am interested in."[44] Winter must have felt that somehow, amid the mutually rising enmity between the U.S. and China, he might continue to serve as the cultural ambassador that he'd always been. He knew the odds against that, but for the time, the possibility of a people's democracy seemed real. True, he admitted in the recent Peiping Conference of All Circles "the reactionaries had been disarmed and suppressed"—a "dictatorship to the reactionaries to be sure. But it is only through such a dictatorship that the rest of us can have democracy."[45]

In the meantime, Winter's friend and champion, David Stevens, was preparing to retire and had gathered together Winter's letters and journal entries, knowing that many readers "could get great pleasure out of your quotations from the scores of writers you have read over the years and from your description of your life in China."[46]

Now Winter's last correspondent at the Foundation was Fahs, who got little pleasure from Winter's continuing complaints against American policy and his insistence that, if we wished to deal with Mao's regime, it must be as equals, not as hanging judges. Indeed, Fahs now believed that Winter had been brainwashed:

> One can conclude from your letter that you are living in an environment in which all the public sources of information and opinion are controlled and poisoned. I am not surprised at this—after all, it is exactly what was forecast in the speeches of Mao Tse-tung on literature of which you sent us translations. I am only disappointed that with your background you don't understand what is happening to your own mental processes. If the leaders in Peking are as deluded on international questions as you seem to be, the next few years will be sad ones for China.[47]

On that note, Winter's connections with the Rockefeller Foundation ended, along with the dreams of peace that had begun them.

CHAPTER EIGHTEEN:
THE CULTURAL REVOLUTION

This political honeymoon was brief. Soon, Mao quickly demonstrated that Communist kindness would be much more limited than that which had enchanted Winter and many other informed observers in the early days of Liberation. In 1951, Mao launched a Three-Anti Campaign that began in Manchuria but soon arrived in Peiping. Ostensibly, its targets were corruption, waste, and bureaucracy, but its eventual victims were widespread. Workers were encouraged to denounce bosses, wives denounced husbands, children denounced parents, and intellectuals denounced one another. Beyond denunciation, there was also murder and rampant suicides. Many, including a number of Winter's colleagues, were sent to work camps, ostensibly on the assumption that shoveling hog shit would help integrate freethinkers into the mainstream of Marxist society.

The FBI began to keep records on Winter as early as August 1950, before his brief honeymoon with the Communists ended, when a news release from China News Agency crossed the director's desk. It quoted Winter as "welcoming the opportunity to add my protest to the latest acts of aggression in Taiwan and Korea by the United States Government," and concluded, "I am convinced that they will eventually be defeated, but I am appalled at the suffering they will cause before they are taught their lesson."[1]

Two years later, an FBI dispatch of July 15, 1952,[2] reveals a chastened Winter:

> He is no longer in sympathy with the new regime and has applied for an exit permit. Since English literature is no longer taught in Chinese universities, he is unable to continue the

teaching he enjoyed. He does not want to become a teacher of elementary English. A sign of his disenchantment with the present state of affairs is that he has given up wearing Chinese clothes and is now seen in Western garb.

A month later, it was reported that he had *not* applied for an exit permit and would not until he had found a job in "some Asian country." The suggestion is that he was looking, but I'd guess that he wasn't looking hard.

A later FBI report[3] summarizes Winter's deteriorating political situation. According to one informant, as a result of the Three-Anti Campaign, he was "separated from his students and colleagues." By 1954, he was forbidden to teach and permitted only to correct examination papers—precisely the fate he had dreaded. In 1957, during the brief Hundred Flowers campaign, the informant says Winter was reinstated as head of his department and was treated well. But Mao later put it, the real aim of his invitation to advance the arts and sciences through free expression of ideas was "to entice the snakes out of their caves." The result, as one of Winter's former students, later an Indian official, told me, was that Winter came out of the episode in "a very poor state psychologically and physically," and, of course, completely disenchanted. His deteriorated state was the result of grillings throughout which the Communists accused him of being an American spy. Now he was adrift in the turbulent waters of Mao's revolution, though he suffered less than many of his Chinese colleagues. Stripped of his connection with the Orthological Institute and the Rockefeller Foundation and maintaining an increasingly precarious connection with his university, he was obliged to walk more and more naked, which meant more and more like any other foreigner. When the Red Guard came for him, by his account, they broke down my door, dragged me by my hair, put their feet on me, and said they would kill me if I resisted."[4]

During his inquisition in 1959-1960, Winter was obliged to testify in writing on a number of subjects.[5] The earliest opens with a brief account of how his acquaintanceship with Wen Yiduo brought him to China. This reminder of his early acquaintance with a man who later became a political martyr may have strengthened his case that he had always been a friend to progressive China.

The document then turns to his relationship with Richards, the Orthological Institute, and the Rockefeller Foundation. He emphasizes that the Foundation temporarily stopped his salary because he was working against the Japanese and ultimately fired him because of his sympathy with the Chinese Communists. It also mentions his diary, which he describes as a voluntary project designed to let the Foundation know of "the terrible suffering of the Chinese people."[6] The aftermath to this inquisition was that Winter was allowed to resume his university job, though that now consisted of writing and editing language exercise and tutoring a few students in literature.

The Communists had put Winter's life on trial and now tolerated but did not quite acquit him. The Korean War made "acquittal" difficult since anti-American feeling, already boiling because of our support of Chiang's regime, had now boiled over into war. And when the Cultural Revolution broke out in January 1968, more serious trouble for him began when his house was raided by cadres led by Chao T-ming, a lecturer in Spanish.[7] According to Professor Yang Zhou-han, author of a famous Chinese history of European literature, Winter told him that Allyn and David Rickett, during lengthy interrogation of their own activities in China, had accused Winter of being a spy.[8] Whether he was reporting to American officials at this time I don't know, but I *do* know that in the 1970s, he made several visits to the USLO (United States Liaison Office), seeking assistance on matters like getting the money his sister had left him in her legacy or renewing his passport. But once there, he would also talk at length about current Chinese political affairs,[9] thus cooperating with American officials in a way he had not done before his ordeals during the Cultural Revolution.

A lot of Winter's property was seized in the January raid, ranging from electronic equipment, including the turntable and speakers that allowed him to listen to the classical music he loved. Several albums of classical records were taken too, along with music tapes. Some trinkets and a few machines were returned, "mostly damaged or broken." "But the irreplaceable things, such as lecture notes and correspondence," which he estimated "would make a pile 25-30cm. high," along with some clothes, were not returned. Winter's inventory of the stolen good ran to more than thirty items and included even a small legacy he had received when his sister died in 1962. Since those funds allowed him to purchase medicine and packages of vegetable seeds for his garden, it had potentially devastating effects on his daily life, in which expert gardening had become an important part of his routine.

Winter had always been a superior gardener, an intellectual who needed to dig in the dirt, but the activity must have taken on even higher importance at a time when he had so little to fall back on. When a box of dahlia tubers that he'd asked Bill and Delia Jenner to send him arrived frozen and rotten as a result of their long passage from London through Russia, he expressed his deep disappointment.[10] He had requested them by name: "House of Orange, Popular Guest, Giant Spider, Miss Universe." Happily, as it turned out, he could still plant dahlias because the head gardener of the Altar of Heaven gave him some very fine varieties."[11]

Chao Te-ming, who had led the raid against Winter, eventually paid heavily for his actions, which included "borrowing" money from Winter by demanding it. Far worse, from January 8, 1969, to April 12, 1969, he kept Winter imprisoned in a university building; and for thirteen hours a day, Winter was obliged to sit and confess his "crimes."[12] It stretches the imagination to think of this man who faced down a Japanese soldier whose bayonet was ready to stab him in the stomach being obliged to sit and confess, but Winter's education in humility was well under way.

He was also obliged to write a summary of his academic career. Even under the humiliating circumstances, his account of his teaching reflects his pride in long-sustained accomplishment. He speaks somewhat generally of the great numbers of research students and young teachers that he had trained, but several people whom I interviewed were more specific. Professor Chuan Hsiung-chao, for example, noted that in a class Winter taught back in the early thirties, of the eight students who studied French with him for four years, half went on to become professors themselves.

The list of publications that Winter provided to the authorities was a little inflated. (For whatever reasons, Winter never published, although his correspondents at the Rockefeller Foundation often urged him to revise his diaries into a book.) Thus, his bibliography includes essays he wrote going back in his undergraduate days and at the University of Chicago and lists English texts for Chinese students that he wrote or edited and two books that were basic to Richards's program in China: *A First Book of English* and *A Second Book of English*. Richards, as was his custom, failed to acknowledge Winter's considerable contributions to these works, just as he had failed to acknowledge Jameson's work at all, thus probably helping to bring about Jameson's resignation.

Winter explored in detail his relation with the Guomindang because his meeting with Chiang Kai-shek on behalf of the living Buddha made up the gravamen of the case against him. Readers will recall his dealings with Hsiung Ting, whom he had helped sneaking a code book past the Japanese and buying guns for the GMD from Japanese traitors in the early '40s.[13] Hsuing Ting had convinced him that he would be of more use against the Japanese if he had the backing of the government in power, and it was in this context that he brought the living Buddha to Chiang's headquarters and had received Chiang's thanks for his help against the Japanese. At the time, Winter believed he was working for the Chinese rather than for one side of a simmering civil war.[14] He retells the story in great and honest detail and also appends a selective summary of his correspondence from 1940 to 1960 with Richards and officers of the Rockefeller Foundation. He includes a number of letters in which he attacks the policies of the American government and also includes a partial index of his diaries, again emphasizing that their purpose "was to show the terrible sufferings of the Chinese people."

Elsewhere, in these "self-criticism" documents, he provided a list of people who visited him in the first six months of 1960. These included Jacques Pimpaneau, who went to come a professor at l'Institut national des langues et civilisations orientales; Michel Cartier, who also would write about China; David Dubois, son of the founder of the NAACP; and Marcella Yeh, at the time an American expatriate and poet. For all the political pressures on him and his semiostracism from colleagues, Winter continued to be a magnet for foreign intellectuals. Some students were also allowed to visit, as well as Li Fu-ning, at the time vice dean of the Foreign Languages Department and later chairman of the English Department.

Winter survived these inquisitions, not without mental and physical costs, and, with an unselfishness widely remarked upon, went on writing language texts, prepare exercises, and gladly doing kinds of humbling work of the kind he once did for Richards. At the same time, he avoided some of the official intrusions that his Chinese colleague had to accept— regular bed checks, for example. He refused to answer "the midnight knock," and after he mentioned his refusal to a party official who had been his student and visited him regularly, the forced visits stopped.[15] In such circumstances, he read eight to ten hours a day, sometimes typing out passages from what he was reading, including long excerpts from his sometime friend Joseph Needham.

While Winter was generally isolated from his colleagues, some, such as Professor Zhang Xingbao, his longtime colleague in the English Department, were allowed to visit him on work-related matters, although she sometimes mailed borrowed books back to him rather than delivering them in person. Zhang Xingbao remembers how he worked with her on sentence examples in a Chinese-English dictionary to attune them with the political dogmas of the time. But while he was generous with his books and in his editing of dictionaries and language texts, she knew that if she visited him to borrow or consult, she would have to stay a long time. "He liked to talk. He enjoyed an audience."[16] Until the Cultural Revolution began in 1968, he was allowed to gather audiences as he had done much earlier in Evanston by directing dramatic student performances in which he played the lead roles.

Hippy travelers gave Winter a glimpse of the '60s atmosphere in the U.S., and he didn't much like what he saw, perhaps in the light of the Red Guard movement in China. Such an upheaval, he told his friends the Jenners, reminded him of the Children's Crusades of the thirteenth century.

> From all the corners and pockets of the country, wearing every weird sort of dress, or even no clothes at all, only a G-string, carrying on their backs everything they possess, seeing the world for the first time, so intent on drinking in new impressions that they remain totally indifferent to the long lines of lorries that never stop, indifferent to hunger, cold, sore feet.[17]

But even as he disapproved of the new traveler's seeming fecklessness, he would sometimes oblige them by guiding long lines to the road that took them to sites of interest, such as the West Gate.

On occasion, he would also guide Chinese commuters. On days when no public transportation was available because buses were all consigned to bringing people to a rally, Winter would encounter at each bus station, "several thousand people who had been waiting up to seven hours for a bus that never came." He told them at each stop that there would be no bus that day, and they followed him to their various destinations, and "another thousand or so would join the Pied Piper" until the crowd stretched out behind him as far as he could see.[18] It's the kind of Winter story that, if it isn't perfectly true, it should be.

I was told that Winter was "an intimate friend" of Deng Ying-chao, wife of Chou En-li. He met her through Fu Yi. During early '70s, these people would visit Winter, and from small hints, he knew a good deal of what was happening to everyone. "At the height of the Cultural Revolution purges, there was always a group of workmen working around his house. They did little—pulled things up, and pushed things down—but it was clear from their presence to passing RG that Winter was protected."[19]

During his late years, he delighted in tending his garden, for which friends abroad would send him exotic seeds. Winter's house during this time was surrounded by lotus gardens. He enjoyed walking among them. His interest in Adele Davis's nutritional advice continued and, in 1980, even self-published a small pamphlet entitled *Nutrients Essential to Human Health*.[20] He still saw some old colleagues and foreign visitors, but his hunger for gossip had abated, and he treasured his solitude. I believe that he finally enjoyed real peace in these waning years, knowing the serenity and balance that he had admired in Chen Daison.

For all Winter's attention to diet (or because of it), in 1973, he was hospitalized for one hundred days with spastic colon and acute gastric dilation. During that stay, he told the Richards he was "pinned to his bed like a dead moth" with a needle dripping into his veins. Later, back in the saddle, he built a cold frame in which to grow kale but couldn't find rice straw to make mats that would protect it from the cold at night. He mentioned the problem to a young friend he bumped into, and the friend promised to get him the rice straw from his commune. He ran a serious risk of putting himself out for a class enemy, but one evening, just after dusk, the friend arrived at his door with a pile of straw over his head.[21]

In 1974, when the heat of the Cultural Revolution had somewhat diminished, Winter wrote to the Richards that one could once again speak of Confucius and Mencius. He had also taped for Shanai University a book on Basic, "which is to be used throughout the province."[22] To the Richards, he waxed poetic about the absence of herons in Peking. For years, the Peking herons had lived in a grove of evergreen to the north of the city. He remembers watching them fly "in a straight line, and trailing their long legs behind." I was once told that during the Cultural Revolution, a Chinese painter was imprisoned for painting a traditional scene with heavier black tones than were typical; the black was understood, perhaps correctly, as a criticism of Mao's regime. I suppose that in earlier days, had this letter come to the authorities, Winter's nostalgia for the cranes might be similarly understood by officials.

During this period, Winter received many letters from other friends abroad, full of accounts of their everyday lives. These, along with other of his papers, he kept in a secret cache until, at the time of his death, they were given to me. I imagine that they comforted him in his isolation.

And they sent him all sorts of things, from yogurt cultures and flower seeds to books and records for his Phillips player.

We glimpse Winter's isolation through the stories he told the Richards about his daily life. In a restaurant where he stopped, he saw a crowd of workers wearing shaggy sheepskins or long padded gowns, "patched and shiny with age." One of them spoke to him, and Winter recognized him as someone he often waved to when he saw him driving his night soil cart. Now the man surprised Winter by calling out to his friends Winter's age and residence and details of his daily life. When the crew left, they waved, and Winter felt a sensation of human solidarity that he rarely experienced during these dark times.[23]

It was a time when, should Winter ask someone a question, the inevitable answer was "I don't know." A series of violent movements followed, "including one during which Confucius and Mencius were called every dirty name."

Then in 1982, everything changed when he broke his hip and, even after long hospital treatment, could only rarely, and with assistance, leave his bed. In the end, Adele Rickett told me he was a paranoic old man, short-tempered, convinced that even the doctors wanted to kill him. It was two years after his accident, while I was teaching in the English Department of Peking University, that I met him to find that he was all that but far more.

CHAPTER NINETEEN:
SAYING GOODBYE

This book began when I first visited Winter in mid-September 1984, shortly after my family and I arrived in China, where I would teach for a year at Peking University (Beida), where Winter had taught for many years. Ruye Min-yuan went with me, and it turned out that his father, Professor Wang Min-yuan, had preceded us because when we arrived in Winter's yard, he came out of the house, shaking his head. We could hear someone roaring within. Ruye went in to see how bad things were, and in a few minutes, he beckoned us to enter: there is Winter, a big man in a small cot, propped up by pillows, screaming that his servant Wang wants to kill him. If we are really his friends, he says desperately, we'd better act quickly.

When Winter was calmer, Ruye helped him into a wheelchair, and we went outside to his small yard and untended garden under a late-afternoon sun. Now that I could speak with Winter, I asked him if there is anything I could do for him. He answered no: he is in this situation, and the only way I could help him would be by getting him out of it. The nature of the situation, I gathered, was that he is ninety-seven and, since a bicycle accident two years earlier, unable to walk. I didn't yet know that the situation included a hell of self-doubt.

As the afternoon cooled, we went back into the house; and as Ruye put Winter back to bed, I took in the room. The space was cramped, almost squalid, and it smelled of medication and of the man himself. But fabulous objects were scattered around as relics of a livelier past.[1]

Almost at once, Winter began to talk to me with clarity and authority about how he left America in 1921. He started off in Chinese hesitantly. Then remembering my presence, he switched to English to say that when he analyzed, he saw that the problem was the American way of religion. It wasn't so much that people declared themselves religious at the drop of a hat but that they weren't religious at all but just talked about it. The Chinese, he said, really are religious, but they don't talk about it. Winter might seem rarely to have suffered self-doubt in his vital years. Now he said he wanted to blot himself out. Was this a kind of Buddhist leap (he'd always been drawn to the principles of Eastern spiritual texts) in a man whose ego used to call the shots?

Why did people come to see him now? He really wanted to know. Did his life mean anything? A man came to see him, he said, who told him that he was a good man. Winter asked him why he thought him good. The man didn't know, only that Winter would be incapable of doing anything bad. "I didn't think that was a very satisfactory answer," Winter said, perhaps thinking of earlier bouts of egotism and self-indulgence. But when Wang Min-yuan told him that the man had paid him a great compliment, he seemed pleased and relieved.

But he was still haunted. Why had I come? What had I heard about him? When I told him that Wang Min-yuan's younger son, Rujie, whom I had taught back at Wabash, said he was a great and widely influential teacher, Winter smiled. Wang Min-yuan reminded me of how many distinguished writers and professors he had influenced, and his smile continued. But his self-doubt seemed deeper than praise could assuage.

During this first visit, reminscence was larded with hallucination. It was sometimes hard for me to separate hallucination. Ronald Regan had come to visit him and bowed to him in a courtly Chinese way without saying a word. What could that mean? His question was too urgent for me to leave unanswered. I told him it meant that the U.S. was finally honoring him.

Other of his stories rang true. Before Liberation, a former student, Fu Yi, had come to his door to ask for food and water. She was a revolutionary, and the GMD was looking for her. Winter took her in, and shortly later, some men came to his door, and he looked at their shoes and saw that they were good shoes and knew that they worked for the Nationalists—"the enemy." He hurried back in to warn her, locked her in his wardrobe behind his clothes, with a Chinese key so complicated that he had always had trouble opening the wardrobe himself. There he kept her safe until the men left.

Winter warmly reminisced about his gardening days. Once he said his mind was set on crossing flowers. He interbred some marigolds he had brought with him from Germany by train through Siberia (this was fifty or sixty years ago). He crossed them with blue spiked Chinese marigolds and had flowers of every color. His cook saw that he valued them and dug them up to sell to neighboring women who put them in pots. "But they won't grow that way; they all died." He started over but never got the same varieties. There are many flowers in his garden now, including some hardy-looking but ordinary marigolds. The garden hadn't been tended for a long time, probably since he'd been confined to bed two years earlier.

We shook hands when I left, and he told me he hoped to see me again. I'd already made up my mind or fallen under his spell. I wanted to do something for him, and all I could think to do was to tell his story. As I left, I turned back. He lay prone on a narrow bed, a gaunt man nearly immobile, except when he coughed. He was like a great fish washed up on the shore, breathing out his last.

When I bicycled over to Winter's house a couple of weeks later, again, he was obsessed with whether he was a good man and sadly concluded that everything he had done was for the approval of others and not for the good of the world. (The remark makes me reconsider the question of his self-doubt. Had it always haunted him? Had he always been trying to prove something to himself—perhaps that he really *was* a good man?) Now he believes he is being punished for liking men better than women. And he thinks that his servant Wang is being punished because "every day she must have intercourse with men." In fact, she had been a prostitute when he found her on the street being beaten by a small crowd from whom he rescued her. That was thirty years earlier, but they have been together ever since. She was often the object of his rage, and once, his neighbor, Zeisberger, told me he seriously injured himself while chasing her around the courtyard.[2] His anger had always been on a hair trigger and had gotten worse in his semidementia.

When it was time for me to go, Winter calmed himself and asked if my visits to him were worthwhile. I assured him, honestly, that they were. Even on occasions like this, when he wasn't lucid for very long, I was wedded to my notion of getting him to talk about his life and thus enhancing my own. When I reassured him, he grinned at me, and it warmed me to know that I'd brought him comfort.

The prospect of his biography sometimes framed itself around the idea of a last judgment, as if such a judgment of a human being is ever possible. Once Winter asked me if I would write good things or bad things about him, and when I answered good things, he replied: "They won't be true then." He regretted that he couldn't often give me coherent accounts of events: "I think my brain is falling to pieces." And he would hand me fragments. For instance, he sometimes talked about the Basic English project: "One day the whole world will speak one language." This was Richards's dream; Richards was "one of the greatest men I ever knew." At one time, Richards believed that imagination could again come of age, resuming its earlier place as companion to reason, as William Blake had imagined it, and that this could be brought about when the Chinese and Western minds could communicate more deeply. But Richards had also feared, as the Romantics did, that analytical reason would finally murder imagination, and Winter grieved that this had already come to pass: "People seem to be too busy to find what we had in those days." I reminded him of Pound's line, "What thou lovest well remains." He smiled, briefly comforted.

Then he'd return to the dismal entrapment that was the only real constant of his late life: "I'm quite a different person since I was not able to walk. When I was able to walk I could go anywhere—here and here—to see what it was like. Now I don't go anywhere, don't see anything. I think it is very bad not to be able to walk." He achingly missed his own neighborhood "of ponds and water creatures and birds, bamboo and flowers."

Those lost walks sometimes merged with childhood memories of walks in a mythical Crawfordsville overlaid with China: When he was a little boy, he said, he used to take long walks along the water next to the lake. There he would see the ruins of an ancient civilization that had entirely disappeared, except for part of a building. I took this memory to refer to the Empress Xu Ci's ruined Summer Palace, where my wife and I often went with our five-year-old daughter, who found it a marvelous playground, and where, Winter said, he too had, "climbed . . . for amusement."

Winter often recalled past kindnesses to him. Gladys Wang, the famous translator, made him an open invitation to drop over for dinner, and she also often visited him. An anonymous government official, during his visit to the United States, asked him why he kept returning to China, and he answered that he wanted to make the world a better place to live in. When she asked how he spent his free time, he told her that he read. "How many books do you read?" she asked, and he replied, "a book a day." When he got back to China, he received a telegram that read, "a book a day." And so it was: a new book every day in the mail. Yet he'd often insisted, perhaps remembering his early family life in a household of women, that he didn't like women. "My punishment is to be put here, in the charge of a woman." He often spoke that way—as if his room was a prison where he was being punished for being a homosexual. Worse, it was a prison almost without windows. He lay there twenty-four hours a day, he said, staring at "that square [the TV] or whenever there's a light on it. I can see out a little way."

> I have a problem just now. Economy has reduced me to just one assistant, or worker—the one that let you in, who is very extraordinary in one way, if not in many others. When I took her she was not a person at all. She belonged to no class in those days. Chinese all had their classes. She was not even a person. A person like this woman who had no position in society, you could kill without being punished—strike them dead and the law wouldn't touch you. That's impossible almost anywhere in the world now. And the one standing behind you, who let you in, her life became so different when I gave her a personality and called her by a name that she herself, I feel sure, can't remember what she was before that happened . . . . In a sense, this person "didn't exist in those days when she didn't have a class or a name.

When he met her, a crowd was stoning her and hitting her with sticks. He came running at them with his own walking stick, a stout one that he carried at the time for style, not because he needed it. They would have killed her. He scattered them and then took her in because he had saved her and felt obliged to her. I don't know the date of this incident, but it's likely to have happened when Winter could easily identify with those cast away.

Late in his life, Professor Li Fu-ning said something to me that might have eased Winter's doubts, had they been susceptible to reason; when I knew him, I doubt that he'd have been comforted by the words of Li Fu-ning, a student whom he helped go to the U.S. to study while the two were in Kunming. It was Li who told me what might have eased Winter's doubts if they were susceptible to reason:

> I hope you will draw a picture of Mr. Winter as one of the best friends China has ever had, and also please stress the point that he has made very great contributions to change education, and

especially toward the training of Chinese teachers of language. Also his anti-fascist, pro-Communist progressive activities. All these respects deserve our very great admiration.

*   *   *

On the morning of July19, 1985, four days before we were to leave China for home, my wife and daughter and I were at breakfast when Winter's cook, Liang, came by to invite me for lunch that day. Together we rode to Winter's house, pedaling fast because it had begun to rain, Liang ringing his bicycle constantly as we made our way through pedestrian traffic. Despite the rain, strong light came down through the trees, and when we got to the lotus ponds near the house, their leaves were aching with light, nearly translucent.

Winter's servant, Wang, was waiting for us at the open door, with her warm mask of a smile, which remained fixed. A man I've never seen sat in the outer room and smiled as I went through, like a vaguely ominous figure in an Eliot quatrain. Almost immediately, he disappeared.

Winter was sleeping in a chair whose back was held together by wire, before him a tray on which sat two half-finished jars of yogurt and two chocolate biscuit wrappers. Wang and Liang woke him to tell him that I'd come to say goodbye.

For a minute, he looked around him, confused, then he began to talk commandingly, though with an abruptness not quite rational:

"I told them to keep my name out of the papers. I didn't come here on anything political. But now I'm in trouble. I wanted to be small, so that I wouldn't be visible. But now I have become so small that I am practically nothing." As he talks, he stares at a scroll that contains Mao' famous and ominous words: "Let a thousand flowers bloom."

Then after a long silence:

When they interviewed me there were five of us, but the others were so nervous that they could say anything. When he got to me I said, in French "A young man was walking from Jerusalem to Jericho but fell among thieves and they left him for dead on the road. But he didn't die." I wanted to say nothing but was telling them a great deal. A great deal indeed, since they were the thieves, he the young man, this stated in a language they did not understand and in reference to a Biblical story they would not know.

Abruptly, his mind turned to Wang. Outside his window, the bamboo grove he had planted nodded in the odd light, but he waved past the grove and said, "She used to keep a whorehouse, over *there* . . . . She had a wonderful mind to recognize an evil person when she saw him. And if you knew what she was doing, she was a wonderful help. The people she helped were all the worst people in China . . . . She was making it clear by seeing her who her friends were, and they were the people to destroy.

Trying to make clearer sense of his story, I asked, "Who *were* her friends?" "Chiefly, big business wanted to make money out of it. And some were just bad people. But nobody could escape her. She knew which ones to work with or work for but not the reason they were working. The Chinese are a very strange people. They don't say what they are working for, but they never stop working."

I knew that there was more to his story than my limited knowledge and experience could take in, but I was used to being in that position. The longer I stayed in China, the more mysterious and often impenetrable it seemed. It was as if, in the year I'd spent there, I was experiencing a slow and deepening culture shock. The deteriorating Winter was just part of that larger movement.

All through our conversation, I tried to eat the banquet style lunch set before me. In one plate, there was duck (very expensive in Beijing in those days) and a savory eggplant dish. Beside it, Wang had set a salad of green peppers and cucumber and tomato. Then she brought in a bowl of tomato soup, shiny with grease but delicious, and, at the end of the meal, three big slices of watermelon and a bowl of canned pears. It wasn't a Chinese but a Western meal, and I ate with knife and fork. Winter ate nothing.

Through the several layers of confusion that marked what I thought would be our last talk, I longed for something more: maybe that he would rise from the bed and walk, sixty and strong and clear again. Wang interrupted my reflection, telling me, "Eat, eat." And when, being stuffed, I couldn't, she said, sounding like my Jewish bubby, "No good, the food isn't good, of course you don't want to eat it." When I reassured

342   BERT STERN

her that it was delicious, again, she said, "Eat, eat," and I feared that she would start spooning food into my mouth.

Through all this, the old man and I somehow managed to keep talking. Even when twice she brought him bottles of Peking Royal Jelly fortified with ginseng and twice I assured him that it was good medicine, all honey and energizing root, and twice she snapped the neck from the small glass bottle and poured the liquid into a spoon and fed him, still, we kept talking.

"You wanted to write a book about the Chinese and American minds, so that the two people could understand each other better."

"They will anyway, with or without a book." Then back to the recurrent theme.

"What do the Chinese think of me?" he wanted me to ask Wang. And then it all became surreal. "Let that man translate," he said, gesturing to Liang, who had sat quietly through our meal. But no, the mysterious Liang with the milky cataract over his right eye can't. He doesn't speak English. Several times during our conversation, when Winter became disturbed, Liang spoke to him quietly, holding his hand and rubbing his back softly with the other hand. Then Wang returned from the other room where she'd been eating her own meal, and Winter asked his obsessive question in Chinese. She answered, and he translated to me, almost disinterestedly, as if we were not acting out an absurdist drama: "Fu Yi, Mao Tse Dong, Chou En-lai—they all say you are a good man."

"Those are just names," Winter remarks.

"No," I said, "they're people who admire you and are grateful for your work in China." He smiled. "Why should you doubt yourself?" His eyes moisten. Wang speaks again and Winter translated: "When you go back to America, everyone will understand."

Abruptly, now that we'd finished eating, Wang cleared he table, and I started to move it so that I could move my chair closer to Winter. But she waves me aside and moved it for me. Then, just as I was about to say goodbye, she brought us Skippy Cups, which neither of us wants, and for once she didn't persist.

Before I left, I asked Winter a last question. All through our talk, the wind rustled through the bamboo grove that he'd planted years ago, and how they shone on a summer day that had turned sweet and fair.

"Can I grow bamboo like this back home?" He looked at me with fresh interest.

"They have to have the things they like. I started these. I doubt if they'll grow for you there."

"How would I start them?"

"You take a shoot that grows in the fork. You can take it off without breaking it. But it doesn't come up where you plant it. Under the ground, it sends out a lateral shoot, and it will up here and there along the shoot. So you must cultivate all around the shoot when you plant it or else the new plants won't be able to break through."

For once, we were talking on solid ground, in the language of fact sweet to both of us. I took Winter's hand and kissed him on the top of the head.

"Will I see you again?"

I hesitate. I'll be in China for three more days, but no, let it end here because there can't be a proper end. The two of us will never be satisfied.

I left the house and started walking toward my bicycle, but Wang ran after me to load my bag and then give me a string bag, both loaded with cans of pears and cartons of chocolate wafers. I said goodbye, and as I tied the string bag to my handlebars and got on the bike, Liang appeared and insisted on wheeling it till I waved him goodbye and then I was pedaling fast down the sunlit road, past the lotus ponds, the Democracy Building, up the road to home in the Shao Yuan, the dorm for foreigners.

*   *   *

Two years later, I received a formal invitation to attend Winter's hundredth birthday party on December 19, 1987. By that time, my college had launched in Winter's name a scholarship program for Chinese students and were planning to begin a program in Asian studies. So they generously sent me back to the university I'd learned to love during the year I taught there, with its lake named No-name, its wise long-suffering professors and brilliant students, and the brick wall near our dorm that my daughter, Anna, would walk under the mimosa trees as I held her hand.

Bob Winter had always longed to live to a hundred, and now, though having suffered every kind of deterioration, he had triumphed. But the birthday party itself was a kind of nightmare. When I arrived at his house, his room was already packed with dignitaries from the university and the Foreign Affairs Office of the Education Commission. Dewey Pentergrass, an American consul, is there to read a letter to Bob Winter from Ambassador Lord, and there were reporters from the Chinese and American press and from the VOA.

But the ensuing ceremony was more for the guests than for Bob Winter. He seemed already a reluctant ghost summoned up to play its part in this whirlwind of living energies, but he held back, bewildered. All this formal fuss around him obviously didn't concern him at all. He could only feel the shock of so many people, so much demand on his attention, so many flashbulbs. Afterward, in the outer room, I blew out the candles and made a ceremonial cut into the magnificent two-layer cake.

I visited him several times after the ceremony. Though he was more gaunt and confused than when I'd seen him in the summer of 1985, he was still hungry for companionship and able to respond emotionally. He even seemed to take some comfort in knowing that so many people now found his life admirable and even exemplary. Much of his correspondence, including letters to and from Pound and Wen Ito, had been burned after being used as evidence against him during the kangaroo courts of the Cultural Revolution. But many other letters along with his journal survived and came into my possession to leave a record, however spotty, of his relationship and work with many of China's and Europe's best and brightest.

Bob was still alive when I left China a few days after the party, He'd die not long after. Before I left I gave to an assistant dean of the English Department a poem of mine that could be burned with the body. Two hundred people came to the event at the Ba Bao Shan Cemetery, and there was serious talk about erecting a stone for Winter near his house on the campus. It's pleasant for me to imagine it in any of the four seasons, set beside one of the lotus ponds where he loved to walk.[3]

ENDNOTES

Preface

[1] Robert Winter to Trustees of Wabash College, August 30, 1980, RAC Special Collections: Herbert Stern Collection (unsorted).

[2] For many years Zeisberger taught German at Peking University.

[3] Hahn was a famous writer who lived in China from 1935 to 1941. Like Winter, she was also an adventurer.

[4] *China to Me* (Philadelphia: The Blackston Company, 1944), p. 107.

Chapter 1

[1] Winter to Ivor and Dorothea Richards, November 24, 1940. Material like this, unless otherwise indicated, is archived in the Rockefeller Archive Center (RAC) Special Collections: Herbert Stern Collection (unsorted). Winter was a renowned storyteller, and in some of his harrowing accounts, there may be a degree of hyperbole. But the conditions in Kunming were harrowing at this time, there can be no doubt.

[2] Ibid.

[3] Winter to Dr. M. C. Balfour, January 15, 1941 (RAC Special Collections: Herbert Stern Collection) (unsorted).

[4] Winter to Ivor and Dorothea Richards, November 24, 1940. Volume II, 1940-1946, RAC Special Collections: Herbert Stern Collection (unsorted).

[5] Robert Winter, "Report on the Work of the Orthological Institute from March to May 1941," Rockefeller Archives, 601R, RG1, Series 601, Box 48, Folder 405.

[6] Gerard Manley Hopkins, "Pitched Past Pitch of Grief."

7   Gerald Manley Hopkins, "Spelt from Sibyl's Weeds." Winter frequently frames his experiences against quotations of other modernist poets, such as Hopkins, T. S. Eliot, and W. B. Yeats.

8   Winter to Richards, November 11, 1941, Vol. II, RAC Special Collections: Herbert Stern Collection (unsorted).

9   Ibid.

10 Robert Winter, "Terror," typescript (1977?), RAC Special Collections: Herbert Stern Collection (unsorted).

11 Interview, December 12, 1984.

12 Chao Li-Kate, Interview, January 19, 1985.

13 Winter, Interview, December 12, 1984.

14 Ibid.

15 Ibid.

16 Ibid.

17 Interview, March 27, 1985.

18 Ibid.

19 Ibid.

20 Interview, December 12, 1984.

21 *The Wabash*, XXX.13 (May 21, 1910), "The Greek Play *Oedipus Tyrannus*," Presented in English by the Students of Wabash College under the Auspices of the Department of Greek, June 16, 1908.

22 *The Wabash*, XXX.13, May 21, 1910.

23 Ibid.

24 Wabash College *Bachelor*, May 21, 1910, p. 2.

25 Interview, March 3, 1985.

26 Winter to Wang Rujie, January 9, 1982, RAC Special Collections: Herbert Stern Collection (unsorted).

27 Interview, December 12, 1984.

28 *The Evanstonian*, III.1, October 1919.

29 Ibid.

30 Phone interview, November 13, 1986.

31 RAC Special Collections, Herbert Stern Collection (unsorted)

32 Ibid.

33 Memo, Patrick Quinn, Northwestern University Archivist, to William Padden, April 23, 1985, RAC Special Collections: Herbert Stern Collection (unsorted).

34 Memo, Daniel Meyer, Special Collections, University of Chicago, to Peter Dembowski, Department of French, April 3, 1985, RAC Special Collections: Herbert Stern Collection (unsorted).

[35] Quoted by Robert Winter, D2, p. 39.

[36] Ibid., p. 40.

[37] Interview, March 3, 1985.

[38] Wen Yiduo to Liang Shi Qiu, November 26, 1922, *The Complete Works of Wen Yiduo,* vol. 3 (Hong Kong), p. 608.

Chapter 2

[1] John Israel, *Lianda: A Chinese University in War and Revolution* (Stanford, CA: Stanford University Press), p. 165.

[2] Ibid., p. 166.

[3] Interview with Li Fu-ning, November 1987.

[4] Ezra Pound, "The Rest," *Personae* (New York: New Directions, 1971), pp. 92-3.

[5] Winter to Wang Ru-jie, January 9, 1982, in my possession.

[6] Israel, op. cit., p. 167.

[7] "Sources of Conflict," *So Much Nearer* (New York: Harcourt, Brace & World, 1968), pp. 231-32.

[8] Israel, op. cit., p. 168.

[9] Vera Schwarcz, *The Chinese Enlightenment: Intellectuals and the Legacy of the May Fourth Movement of 1919* (Berkely: U of Cal Press, 1986), p. 7.

[10] E. R. Hughes, *The Invasion of China by the Western World* (New York: Barnes & Noble Inc., 1968; 1st ed. 1937), p. 178.

[11] Schwarcz, p. 122.

[12] Ibid., p. 8.

[13] D2, p. 23. The diary originally came to me in the two volumes that Winter kept with him until he died. There is also a one-volume version in the Rockefeller Center Archives. Because there are some slight variations between the two versions, I will refer to the two-volume version except for material found only in the single volume.

[14] D2, p. 23.

[15] Ibid., p. 276.

[16] D, p. 90, quoting Richards, *Science and Poetry.*

[17] John Blofeld, *City of Lingering Splendour: A Frank Account of Old Peking's Exotic Pleasures* (London: Hutchinson & Co., 1961), p. 79.

[18] D2, p. 48.

[19] "57 Years Inside China: An American's Odyssey," *Asia,* II.5 (Jan/Feb 1980), p. 11.

[20] D2, p. 24.

[21] Ibid.

[22] D, p. 107.

[23] D, p. 43.

[24] Accounts of the incident vary considerably. See Ka-che Yip, "Nationalism and Revolution: The Nature and Causes of Student Activism in the 1920s," China in the 1920s: *Nationalism and Revolution,* ed. F. Gilbert Chan and Thomas H. Etzold (New York: New Viewpoints, 1976), p. 103; Vera Schwarcz, *The Chinese Enlightenment: Intellectuals and the Legacy of the May Fourth Movement of 1919* (Berkeley: U. of California Press, 1986), pp. 147-148; Jonathan D. Spence, *The Gate of Heavenly Peace: The Chinese and Their Revolution, 1895-1980* (New York: The Viking Press, 1981), pp. 183-4.

[25] Schwarcz, pp. 145-146.

[26] D 2, p. 39.

[27] D 2, p. 50.

[28] D 2. p. 15.

[29] Ibid.

[30] Ibid.

[31] D2. p. 16.

[32] *Collected Poems* (New York: Harcourt, Brace & World: 1949), p. 32.

[33] D 2, p. 14.

Chapter 3

[1] Chapter 1, supra, 15ff.

[2] For an excellent supplementary discussion of the ferment of this era Wen-Han Kiang, The Chinese Student Movement (New York: King's Crown Press, 1948).

[3] Vera Schwarcz, op. cit., p. 5.

[4] Quoted by Schwarz, p. 1.

[5]

[6] Hinton, William. Hundred Day War: The Cultural Revolution at Tsinghua University (New York: 1972), p. 21.

[7] E-Tu Zen Sun, Cambridge History of China, vol. 13, chapter 8.

[8] My subsequent account of this Tsinghua community relies heavily on Janet Smith's unpublished memoir entitled "Memories."

[9] One informant told me that this was not the case.

[10] Telephone interview with Dorothy Gaylord, November 13, 1986.

[11] Ibid.

[12]   Liang Ch'i-ch'ao, Reflections on a Trip to Europe, in Yin-ping-shi ho-chi, chuan-chi, ts'e 5, 1-62 (Shanghai: Chuan-hua, 1936).

[13]   For a fuller account of Liang see Levenson, Joseph. Liang Ch'i-Ch'ao and the Mind of Modern China (Los Angeles: University of California Press, 1970).

[14]   E. R. Hughes. The Invasion of China by the Western World (New York: Barnes & Noble, 1968, 1st ed. 1937), p. 176.

[15]   Wabash College Archives, 378.7-823, Spring 1909.

[16]   D1, 32.

[17]   The Communists would later deemphasize the significance of the May Fourth Movement because they feared the prospect of mobilized students criticizing the government. It is also true that this movement, like other of the student risings about which I will speak later, affected only the educated elite but did not touch the majority of Chinese.

[18]   Spence, Gate of Heavenly Peace, op. cit., p. 194.

[19]   Ibid., p. 195-96.

[20]   Ibid., p. 234.

[21]   Spence, op. cit., p. 236.

[22]   Schwartz, op. cit., p. 158.

[23]   Schwarz, op. cit., p. 177.

[24]   Ibid., p. 182.

[25]   Ibid., p. 183.

[26]   Ibid., p. 186.

[27]   Ibid., p. 194.

[28]   William Butler Yeats, "Nineteen Hundred and Nineteen," The Variorum Edition of the Poems of W. B. Yeats (New York: The Macmillan Company, 1968), p. 485. In his diaries, Winter often turns to Yeats to express his own reaction to the violent assault on everything he believed.

[29]   Schwartz, op. cit., p. 70.

[30]   Interview with Li Fu-ning, November 1984.

[31]   Harold Shadick to me, March 7, 1989, including a short essay, "Remembering Robert Winter," RAC Special Collections: Herbert Stern Collection (unsorted).

Chapter 4

[1]   For an excellent study of this subject, see Rodney Koeneke's *Empires of the Mind: I. A. Richards and Basic English in China, 1929-1979* (Stanford, CA:

Stanford University Press, 2004). Koeneke's focus allows limited attention to Winter.

[2] Ibid., p. 596.

[3] *Climbing Days,* quoted by Russo, p. 596.

[4] Interview, March 27, 1985.

[5] Quoted by William Empson, *The Magdalene Magazine and Record* (Winter 1979-80), p. 3.

[6] Russo, op. cit., pp. 676-77.

[7] Richards, *Basic in Teaching: East and West* (London: Kegan Paul, Trench Turbner & Co. Ltd., 1935), p. 23.

[8] Vera Schwarcz, op. cit., *The Chinese Enlightenment: Intellectuals and the Legacy of the May Fourth Movement of 1919* (Berkeley: University of California Press, 1986), p. 199.

[9] Russo, op. cit., p. 467.

[10] John Fairbank, *Chinabound: A Fifty-Year Memoir*, op. cit., p. 42.

[11] Richards, "The Future of Reading," in *The Written Word,* ed. Brian L. McDonough (Rowley, MA: Newbury House, 1971), p. 32.

[12] Richards, *Mencius on Mind: Experiments in Multiple Definition* (Westport Connecticut, 1964; 1st ed. 1932), p. 92.

[13] Geoffrey Hartman, "The Dream of Communication," in *I. A. Richards: Essays in His Honor,* ed. Reuben Brower et al. (New York, 1973), p. 173.

[14] Richards, "Sources of Our Common Aim," *Poetries: Their Media and Ends,* ed. Trevor Eaton (The Hague, 1974), p. 169.

[15] Ibid.

[16] Ogden, quoted by Richards, "Toward a World English," *So Much Nearer* (New York: Harcourt, Brace & World, 1968), p. 244.

[17] *Psyche,* XII, 4 (April 1932), p. 83.

[18] For a detailed study of the Rockefeller Fuondation's activities in China, see Frank Ninkovitch, "The Rockefeller Foundation, China, and Cultural Change," *The Journal of American History,* vol. 70, no. 4 (March 1984), pp. 799-820.

[19] Letter from Arthur Hummel to David Stevens, dated September 26, 1933, Rockefeller Archives RG1.1, Series 200.

[20] Raymond B. Fosdick, *The Story of the Rockefeller Foundation* (New York, 1952), p. 249.

[21] Richards, *Basic English and Its Uses* (New York: W. W. Norton & Company, 1943), p. 6.

[22] Ibid., p. 12.

23 R. D. Jameson, "The Present Position of Basic in China," RA, RF RG1.1, 601R Orthological Inst., 1935-1936, Box 48, Folder 397.

24 Ibid.

25 Ibid.

26 Ibid., p. 10.

27 In the long run, that view was never dispelled, according to remarks made to me by several of my Chinese interviewees.

28 I. A. Richards, letter to David Stevens, June 20, 1936, RAC Special Collections: Herbert Stern Collection (unsorted).

29 Ibid.

30 Richards to John Marshall, June 19, 1936. Rockefeller Archive Center, Special Collections: Herbert Stern Collection

31 Ibid.

32 Ibid.

33 Richards to Stevens, July 21, 1936 RF, RG 1.1, Series 601R Orthological Institute, May-December 1936, Box 48, Folder 398.

34 Ibid.

35 Richards, letter to Marshall, December 17, 1936.

36 Ibid.

37 The reader can find pictures of Winter's furniture on pp. 80, 81, 98, and 100-191 of George Kates's *Chinese Household Furniture* (New York: Dover Publications, 1948).

38 John Blofeld, *City of Lingering Splendour* (Boston: Shambala Press, 1958), p. 171 ff.

39 Ibid., p. 248.

40 Ibid., p. 202.

Chapter 5

1 Richards to Stevens, February 13, 1937, Box 48, Series 601, RG1, Rockefeller Foundation Archives (RAC).

2 Ibid.

3 Richards to Stevens, February 3, 1937, RAC, 601R, Box 48, Series 399.

4 Ibid.

5 "Sources of Our Common Aim," *Poetries: Their Media and Ends,* ed. Trevor Eaton (The Hague and Paris, 1974), p. 168.

6 Richards to Marshall, April 24, 1937, Special Collections: Herbert Stern Collection, RAC (unsorted).

7   Robert Winter, "Notes on the Orthological Institute of China," enclosed with letter to Dr. Houghton dated January 18, 1939, Special Collections: Herbert Stern Collection, RAC (unsorted).

8   *I. A. Richards: His Life and Work* (Baltimore: Johns Hopkins Univ. Press, and London: Routledge and Kegan Paul, 1989), p. 420.

9   It is interesting to me that the poet Rilke had his own dream of peace, to be accomplished by transformative poetry. Rilke wrote in a letter that the task of the artist-intellectual in a postwar world would be "to prepare in men's hearts the way for those gentle, mysterious, tembling transformations, from which alone the understandings and harmnonies of a serener future will proceed." Quoted in Rainer Maria Rilke, *Duino Elegies*, trans. J. B. Leioshman and Stephen Spender (London: Hogarth Press, 1957), p. 16.

10 Dorothea Richards to me, January 15, 1985. RAC Special Collections: Herbert Stern Collection (unsorted).

11 Photos and descriptions of Winter's furniture can be found on pp. 80, 81, 98, and 100-191 of Kates's *Chinese Household Furniture.*

12 John Blofeld, *City of Lingering Splendour* (Boston: Shambhala Press, 1988), p. 80.

13 Letter from Richards to Stevens dated August 21, 1937; Box 481, Series RG1, RAC Series 601, Folder 400.

14 Letter from Richards to Holland D. Roberts (President, the National Council of Teachers of English), July 27, 1937, Box 578, Series 601 IAR, RAC.

15 Richards to Stevens, September 1, 1937, Box 48, RG1.1, Series 601R, RAC.

16 Richards to Stevens, August 21, 1937, Box 48, Series 601R, RAC.

17 Barbara Tuchman, *Stillwell and the American Experience in China* (New York: The Macmillan Company, 1985), p. 192.

18 Telephone interview with Dorothy Jameson, November 13, 1986.

19 "Some Teachers of English in China: I. A. Richards, William Empson, Robert Winter, and Wu Mi, talk delivered at Wabash College, Spring 1986, RAC: Herbert Stern Collection (unsorted).

20 Fairbank to Alger Hiss, *Chinabound*, op. cit., p. 197.

21 Ezra Pound, *The Cantos of Ezra Pound* (New York: New Directions Book, 1950), canto 113.786.

22 Russo, op. cit., p. 427.

23 Winter's editorial notes on *First Book of English* run some twenty single-spaced pages. Rockfeller Archive Center, Special Collections: Herbert Stern Collection (unsorted).

Chapter 6

[1]   Theodore White and Annalee Jacoby, *Thunder Out of China* (New York: William Morrow and Company, 1980], p. 58.

[2]   Ibid.

[3]   This account of Winter's efforts to defend the university is based on a report by Winter dated October 11, 1937, and presented to the Peace Preservation Committee, and letter to Mr. F. Shima, Third Secretary, Japanese Embassy, Peiping, RAC Special Collections: Herbert Stern Collection (unsorted).

[4]   Regarding Winter's fearlessness, in a letter dated January 15, 1985, Dorothea Richards told me that "he was completely fearless and when the Japanese were taking over Peking . . . he is said to have knocked a Japanese's teeth out who was beating up his rickshaw coolie," RAC Special Collections: Herbert Stern Collection (unsorted).

[5]   Tuchman, op. cit., p. 156.

[6]   Tuchman, p. 156.

[7]   Richards to Winter, 1938, Box 579 960 IAR, Series 601.

[8]   Richards to Winter, January 1938, Box 579 960 IAR, Series 601.

[9]   Pollard to Stevens, February or March 1938, Box 579 960 IAR, Series 601.

[10] Shui to Richards, "Friday the 11th" (1938), Box 579 960 IAR, Series 601.

[11] Richards to Stevens, April 4, 1938, Box 48, Series 601, Folder 401.

[12] *The Years that Were Fat*, op. cit., p. 258.

[13] Professor Yang Zhou-han told me in an interview that the story was a legend and that the box in fact contained books.

[14] Robert Payne, *Chinese Diaries, 1941-46* [Weybright & Talley, 1970], p. 8

[15] Ibid., p. 365.

[16] Hahn, *China to Me* (Philadelphia: Blackstone Co., 1944), pp. 106 ff.

[17] Winter to Hsieh 1939, RAC, Special Collection: Herbert Stern Collection (unsorted).

[18] Incidentally, Pei was the codiscoverer of the famous "Peking Man" skull, later shown to be a hoax.

Chapter 7

[1]   Interview with Yang Zhopu-han, n.d.

[2]   For another account of the daily experiences of an American teacher during this period, see Edward Gulick, *Teaching in Wartime China: A Photo-Memoir, 1937-39* (n.p.: University of Massachusetts Press, 1995).

[3]   Pollard to Stevens, October 21, 1940, Box 48, Series 601, RG1, RAC.

4   Balfour to Stevens, September 19, 1940, RG1, Series 601, Box 48, Folder
    404, RCA.

5   Ibid.

6   Winter to Stevens, April 18, 1939, RG1, Series 601, Box 48, Folder 396,
    RCA.

7   Statement by Winter, September 15, 1959, RAC Special Collections:
    Herbert Stern Collection (unsorted).

8   Winter recounts this misadventure in a letter to Richards, January 22, 1940,
    Box 48, RG1, Series 60.

9   "C" is almost certainly Chen Daisun, the prominent economist who, like
    Winter, was a lifelong bachelor. For Winter's account of his serenity, see
    supra, p. 91.

10 Winter to Dorothea and Ivor Richards, November 1940. RAC Special
    Collections: Herbert Stern Collection (unsorted). The subsequent account
    of the truck ride is in the same letter.

11 See p. 11, supra.

12 Ibid.

13 Richards to Winter, November 1940.

14 Ibid.

15 Prideaux-Brune to Balfour, Winter, December 1940, RAC Special
    Collections: Herbert Stern Collection (unsorted).

16 Balfour to Stevens, December 17, 1940.

17 Quoted in a letter from Balfour to Stevens, September 19, 1940, RAC
    Special Collections: Herbert Stern Collection (unsorted).

18 Richards to Stevens, November 1940.

19 Stevens, Diary, November 2, 1940.

Chapter 8

1   Winter to Stevens, November 1940, RG1, Series 601, Box 48, Folder 404.

2   Balfour to Prideaux-Brune, November 9, 1940.

3   Stevens to Prideaux-Brune, November 15, 1940.

4   Prideaux-Brune to Winter, November, 1940.

5   Winter to Balfour, January 5, 1941, Box 48, Series 60 RG1, Folder 405.

6   Interview with Chen Deisun, May 1, 1985.

7   Winter to Balfour, January 5, 1941, Box 48, Series 601, RG1, Folder 405.

8   D 2, p. 35 ff.

9   Interview with Li Fu-ning, November 1984.

[10] Richards to John Marshall, in interview, March 11, 1941. RG1, Series 601, Box 48, Folder 405.

[11] Richards to Winter, March 1939.

[12] Winter to Elizabeth Winter, 1941, RAC Special Collections: Herbert Stern Collection (unsorted).

[13] English Version of the Official Authorization Granted to the Orthological Institute of China to Minister on Behalf of the Yunnan Commission of Education an English-Training School.

[14] Balfour to Stevens, April 15, 1941, Box 48, Series 691R, Folder 48, RAC.

[15] These lines come at the end of T. S. Eliot's "Burnt Norton."

[16] Winter's translation of a line in Mallarmé's "Le vierge, le vivace et le bel aujoud'hui."

[17] Lines from Eliot's "The Wasteland."

[18] The first and last sentences are from T. S. Eliot's "The Wasteland."

[19] This line is from Shakespeare's *King Lear,* Act 1V.

[20] The line alludes to "The Battle Hymn of the Republic," an American Civil War song.

[21] The last sentence is from Gerard Manley Hopkins's "Terrible Sonnet," "No Worst, There Is None."

[22] The line is from T. S. Eliot's "Preludes."

[23] From G. M. Hopkins's "Spelt from Sibyl's Leaves."

[24] Winter to Stevens, May 28, 1941 (cover to "Report on the Work of the Orthological Institute from March to May 1941), Box 48, Series 601R, Folder 405. For a rich study of conditions at Lianda University caught up in war and revolution, see John Israel's *Lianda: Chinese University in War and Revolution,* where we experience not only the horrors Winter describes but also a struggle I can only call noble to "uphold a model of higher education, based largely on the American model, sought to preserve liberal education, political autonomy, and academic freedom." Winter was a senior member of the youngish faculty, where he taught courses in English literature and taught Shakespeare by reciting long passages using different voices and intonations to depict each character—this while carrying on his complex duties at the battered Orthological Institute.

[25] Ibid.

[26] Ibid.

[27] Ibid.

[28] Winter to Wu Fu Heng, May 1941, RG1 Box 48, Series 601, Folder 405.

29   This and the subsequent account of the raids are in "Report of the Work of the Orthological Institute from March to May 1941," Box 48, Series 601R, Folder 405, RAC.

30   Rickett and Fairbank accounts from phone interviews.

31   Winter to Stevens, Summer 1941, RG1 Box 48, Series 601R, Folder 405, RAC.

32   Winter to Richards, November 11, 1941.

33   Winter to Richards, November 11, 1941, vol. II, RAC Special Collections: Herbert Stern Collection (unsorted).

Chapter 9

1   Winter to Richards, March 12, 1942, RAC Special Collections: Herbert Stern Collection (unsorted).

2   Ibid.

3   Ibid.

4   Winter to Richards, November 18, 1942, Box 49, Series 601R, Folder 406, RAC.

5   Stevens to Winter, April 1942.

6   Richards to Winter, May 27, 1942, RAC Special Collections: Herbert Stern Collection (unsorted).

7   Ibid.

8   Winter to Stevens, August 10, 1942, RAC Special Collections: Herbert Stern Collection (unsorted).

9   Winter to Richards, November 18, 1942, Box 48, Series 601R, Folder 406, RAC.

10   John Blofeld, *City of Lingering Splendour,* op. cit., p. 202.

11   Winter to Stevens, November 18, 1942, Box 49, Series 601R, Folder 406, RAC.

12   Winter to Stevens, August 10, 1942, Box 49, Series 601R, Folder 406, RAC.

13   Ibid.

14   Ibid.

15   Winter to Stevens, December 25, 1942, RAC Special Collections: Herbert Stern Collection (unsorted).

16   Fairbank, *Chinabound,* op. cit., p. 193.

17   Emily Hahn tells Corin's story at length and with different emphasis in *China to Me,* op. cit., pp. 120ff.

18   The Executive Committee of the Rockefeller Foundation budget proposal, with a skeptical note from Stevens, February 1943, Box 49, Series 601R, Folder 407, RAC.

19   Marshall cable to Balfour, March 1943.

20   Balfour to Marshall, March 16, 1943.

21   George B. Cressey, head of the American Cultural Relations Program in Kunming, memo copied to RF March 1943.

22   Fairbank to Balfour, October 8, 1943, RAC Special Collections: Herbert Stern Collection (unsorted).

23   Balfour to Marshall, Fall 1943, RG1, Series 601, Box 48.

24   Winter to Balfour, March 9, 1943, Box 49, Series 601R, Folder 49, RAC.

25   Winter to Richards, April 13, 1943, Box 49, Series 601R, Folder 407, RAC.

26   Winter to Balfour, April 22, 1943, Ibid.

27   Wilma Fairbank to Stevens, May 18, 1943, Box 49, Series 601R, Folder 407, RAC.

28   Winter to John Fairbank, April 11, 1943.

29   John Fairbank to Winter, April 21, 1943.

30   Stevens to Wilma Fairbank, April 1943, Box 49, Series 601R, Folder 407, RAC.

31   Charles Thompson to Stevens, April 1943.

32   Stevens to Raymond B. Fosdick, May 1943.

33   Marshall to Stevens, June 28, 1943, Box 234, Series 200, Folder

34   Richards's phone call to Marshall, June 28, 1941.

Chapter 10

1   Balfour to Marshall, August 21, 1943, RAC Special Collections: Herbert Stern Collection, (unsorted).

2   D 2, p. 36.

3   Russo, *I. A. Richards: His Life and Work*, op. cit., p. 438.

4   Several Chinese scholars I've spoken to made light of the Basic project, not for political reasons but because educated Chinese delight in the nuances of their language and are impatient with language systems that would eliminate nuance. It's also true that systems like Basic and Esperanto, and the Romanization of Chinese words, reflected the fact that most Westerners in China couldn't read or write Chinese characters and "pushed any system that would get the Chinese away from writing in that thousand-year-old system." Finally, though Basic had a more rational basis, it also had similarities with attempts during the American occupation of Japan to begin

writing everything (street names, shop signs, etc.) in a Romanized system to do away with Japanese syllabic writing *(kanna)*. (My thanks to Professor Ron Suleki of Emerson College for these observations.)

5   Willys R. Peck to David Stevens, September 30, 1943, RAC Special Collections: Herbert Stern Collection (unsorted).

6   Fairbank report to State Department Far Eastern Section, February 1943, RAC Special Collections: Herbert Stern Collection (unsorted).

7   Stevens to Charles Thompson, November 24, 1943, RAC Special Collections: Herbert Stern Collection (unsorted).

8   Raymond Fosdick to Balfour, July 8,1943.

9   Balfour to Fosdick, July 17, 1943.

10   Interview with RW, January 1985.

11   F. T. Ching (Chen Fu-tien), an American citizen and Harvard engineer, who had gone on to teach English at several Chinese universities, including Tsinghua, and who now headed the Lianda English Department; and C. Y. Lin (Chin Yu-lin), China's leading logician.

12   Marshall to Winter, March 1944, RAC Special Collections: Herbert Stern Collection (unsorted).

13   Winter's account to Red Guard of his relations with the Guomintang and with the Rockefeller Foundation, September 25, 1959, RAC Special Collections: Herbert Stern Collection (unsorted).

14   Fairbank to Stevens, November 10, 1943, RAC Special Collections: Herbert Stern Collection (unsorted).

15   Marshall to Stevens, January 6, 1944, RAC Special Collections: Herbert Stern Collection (unsorted).

16   Winter's account of his relations with the Rockefller Foundation, November 18, 1959, RAC Special Collections: Herbert Stern Collection (unsorted).

17   Stevens to Mei I-chi, February 16, 1944, RAC Special Collections: Herbert Stern Collection (unsorted).

18   Stevens to Peck, June 1, 1944, RAC Special Collections: Herbert Stern Collection (unsorted).

19   John S. Dickey to Stevens, September 7, 1944.

Chapter 11

1   Jin Ti, "The Little Balcony (A Leaf from a Diary)." The piece was published in a Chinese newspaper and forwarded to Stevens by Winter in a letter dated August 25, 1945 (Special Collections: Herbert Stern Collection [unsorted]).

[2]   Interview with Jin Ti in Tientjin, January 11, 1987.

[3]   Ibid.

[4]   *Chinabound*, op. cit., p. 193.

[5]   Winter to Stevens, April 6, 1945, RAC Special Collections: Herbert Stern Collection (unsorted).

[6]   Winter to Stevens, October 15, 1945, vol. 2; letter to Mrs. Webster, August 20, 1945.

[7]   Excerpts from Balfour's Diary, Kunming, May 2, 1945 (RAC 601R, Tsinghua, Humanities, Box 49, Folder 414).

[8]   Inter-Office Correspondence, H. M. Gillette to John Marshall, May 1, 1945, RA Special Collections: Herbert Stern Collection (unsorted).

[9]   Stevens to Balfour, August 24, 1945.

[10] Winter to Stevens, August 18,1945.

[11] Stevens to Winter, September 26, 1945.

[12] Winter to Stevens, October 13, 1945.

[13] *Chinabound*, op. cit., p. 222.

[14] Winter to Marshall, May 16, 1945, RAC Special Collections: Herbert Stern Collection (unsorted).

[15] Winter to Stevens, August 18, 1945.

[16] Winter to Stevens, September 5, 1945, RAC Special Collections: Herbert Stern Collection (unsorted).

[17] The group began among officers at the Whampoa Military Academy and, under the direction of Chiang Kai-shek, sought to lead the GMD down a fascist road. It also constituted a secret police agency for the GMD.

[18] Lloyd E. Eastman, "The Kuomintang in the 1930s," in *The Limits of Change: Essays on Conservative Alternatives in Republican China*, ed. Charlotte Furth (Harvard University Press, 1976), p. 195.

[19] Ibid., p. 311.

[20] John Israel, "The Idea of Liberal Education in China," in *The Limits of Reform in China*, ed. Ronald A. Morse (Boulder, CO: Westview Press, 1983), p. 91.

[21] Ibid., p. 92.

[22] John King Fairbank, *Chinabound*, op. cit., p. 259.

[23] Payne, *Mao Tse-tung* (New York: Weybright & Talley, 1969), p. 250.

[24] Ibid.

[25] Diary, 2, p. 40.

[26] Jonathan Spence, *The Gate of Heavenly Peace* (New York: Penguin, 1982), p. 317.

[27] Ibid.

28   Ibid., p. 339.

29   Ibid.

30   Diary, 2, p. 42.

31   Ibid., p. 40.

32   Winter to Stevens, August 18, 1945, RAC Special Collections: Herbert Stern Collection (unsorted).

33   Ibid.

34   John Israel, "Southwest Associated University: Preservation as an Ultimate Value," in *Nationalist China During the Sino-Japanese War, 1937-1945,* ed. with an introduction by Paul K. T. Shih (Hicksville, New York: Exposition Press, 1977), 150. See also Israel's *Lianda: A Chinese Universityin War and Revolution,* op.cit., pp. 337 ff.

35   Eastman, "The Guomintang in the 1930s," in *The Limits of Change: Essays on Conservative Alternatives in Republican China,* ed. Charlotte Furth (Cambridge, MA: Harvard University Press, 1976), p. 195.

36   John Israel, "The Idea of Liberal Education in China," in *The Limits of Reform in China,* ed. Ronald A. Morse (Boulder, CO: Westview Press, 1983), p. 92.

37   Winter to Mrs. Webster, August 20, 1945, RAC Special Collections: Herbert Stern Collection (unsorted).

38   D, 1, p. 14.

Chapter 12

1   For reasons I have not been able to discover, both copies are missing substantial sections: pages 70-79, 120-242, and 290-310. In the Rockefeller copy, an annotation at the start of the diary simply indicates that these sections were "not received for filing."

2   U.S. Congress, Senate, Committee on Armed Services and Committee of Foreign Relations, Hearings on Military Situation in the Far East, 82nd Congress, 1st Sess., 1951, p. 1770.

3   "Relations with the Kuomingtang," dated September 25, 1959, document in my possession that we originally wrote to placate Winter's Red Guard accusers.

4   D2, p. 47.

5   Winter to Stevens, March 4, 1947, RAC Special Collections: Herbert Stern Collection (unsorted).

6   Winter to Stevens, January 12, 1947.

7   Stevens to Winter, January 9, 1946.

[8] Stevens to Winter, February 10, 1947.

[9] Merle Goldman, *China's Intellectuals: Advise and Consent* (Cambridge, MA: Harvard University Press, 1981), p. 3.

[10] D1, p. 24.

[11] John Fairbank, *Chinabound*, op. cit., p. 229. Fairbank observes that something besides idealism was at stake here. Americans under such conditions "would have forsaken their books and turned to reconstructing their living conditions." But these Chinese scholars accepted the primitivism of their conditions and went on with their work because "the scholar's role was deeply ingrained into the social structure and everyone's expectations." If scholars "had broken out of it by becoming amateur carpenters, bricklayers, or plumbers in their own interest, they would have been subverting the social order and soon become déclasse and targets of local suspicion, if not abuse."

[12] Winter to Stevens, September 5, 1945, RAC Special Collections: Herbert Stern Collection (unsorted).

[13] Robert Payne's *Chinese Diaries, 1941-45* (New York: Weybright and Talley, 1970; 1st ed. 1945), p. 289. My account of this episode derives primarily from Winter's treatment of it in his diary, which was an immediate response to the events, but I also draw on pp. 284-291 of Payne's *Diaries*, op. cit. John Israel's account of "The December First Movement" in *Lianda: A Chinese University in War and Peace*, op. cit., is also invaluable.

[14] On an unnumbered page of the diary that appears after page 31 of the RF version, Winter had written, "There are, up to today (December 7), fourteen students dead." Presumably Winter had heard a rumor to this effect, but it was unfounded. In a letter dated March 15,1988, Professor John Israel told me that "fatalities were limited to the original four."

[15] The reference to the university auditorium on page 32 of the diary was apparently a slip on Winter's part for "the university library." The university had no auditorium.

[16] D32. This page appears only in papers Winter marked as "Vol. 2," Rockefeller Special Collections: Herbert Stern Collection (unsorted).

[17] D2, p. 68.

[18] Ibid.

[19] D, p. 35. This page is only found in the one-volume copy of the diary, RAC Special Collections: Herbert Stern Collection (unsorted).

[20] D1, p. 47.

[21] D1, p. 25.

[22] D1.

23 Ibid.
24 Ibid.
25 D, p. 51.

Chapter 13

1   Interview with Wang Shi-ren, January 7, 1987.
2   Winter to Roxby, February 25, 1946, RAC Special Collections: Herbert
    Stern Collection (unsorted).
3   Roxby to Winter, February 20, 1946.
4   Winter to Roxby, February 25, 1946.
5   John Israel, *Lianda*, op. cit., p. 18.
6   D1, p. 34.
7   D1, p. 2.
8   D2, p. 4.
9   D1, p. 42.
10 D1, p. 4.
11 D1, p. 42.
12 D1, p. 11.
13 D1., p. 6.
14 D1, p. 42.
15 D1, p. 8.
16 Ibid.
17 D1, p. 24.
18 D1, p.
19 D,1, p. 36.
20 D1, p. 47.
21 D1, p. 48.
22 Winter to Stevens, January 9, 1946, RAC Special Collections: Herbert Stern
    Collection.
23 D1, p. 2.
24 Diary 1, p.
25 John Israel, "The Idea of Liberal Education in China," in *The Limits of
    Reform,* ed. Ronald A. Morse (Boulder, CO: Westview Press. 1983).
26 Winter to John Marshall, May 5, 1945, RAC Special Collections: Herbert
    Stern Collection.
27 Ibid.
28 Ibid.
29 Ibid.

30 D2, p. 2 et seq.

31 D2, p. 4.

32 That Winter was openly gay there seems no question, according to many of my informants. To my regret, I have almost no information about Winter's homosexual relations, though many of his former colleagues whom I interviewed remarked that he sometimes gave free play to anger and lust. Even toward the end of his days, I was told, the English Department of Peking University had to stop sending students to him for Winter's companionship and their own edification because he would molest them. One of my Chinese informants became very angry when I brought the matter up and said that it was "the worst thing you could say about a person." That may have been especially true during the Cultural Revolution. Yet even during the early years of Liberation he was able to indulge his sexual hunger without hindrance, and I was told that in the '70s, when Winter was in his eighties, when he had to renew his residential permit, a Beijing police chief would sometimes visit him and offer to get him boys. R. D. Jameson's widow, Dorothy Gaylord, told me that Winter was "a blatant homosexual," who told her once that the Communists "like their pleasures like everyone else." For an enlightening account of attitudes toward gays in the first half of the twentieth century, see Wenqing Kang, *Obsession: Male Same-sex Relations in China, 1900-1950* (Hong Kong: Hong Kong University Press, 2009). D. E. Mungelo *(Western Queers in China: Flight to the Land of Oz)* has also written on the subject.

33 D2, p. 5.

34 Russo, op. cit., p. 426.

35 D2, p. 6.

36 D2, p. 8

37 D2, p. 6

38 D2, p. 6.

39 D2, p. 7.

40 D2, p. 8.

41 D2, p. 41.

42 D2, p. 9.

43 D2, p. 41.

44 Professor Ron Suleski of Suffolk University informs me that the U.S. supplied the Nationalists with large numbers of machine guns, which were later captured by the PLA and used in the liberation.

45   Many of these "tommy guns" are now on display in the military museum in Beijing. They were captured by the PLA from the Nationalists and used against them.

46   D2, p. 9. Professor John Israel called my attention to Shen Zui, "Nei-mu zong de nei-mu ("The Plot within a Plot," *Nan Ch a True Record of Political Assassinations), Hong Kong: Zhongyubashe,* 1985.

Chapter 14

1   As the city was known until 1946, when the name reverted to Beijing/ Peking.

2   D2, p. 14.

3   Winter to John Marshall, RAC Special Collelctions: Herbert Stern Collection (unsorted).

4   D2, p. 56.

5   John Fairbank, *Chinabound,* op. cit., p. 343. Winter reported in January 1947 that Chiang Kai-shek, his brother-in-law T. V. Song, and Guomindang finance minister H. H. Kung had pocketed $2 billion from the national treasury, a theft that had been exposed and that was known to General Wedemeyer. Winter supposed that Truman would put an "iron curtain" around the facts of this financial crime so that he could then go to Congress for another ten to twenty million dollars a month in aid to China, "which perhaps will not do much harm and certainly will not do much good" (Winter to Burton Fahs, January 9, 1947. RA Box 50, Folder 415).

6   D1, p. 47.

7   D2, p. 81.

8   Joseph McCarthy, *The Story of General George C. Marshall* (Copyright 1952 by Joseph R. McCarthy), p. 128.

9   D2.

10   D2, p. 82.

11   D2, p. 24.

12   D2, p. 25.

13   Winter to Stevens, January 12, 1947, Box 50, Folder 415.

14   Winter to Fahs, January 9, 1947. RAC, Box 50, Folder 415.

15   Ibid.

16   The daughter of Southern Baptist missionaries in a coastal town on the Shandong Peninsula, she went on to work with Rewi Ally (himself a pro-Communist activist and writer) during the Japanese occupation in organizing the Chinese Industrial Cooperatives. A political activist

all through her life, she wrote many books about China, some of them autobiographical, and also edited and translated many Chinese works.

[17] D2, p. 28.

[18] D2, p. 37.

[19] D2, p. 28.

[20] Ibid., pp. 28-9.

[21] Ibid., p. 29.

[22] D2, p. 30. Back in Kunming, the Gaponoviches lived next door to Wen Yiduo, and the wife was an eyewitness to Wen's assassination.

[23] John Fairbank, *Chinabound*, op. cit., p. 315.

[24] Stevens to Winter, February 10, 1947. RAC, Box 50, Folder 415.

[25] Winter to Stevens, March 4, 1947.

[26] D2, p. 30.

[27] D2, p. 37. The *Kuan Tzu (Guanzi)* is a vast compilation of Chinese philosophical thoughts named after the seventh-century BCE philosopher Guan Zhong.

[28] D2, p. 107.

[29] Vishnu expresses the animating and preserving principle.

[30] D2, p. 36.

[31] D2, p. 33.

[32] D2, p. 33

Chapter 15

[1] For a lively treatment of inflation and currency devaluation under the Kuomindang, see Lilliane Willens, *Stateless in China* (Hong Kong: Earnshaw Books, 2011).

[2] Winter to Stevens, January 12, 1947, RAC Special Collections: Herbert Stern Collection (unsorted).

[3] Stevens to Winter, February 10, 1947.

[4] Cable from Mei to RF, February 14, 1947.

[5] Marshall to Mei, February 27, 1947.

[6] Winter to Stevens, March 4, 1947.

[7] "Inter-office Correspondence," Stevens to officers, March 21, 1947, RAC Splecial Collections: Herbert Stern (unsorted).

[8] Jack Belden, *China Shakes the World*, op. cit., pp. 401-02.

[9] Just previous to coming to the foundation as assistant director of the Humanities Division, had served as acting chief of the State Department's Division of Research for the Far East.

[10] Ibid., p. 400.

[11] Quoted by Susan Pepper, *Civil War in China: The Political Struggle, 1945-1949* (New York: Rowman & Littlefield, 1999), p. 401.

[12] The perception of students as the conscience of the nation is a long-established value held also by Korea and Japan and going back much farther than May Fourth. Professor Ron Suleski of Suffolk University informs me that this deep tradition is one reason why "the students could quickly gain so much national support, and a reason why the government was especially powerlesss to control the students, since public perceptions were to automatically support them."

[13] Belden, op. cit., p. 402.

[14] Pepper, op. cit., p. 71.

[15] D, p. 263.

[16] D p. 264.

[17] Mei to Fahs, August 25, 1947, RAC Special Collections: Herbert Stern Collection (unsorted).

[18] Winter to Stevens, October 2, 1947, op. cit.

[19] O. Edmund Clubb, *Twentieth Century China* (New York: Columbia University Press, 1972; 1s ed. 1964), p. 283.

[20] Pogue, George C. *Marshall: Statesman, 1945-1959,* vol. IV (New York: Viking, 1987), p. 270.

[21] Winter to Stevens, November 25, 1947, RAC Special Collections: Herbert Stern Collection (unsorted).

[22] Fahs to Winter, March 2, 1948, RAC Special Collections: Herbert Stern Collection (unsorted).

[23] Fahs to Winter, March 2, 1948, RAC Special Collections: Herbert Stern Collection (unsorted).

[24] Barbara Tuchman, *Stillwell and the American Experience in China, 1911-45* (New York: Macmillan, 1971), p. 528.

[25] Winter to Fahs, March 13, 1948, RAC Special Collections: Herbert Stern Collection (unsorted).

[26] Ibid.

[27] D, p. 265.

[28] D, p. 118.

[29] *Civil War in China*, op. cit., p. 74.

[30] Winter to Stevens, March 14, 1948, RAC Special Collections: Herbert Stern Collection (unsorted).

[31] Winter to Fahs, March 13, 1948, op. cit., and D, p. 267.

[32] See page 36, *supra*, for a more detailed account of this story.

33 D, p. 267.
34 *The Nation,* October 18, 1947.

Chapter 16

1 Diary, p. 246.
2 Interview, n.d.
3 Telegram from USLO Peking RUEHC/SecState, May 3, 1974. For some five years David M. Kendall and Laura P. Masurovsky of William and Connolly in Washington, D.C., pursued a Freedom of Information Act requesting the FBI's release of documents concerning Winter. What the FBI finally released was incomplete and heavily censored but remains an important source of information on Winter after his correspondence with the Rockefeller Foundation ended.
4 Winter to John Marshall, June 26, 1948, RAC Special Collections: Herbert Stern Collection.
5 Winter to David Stevens, June 27, 1948.
6 Jack Belden, *China Shakes the World,* op. cit., p. 397.
7 Ibid., pp. 397-38.
8 Ibid., p. 405.
9 Ibid., p. 407.
10 Ibid.
11 D2, p. 58.
12 D2, p. 57.
13 See p. 39, supra.
14 D2, p. 58.
15 D2, p. 48. The description of the boys as languid and androgynous is probably colored by Winter's gay temperament.
16 D2, p. 59. Robert Payne, *Contemporary Chinese Poetry* (Oxford: Routledge, 1947), pp. 12 ff.
17 D2, p. 40.
18 See p. 174, supra.
19 Ibid.
20 D2, p. 41.
21 Ibid.
22 Ibid., 41.
23 D, p. 42.
24 In 1960, Wu's Beijing opera *Hai Rui Dismissed from Office* became a great success. The attack on it on the ground that it obliquely criticized Chairman

Mao was one of the early shots of the Cultural Revolution. Wu Han was imprisoned, and his death may have been the indirect result of beatings by prison guards.

25 Ibid.

26 See p. 162 supra for the complete poem.

27 D2, p. 43.

28 D2, p. 44.

29 D2, p. 45.

30 D2, p. 70.

31 D2, p. 72.

32 Ibid.

33 See p. 109, supra.

34 D, p. 90.

35 D2, p. 260.

36 D, p. 261. The paired sketches may have been influenced by Tennyson's "Northern Farmer: Old Style" and "Northern Farmer: New Style."

37 D, pp. 261-2.

38 Belden, op. cit., pp. 404-05.

39 Susan Pepper, *Civil War in China: The Political Struggle, 1945-1949* (Berkely: University of California Press, 1978), p. 227. Professor Ron Suleski of Suffolk University informed me that when young, Hu Shi "was in the forefront of the reformist camp, calling for changes in values, perceptions and attitudes. As he grew older he fell behind the crest of reform waves, so in old age he could be used, because of his good English, to represent the discreditedand defeated Nationalists . . . . He also seems to have had a number of female lovers . . . and when word of that got out, he had less luster with idealistic students in China," and ended up a discouraged man. For a good account of him, see Chou Min-Chi, *Hu Shih and the Intellectual Choice in Modern China* (Ann Arbor: University of Michigan Press, 1984).

Chapter 17

1 Winter to Burton Fahs, July 16, 1948, RAC Special Collections, Herbert Stern Collection (unsorted).

2 Winter to Fahs, September 3, 1948. Ibid. In these accounts, Winter put down what he heard, and as well connected as he was, he heard a lot. Some of the material in this chapter I'm unable to confirm, and some, as Fahs says, are mere rumors. But Winter's reports on things he had experienced

directly are reliable, and so is much of what he picked up from the grapevine.

3 Fahs to Winter, December 2, 1943.

4 Nancy B. Tucker, ed., *China Confidential: American Diplomats and Sino-American Relations, 1945-1996* (New York: Columbia University Press, 2001), p. 62.

5 One active member of the pro-Chiang China lobby, Alfred Kohlberg, called the White Paper "the story of the American betrayal of the Republic of China" (Ross Y. Koen, *The China Lobby in American Politics* [New York: Octagon Books, 1974], p. 167.

6 D2, p. 101.

7 D2, p. 74 (313).

8 D 2, p. 101.

9 D2, p. 77.

10 D2, p. 97.

11 D, p. 323.

12 Ibid.

13 Ibid.

14 D, p. 330.

15 Ibid.

16 Winter to Stevens, April 19. 1949, RAC Special Collections: Herbert Stern Collection.

17 Ibid.

18 Interview with Li Fu-ning, November 1984, who confirmed that Winter, though he had made pages of notes for the course, was no expert in this subject.

19 Interview with Wang Shi-ren, January 7, 1987.

20 Ibid.

21 Letter to Delia and Bill Jenner, January 19, 1967, RAC Special Collections: Herbert Stern Collection (unsorted).

22 Ibid. Winter also self-published and had handsomely bound monograph called *Nutrients Essential to Human Health*.

23 Letter to Bill and Delia Jenner, August 22, 1965.

24 Millet sustained Mao and his army through the revolution. It was a grain one ate when nothing else was available.

25 Winter to John Balfour, August 1, 1949, RAC Special Collections: Herbert Stern Collection (unsorted). In this eleven-page letter, Winter gave a detailed account of the situation at Tsinghua and his own place in it.

26 Ibid.

27 Winter to Balfour, August 8, 1949. That same question would evolve into "Who Lost Vietnam," and Iraq and Afghanistan.
28 Winter to the Housing Committee, Tsinghua University, August 26, 1949, RAC Special Collections: Herbert Stern Collection (unsorted).
29 Ibid.
30 Ch'i-sun Yeh to Winter, enclosed with letter from Winter to Marshall, dated August 28.
31 D, p. 332.
32 Interview of I. A. Richards by John Marshall, November 1, 1950, RAC 1.1/200/235/2798.
33 Telephone interview of I. A. Richards by Charles Balfour, November 17, 1950. RAC, Box No. 235, Series 200, Folder 2798 RG1.11.
34 D, p. 337, quoting from Fairbank, *The United States and China*, op. cit.
35
36 D, p. 338.
37 D, p. 339. Winter quotes from Thien Cien.
38 D, p. 342.
39 Winter to John Marshall, September 7, 1949, RAC Special Collections: Herbert Stern Collections (unsorted).
40 Vol. 3, RAC Special Collections: Herbert Stern Collection (unsorted), p. 346.
41 Vol. 3, Stevens to Winter, February 14, 1949, RAC Special Collections: Herbert Stern Collection (unsorted).
42 Vol. 3, R. P. Burden to Winter, March 25, 1949.
43 Vol. 3, Burden to Winter, June 1, 1949.
44 Vol. 3, Winter to Fahs, October 7, 1949.
45 D, p. 351.
46 Stevens to Winter, November 10, 1949, RAC Special Collections: Herbert Stern Collection (unsorted).
47 Fahs to Winter, April 30, 1950.

Chapter 18

1 Memo to the director, March 21, 1955, FBI file no. 100-370862-3.
2 Excerpt from FBI file dated July 15, 1952, file no. #138.946G (Hong Kong) / 96.
3 FBI file dated September 16, 1963, no. 100-370862-22.
4 *Chicago Tribune*, August 7, 1979. Someone had copied the *Tribune* story in neat longhand and sent it to Winter.

5   These documents came to me in a group that I have gathered under the title "Self-Criticism." A copy is filed with the Rockefeller Foundation together with all my other supporting documents. Tolef Ås told me in an interview (n.d.) that Winter wrote a two-hundred-page essay on his stay in China, but this was not among the papers I acquired, and Ås may have been referring to the diaries.

6   Document dated November 18, 1959.

7   Letter from Winter dated August 25, 1971, addressed to "Comrade Chang Hüeh-shu," or the University Party Committee, "Comrade Kuo, "of the Revolutionary Comitte of Peking University, and Comrade Tao, a Political Instructor of the University Xi Yu Xi. RAC Special Collections: Herbert Stern Collection (unsorted).

8   Interview with Prof Yang Zhou-han (author of a famous history of European literature), March 6, 1985. Adele Rickett told me in an interview that although she had not actually fingered him, she was subjected to "rigorous questioning," and many of her and her husband's circle of friends fell into trouble because of the association. People who had been exposed to Western education were already likely to be suspect, and if, in addition, they were known to have associated with confessed spies, they were likely to become pariahs. Others could now be harmed by secondary contamination from them. During the antirightist campaigns particularly, people like Winter, who had once enjoyed so rich a circle of friends, became more and more isolated.

9   See, for example, the telegram from USLO to the State Department, Dispatch #99, July 15, 1952, file #138.946G (Hong Kong)/96 (RAC: Herbert Stern Collection) in which Winter discussed details of the current anti-Lin, anti-Confucius campaign, and the May 7 schools, in which officials and university professors could be assigned to physical labor in the countryside as part of their "rehablitation."

10   Letter to the Jenners, March 10, 1966, RAC Special Collections: Herbert Stern Collection (unsorted).

11   Letter to Bill and Delia Jenner, December 3, 1965.

12   Eventually Chao, though earlier a favorite of the Red Guards, was sent to the countryside to rehabilitate himself by herding pigs and serving food to teachers. Thus, in a kharmic circle, the man who had caused Winter to lose face got a heavy dose of his own medicine. (My interview with Chao Li-kate, January 5, 1987.)

13   See p. 91 supra and Robert Payne, *Chinese Diaries, 1941-46* (Weybright & Talley, 1970), p. 8.

14 See supra, p. 92.
15 Department of State Telegram from USLO, Peking to the Secretary of State, dated June 1974.
16 My interview with Zhang Xingbao, June 23, 1985.
17 Letter to Delia and Bill Jenner, January 19, 1967, RAC Special Collections: Herbert Stern Collection (unsorted).
18 Ibid.
19 Interview with Tollef Ås, n.d.
20 RAC Special Collections: Herbert Stern Collection (unsorted).
21 Winter letter to Ivor and Dorothea Richards, November 10, 1971.
22 Letter to Ivor and Dorothea Richards, March 5, 1974.
23 Letter to Ivor and Dorothea Richards, September 27, 1976.

Chapter 19

1 For a detailed description of these, see my introduction.
2 In another version of the story, I heard that injury resulted from his furiously chasing the cook.
3 I've been sunable to find out if the stone stands.

INDEX

Richards, Ivor, 14, 18-19, 26, 46, 54,
70, 75, 83-85, 87-88, 110, 112,
145, 195, 233, 241-42, 255,
293, 316, 320
Rock, Joseph F., 113, 255
Rockefeller Foundation, 20, 67-68,
91, 112, 114, 116, 119, 126,
136-37, 139, 145, 186-87,
191-92, 196, 198-200, 207-9,
211, 216-19, 231-34, 274-75,
280-81, 315-16, 319-20, 328,
330-31
Rose Hsiung. *See* Hsiung Ting

S

Schwarcz, Vera, 50, 79, 86
Shadick, Harold, 82-83
Shima, F., 119, 121-22
Shui, T. T., 143-45, 220, 241
Skinner, Geraldine, 133
Smith, E. K., 68, 71, 96, 134
Southwest Associated University. *See*
Lianda
Stevens, David, 91-92, 105, 107, 110,
125, 138, 167, 184, 193, 196,
200, 209, 217, 233-34, 250,
252, 259, 265, 274-75, 282,
284, 289, 296, 325
Stillwell (General), 211, 285-86
Suleski, Ron, 363n, 366n, 368n
Sun Yat-sen, 43, 48

T

Tai Li, 127, 131-33, 305
Takeda, 118-19, 122
Tietjens, Eunice, 40
Tolstoy, Leon, 55, 323-24

Tong, Hollington, 130, 132-33
Trimurti, 152, 193, 271-72
Truman, Harry, 264, 288-89, 364n
Tsinghua University, 42, 45, 91, 111,
122, 125, 128, 145, 266, 274
Tuchman, Barbara, 111, 124
Tu Kung-sun, 51-52
Tyler, Charlotte, 108, 112

V

Voice of Democracy, 184

W

Wabash College, 9, 12-13, 28, 31, 75
Wang Min-yuan, 13, 335-36
Wedemeyer, Albert C., 280, 283, 285,
364n
Wen Yiduo, 39-44, 51, 64-67, 76,
112, 116, 144, 152, 223-26,
248-49, 258-59, 270, 276,
280, 294, 297, 301-4, 312,
321, 328
West, Rebecca, 229, 310
Winter, Robert
death of, 30, 231
diary of, 231-33
Wong-Quincey, J., 69, 82
Wu Mi, 44-47, 53, 62, 81, 291

Y

Yeats, William Butler, 81, 145,
238-39, 267-68
Yenching University, 82, 137, 139,
182, 295
Yunnan University, 310, 312

Z

Bert Stern, Emeritus Professor at Wabash College, has also taught at Thessaloniki and Peking Universities. Stern's poems and essays, personal and critical, have been published in anthologies and in journals including *Southern Review, Kenyon Review, New Republic, Poetry, and The American Poetry Review,* and in two collections of poems, *Steerage* and *Silk/The Ragpicker's Grandson.* His pioneer study of the poet Wallace Stevens was published by the University of Michigan. He lives in Somerville, Massachusetts, where he co-edits Off the Grid Press with his wife, the poet Tamlin Neville. The two also teach in an alternate sentencing program called Changing Lives Through Literature. A Chinese edition of this biography is being concurrently published by Peking University Press.

CPSIA information can be obtained at www.ICGtesting.com
Printed in the USA
BVOW05s1725280115

385394BV00004B/233/P